SERVING SINGAPORE
My Journey

SERVING SINGAPORE
My Journey

V K Rajan

Ministry of Foreign Affairs, Kingdom of Bahrain

World Scientific

NEW JERSEY · LONDON · SINGAPORE · BEIJING · SHANGHAI · HONG KONG · TAIPEI · CHENNAI · TOKYO

Published by

World Scientific Publishing Co. Pte. Ltd.
5 Toh Tuck Link, Singapore 596224
USA office: 27 Warren Street, Suite 401-402, Hackensack, NJ 07601
UK office: 57 Shelton Street, Covent Garden, London WC2H 9HE

British Library Cataloguing-in-Publication Data
A catalogue record for this book is available from the British Library.

SERVING SINGAPORE
My Journey

Copyright © 2020 by World Scientific Publishing Co. Pte. Ltd.

All rights reserved. This book, or parts thereof, may not be reproduced in any form or by any means, electronic or mechanical, including photocopying, recording or any information storage and retrieval system now known or to be invented, without written permission from the publisher.

For photocopying of material in this volume, please pay a copying fee through the Copyright Clearance Center, Inc., 222 Rosewood Drive, Danvers, MA 01923, USA. In this case permission to photocopy is not required from the publisher.

ISBN 978-981-120-557-6

For any available supplementary material, please visit
https://www.worldscientific.com/worldscibooks/10.1142/11422#t=suppl

Desk Editor: Sandhya Venkatesh

Typeset by Stallion Press
Email: enquiries@stallionpress.com

Printed in Singapore

AUTHOR'S NOTE

This book is much more than an autobiography. It is an active insider's account, from a vantage point of view, of how Singapore succeeded in achieving a First World developed status, starting with so little and in the most unpromising of circumstances, while many other countries, which were so abundantly endowed with human and natural resources, foundered.

The idea of writing this book came late. I had not kept detailed written records of events, and my involvement in them, as they unfolded in the course of my long service, except for a small collection of some documents, papers, letters and photographs that have survived my frequent moves for my postings abroad.

Many friends from different walks of life, both at home and overseas, had been urging me to write this book. Among them were my colleagues in the Civil Service of Singapore, where I served for more than 42 years, foreign diplomatic colleagues with whom I had interacted at home and abroad, as well as academics and officials who attended my keynote addresses, lectures, presentations and panel discussions which I undertook at the invitations of government ministries, media, universities, think tanks, professional bodies, and community organisations in the countries I served during my career in the Foreign Service. In sum total, their argument was that the knowledge, observations and the practical experience I gained while serving in the Executive Service, Administrative Service and Foreign Service at different stages of Singapore's development — including the transition from British colonial rule to self-government, the short-lived years in the Malaysian federation and finally as an independent Republic — were unique in many ways and, therefore, should be recorded for the benefit of others. I was lucky to have had the opportunity of being both an insider and an active participant in the events that unfolded during the crucial years of Singapore's development.

After much thought and reflection over many years, I decided to write this book. Getting started was difficult, especially in tracing whatever material I had, organising them in some order, and recalling and recording my experiences, recollections and reflexions, as accurately as possible. This has taken some time to complete. I believe that the readers, both at home and abroad, including practitioners and academic researchers, who have an abiding interest in public administration, will find this book beneficial. Hopefully, they will be inspired by my story.

I acknowledge, with grateful thanks, the invaluable help, assistance, and encouragement I received from many colleagues, friends, acquaintances, and many others who have helped me in this effort. Every effort has been made to list all those who have assisted me in one way or other in the "Acknowledgement" page. I may have unintentionally missed out few names, I seek their understanding in this regard.

Finally, I must state here that the views, impressions, assessments, opinions, and reflections in the book are mine. They do not necessarily reflect the policies, official or otherwise, of any institutions, organisations and entities, whether in the public sector or in the private sector.

In memory of my beloved Parents
who
sacrificed much for their children

ADVANCE PRAISE

It is my great pleasure to recommend this fascinating account of a lifetime's work in the service of the Republic of Singapore, and a first-hand encounter with the emergence and growth of a truly remarkable and inspirational nation. VK Rajan has such a wealth of experience, and so many compelling and illuminating insights, that each chapter brings a new perspective on issues and challenges that remain relevant around the world to this day.

In the Kingdom of Bahrain, we have also been fortunate to have benefited from Mr. Rajan's experience and insight, through his work at the Ministry of Foreign Affairs, Bahrain and I personally have greatly welcomed and appreciated the depth of his practical knowledge and understanding. Indeed, it has always been very apparent that he is a truly dedicated, talented and yet humble public servant, whose pride in his country's achievements and principles shines clearly in every page of this book. Step by step through each chapter, his unique journey is recounted in a vivid yet concise manner so that every reader can benefit, and learn, from the historic developments Mr. Rajan has witnessed.

I, therefore, have no hesitation in recommending *Serving Singapore — My Journey*, in the hope that other readers will find in it new perspectives, unexpected lessons, or perhaps simply a spark of insight that challenges their preconceptions and fires their own thoughts and analysis in new directions.

Khalid Bin Ahmed Bin Mohamed Al Khalifa
Minister of Foreign Affairs
Kingdom of Bahrain

FOREWORD

I thank my friend and colleague, Mr VK Rajan (VK), for inviting me to contribute a foreword to his inspiring autobiography.

VK Rajan started life in very humble circumstances. His parents ran a small provision shop in rural Singapore. His family lived in an *attap* hut, with no electricity, running water and modern sanitation.

Fortunately for VK, he was a bright boy and did well in school. After obtaining his A-Level certificate, he joined the Executive Service. He managed to earn a law degree and obtain admission to the English Bar, as an external student. He was promoted from the Executive Service to the elite Administrative Service and to the Foreign Service.

He had a stellar career in the public service of Singapore. He was the Private Secretary to President Benjamin Sheares. He was an outstanding Chief of Protocol. He also served, with distinction, as our High Commissioner to New Zealand and Ambassador to Egypt. I have enjoyed his reflections on those experiences and the lessons he learnt.

VK Rajan's life story is another case of the Singapore Dream come true.

Professor Tommy Koh
Ambassador-At-Large, Ministry of Foreign Affairs
Professor of Law, National University of Singapore

FOREWORD

VK Rajan (Rajan) has been a buddy of mine for close to 60 years. I have known him since his early days in the Civil Service.

Despite going up the civil service ladder with several promotions, and eventually being the Head of Mission in New Zealand and in Egypt (with concurrent accreditations to several other countries in the region), he always stuck to a Spartan lifestyle. Humble, obliging and dedicated to social work. That is the quintessence Rajan.

The book spans his entire career in the civil service and the diplomatic service. What we have been treated to is not only a historiography but also pictorialgraphy, if I can use the word liberally. There are lots of fascinating photographs with Rajan in the company of Prime Ministers, Queen Elizabeth and Pope Paul ll.

He travels through decades, tracing Singapore's own growth from self-government in 1959, the country's sojourn in Malaysia, to being an independent republic. He also played a major part in setting up Singapore's diplomatic missions abroad. His glory came with the organisation of the Commonwealth Heads of Government Meeting in Singapore in 1971.

As Private Secretary to President Sheares and later as Head of Protocol in the Ministry of Foreign Affairs, we get an inside view from Rajan's vantage point. He has adopted a prose style which is lucid, clear and simple.

One commendable achievement on his part was the setting up of a kindergarten for Tamil students — Saraswathy Kindergarten. He did so when he was the Chairman of the Hindu Endowments Board, Singapore. To him, religion must go hand-in-hand with social service so that communities are uplifted. Rajan sees everybody in equal terms and has no bias on religion, language or class. He is a true Singaporean, the likes of which are diminishing.

After retirement, he has had many offers from other countries to organise their protocol office or train their civil servants. He is currently with the Bahrain government sharing his expertise in diplomacy and a functioning civil service.

I did not put down the draft memoirs, which Rajan allowed me to take a look at.

I am sure every reader will be excited to read and be enlightened by Rajan's memoir.

Dr Gopalan Raman
Senior Consultant
Withers Khattar Wong LLC

REVIEW

V K Rajan has written a personal and fascinating account of his long career in the Singapore Civil Service. He encountered and worked with many pioneer political leaders of Singapore. He interacted with numerous foreign leaders over the years in different capacities, including as Chief of Protocol at the Ministry of Foreign Affairs and as Singapore's ambassador to several countries. He heard and saw at close quarters how royalty, top decision-makers and brilliant minds talked about Singapore, and how some of our pioneer leaders dealt with bilateral relations and policy matters. With his long experience in the Civil Service and with an eye to the developments past and present, V K Rajan also shared his thoughts on the issues facing Singapore and its future as an independent small state. His devotion to Singapore and what it has achieved comes through clearly. This reflection on V K Rajan's life is impassioned, inspirational and instructive. It is wonderful reading, especially for those interested in Singapore's history in the early decades of independence."

— Ambassador Ong Keng Yong Executive Deputy Chairman
S. Rajaratnam School of International Studies Singapore

COMMENTARY

I enjoyed reading Ambassador Rajan's book *Serving Singapore*. He is a dedicated person who made his way up in life, in spite of the harsh living conditions he encountered as a child and as a young man.

The same dedication is reflected in his career. He did not perceive it simply as a job but rather as a mission to serve his country, Singapore, from its difficult birth to its maturity as a prosperous and successful nation.

His mission did not end with his retirement, instead he went on to reflect on his journey and share those reflections with others in this book.

We should be grateful to Ambassador Rajan for sharing with us his reflections and his experience, which are useful to individuals and nations alike.

Thank you Ambassador Rajan.

Dr Ibrahim Ali Badawi
Ambassador (Retired)
Republic of Egypt

COMMENTARY

I first met VK Rajan *ji* in 1997 when I accompanied my husband on his posting to Egypt. Singaporeans living overseas then were hurtfully labelled as "quitters" by one prominent Singaporean. Ambassador VK Rajan, however, embraced his flock living in Egypt warmly. He recognised, even in those days, that overseas Singaporeans were unofficial representatives of their country, and the adage that "you can take a person out of the country, but you can't take the country out of the person" rung true. Additionally, Mrs. Vijaya Rajan was like our *ibu* or *kakak* (mother or elder sister in Malay), dishing out her legendary Indian cuisine with love to us Singaporeans of diverse ages. It bears highlighting that Mrs. Rajan is vegetarian, but that did not stop her from feeding us carnivores with delectable meat dishes; a testament of her kindness. Mr. and Mrs. Rajan's care was an umbilical cord to home.

It was not only about food and socialising, though. During our time in Egypt, there were gruesome terrorist attacks on foreigners in Egypt. In the aftermath of the September 11 2001 terrorist attacks in the US, there were also the US retaliatory "war on terror" invasions of Afghanistan and Iraq. During a volatile time in the Middle East, it was reassuring to have a caring ambassador with us.

I was born in the year that VK Rajan *ji* started his first day of work in his long career in the civil service. That was also the year

Singapore became self-governing. It is not lost on me that in the twenty plus years as I progressed from wearing cloth diapers to becoming a lawyer like him, he and his colleagues had been painstakingly paving a better Singapore for us. Although some two decades separate us, I am old enough to know the difficult conditions in Singapore that Mr. Rajan grew up and worked in, as described in his book.

This book is unputdownable for various reasons: readers get to read about historic events from the unique perspective of (extra)ordinary civil servants like Mr. Rajan; there are interesting details of their hard work behind-the-scenes, without which the brilliant ideas of leaders could not have been efficiently effected; and it is a personal account of the values that undergird the integrity of Mr. Rajan and those of his ilk, values which seem to be at risk of extinction in this age of instant gratification and self-absorption. And the photos and documents are priceless!

Thank you, VK Rajan ji for taking me along on this insightful journey of yours.

Ms. Agnes Sng
Lawyer, and founding President of
Singapore Club in Cairo (2000 to 2003)

COMMENTARY

Being a Singapore permanent resident and married to a Singaporean, I have spent altogether more than 20 years in Singapore, with some intermittent years on overseas postings. In my work as regional director, I have had regular contacts with many diplomats with different characters. My acquaintance with V K Rajan, then ambassador to Egypt, was remarkably pleasant from the beginning. Unlike many career diplomats from other countries, V K Rajan was not throwing his weight around as a higher being but came across as approachable and plain speaking with all the people he had to meet. But I sincerely admired his unusual attitude vis-à-vis people he was not obliged to meet. These were, for example, the numerous Singaporean and Malaysian students in the Cairo universities who were regularly invited to embassy functions. And they did not come only for the glorious food organised by Mrs. Rajan; their experiences in Egypt was being taken seriously and there was open dialogue.

Mr. Rajan's book covers a wide range of topics, among which his insights into the development of Singapore and the political, economic, and social factors behind the success story are especially important. Since my first arrival in 1986, I have been a student of Singapore's and Southeast Asia's special dynamics. The book is filling quite several voids in my understanding and will help a lot in my continuing effort to write comments and analyses on the region. Thanks, V K Rajan, for extending your friendship and sharing your insights with me.

Dr. Wolfgang Sachsenröder
Researcher and Managing Editor,
Political Party Forum Southeast Asia

ACKNOWLEDGEMENTS

I owe a debt of gratitude to many people for their encouragement, advice, suggestions and assistance in getting this book written, published and to launch it. I have made every effort to acknowledge them here. If I have inadvertently missed out some of them, I seek their kind understanding.

My gratitude and special thanks to His Excellency Shaikh Khalid Bin Ahmed Khalifa, Minister of Foreign Affairs, Bahrain, for so graciously contributing a "Commentary/Recommendation". I am also grateful to Professor Tommy Koh, Ambassador-At-Large, Ministry of Foreign Affairs and Professor of Law, National University of Singapore, for his Foreword; Ambassador Ong Keng Yong, Executive Deputy Director, S Rajaratnam School of International Studies for his Review and also for his kind gesture in agreeing to launch this book; Dr. Gopalan Raman, Senior Consultant, Withers Khattar Wong for his Foreword; and Dr Ebrahim Ali Badawi, Retired Ambassador, Egypt, Ms Agnes Sng, Lawyer and President of the Singapore Club in Cairo (2000–2003) and Dr. Wolfgang Sachsenroder, Researcher and Managing Editor, Political Forum South East Asia, for their Commentaries.

I thank Mr Wong Kan Seng, former Deputy Prime Minister and former Foreign Minister and Ambassador Darry Deskar, Distinguished

Fellow, S Rajaratnam School of International Studies for their help in launching the book.

I also record my gratitude and appreciation of the kind help and prompt assistance I received from Ms Yeong Yoon Ying, Director (Special Duties), Ministry of Communications and Information; Ms Chang Li Lin, Press Secretary to the Prime Minister, Prime Minister's Office; Ms Seraphim Cheong, Head Media and Communications, Office of the President; and Ms Sheila Ng, Senior Manager Civil Service College, to secure the necessary permission to publish the images seen in the book.

I thank the Ministry of Foreign Affairs, in particular, Mr Ong Eng Chuan, Deputy Secretary (Management) for his assistance.

I also extend my thanks to my schoolmates, Harold Seah, Mohinder Singh and R Diviyanathan for painstakingly reading through the first draft of the manuscript.

A big thanks to the team at World Scientific Publishing: Dr KK Phua and Mr Max Phua for agreeing to publish the book; Ms Sandhya Venkatesh for her guidance and editing; Ms Ugena See for her coordination of logistics and Ms Judy Yeo for her initial work in getting the process started.

I also owe a debt of gratitude to the energetic staff of the S Rajaratnam School of International Studies, especially, Ms Chew Peck Wan, Ms Maureen Lee and Ms Pauline Liew, amongst others, for their hard work in organizing the book launch.

I must thank many more people who have encouraged me to write the book and others who have assisted in many incidental matters during the process of writing the book and later in launching it. Among them are (not in any particular order):

Ambassador Hasan Riyadh Al Zayani, Ministry of Foreign Affairs, Bahrain
Mr Ahmed Janahi, Ministry of Foreign Affairs, Bahrain
Mr Ong Tiong Pin, APCO Architects Ms Lai Yoke Lan and her colleagues in National Archives Singapore
Professor (Dr) Mona Zaki, American University in Cairo (AUC)
Professor (Dr) Valsan AUC
Professor (Dr) Ali Hilal Dasuki, AUC
Professor (Dr) Mohamed Salim, Cairo University
Ambassador Dr Warawit Kannithasen, Thailand
Mr Ong Tze Boon, Ong Teng Cheong Collection
Mr Lee Chiong Giam, Deputy Secretary, Ministry of Foreign of Affairs
Ms Jessie Tham, Ministry of Foreign Affairs
Ms Joyce Lim, Ministry of Foreign Affairs
Mr Ricky Sim, Managing Director, SunChest Property Consultants Pte Ltd
Mr Teh Gim Teck, Director, Gimtronic Engineers
Mr Satanu Gupta, retired civil servant
Mr Abdalla Nabeel Mohamed Shams, Ministry of Foreign Affairs, Bahrain
Mr Hassan Abdulameer Albakali, Ministry of Foreign Affairs, Bahrain

There are many more people based in Singapore and overseas and among them are government officials, diplomats, academics, political leaders and authors, who have encouraged and supported me in this endeavour. I have not been able kept in touch with all of them. Some have sadly passed on. My heartfelt thanks to all of them wherever they are.

CONTENTS

Author's Note	v
Advance Praise	ix
Khalid Bin Ahmed Bin Mohamed Al Khalifa	
Foreword	xi
Tommy Koh	
Foreword	xiii
Gopalan Raman	
Review	xv
Ong Keng Yong	
Commentary	xvii
Ibrahim Ali Badawi	
Commentary	xix
Agnes Sng	
Commentary	xxi
Wolfgang Sachsenröder	
Acknowledgements	xxiii
Chapter 1 Winds of Change	1
Chapter 2 Childhood Days	5
Chapter 3 First Day at Work	41
Chapter 4 Civil Servants Get the Shock	47

Chapter 5	Political Education	53
Chapter 6	Initial Reforms	57
Chapter 7	Building a Nation	67
Chapter 8	The Battle for Merger	73
Chapter 9	Sojourn in Malaysia: A Failed Venture	81
Chapter 10	Forever Independent & Sovereign	85
Chapter 11	Recognition & International Role	95
Chapter 12	Swimming Against the Current	127
Chapter 13	Setting High Standards	133
Chapter 14	Form Versus Substance	145
Chapter 15	Relations with Neighbours	169
Chapter 16	Slums to Shining Metropolis	281
Chapter 17	"Innovate or Evaporate"	293
Chapter 18	Fiscal Discipline	329
Chapter 19	Learning from the Master	343
Chapter 20	Food in Diplomacy	353
Chapter 21	Success and Failure	367
Chapter 22	Power of Knowledge	381
Chapter 23	Western Democracy: Can It Deliver?	393
Chapter 24	Singapore Model	441
Chapter 25	The Future	467

Chapter 1

WINDS OF CHANGE

A journey of a thousand miles begins with a single step.
                                                    Lao Tzu

Monday, 14th December, 1959 was a fine, sunny and breezy morning when I took that first step. With confidence, enthusiasm and pride, I walked-up the steps of the City Hall frontage at about 8.30 A.M. to report for duty as Executive Officer in the newly-formed Ministry of Culture, located on the 3rd floor. The minister was Sinnathamby Rajaratnam who later became the foreign minister. Thus, began my long journey and career in the civil service that spanned more than 42 years.

Singaporeans know the year 1959 as a momentous year — the year Singapore attained self-government, following first general election, under universal suffrage on 31st May. The Peoples' Action Party (PAP), led by Mr Lee Kuan Yew, assumed office on 3rd June. A journalist by the name of Vernon Bartlett wrote in *The Straits Times* in June of that year that Lee Kuan Yew then was the youngest prime minister in the Commonwealth and, probably, in the world, as well. The scale of the victory stunned many observers and even the British were probably surprised at the massive landslide.

DAWN OF A NEW ERA

The Second World War brought destruction and suffering on a scale never before experienced by mankind. In Asia, the Japanese invasion and occupation were brutal and vicious. However, one unintended outcome was that people subjugated and oppressed by colonial powers for so long realised that colonial regimes were not invincible. With Japanese surrender on 2nd September in 1945, the anti-colonial struggle gained greater momentum in Singapore, as elsewhere in Asia. The torch for independence was lit; it was a not a question "if" but "when" the oppressed masses would break free. The unfolding drama in India, China, Indonesia, and Vietnam had a profound effect in shaping the events of the time and were a harbinger of a resurgent and vibrant Asia. Before the War, when people referred to Malaya they generally included Singapore as well. Singapore, Malacca and Penang were administered as **"Straits Settlements"**. After the War, Singapore became a **"Crown Colony"**. Singapore was ruled by the **British Military Administration** from 1945 to 1947.

JAPANESE OCCUPATION

The Japanese propaganda was to create a **"co-prosperity sphere"** in the countries they invaded and occupied; instead what they created was **"co-poverty sphere"** through systematic brutality, which was well-documented and needs no narration here. Many people lost all they had, and many families were destroyed; yet there were also a few who made their fortunes by whatever means they could. My parents lost all of what they managed to save to give us children a good start and, in this regard, their struggle continued. Singapore suffered much loss of life and destruction from the Japanese invasion and occupation largely due to the supreme over confidence of the British rulers. They openly derided the Japanese and said the Japanese were short-sighted and could not fly aircrafts properly during the day, never mind flying them at night. President Sheares told me that during a visit to their hospitals in Kyoto in the 1930s, he found the Japanese were much more advanced, not only in medicine but in all other fields as well. Upon returning home, he told his colleagues what he saw and his belief that the British were not only fooling the natives (as we were termed) but themselves also. As if to prove the point, the Japanese bombed Singapore at night, while the British officer, who had the key to turn off city lights and to enforce a black-out, was reportedly enjoying himself dancing at the **Raffles Hotel**, the centre of British social life then. The pictures of the carnage in Battery Road caused by Japanese bombing show horrible scenes. Sheares shared many more important observations with me and I will refer to them later.

THE AFTERMATH

In the settling of scores that followed in the aftermath, those who had collaborated with the Japanese paid a terrible price. They were hunted down and killed like animals. Those who witnessed the scenes told us blood curdling accounts of the ruthless slaughter of "collaborators" who begged for mercy.

Picking up the pieces for the vast majority of the people was not easy or smooth but the relative peace enabled rebuilding. Life was still tough: food was in very short supply and many items were unaffordable, even if available. **There was rationing of essential commodities — rice, sugar and condensed milk**. If I remember correctly, it was about a *kattie* of rice (low grade) per person per week and one condensed milk tin per family per week. Hardship was prevalent. In those days, the weight measurement was *16 tahils* made one *kattie* and *100 kattis* made one *pickul;* one *kattie* was probably about 0.5 kilograms in present day weight measurement.

Transport was difficult. I remember my elder brother and I used to cycle (myself riding pillion) to the shop, which was the government appointed dealer, to collect our family ration. We had to produce the **family ration card which was pink in colour.** The shopkeeper was not a pleasant fellow. If anyone dared so much as to check the weight, i.e. to ensure there was no shortchanging, he would go into a rage and chase the person out. Besides, his premises were not clean; many a time we saw his dogs with scabies (skin disease) sleeping on top of the bags of rice. Nobody dared to question him as it would have been extremely unwise to do so. In those days, hoarding and black market dealings were not uncommon.

Yet, very few complained; we went about our daily grind and did the best we could to survive, in the hope that things would get better. Anyway, when all of life was a struggle, what could we complain about, and to whom?

Chapter 2

CHILDHOOD DAYS

The earth provides enough to satisfy every man's needs, but not every man's greed.

Mahatma Gandhi

Nature never did betray the heart that loved her.

William Wordsworth

The memories I have of my early childhood is growing up in our small ancestral village, then named Aliyanilai (which roughly translates to "eternal settlement"), in Tanjore District of Madras Province, later called Tamil Nadu, in India. This happened quite by accident. My parents took me, then about eight months old (as I understood later from my mother), and my two elder siblings for what was intended to be a short trip. It was some time towards the end of December 1939 or early January 1940. However, not long after, sea transport between India and Singapore stopped and, therefore, we could not return to our home in Singapore. It was one of the consequences of the War. Reminiscing those years, decades later, my mother remembered that "Poland was burning" at the time we left for India. (War films and German archival footage, which I saw later in adult life, showed **Adolf Hitler's** storm troopers torching buildings, many of them in the Jewish quarter, with flame-throwers shooting ferocious flames.) Thus, we were stranded in the village. Even after the Japanese surrender, and the return of the British to Singapore, there was quite a delay in the resumption of passenger ship services. Almost all available ships had been commandeered and most of them converted to troop-carriers to serve the War effort.

My parents did not have much savings or any relatives who had resources to spare. However, it was not too difficult to get going, as both my father and mother were natives of the village, having been born and raised there. Their first-born son, Sivasamy (my eldest brother), was born there sometime in the 1920s. All the remaining four sons, namely Kannusamy, Meiyappan, myself and Shanmugam, were born in Johor Bahru. I have explained this below. I remember our family friends telling my mother that, among all her children, Sivasamy was the brightest. Apparently, so early in his very brief existence, he had shown many promising signs and impressed people around him. Alas, fate had a different destiny for him. He did not live to see his second birthday. It must have taken my mother a very long time to get over the loss, if at all. I have heard of a saying that "Time gilds with gold the iron links of pain." As decades went by, my mother's reminiscences of him became less.

Life in the village was very simple and agrarian with daily engagements with nature for a variety of needs. Most of the dwellings were mud huts with thatched roofs and had mud floors. Cooking was done on open fires in mud-hardened stoves and the utensils were made of either clay or wood e.g. cooking pots, drinking vessels, ladles and others. There was one interesting cutting instrument. It consisted of a thin iron plate securely mounted in a vertical position near one end of a thick piece of wood measuring, approximately $2 \times 6 \times 12$ inches. The women folk sat on the wooden board and cut or sliced the vegetables and meat (when available) using the sharp side facing them. They also made rice flour by pounding rice in a circular wooden block with a circular well in the middle. They used long suitable wooden poles with steel ends to pound the rice. For grinding, a different tool was used. A granite block, with a similar circular well in the middle, had a short granite stub and its rounded end sat snugly in the well. The top end, chiselled to the size of a palm, was rotated in a circular motion and the dripping rice was fed into the narrow space in between. Thus, they could grind the rice to any specification required. They did it with ease and quite deftly. In those days, it was a must for girls to learn these skills at a very young age. It was unthinkable that any prospective mother-in-law would accept a girl without such skills as her daughter-in-law! These skills were part of the culture and their use in daily routines kept the women folks lean and healthy, as well. My mother was naturally slim and she used all these skills daily, even in Singapore, until the 1970s.

People in the village did not have much; it was a sort of day to day living for most. They toiled in the fields, almost from dawn to dusk, planting and growing crops such as paddy, ground nuts, maize, millet, and a variety of vegetables, and tended to livestock that typically included oxen, cows, goats, sheep, and chicken. The oxen were beasts of burden for ploughing and for pulling (bullock) carts. Not everyone owned a plot of land, and if they did, it was often small in size. Cooking was done in earthen pots with wooden utensils and banana leaves served as plates. They had very little else. Some of them did seasonal work, toiling for landowners for meagre wages. It is no secret that for centuries, and all over the world, landowners in similar agrarian settings were not kind to the humble, illiterate, and simple peasants whose blood and sweat helped to create the wealth of the landed gentry.

I enjoyed just like other kids around me did and in any case, I had not known any better or different then. It was not uncommon to see very young children, ages one to three, running around naked. I was probably not an exception either. Such was the poverty.

My first and most important step into the world of knowledge began with my father making me regurgitate the Tamil alphabet — 216 in all. My memory is that, when I was about 4-years-old, my father took me to a village teacher to learn Tamil and I was wearing just shorts which were sewn from clothes that my parents had brought with them from Singapore.

The teacher sat on raised ground under an old banyan tree. We students sat on the ground. Neither the teacher nor the students had any writing materials and there was no blackboard either. He had a slate (a wooden-framed tile about the size of today's A4 size paper) and a slate pencil to write with. He would write on it and show it to us and we had to "write" that on the sand in front of us. He also kept his small stick handy as a warning to pay attention and did not hesitate to use it, if he felt irritated. He told us fables like the **"fox and the crow"**, describing how the cunning fox tricked the crow perched on a branch to sing and when it did, the food in the crow's mouth fell to the ground whereupon the fox made off with it! A little information about the teacher: He had no formal schooling himself and had no salary. The parents would pay him in kind, like paddy during harvest, or other produce and some token of appreciation during **Deepavali**, the most important festival for Hindus. All these were not much in quantity but they helped him to keep his home fire burning. He, like others around, had his own work. Classes were usually about two hours' long and irregular at times; nevertheless, his dedication was not in question.

My formal education began a few months later. My father sent me and my elder brother to a school (of sort) conducted by a Brahmin elderly man in his house in a neighbouring village named **Sellatoor,** about three miles away. There the ambience was better. Again there were no textbooks, blackboards and writing materials. However, if I recall correctly, some students had simple basic books with illustrations of objects and people with simple relevant text. My brother and I were lucky (or privileged) in many ways: we wore simple shorts and shirts, and had some primary school books which my brother used in Singapore. They were merely pictorial with appropriate words, for example *"rambutan"*, which our teacher pronounced a little differently because there was no such fruit there. School was for a full day. We would start from our home at about 9 A.M. or thereabout, walk the distance along the footpath, cross a stream and reach the school probably around 10 A.M. In those days, folks based the time by the position of the Sun and sometimes also by the arrival of the bus on the typically unpaved road. People used to say that the bus operator, a private company known as TVS (I came to know much later that they were the initials of the owner), ran very punctual schedules. Those were still the days of the British Raj! There were no clocks in the homes, not to mention wrist watches. Yet, it was not a problem for people in the village.

Despite the poverty and simple life, people were generally happy. There was a strong community spirit, they lent helping hands when needed, came together to celebrate social and religious events, and to settle disputes of whatever nature, in sessions presided by recognised elders (the **panchayat**). Villagers coming together for any event often took place under the old banyan tree within the village which was often the focal point. While the saying that **"nothing grows under the banyan tree"** is as true today as it has always been, I have, however, seen many activities taking place under the cool shade provided by its large spread of green canopy, projecting an aura of timelessness!

The most important thing for me, however, was the sacrifices made by my mother. She used to wake up very early, between 4.30 A.M. and 5 A.M., at the first crow of the cockerel. He was the most important time-keeper, who usually never failed (probably, he had his own reasons as well, such as to wake-up his harem of hens since the "early bird catches the worm"). If rarely and for some reason, the cockerel was amiss with his timing, he was roundly blamed and no excuse was allowed for his late nights! However, the cockerel was also blamed for no fault of his. Folks who could not or did not want to wake-up early often gave the lame excuse that the cockerel let them down!

My mother would clean the house and put the traditional *kolam* which are patterns made on the floor in front of an entrance using white rice powder. Later, I learnt its meaning and purpose. Apart from cultural aesthetics, it was also an offering of food to insects like ants, a reminder of the Hindu religious belief that all of God's creations deserve respect. She would then prepare food, often rice with water added and kept overnight, vegetables and pickle for us to carry and eat at lunch time. Sometimes, maize would substitute for rice. Occasionally, we would have fish or crab curries — a real treat. She would also make similar preparations for my father and grandfather. After finishing all the household chores, including washing clothes, she would take the food to my father and grandfather working in the fields, in time for their first meal of the day, around noon. She would also help in their work by removing weeds and keeping the flock of cunning and daring crows away from the rice stalks. The scarecrows (human effigies) were not much of a help to scare them away. She would return home around mid-afternoon to resume housework. More details of their hard lives later.

I have many happy memories of my years in the village, which was surrounded by nature. However, there were also dangers which young children cannot realise or understand. A proverb in Tamil goes something like this: "A young calf does not know fear". I had some near fatal encounters. Below are a few that I can remember.

When I was an infant, my mother used to keep me by her side when she slept at night. Everyone used to sleep on the floor, some on straw mats and others just on the bare floor. One night, she left me for a while to attend to something and when she returned she noticed that the home-made pillow was raised and two small eyes were gleaming from beneath. Realising the danger, she immediately deftly picked me up and alerted her father (my grandfather) sleeping nearby. He had much experience in dealing with such dangers and dealt with it effectively. It was a young cobra and it paid the price for its daring intrusion (Later in my adult life, I learnt from a documentary that on the very day a cobra hatchling breaks free from the egg shell, it has enough venom to kill a person. When fully grown, it would pack enough venom to kill about 40 persons!).

When I was about 4 or 5 years old, I remember groping the ground under the mango trees to pick up ripe fallen mangos, before day break, just to be ahead of others who would also come for the sweet and aromatic fruits. Sometimes there were rustlings among the dried leaves, and it could have been anything, for example, a rodent, squirrel or even a venomous snake and they were also there for the fruits. My parents did not approve of it, but I could not resist the urge to pick the mangoes and, on a lucky day, I could earn a few *annas* (16 *annas* made 1 *Rupee* which **then** was $0.66 in Singapore. In 2018, the rate was 1 Rupee to just 2 cents!). It was a foolhardy thing to risk life thus.

However, there is also a paradox. Cobras are revered and normally people avoided killing them, unless it posed serious danger to humans in the particular situation. Lord Shiva when He is depicted in human form, has a cobra loosely coiled around His neck, and is striking a majestic pose. I do not have the depth of knowledge in this regard to explain the precise purpose and meaning. However,

I think it represents one aspect of His omnipotence (in the Hindu pantheon, Lord **Shiva** is the destroyer, Lord **Brahma** is the creator and Lord **Vishnu** is the protector). I have seen folks placing milk in a small vessel, and sometimes an egg as well, at the foot of the earth mound home of the cobras, as offerings. While I have not seen the cobra coming out to drink the milk and swallow the egg, it does not mean that it did not happen. In later years, I have seen video footage of the reptile consuming milk. Cobra idols are also worshipped in some temples.

The most serious incident at that time was when I fell into a well while trying to draw water from it. My father, who was working in the field very close by, must have heard the thud when I hit the water, and jumped in to save me. Apparently, he was struggling to keep both of us above water while swimming in a stationary position within the confined space. Again, as my good fortune would have it, a close neighbour tending to his field in an adjacent plot heard my grandmother's loud wailing and rushed to help. He lowered a big bucket (fixed to a harness for lifting water for irrigation). Thus, he saved both of us in the nick of time. Needless to say, I received a sound thrashing afterwards for what I had done and I deserved every bit of it. In the context of life in the village, climbing small trees and sustaining the occasional falls were dismissed as part of the growing up process. Anyway, much of the time our parents were too busy away at work to supervise us, whose mischief sometimes had no limits.

However, all the above mishaps paled in comparison to my very close brush with death when I was serving in our High Commission in Canberra in 1982. I was returning home after attending an official function at the Papua New Guinea High Commission at about 6 P.M. on a bright summer day. I stopped at a main intersection for the traffic light and when it turned green I drove forward. All I can remember after that was waking up in Royal Canberra Hospital with pain in my chest, more than an hour later, surrounded by a police officer, doctors and nurses. Probably still in some sort of shock, I asked the police officer why I was there and what happened to my car. He responded by saying "Sir, you should not worry about your car now". I then realised that something horrible had happened. A few hours later, when I had gained back my full memory, he recorded a statement from me on my recollection of what I then knew was a very serious accident. He was in charge of the investigation and all he would tell me was that I was involved in serious road crash and that I was very lucky to be alive.

Police investigation established that my car was hit on the driver's side by a huge interstate transport truck (running on 28 wheels and locally known as "road train") which ran the red light. The police found that my car had been tossed or dragged for more than 50 feet and finally came to a rest facing the wrong direction. It was a complete wreck. The police found the driver was driving his truck while one of his legs was in plaster and he had to use crutches to alight from his vehicle. He was suspected to be under the influence of opiate drugs. These "truckers" frequently flouted laws requiring mandatory rest stops after more than 6 hours of continuous driving. They took drugs to keep themselves awake while at the wheel. The fact that my Mercedes car was new (7 months old then) and I was wearing a seat belt, saved me from the jaws of death. The Almighty had also intervened to save me. (About six months later, the Chinese Defence Attaché in Canberra was killed on the spot at the same intersection in a motor accident in similar circumstances.)

There were many people who could not believe that I survived the crash with just broken ribs. I spent several days in the hospital. I asked my wife to retrieve my brief case, driving licence and other personal belongings from what remained of my car, which was at the

Mercedes agent's premises. It was towed there on my instruction. My wife cried when the agent asked her why she wanted the driving licence of a dead person. He apologised to my wife when he learnt that I was very much alive. The car was a total wreck and was written off by the insurers. Also, it is during such times that you realise who your real friends are and how much they care for you. Upon hearing the news of the accident, our close friends, an Australian couple, David and Robyn McConocky, rushed to the hospital with my wife and children, and assisted us during that difficult time. There were also a few visits from some of my friends in the Department of Foreign Affairs and Trade. Many of them also sent me get well cards stating "we want to see you back in the Department soon". It was indeed touching. Sadly, David succumbed to illness a few years later. We miss him.

Back to life in the village. I was also able to make myself useful to those who mattered to me. I recall quite vividly to this day accompanying my grandfather, together with his few cronies, to catch fish in the streams, in small lakes and in the tank (large earthen dam to collect and retain rainfall for community agricultural use). The fishes caught in the net were thrown to the bank and my job was to pick them up and put them into the straw basket which had a narrow neck. I had to do it quickly to prevent the fish from jumping back into the water. Once, I was injured by a fish when it hit me in the right upper arm. Its sharp protruding fin on its side (its defensive armour) punctured my skin and caused pain. My grandfather came out of the water and took another type of fish (which was "female") and rubbed its saliva on the affected part, whereupon the pain stopped immediately. I was very fond of my grandfather, from whom I learnt much, simply by observing him. He was never harsh with me, except on one occasion. I went missing, probably during a religious gathering, and when the search party found me and brought me to him, he gave me a tight slap. Still my fondness for him never waned and I missed him much after I left the village. Decades later, I sent him a box of good quality cigars (locally known as *"chroot"*) from London during my posting there (details below). According to stories that reached me, he had gone a round telling almost everyone in the village how proud he was of his grandson. He passed away at the ripe old age of about 100 or 102. I was told that till the very end, he was not bedridden and had reasonable memory for his age.

Village elders had a treasure trove of knowledge and experience, passed on to them by generations of ancestors from ancient times, in treating ailments and injuries, mainly by herbal preparations. Nature has many useful plants and also holds secrets in this regard. We "brushed" our teeth most of the time with a small twig broken off from the branches of neem trees. Sometimes, clay was used to do so. Toothbrushes and paste were never heard of. The neem tree and its leaves still have medicinal value. The abundance of neem trees that grow in the Gulf states came from India about 200 years ago, according to some observers. In our village, as was elsewhere, there was a medicine man practising traditional medicine, using plants and oils like gingelly oil, neem oil and castor oil extracted from the plants and their seeds. People in the village relied on the medicine man. In my observation, he was able to cure many common ailments, for example, vomiting, diarrhoea, headache, and simple injuries. He was, for all intent and purposes, the "doctor" in the village. The nearest formally-trained doctor was several miles away in a small town. The sick, even if they could make the long journey by foot, could not generally afford the cost.

There was also a very unusual but serious incident I witnessed and participated in. One evening, I was in a group of about 4 or 5 people returning from a neighbouring village, after having done some manual work there. As we neared the big tank, we heard cattle bellowing and from the sound it seemed to be in distress. The light was fading and when we reached the animal, we were shocked to find that it was stuck in deep mud, apparently while trying to reach for the only remaining small puddle of water around. All its legs had sunk into the mud, which was akin to a quicksand situation. We set to work immediately to lift the cow out of the treacherous mud, which was the result of the prolonged drought. It was a very difficult operation because we ourselves were in danger of getting stuck. As luck would have it, we had some poles and some ropes with us and managed to lift the cow out of the mud after much struggle. The grateful cow trotted away to its home and disappeared in the closing darkness. We could not have left without helping the poor beast. Most probably wolves, foxes, iguanas, and the like would have devoured the helpless animal during the night (It was not uncommon then for nomadic herdsmen to lose a sheep or two to wolves and foxes during the night, if the animals were not properly penned and guarded). The news must have spread quickly as the owner made a trip the next day to thank us. A cow, like a cobra, is also a revered animal.

Simple as it might appear, this system had profound meaning and a message for humanity: the importance of community belonging, a spirit of caring, sharing both joy and sorrow, valuing the need to live in harmony with nature, and the belief that a balance between the spiritual and the material is necessary for fulfilment in life. Alas, having survived the onslaught of time since ancient days, **"progress", "modernity"** and **"globalisation"**, especially since the early 20th century, have become the death-knell for what I believe to be one of the best systems ever designed by men and women for harmonious living among themselves and with the environment. In this context, it is worth recalling **Mahatma Gandhi's** warning: **"The earth provides enough to satisfy every man's needs, but not every man's greed."** Now, and almost a century later, it does not require a genius to realise how prophetic he was. The effect and consequences of insatiable greed and an unbridled lust for power are damaging Mother Earth, thereby, threatening the very survival of the human species, naysayers notwithstanding. It makes me wonder if *homo sapiens* can avoid self-destruction?

All in all, my memory is that life, even at that tender age, was neither uneventful nor unhappy. Often, I look back to those days with nostalgia.

Before I end my narrative on my experiences in the village, I would like to share some interesting facts and observations of changes that have taken place since. During the 70 years that have elapsed, I made three or four very short trips to the village, mainly pilgrimages to temples, the last one being early in 2018. I noticed many things had changed: population in the village had shrunk due to migration to urban areas and overseas in search of jobs, mostly low-skilled; noticeable increase in primary education among the young; more mobility mainly through motor cycles ("two-wheeler" in local parlance); electricity in almost all dwellings (even if supply was intermittent), television sets in almost in every home; somewhat improved roads; and some prosperity in terms affordability of basic household items, thanks largely to remittances from abroad. However, the most spectacular development was the revolution in communication connectivity. One would be hard put to find anyone in the village now (indeed in the whole country) without a mobile telephone. In this regard, the world has come to the village and the isolation, if it could be termed "splendid", has come to an end.

Be that as it may, a very serious problem has also developed in the meanwhile and that is water scarcity. The shallow wells that had plentiful good clean water, used for both domestic and irrigation needs, had dried out. I found weeds and shrubs, the hardy variety, growing in them. The deep well which my father had constructed to provide water for the small temple (dedicated to **Lord Vinayagar**), which he also built, and for the use of nearby residents also had similarly dried up. I felt saddened. Bore wells, unheard of before, had replaced the traditional wells and, with each passing year, the bore had to be deepened, some as deep as 500 metres. Water was pumped up by motor whenever electricity came on. In many villages, even bore wells had to be abandoned owing to unsustainable depths and water contamination by intrusion of sea water and/or sulphur. This has become a serious national problem there. I will refer to this later.

However, amidst all these changes, the mighty cockerel had stood his ground. Even in this age of technology, I noted that the cockerel was still the most efficient timekeeper and reliable "alarm clock" for the villagers. They were unwilling to trade him for the mechanical version. Besides, his prowess and virility in procreation is still valued, but only until old-age consigns him to the curry pot. Owning big, strong, and aggressive cockerels is a status symbol and a money-earner, as well. The birds with razor sharp blades attached to their ankles fight each other during wagers and often resulting in injuries, occasionally serious enough to maim or result in death of either or both birds. Blood sport and cruelty aside, these birds are still very useful.

RETURN HOME

My father's constant worry was the small provision shop and the few possessions he had left behind in the care of a close relative of his, who was under my father's employment as a bookkeeper for many years. Sometime in 1946, the steam ship service resumed, and, after much effort, my father managed to get passage to

Singapore. He left us, telling us that he would send for us as soon as he had earned some money. About a month later, my father's letter arrived. The news was not good. He had lost much of what he had left behind. My understanding was that the relative to whom he had entrusted his business, had run it to the ground and built a dairy business for himself, some three miles away in Kranji. That was another big blow and setback for my parents. They had not expected the person, to whom they had given a job when he came in search of one and stayed with them for several years, would do what he did.

A few months later, my father arranged for the rest of the family to join him. I can remember my excitement upon hearing the news of our travel by steam ship. My mother arranged with a tailor in the nearest town to stitch a few shirts and trousers for all the boys (four of us) and she bought a few cotton sarees for herself. Affordability, and not quality, was the issue at hand. We travelled by bullock cart to the train station that was some distance away and from there by train to the town of **Nagapattinam**, where the port was located. As far as I can remember, it was my first train journey. We stayed in the town for a few days to complete the necessary documentation.

On the date of departure, we proceeded to the port with our few possessions in a bullock cart. Boarding the ship (its name I remember was "SS Rajula" operated by the **British India Steam Navigation** company) was not easy. The port had no wharves for the ship to dock at and so it was anchored some distance away at sea. All the passengers were loaded (or herded) into few launches tied together and rowed to the ship by many tough looking oarsmen, taking advantage of favourable tides and currents as much as possible. On arrival alongside the ship, the launches were manoeuvred one after another to an inclined ladder on the side of the ship.

Passengers boarded one by one by catching the ladder and climbing up, with a little help from ship's crew. Children had to be carefully assisted. Usually, men working on the launches relied on the waves to lift the launch to the height required to catch the bottom rung of the ladder. Therefore, the condition of the sea at that precise time was important. I had heard of instances when boarding the ships had to be aborted or postponed due to unideal conditions. We got onto the ship alright but not without an unexpected additional cost. About mid-way between the shore and the ship, the oarsmen slowed down the launches, almost to a standstill position, and asked for cash as offerings (if I remember correctly to a well-known Muslim shrine in that town) to get blessings for our safe journey. It was a blackmail of sorts; all the passengers gave whatever they could spare, and the launches resumed the speed!

The voyage took five days. We travelled on deck, as did most of the passengers. Bunks and cabins, even if they were available at that time, were beyond our means. It was communal living with just enough space to sleep and store a few possessions. There were no separate sleeping areas or bathing facilities for women and children. People devised some arrangement whereby the women and children would bathe first while some men stood guard outside to alert and warn other male passengers to use the facility later. We bathed in sea water and drinking water was rationed. The most memorable thing for me was the food. The rice was of the lowest quality and had a distinct unpleasant smell, and the curry was equally unappealing. There were no recreation facilities and all one could do to stretch their legs was to walk along the railings. Many had story telling sessions and others, in search of easy fortunes, did what they normally did — gambled. Very long and idle hours in crowded conditions created/caused other problems as well.

On the fifth day, we landed in Penang and were taken in boats to a desolate island where we were quarantined for two days. It was common in those days for passengers from the Indian subcontinent to be thus quarantined and the reason given was, to prevent the spread of infectious diseases. We stayed in barrack-like sheds and slept on the cement floor. Water was plentiful and available in long concrete-made tanks. We kids frolicked in the cool clean water which was pouring out from pipes about three inches in diameter. Food was better than what we had on board the ship and it was the first time ever that I tasted coffee (black) and bread, rationed as they were. On the third day of our stay in that island, we were transported to Prai on the mainland to board trains or other means of transport to reach destinations in Peninsular Malaya and Singapore. We boarded the train for our long journey at nighttime and it arrived at the Johor Bahru station the next morning. My father came with a small open lorry and took us to our home in Marsiling. It was a short distance, about two miles. We crossed the Causeway and we were home. Thus, I began my new life in Singapore.

One final thought on the train journey. Those days the train journeys were not entirely safe. The **Malayan Emergency** had been declared and members of the **Malayan Communist Party** (commonly referred to as "terrorists") used to derail trains as part of their violent campaign to overthrow the British Raj. Passengers were warned by railway staff that if the train made any unscheduled stops on the track, never to leave the train. The last wagon in the train was a big pillbox type steel-plated structure with small lateral apertures for the armed guards inside to engage and shoot the terrorists whenever they attacked the train. My understanding was that it was not very effective and there were occasions when it proved to be a death trap for the guards who were supposed to protect the passengers. The rail network was then known as the "Malayan Railway" (MR); later when *Bahasa Melayu* replaced English, the name was changed to "*Keratapi Tanah Melayu*" (KTR), which meant the same in translation.

RUSTIC SURROUNDINGS

Marsiling then had a rustic charm. In many ways, things were different from the village, Aliyanilai, but in one important respect it was the same. Again, we lived surrounded by nature and I liked that very much. English poet, **William Wordsworth** (1770–1850), wrote **"Nature never did betray the heart that loved her"**. I grew up in a pre-war house made of wooden planks with a roof made of *attap* (thatched leaves) and some corrugated iron sheets. It had no number until the 1950s when the Rural Board allotted it the number "24". It was situated at the edge of a vast rubber plantation in a secondary forest, owned by the Bukit Sembawang Rubber Estates. We had both the small shop and the living accommodation in the same building. There were no other dwellings nearby, except for the estate conductor's office where the latex, brought by the tappers (who were mostly Indians and Malays), would be checked and weighed, usually between 10 A.M. and mid-day. The latex would then be mixed with ammonia and left in open rectangular tanks with vertical tin-plates, to coagulate. The coagulated latex slaps were then pushed through mechanical rollers to be pressed into sheets and taken to be smoked in a wood-burning smoke house. The sheets were then checked and packed in bales for export (Export price was quoted "RSS __ cents per bale fob" where "RSS" was abbreviation for "Ribbed Smoked Sheet").

Apart from these, the only people activity was the estate workers patronising my father's small provision shop, that sold basic necessities, and the occasional motor vehicles and bicycles passing along Marsiling Road, which then was about four miles long, running through forests, streams and swamps. That road took us to Woodlands Road and then all the way to the city, 16 miles away.

In those days, the different communities largely kept to themselves and interacted in their own languages and dialects. Among the

Malays, there were Javanese and Boyanese who had their own dialects; the Indians were mostly Tamils with a few Malayalees; and among the Chinese, the dialects were Hokkien and Hakka. There was no sense of belonging, much less loyalty to Singapore. They were more concerned with the developing situations in their motherlands. For many of them, their stay in Singapore was only to make enough fortune to enable them to return to their motherlands for retirement. In this sense, there was no citizenship and the different communities just co-existed.

There would be a small gathering of estate workers' families in the late afternoons to listen to the radio news and entertainment programmes. Owning a radio set was beyond reach for many of us. Transistor radio was invented much later. Even a gramaphone (to play music records) cost about $100 which was a lot of money for us rural folks then. The **Department of Information Services** (DIS) provided **radio sets for community listening** — a GEC radio set with a horn speaker. Our shop was chosen as the area to operate the set. It was battery powered (the bulky car battery type) and was recharged every week by a DIS appointed contractor. I enjoyed listening to local and foreign broadcasts. It helped me to develop a lively interest in current affairs at a very young age.

NO BASIC AMENITIES

We did not have basic amenities: there was **no electricity, no tap water and no toilets** which was not an uncommon situation in rural areas at that time. Even in the urban areas not every household had flushing toilets. I can still remember night soil vehicles from the then **Municipal Council** lining up in Albert Street in the morning, usually around 7 A.M., to collect **night soil buckets from dwellings** in the area, including Selegie Road, for disposal at sewerage treatment plants. A typical vehicle would have about 100 compartments, much like the safety deposit boxes on the walls in a bank vault. The night soil removers rode standing on the rear of the vehicle clinging to a bar. It was a common sight in the city then. As the vehicles passed by, there would be the strong smell of *Jay's fluid*, a sort of anti-septic used to sanitize the buckets' contents and suppress the foul smell.

We drew water from the Estate's well located some 200 yards from our house. As per division of duties in the family, fetching water was my job. After school and usually in the afternoon, I would do a few trips to the well with two empty four-gallon drums, fill them up and fasten them to either ends of a pole (*kaanda* as it was known then) and carry it on my shoulders. It was a quite heavy load but manageable. Occasionally, I would be rewarded with a small tumbler of coffee, a luxury given our situation then. In those days, coffee was a mixture of about 50% coffee beans and 50% maize (a cheaper variety would have even more maize and less coffee beans) roasted in an improvised drum rotated by hand over a wood fire in the back streets of the city. Nescafe and the like were unheard of then and, even if available in the city, it was beyond the reach of folks like us.

The toilet was a hole in the ground some 50 yards away. Low walls made of wooden planks clobbered together, provided privacy of sorts. At night, a torchlight or an oil lamp was necessary to get there. About once in two months or so, a vegetable farmer would come and scoop up the faeces and carry it away to be used as fertiliser to grow vegetables. He would pay about 50 cents for it. Not a bad arrangement, I would say. There was a big Chinese community some distance away engaged in vegetable farming and pig and chicken rearing. They were relatively more prosperous than other communities.

The vegetables in those days were actually "organic"! In any case, chemical fertiliser was not common and, even if available, was unaffordable for many in the circumstances then.

NIGHTLY SYMPHONY

At night we lit kerosene lamps. We had a German made *petromax* pressure lamp that provided enough illumination. I would study till about 10 P.M. There were so many mosquitoes around that we had to burn mosquito coils to keep them at bay. We slept inside mosquito nets but the frustrated and blood thirsty insects would keep up with their nightly "symphony" and try to find a gap in the net to get in. We used to spray DDT (later banned for being harmful to health) to repel the mosquitoes, but success was only temporary. In any case, we would be so tired by then and would slip into slumber. Vector borne diseases like malaria were quite endemic and the Health Department employees would spray oil in ditches regularly to prevent mosquito breeding. Fumigation technology came about 25 years later!

SCHOOLING

I began my primary education a bit late and in a private school, Public English School, in Johor Bahru. One might ask why Johor Bahru since my family has never lived there. Johor Bahru town was very near, and therefore, was where we went for most of our needs, including marketing, medical care, primary schooling, cinemas, and for mothers to deliver babies. I understood from my mother that the Johor General Hospital then was of a good standard and the obstetrician who delivered me was a British woman. Most people who could afford hospital delivery costs then, went to that hospital. The city area in Singapore was far away and travel costs would have been very expensive and taken very long. In late 1940s, I remember the bus fare to Johor Bahru was 5 cents and could reach there in less than 15 minutes. The bus fare to reach the urban centre in Singapore cost about 50 cents and took about 45 minutes or more to get there, depending on the wait for the bus. There was no immigration control, no passports and no customs checks. People moved easily and effortlessly in both directions. Crossing the Causeway by foot was also quite common then. The only identification document was an Identity Card (IC) that people above the age of 12 were required to carry by law and had to be produced when asked to do so by police personnel. The IC was introduced by the British when the Emergency was declared, and the purpose was to isolate communists. It was the forerunner of our comprehensive data management system and very important security tool, the NRIC (National Registration Identity Card). It also gave us a head start in the pioneer development of "**E-Government**". One final thought on the Causeway: it was built by the British to connect people on both sides and not to keep them separate. However, Singapore's separation from Malaysia necessitated the control measures and mechanisms that have been in place ever since. These are normal arrangements between sovereign states.

This was the beginning of my formal education journey. There were classrooms fitted with blackboards and chalk pieces to write with. We had a text book, an exercise book to write in and were given homework. Above all, there were bucket system toilets. It was, overall, a very different environment than the one I was used to in the village. It was the first time I went to school wearing a proper shirt and shorts and above all, wearing shoes. The school did not have a uniform but it had a badge with name of the school engraved on it. I washed and "ironed" my school clothes. The "iron" was a glass bottle filled with hot water and it was rolled over repeatedly on the fabric to straighten out big creases. Much later, my father bought an iron made of brass which was heated by burning charcoal pieces inside it. In order to save costs, we used dried hard coconut shells, instead. There were problems in this. Care had to be taken not to overheat the baseplate in order to avoid damage to the fabrics. Also, the ash inside would drift outside and land on the fabric. The shoes were made of white canvass with crepe rubber soles. Every three or four days, or sooner if necessary, I "polished" my shoes. The process was to apply white lime after having cleaned the shoes with soap and water and leave them out in the sun to dry. As a rule, I made every effort to turn up to school neat. As an aside, I would like to say that this practice has not left me. Even to this day, I still wash my own clothes most of the time and iron them. It is not as labour intensive as it was before. The machine does the washing and I do the rest. Occasionally, I lend a helping hand to other members of my family in this regard. Also, I continue to polish my shoes. I like doing all these things. It is just a matter of routine.

As a short digression, I want to share two anecdotes on the need for good grooming. The first one was when I was in **Abu Dhabi** to call on a senior official in the government there. I was then the Ambassador to **Egypt** and concurrently accredited to a few other countries, including United Arab Emirates, for which Abu Dhabi is the capital. Before leaving the hotel, I noticed that the Third Secretary, who I had brought with me to be at the call, as part of his training, was wearing old shoes and one had a noticeable cut. It also appeared that it had not been polished for a long while. I told him that he could not come with me wearing those shoes, whereupon he said that his new pair of shoes was packed in the baggage which had not yet arrived from Singapore. I instructed him to get a new pair of shoes quickly and he did, not very willingly I must say. The second occasion was when I was the Chief of Protocol. A protocol officer (a retired army officer) turned up one day to office with his shoes in a similar condition. Unlike the Third

Secretary mentioned above, who was relatively new in the service, this officer had served long years in the army. In his case, I told him to leave the office and come back wearing a presentable pair of shoes. Indifference and sloppiness of this nature in diplomats and protocol officers would not earn them respect from those they have to deal with in the line of duty. Besides, it would also not reflect well of our country. Our civil servants were fairly well rewarded, much to the envy of counterparts in many other countries. Further, remuneration schemes also provided special additional allowances such as "Outfit Allowance" for foreign service officers and "Representational Allowance" for protocol officers. I believe the remuneration package is still the same with adjustments for inflation. Therefore, it was not a question of cost or affordability. In my opinion, it was just a matter of discipline. In my training sessions for diplomats and protocol officers, conducted both at home and abroad, I always emphasised on the importance of good grooming, amongst other requirements. It is one of the tools for small states to punch above their weight.

I devoted as much time as I could, to learn as much as possible, and as quickly as possible. Going to school was an opportunity not to be missed. As could be expected in any school, there were few pupils who did not show similar commitment. It could have been that the boys led comfortable lives and did not see the importance of education, or that the parents of some of the boys kept them in school in order to prevent them from getting into undesirable activities out in the streets. There were many pupils who were four or five years older than me, of bigger build, and had quarrelsome dispositions. I suspected a few were gang members, as well. As much as possible, I kept away from them and ignored their occasional taunting. In this regard, the situation improved later when some of them needed me to help them in the lessons. The school was run and managed by an Indian couple, probably in their middle age, and who owned the real estate as well. I must say, to their credit, they were dedicated teachers to the extent possible, given the fact that it was a private operation for profit. One important factor was that they employed university undergraduates on long vacations looking for temporary jobs. Even though they were untrained as teachers, I found them good in imparting knowledge. It was there that I first met **K R Chandra**, who was an undergraduate in the then University of Malaya at the Bukit Timah Campus. During the short time he taught us, I enjoyed his lessons. After graduation, Chandra joined the Civil Service and rose to the topmost position of Permanent Secretary. As it happened, he was later my boss in the **Land Office** when he was the **Commissioner of Lands** and I a **Deputy Collector of Land Revenue**.

It is a fact that the private schools generally could not match the quality of Government schools in Singapore in terms of the curriculum, skills development, teaching quality, student progression, and many more related aspects, including sports facilities (In some countries, however, the opposite situation may hold true). Noting that I was doing not too badly in school (I scored first in examinations), and that I was a keen learner, our family friend and the "Estate Conductor", whose name was **C K Sundaram**, persuaded my father to enrol me in **Bukit Panjang Government English School** which was the nearest government's school, about six miles away. He, my father, and I went to see the principal of the school, **C A Peterson**, a Eurasian man. He was a stern man and his initial observation was that I was above the age limit. However, after looking at my report cards and giving me a brief oral test, he agreed to admit me to Standard Four. That year was 1952 and it was a very big break for me indeed. Initially, it was tough going, especially in subjects like algebra (a subject I had not even heard of until then), but with help from our family friend's daughter, who had completed her SSLC (Secondary School Leaving Certificate) examination in India, I managed.

The year 1952 was momentous, not only for Singapore, but also for the entire **British Empire**. That year, King George VI died. There was an official mourning period marked by solemn ceremonies. I remember the "royalists" in the population grieved along with the colonial officers. There were many so called "western-oriented gentlemen" who tried to be more British in their ways than even the British themselves. In school, we had solemn speeches by the headmaster who wore a black armband and showed genuine grief. The local teachers also did the same, but perhaps, not as enthusiastically.

Princess Elizabeth was then crowned Queen Elizabeth II the following year (1953), which was even more momentous for the British. The spectacular coronation ceremony in London was also an occasion to impress the British Empire, especially the natives in the far flung colonies, with Britain's "power and glory" or what remained of it. As elsewhere in the Empire, there was much celebration in Singapore. Costly, well decorated and illuminated arches festooned with the portrait of the Queen, Union Jack flags, buntings and banners were erected in many places, mainly in the city area. Many ceremonies, with pomp and pageantry, were held to mark the occasion. Schools also commemorated the occasion. One girl in our class, I think her name was Ooi Siew Eng, was dressed like the figure Britannia seated in a make-believe chariot on the stage and holding a wooden sceptre. A few boys, me included, stood behind her wearing khaki shirts and trousers, British Army berets as headgear, and holding wooden swords which we made in our "art & craft" class. The berets were sourced from second-hand vendors in Sungei Road which was then a very popular place for affordable paraphernalia of used and sometimes discarded items. It was like a flea market. As mentioned above, such events were intended to awe the natives of the imperial rule. In 1877, **Queen Victoria** was proclaimed **"Empress of India"** in a Delhi *Durbar,* after the whole

Indian subcontinent was brought under British rule. India was the biggest and most prized possession of the British Empire, not to mention the "*Kohinoor* diamond" (probably the best and the biggest of its kind and unmatched in value by any other) is set in the British monarch's crown (Incidentally, I have heard that India claims ownership of the Kohinoor and demands its return). However, there were already signs of decline of that "power and glory" after World War II, especially with Indian independence. It was big blow to all those who had firmly believed that the sun would never set on the British Empire!

There was no television broadcast service in Singapore then. It came much later (more on this later). Even in Britain, the service was inaugurated only in 1951, according to some records. An organisation known as "**Pathe News**" filmed, in black and white, important events in Britain and then cinema theatres used to show the films just before the main screening. I remember watching the news reel of the coronation ceremony of Queen Elizabeth II at a special screening in the **Odeon Theatre** in North Bridge Road. It was free of charge and I think it was arranged for by the Ministry of Education for school children. It was quite a treat as it was the first time many of us watched a film in such comfort!

In 1953, I sat for the public examination for entry to secondary school. My scores earned me a place in **Victoria School** in Jalan Besar where I began my secondary education at Standard Six in 1954. Costs for my parents were going up then and I am so grateful that they made sacrifices to keep me in school to complete my secondary education.

Victoria School was very far from Marsiling Road and I completely depended on buses for the commute to school. I walked for about 15 minutes to Woodlands Road to board the **Green Bus** and when it reached near Jalan Besar about 30 minutes later, I had to change to a **Singapore Traction Company** bus to reach school. It would take about 60 to 70 minutes in total, to get to school on a normal day. I had to leave home shortly after 5 A.M., while it was still dark, to reach school on time.

Relying on public transport had its own problems. Strikes were frequent and heavy rains would cause floods, causing further difficulties. When the transport was crippled, I could not reach school on time or sometimes at all, but these were not often. I never played truant and had no problems with my teachers in this regard. I liked being in school though I cannot say that I was a bookworm or very studious.

We were simple rural folks but with strong family and work ethos and values. My parents realised quite early in their life together that education was key for their children to do better than them in life. I would like to narrate an anecdote here. I had a fascination with photography, an unusual and expensive hobby to adopt, given our economic conditions. Not wanting to approach my father directly, I persuaded a family friend, the Estate Conductor (manager of the rubber plantations), to speak to my father about buying the cheapest camera available for me and, for my father's favourable consideration, I offered a deal of sorts. I promised to study very hard and if I achieved the first rank in my class examinations, my father would buy the camera for me. I delivered my side of the deal.

We, my father, the family friend and I, made the long bus journey to "Amateur Photo Stores" in North Bridge Road (opposite St Andrew's Cathedral). Our friend conducted the bargain in English (he was the only English educated person around for miles in Marsiling then) and asked the salesman for the cheapest camera on the shelf. After taking a look at us, he probably correctly assessed that it would be a waste of his time to try to sell us higher priced ones. It was a box camera named "Gevabox" that was made in Germany and cost $11.00, not an insignificant amount for my parents. The camera was a tough black ceramic box measuring about 5 inches by 7 inches by 4 inches — the two parts, front and back, were secured by built-in metal fasteners or clips. The two parts had to be separated to load the film and closed tight to not let any stray light in. It would be opened again only after all the 12 frames in the film had been exposed. After each exposure the spool had to be turned slowly in the direction indicated by a picture of a finger in a small hole at the back of the camera, until the next frame number appeared — an indication that the camera was ready to take the next photograph. The apparatus consisted of a small lens, a simple aperture control knob to allow either level 16 for bright sunlight or level 8 for not so bright or hazy conditions. The knob was pulled or depressed as required. There was a small glass square on top, which was the viewfinder. The one speed (1/60 second) shutter was released by depressing a knob.

Even by the standards of the time (1950s), my camera was very basic and considered by some (the wealthy) as rudimentary at best (In today's world it would not even be recognised as a camera!). In those days, taking fairly good photographs with recognisable images involved a bit of mental gymnastics, even with higher-priced cameras. It was a complicated and tedious process and required effort and patience. There were several requirements and the most important among them was loading the chemical coated paper film into the camera on spools behind the lens, which was in front, letting the right amount of light in through the lens, and accurately setting the distance between the camera and the object (focus) by turning the lens. As my camera was so basic, only three distance settings were available — 8 feet, 16 feet and infinity. In short, if the film was exposed for long, the picture would turn out very dark, or vice versa. And if the focus was not accurate, the images would be blurred. The combination had to be correct to produce sharp pictures on the chemical coated paper behind the lens.

Having exposed the frames, the film had to be rewound and taken out of the camera under a dark cloth. Loading and unloading had to be done in darkness. The film was then taken to a photo studio to be developed and printed. The process involved a dark room where the film was unwound and treated with chemicals to develop "negatives". The negatives were then loaded frame by frame into a "printer" which produced the images in black and white on appropriately sized white paper with chemicals. After that the paper was immersed in water and left in it for some time and the water was frequently agitated to get a proper "wash". The photos were then hung out to dry. Usually the photos could be collected from the studio after two or three days. Other factors for taking very good photos were a knowledge of film speeds, e.g. commonly ASA 100, 200 & 400 for different light intensities, "depth of field", and "exposure value". Few enthusiasts who adopted photography as a serious hobby and those who could afford it, had their own dark rooms and developing and printing facilities.

As readers would note, all these have been rendered obsolete, unnecessary, and primitive by technology. In this digital world, even a visually impaired person can take near perfect pictures with a mobile phone. However, I still keep my old cameras and the accessories, much to the annoyance of my wife, as a reminder of bygone times and my dabbling in photography. They have not lost their usefulness but have been made impractical by advancements in technology and the development of artificial intelligence. In any case, the manufacturers of film ("Kodak", "Ilford" and few others in those days) have stopped manufacturing them. However, photographs of that time did not lie, the images were genuine. Fast forward to present day, digital photos can be manipulated to change the images to suit the intended purpose — they can be "faked". **In this regard, old is gold!**

HELPING THE FAMILY

After school, I would help out at our shop, especially in delivering provisions on bicycle to customers. When not doing this work, I would help my mother by chopping firewood used for cooking, cutting grass for the cow we had, going to Johor to sell the jasmine flowers which she grew in the back garden and drawing water, which I mentioned earlier. I would also help my father in his beetle leaf plot when necessary. My other duties were to help my mother look after the chickens we reared. My mother would let out the chickens from the coop at dawn and I would secure them in the coop at dusk. Sometimes, we lost chickens to pythons and birds of prey. Selling portions of the garden produce, milk, chicken, and eggs supplemented our family income. All in all, it was quite a busy, but not an unhappy, life. As much as possible we were self-sufficient and that had many benefits. I became a handy man of sorts. I remember making stools to sit on from whatever wood I could find. One source was wooden crates containing condensed milk tins ("Blue Cross" and "Milkmaid" brands). After stacking the milk tins on the shop shelf, I would immediately claim the empty crate which I used for a variety of purposes around the house working with my very simple tools — a hammer and recycled nails. I later bought my first electric "Black & Decker" drill (which lasted 40 years) during my posting in London. Slowly since, I have built up my toolbox, not only to carry out simple electrical, masonry and plumbing works around the home, which my wife found useful, but also to service my car. I was a simple mechanic with just enough knowledge to change oil, clean/replace spark plugs, change oil and air filters, adjust and service the brakes and the like.

My wife provided the necessary assistance. Getting under the car was tedious work but the joy of being able to do so and ensure quality work gave me enormous joy. I still have the tools, but today's motor vehicles are the creation of very sophisticated computers and require sophisticated computers to diagnose, analyse, and rectify the faults in them. Not a job for a DIY mechanic like myself anymore!

On Sundays, and during school holidays, I would devote more time for all these activities. I used to trap wild fowls in the forest. The birds made a tasty soup. I had to be vigilant to prevent my catch from being stolen by others. I would also fish both at the streams and at sea (at the Causeway) with improvised hooks, sewing threads and a bamboo stick. Primitive as it was, I had some success. Returning home empty handed would not have pleased my parents, especially because of the time wasted. There were some wild animals in the forest then. One day, a group of boys caught a mouse deer after a chase. The animal looked terrified. It provided a great feast for some families on that day. However, there was always an ever-present danger from snakes and occasionally pythons. One day, a cobra slithered into our shop and hid itself in the space where the money till was located. My brother spotted it by chance, and he had a very narrow escape. For its audacity, the snake paid with its life.

As much as possible, I devoted 8 P.M. to 10 P.M. to my studies.

My father and mother worked very hard and were very disciplined about working from around 4 A.M. until 10 or 11 P.M. day in, day out. I cannot recall them ever taking a holiday, not that they could afford it. My father was quick tempered and often I would get into trouble with him over some lapses. Once, he hit me so hard that I fainted and collapsed. My mother was so concerned that she got him to promise that he would not hit me so hard again. He kept his word.

Be that as it may, they toiled so hard to give their children basic food on the table. My mother's life as a very young child in India is a heart-wrenching account. Her mother died when she was five and her father, a kind man according to my mother, remarried. Her stepmother did not care much for my mother. The family was very poor, and my mother was sent to work for a family who treated her very cruelly, made her do all the housework and toil in the field from morning until dusk. All she was given was one meal, consisting of a handful of rice leftover from the previous night and a few dried chillies!

After a few years, she could take it no more and ran away. She begged her father not to send her back and told him that she would kill herself if she was sent back. He relented. The account of her suffering so much at such a tender age is deeply embedded in my memory and brings tears to this day. Sometimes, I feel guilty for not spending much time with my parents during their twilight years when I served abroad.

As mentioned earlier, my parents were natives of the village, Aliyanilai, which was in Madras Province (later Tamil Nadu) in India, and were hardy people. Soon after their marriage, they went to Ceylon (Sri Lanka) to work as tea pickers in a tea plantation in Kandy (I am inclined to think that India's human resource contributions, which in many ways empowers much of the world now, is not a recent development). Their earnings were meagre and depended on how much tea leaves they picked and also how well they were picked. They worked long hours and could hardly make ends meet, but still they were better off than those they had left behind in their village. However, danger came in the form of malaria which was very prevalent in Ceylon then. My mother was struck by the dreaded disease and many of her co-workers believed it was a miracle she survived. Many a time they went to check whether she was still around, as many others had succumbed to the disease. There was then no medicine to cure and, even if it was available, they would not have had the means to pay for it. They then decided that they had had enough of that life and returned to their village. (It might be of interest to readers that malaria was endemic in both Singapore and Malaya in the past. People bitten by the particular female mosquito (*Anopheles*) suffered agonising pain, alternating between extreme cold and high fever and if I remember correctly, the only medicine that was around was "quinine" and it was not very effective from what I heard. According to one record it was only in the early 1980s that our Government secured the WHO certification that Singapore was free from the disease.)

Soon after, my grandfather (mentioned earlier), who had come to Singapore and worked as a labourer, arranged for my father to come to Singapore to find employment. According to my father's recollections, it was sometime in early 1920s that he set foot in Singapore. If I remember correctly, he told me that he came on an "assisted passage" and billeted along with 20 or 30 men, all from the same close knit villages back home, at a small dwelling unit No. 8 (or 16 I cannot recollect) in Upper Dixon Road, close to the junction of Serangoon Road. They all lived together and, as far as possible, helped each other, as newly arrived immigrants often did.

Initially, my father worked as a Public Works Department labourer, in a team, employed to build roads, and later as a rubber tapper. A few years before his death, he spent some time with me, describing his early life in Singapore. He told me many anecdotes of his work experiences then (It brought me tears). The common thread was hardship but a few, to me, were somewhat hilarious as well. He did not like the heavy road building work, especially during the mid-day heat. One day, my father's team was laying gravel and pouring hot bitumen in Kerbau Road when a European supervisor came and ordered the team to rip off everything and do it all over again, just because he noted a very slight soft patch when the steam roller went over.

On that day my father decided that there must be a better way of eking out a living, if only he could find some other work. Most in his team tried to ease their hardships by drinking toddy daily in the evenings, in government run toddy shops. My father did not think that that was a panacea and did not want to succumb to that. He was so angry with his situation that he just "disappeared" for a few days, without telling my grandfather or anyone else, and went around looking for other more congenial work. His search for work was futile and when he "resurfaced" my grandfather was furious about what he did. But the shocker for my father came when he learnt that my grandfather had spent all the meagre savings he had left with him for safekeeping, and even a bit of his own money, in searching for my father. Apparently, he had sent out a few of his friends as search parties and, as it turned out, they did very little searching and spent the money enjoying themselves in parties of their own, probably to find some respite from their own hardships!

Once, in between two jobs, my father worked as a coconut gatherer in Bedok. He told me that tigers had been sighted in that area, as it was a dense jungle then. A monkey owned by a Malay man would pluck the mature coconuts and drop them to the ground. One day, a coconut narrowly missed my father. Whether the monkey did it on purpose was difficult to tell; probably it was showing its own frustration over its captivity and bad treatment by its owner. In any case, my father could not earn even the 3 cents required for the most basic meal! He then decided that he had had enough. Not only did he have to keep himself alive but he also had to support my mother who he had left behind in India.

THE BREAK

One day, my father took a bus and headed towards Johor to seek a better job. As the bus passed Marsiling Road, he got down and asked the people there whether there were any jobs available. There were none but the rubber estate conductor told him he could restart the small provision shop, which was abandoned by the previous operator, owing to ill health — malaria. My father's previous experience included rubber tapping and tea picking, and none in running a provision shop, but he decided to give it a go. Those were the Great Depression years (1929–1936) and demand for rubber, along with other primary commodities, around the world had collapsed. Many rubber tappers in Malaya and Singapore, and those associated with the industry, were being repatriated to their homelands, mainly to India, on free passage, as the economic conditions were bad and deteriorating. My father, however, did not avail himself of the free passage because the situation in his native village was not much better either. Therefore, he decided to take his chance in Singapore. He later sent for my mother to join him. They had 5 children, all boys and I am the fourth. At the time of this writing, my parents and all my siblings are no more. More on this later.

SPARTAN LIFE

I never tasted cheese, and many other foods which children these days take for granted, until I went to work. However, the silver lining was that it kept me lean and healthy (even if hungry at times). Life is not without ironies; when young not everyone has the means to afford the few things they crave, but when they can afford it in later life, their health might not permit it. However, compared to the hardship and suffering endured by my parents, I must say we children led relatively comfortable lives.

Chapter 3

FIRST DAY AT WORK

On arrival at the Ministry of Culture, the first person I saw was the Office Keeper, Santhanan, who was seated near the entrance and I informed him of my purpose. Many government departments then did not have staff designated as receptionists. Whoever was around was expected to chip in and do the job. He took me to an officer (an Executive Officer in charge of general administration) who then led me to the Assistant Secretary (an Administrative Service Officer) and who was the head of the personnel and finance sections and my immediate supervisor. After a short briefing, I was introduced to other heads of sections.

When the introductions were over, I arrived at the finance section that I was to take charge of. It was staffed by a Higher Clerical Officer (nearing retirement then) and a Clerical Officer (a lady) with about five years of experience in the service, both in Division Three. I was recruited into the General Executive Service (GES) in Division Two. In those days the Government was probably the biggest employer, and civil servants had a certain status in the community. As far as I knew, I was the first person to enter government service from the remote kampong where we lived.

In those days, jobs were scarce and therefore, competition was very intense. Recruitment to GES was done through a competitive examination. In that exercise, I do not know how many applied, but no more than 50 candidates were selected to sit for the examination. After the exam, we discussed the questions, as candidates often do, and to my horror none of the others had attempted the questions I had selected. It was **"Is Western democracy suited to Asian Countries? Discuss"** They had avoided it because they considered it difficult to score in and did not think that I had much of a chance. To cut the long story short, when the results were announced in the Government Gazette in June 1959, I was one of the 10 or 12 people who passed and qualified for an interview by the Public Service Commission — the next hurdle — in which I was also successful. I considered myself lucky. My classmates were happy that I managed to get the job. I will refer to this in a later chapter.

My designation was Executive Officer (Finance) — abbreviated as EO(F). There was no job description, but that was not uncommon in those days. All I gathered was that, as head of the finance section, I was responsible for the financial management of the Ministry headquarters, as well as the departments under the Ministry's charge — the Broadcasting (only Radio as there was no Television then) Department, Government Printing Office, Raffles Library and Raffles Museum (later changed to National Library and National Museum, respectively). It all seemed quite daunting to be just out of school and thrust into a position that required some knowledge and experience of government procedures, especially concerning financial management, all of which were regulated by **"General Orders"** and **"Colonial Regulations"**.

Learning the ropes quickly and performing well was all that I was concerned with and there was certainly no luxury of time. Much depended on my success in this regard. Initially, it was tough; the body language of some of my officers was envy and a few, especially the elderly, were not cooperative. I suppose the unease on the part of some and envy among others, was understandable.

Here was a person, straight out of school, appointed to a Division II supervisory position. Some amongst them must have felt that they should have been promoted!

However, there was one officer, a Clerical Assistant by the name of **N Raman**, who saw my plight and was very helpful. He taught me aspects of the office routine and internal communications like writing minutes. I am always grateful for his help. Naturally, it entailed long hours, but my enthusiasm and determination never waned. Not succeeding was never an option for me.

Air-conditioning was not common as, at that time, it was a recent invention and costly as well. In the office I worked, only few very senior officers had window unit air-conditioners in their rooms. All others worked in open spaces which had "GEC" fans hanging from ceiling at about 20 feet intervals. Those who had their desks near or under the fan naturally felt relatively more comfortable. All buildings had windows left open throughout the day. (Pollution was not heard of and not a problem then, either.) Working hours then were:

(i) Monday to Friday 9.00 A.M. to 4.30 P.M.
     Lunch break was from 1.00 P.M. to 2.00 P.M.
(ii) Saturday from 9.00 A.M. to 1.00 P.M.

These working hours set up by the British colonial administration were changed to 8.30 A.M. to 5.00 P.M. on Monday to Friday and 8.30 A.M. to 1.00 P.M. on Saturday, in the early 1960s.

As mentioned earlier, travel time took about 90 minutes each way. The bus companies — **Singapore Traction Company (STC), Green Bus Company, Hock Lee Bus Company and Tay Koh Yat Bus Company** — were all private operators and their workers were mostly controlled by militant trade unions, which were widely believed to be either pro-Communists or communist sympathisers. Hence, strikes were frequent; conductors pocketed sizeable amount of fares collected from passengers by not issuing tickets; and the company appointed ticket inspectors were prevented from doing their jobs by threats and intimidation. I remember one STC ticket inspector was shot and killed for insisting on doing his job. The colonial administration was either powerless or indifferent in this matter. Later, with the PAP government in charge, the transport system was rationalised and amalgamated to form a single, efficient and convenient network, but it took some time. Once developed, there were no more strikes.

In tandem, a pioneering policy of increasing the cost of private ownership and using motor vehicles was implemented, to reduce traffic congestion and gridlock — problems that continue to plague many major cities around the world, with consequent loss of productivity, forcing many governments to take very drastic measures to stem the serious problem of congestion and pollution threatening the health of the population. A few countries e.g. Brazil which tried to solve the problem by building a new capital deep in the interior did not meet with much success. In my experience and observation, Singapore would also be in a similar situation now, if we had not implemented comprehensive transport policies in early 1970s, soon after Singapore attained independence. Owing to lack of political will on the part of the leaders in many countries, the people were overwhelmed by massive problems. As a result, the leaders did not get full support and cooperation from the people. Consequently, the countries experienced only limited success in economic development despite having abundant human and natural resources and the serious consequences arising therefrom have produced only limited success owing to several factors, including lack of public support and cooperation.

My concern then was not the length of time taken to reach my office on normal days. That is a merely matter of getting up early. The bigger problem was when it rained or when buses drivers went on strike or buses broke down. Even on other normal days, arriving at the office without too much sweat (from the heat and humidity) had to be taken care of. However, spending that much time on transport was both tiring and unproductive. About a year later, I bought a motorcycle with a government loan. That eased the problem considerably and made me more mobile as well.

Lunch time was a more social event then. Friends would gather and engage in seemingly endless chats, mostly about work and food. Around City Hall, like many other crowded places in Singapore then, there was no dearth of hawkers peddling wide varieties of food. I can still remember my lunch on the first day — **rice, a piece of fish, one vegetable and a** *"teh o"* (tea without milk), **all for 45 cents** — at the then **Hock Lam Street** in North Bridge Road. Under the urban renewal programme, Hock Lam Street and all the pre-war tenements around it were swallowed up by Funan Centre, which in turn has come under the wreckers' hammer recently. Such is the relentless pace of renewal and change in our homeland.

Boat Quay was another favourite place for office workers in the vicinity. Hawker stalls at the edge of the **Singapore River**, from Cavenagh Bridge to roughly where the UOB building now stands, dished out all types of local food. Food vendors had very limited clean water and some used the river water to supplement. Food remnants and waste were also dumped into the river, not to mention human waste from the squatters further afield the river. For washing dishes, they simply scooped up the river water. Hygiene then, by today's standards, was very poor and unacceptable. There were no canned drinks at that time. The drinks seller, usually a hawker with a tricycle, would scoop a small glass of aerated water (orange concentrate mixed with water) from a container with a big block of ice floating in it. The cost was 5 or 10 cents depending on the size of the glass. A slice of papaya was 10 cents. After use, the glasses were dipped into a pail of water and placed ready for next customer. Also, after peeling the skin, the papaya was "cleaned" by dipping into the same pail of water, which was used for the whole day. It was not that water was all that scarce; the hawker, whether peddling on a tricycle or carrying his wares on his shoulders just had only one pail of water. We must have built a good resistance to whatever bacteria that was present! Strangely, food poisoning was not a problem then.

After a quick lunch, we would go into the nearby Chartered Bank (Battery Road), one of the very few premises with air-conditioning then, to cool ourselves before trotting back to our office in City Hall. This bit of luxury did not last long for me. When I started my part-time law studies, I gave myself 15 minutes for lunch and the remaining 45 minutes to reading my books under a shady tree in the Saint Andrew's Cathedral grounds. (I was offered a place in the then University of Malaya in Singapore to read law, but I could not afford the cost. There were no scholarships or bursaries available then. Also, my application for "**No Pay Leave**" was turned down by the Ministry of Finance. The only alternative was to do it part-time and by self-study. Therefore, I enrolled with the **University of London to read law as an External Student and later with Lincoln's Inn to do the Barrister-At-Law Course**.)

It was against this backdrop that I began my long career in the Civil Service.

Chapter 4

CIVIL SERVANTS GET THE SHOCK

I say to the civil service and their present, rather inept, leaders who have begun what they believe to be revolutionary movement against the government, that if nothing else more catastrophic happens to them than the loss of allowance in the top brackets of the civil service, and the fact that they have to face fiercer competition from the non-English educated they should go down on their bended knees and thank the Gods that their souls have been spared.

Prime Minister Lee Kuan Yew

THE CHALLENGES FOR THE NEW GOVERNMENT

The problems faced in Singapore were immense: poverty, inadequate health care, serious unemployment, limited educational opportunities and many more. All these on top of serious political problems, especially the challenge from the Malayan Communist Party (MCP). Despite these concerns, there was a mood of general excitement among the populace, even if not many knew what the future had in store for them.

Within days of assuming office the PAP Government announced a **pay cut for civil servants**. At that time the salaries consisted of two elements — basic pay and a variable component known as Cost of Living Allowance (COLA), which (as far as I can recollect) was 30 per cent of the basic pay, subject to a maximum $150 per month for officers who were single, $240 per month for married officers and $400 per month for married officers with children. The rate of cut in COLA varied depending on the total amount of salary. The bottom rung suffered much less than those in the higher brackets. Those at the very top lost the whole COLA. Daily rated workers were not affected.

Many senior officers were also required to participate in community programmes such as street cleaning campaigns. In my view, the leftists and pro-Communists elements within the PAP probably pushed the moderate leadership to institute this measure as a form of punishment. For many senior civil servants who did not even know how to make a cup of coffee, which was made and served to them by servants, never mind holding a broom and sweeping the floor at home, it must have been humiliating and distressing! For some, it was a deflation of ego.

The Government's official explanation for the pay cut was that there was not much money then in the kitty and they could not afford the wage bill. Another reason given was the departing colonial administration did not leave a healthy Treasury. However, doubts regarding Government's motive lingered.

There were several reasons making the rounds then, and among them were:

a) It was an act of vengeance by the Government to punish the English educated civil servants, whom the PAP believed did not, by and large, vote for the Party; and
b) There was a perception that the civil servants were not in tune with the new reality and not very sympathetic to the programme of the PAP government.

There was unhappiness and some leaders in the civil service union thought the pay cut was "unconstitutional" and a few were vocal in their opposition. They probably did not anticipate the fierce admonishment from none other than the Prime Minister.

Addressing the First Legislative Assembly, **Prime Minister Lee Kuan Yew** (hereafter also referred to as "PM Lee", "PM", or "Lee Kuan Yew") warned:

> "…I say to the civil service and their present rather inept leaders who have begun what they believe to be revolutionary movement against the government, that if nothing else more catastrophic happens to them than the loss of allowance in the top brackets of the civil service, and the fact that they have to face fiercer competition from the non-English educated then they should go down on their bended knees and thank the Gods that their souls have been spared…"

excerpt from the
Legislative Assembly Debates State of Singapore,
First Session of the
First Legislative Assembly Part 1 of First Session Column 368

The warning could not have been more chilling, especially for the senior ranks of the civil service. The quiet whisper among the civil servants was that **PAP** stood for **"Pah" "Addie" "Pukkol"** which in **Hokkien, Tamil and Malay**, respectively, meant the same: **"beat"**.

The intended effect was profound at all levels. There were many among the population who believed (mistakenly in hindsight) that the PAP was communist inspired, if not a communist outfit. The feeble Singapore Peoples' Alliance opposition, consisting of three or four members, kept on insisting that that the PAP must officially declare in the Legislative Assembly that it was **"anti-communist"** but the PAP leadership refused and declared itself as **"non-communist"**. It was a clever and necessary strategy in the circumstance because the communists and their fellow travellers had strong influence within the Party. With shrewd and courageous strategy, Lee Kuan Yew and his moderate colleagues were able to ride the Communist tiger without being devoured by it.

However, in my view, I believe it was, perhaps ironically, the beginning of the enduring "partnership" between the Government and the civil service that developed in the years to come, and was one of the important factors in the transformation of Singapore from **"Third World to First"** (memoirs by Lee Kuan Yew).

There were some tensions in the civil service in the immediate aftermath. We would try to relieve stress by telling jokes among ourselves in quiet whispers. One among the many that was making the rounds, went like this: the Minister for Health, Ahmad Ibrahim, who was a fireman in the Fire Brigade before his election, was on a familiarisation tour of Kandang Kerbau Hospital and, when told that he was approaching the labour (maternity) ward, the Minister skipped it saying "Byrne is responsible for labour"! (For the information of the younger generation, KM Byrne was the Minister for Labour in the Cabinet then.)

More than a year later, in 1960, the Government restored the pay cut, not fully retrospective but with six months back pay. We were naturally very happy to receive the back pay. My salary then was $225 per month basic pay. About a year after that, the pay cut was fully restored.

Again there were several views floating around for the change of heart on the part of the Government. Among them were:

- One view was the **"empty coffer"**. It was seen as an ostensible reason. The PAP (especially the Communist and pro-communists within who were influenced by events in China) had perceived that the English educated civil servants had not been generally

very enthusiastic in supporting the PAP in the general election that swept the PAP to a landslide win;
- Another view was that the top leadership — **Lee Kuan Yew, Goh Keng Swee** and **Sinnathamby Rajaratnam** amongst them — were inwardly not too enthusiastic to punish the civil servants but had to satisfy the largely Chinese-educated masses (led by leaders like **Lim Chin Siong and Fong Swee Suan** who were entrenched in powerful **Middle Road Unions**) who were then the backbone of support for the PAP; and
- A more plausible and pragmatic explanation was that the full and unstinting support of the civil service was necessary to implement the development agenda and it was required to deal with serious challenges to the moderate leadership of the Party from within, especially from Communist and pro-Communist elements, and predominantly from the Middle Road Union group. They were then known as "Middle Road Unions", not because they were middle of the road in their policy orientation and action, but because their premises were located at Middle Road!

My pioneer generation has no need to read from historical records to know the dire situation the Government was in at that time. It was a touch and go situation for the Government. A very sick member of the PAP (I think her name was Zahara) was brought in on a stretcher into the chamber of the Legislative Assembly for the voting, to save the PAP which came within a whisker of losing the majority and thereby, being defeated. That lady member succumbed to her illness a few days later. Many of us believed that that was the decisive moment that saved the Government, and Singapore if I may add!

Life then was never dull, peaceful or predictable, that is, for those who were involved in the "life or death struggle" of the political drama that was being played out!

However, there was also occasional comic relief in the Assembly. One opposition Assemblyman, referring to a Government back-bencher, said that it was his lucky strike that he was elected as an Assemblyman. Immediately, the member concerned sprang to his feet and protested loudly saying that he did not smoke **"Lucky Strike"** cigarettes but smoked only locally-made **"Pigeon"** brand cigarettes. The House roared with laughter! In those days, many Assemblymen came from humble backgrounds and did not have formal education in the English language, but they lived among the grassroots and connected with the people very well. Importantly, they were effective vote-getters.

Chapter 5

POLITICAL EDUCATION

The civil servants were neither "civil" nor "servant"

Business as usual for the civil service ended abruptly. Civil servants recruited under the colonial administration to serve mainly colonial interests, especially the preservation of the status quo, needed a mindset change, so as to face the new reality and implement a development-oriented programme. The expectations of the masses were high, the resources were limited and time available to deliver was short.

There was also a belief among the public that civil servants were **neither "civil" nor "servant".** Long queues at government offices and rude, impolite treatment was not uncommon in those days. The irony was that, in those days, letters from the government to the public would begin and end thus:

<u>Beginning</u>
"Sir/Madam"
"I have the Honour to refer to…"

<u>Ending</u>
"I am Sir/Madam, your obedient servant"
(signed by the officer concerned with his name)
and below the signature was "for Colonial Secretary"

The envelopes carrying the letter would be marked "On Her Majesty's Service" (later changed to "On Government Service"). In form they maintained the ethos that they were servants of the taxpayer and were there to serve the public; in practice the situation was a bit different. If I remember correctly, around late 1960s we abandoned the above and the simpler form of "Dear Sir/Madam" and "Yours faithfully" was adopted.

POLITICAL STUDY CENTRE

A department under the Ministry of Finance was set up for the **"political education" of civil servants. The name was Political Study Centre and its Director was George Gary Thompson** (G. G. Thompson), a Scotsman in the British Colonial Service. He was, prior to this appointment, the Director of Information Services which was absorbed into the newly created Ministry of Culture, under Minister Rajaratnam (Raja). The Political Study Centre was located in a government bungalow at Goodwood Hill. As I saw, its task was

(a) To sensitise civil servants, especially at the senior levels, to the new reality, demands, and expectations of the masses;
(b) To understand the forces, political and non-political, at work to undermine development, especially by the communists and pro-Communists;
(c) To build partnerships between the civil service and the political leadership to carry through the development programme; and
(d) To emphasise the importance of integrity and commitment among the civil servants.

Officers in Divisions I & II attended the weeklong course full-time. Thompson was an affable and engaging speaker. One of the important topics he lectured about was the communist threat. Another person who shared his experience with the communists was Gerald

D'Cruz. Overall, we had very lively sessions. I enjoyed the interaction and the exchanges which were interesting, informative, and useful, even if some participants quietly whispered that they were "brainwashing sessions".

This programme continued in some form or other even after independence and ended, I think; sometime in the 1970s. I remember Kishore Mahbubani giving lectures on communism around 1972. By then, structured curriculum and training modules encompassing a broad range of issues and topics had been developed to continually improve efficiency in government operations. **The Civil Service Staff Training Institute** took on this responsibility. This institute has had a few transformations, becoming the **Civil Service Institute** and now the **Civil Service College**, and has expanded its work and scope. It has gained international recognition for its expertise in public administration. As a Trainer (part-time) with the Civil Service College, I have given lectures and conducted training courses on public sector reforms in Singapore for public servants — both our own and from abroad — and senior public servants from many countries in Asia, Africa, South America and many small island nations from around the globe, under the auspices of the **Singapore Technical Cooperation Programme**. As I have mentioned elsewhere, this is Singapore's **contribution to global governance.** Hon Hui Sen, both as Permanent Secretary and later Minister of Finance, initiated many of the policies to train civil servants and increase their productivity.

Chapter 6

INITIAL REFORMS

In colonial times, many civil servants lived beyond their means leading to serious indebtedness.

Many major reforms were undertaken quickly. I list below (not in any particular order of importance) a few of them to give a flavour of the measures implemented.

FIGHTING CORRUPTION

The Corrupt Practices Investigation Bureau (CPIB) set up by the colonial administration was not very effective in fighting corruption. I had seen a policeman demanding a bribe in a threatening manner from a person who was pleading that he had no money. I did not know what the offence was. I myself also had a bad run in with a cop. Sometime in early 1950s, I was riding a bicycle with a pillion in a dirt track off Marsiling Road. The cop chased me on his bicycle and booked me for carrying a pillion. I argued with him in Malay that it was an *"ulu"* or desolate area and asked him to let me off. He would not listen and issued a summon. He knew I had no money. My father had to take me to the traffic court in Sepoy Lines to pay the fine of $5.00. I got a sound thrashing from my father. In those days, police constables went on beats in the areas under their jurisdiction as part of their work, to maintain peace. They rode bicycles. That cop was one of those on beat and would sign the record book kept in a tin box nailed to the wooden pillar in our shop. When my father asked him why he did what he did, considering he and his colleagues never bothered to summon others who carried pillions, he told my father I was "*sombong*", meaning showy. That resulted in further thrashing from my father! Mostly, if not all, the policemen then were Malays from *kampongs* in Johor and were not fluent in English.

Much has been written on corruption during the colonial era, and therefore, it is not necessary for me go into details. Suffice to say, the government revamped the CPIB, provided more effective powers and tools through the **"Prevention of Corruption Act"** and hired honest and dedicated officers. More importantly, CPIB was brought under the Prime Minister's Office.

REVAMPING OPERATING PROCEDURES

A review of the rules and regulations and an implementation of the necessary changes was undertaken. Until then, the civil service operation was governed by Colonial Regulations (CR) and General Orders (GO). A team that included a Canadian expert (I think his name was Deshant) was appointed around 1962. It had consultations with ministries, and I remember attending one of those sessions with my then boss **S T Ratnam**. The team came up with a comprehensive scheme to replace CR and GO; it also included important mechanisms to improve accountability. The result was the introduction of "Instructions Manuals" for civil service operations. It was no longer waiting for orders but applying instructions proactively and intelligently. (In one of my lectures on Public Sector Reforms in Singapore at the Civil Service College, for senior officials from many Asian and African countries, a participant (a magistrate) from Brunei asked me whether Singapore would be able to write a similar manual for Brunei. My response was we would consider it if there was an official request. Nothing was heard of since. Monarchies are used to ruling by decrees, orders, and edicts. It is easier for republics to change. However, even other countries which are republics have not changed much and are firmly rooted in the past; for example, countries like India still use outdated laws and archaic terminologies introduced by the British Raj. Even at present, outdated terms like "Appointment Order" are still in use.

A committee was appointed to inquire into government expenditure. My recollection is that it was headed by **Dr B R Sreenivasan** who was also appointed to head the **Malayanisation Commission**. At that time, there were still many expatriate officers (mostly British and a few from Australia and New Zealand) serving in Singapore. In addition to Thompson mentioned above, there were many others. I can remember a few: **N V Casey** (Comptroller of Income Tax), **Buttrose** (a senior Judge) and **Armitage** (Director of Audit). They were gradually replaced later by local officers under the Malayanisation Scheme. Younger readers might ask why is it called "**Malayanisation**"? Under the British colonial rule, Singapore was administered as part of Malaya and people from across the Causeway could apply for jobs in Singapore on equal footing with Singapore residents.

When the government imposed pay cuts, it also froze all new staff recruitments and the purchase of special expenditure items for which there were provisions in the budget. In those days, the budget consisted of three sections: **"Personnel Emoluments" (PE), "Other Charges Annually Recurrent" (OCAR) and "Other Charges Special Expenditure" (OCSE).** It enabled detailed scrutiny and control of expenditure. The purpose of the freeze was to conserve funds and to reallocate them to higher priority areas, in line with the new development strategy. However, when it was absolutely necessary to fill a frozen post, a very convincing case had to be made out to the Ministry of Finance to unfreeze the post, before recruitment could proceed.

CONSERVATION OF RESOURCES

Programmes were also launched to save water and conserve electricity. There were campaigns against water and electricity wastage. We had two instances of water rationing in 1960s. There were circulars asking civil servants to conserve electricity. Posters were displayed in the offices, instructing staff to turn off lights when they were not required, and in toilets, to use minimal amounts of water and to turn off taps fully. Posters in public places had slogans like "save water" at the top, and a dripping tap below ending with words like "every drop counts!". In later years, the Public Utilities Board ran the programme through more innovative ways. Many countries that are more abundantly endowed are paying the price for not biting the bullet. During my term as Ambassador to Egypt, the Minister of Agriculture there told me that he was in favour of such measures, but his cabinet colleagues were against it. Their reason was "water is Allah's gift" and, therefore, it is wrong to make people to pay for it. I observed much wastage. Soon after my arrival in Egypt, Nile TV interviewed me. Just before it started, I went into the washroom. The tap was leaking, and sizeable amount of water was going to waste. I tried to turn it off, but it did not work. I reported it to one of the staff members, but he did not appear concerned. About a year later, Nile TV interviewed me again and, coincidentally, in the same studio. I went to freshen up in the same washroom and to my great surprise water was still flowing out of the same tap! Nobody had attended to it. To me, Egypt was wasting water at the expense of other upstream riparian states. The Ethiopian Ambassador told me "it is our water they are wasting". In later years, the upstream states started to insist on drawing their fair share and Ethiopia started to build dams, the big one named "Renaissance Dam", on its side of the river Nile to irrigate its parched land and for power generation. Finally, Egypt realised the seriousness of the problem and that it could no longer rely on its big power status and military strength to overcome the problem.

INDEBTEDNESS

In colonial times, there were many cases of civil servants living beyond their means. On pay days (usually during the last two days of the month) money lenders would hang around the offices to collect their dues. In case anyone tried to give them a slip, they made sure every exit was covered. Our salaries were paid in cash. I remember that we had to seek police escorts from the then Guards and Escorts Unit to accompany two officers from each department to collect the cash from the Accountant General's Office in the CSO (**Chief Secretary's Office**) in Empress Place (which is now the Asian Civilisation Museum). I and my Higher Clerical Officer would arrive at the appointed time slot, collect the pay packets, acknowledge receipt and return to the office with the guards. Much manpower and labour was involved. Years later, the practice ended when, with encouragement from the government, civil servants opened bank accounts and their salaries for that month were credited to their bank accounts on the 12th of each month.

The Government acted swiftly and established rules against indebtedness. All civil servants were required to declare their assets and to state whether they were in debt. False declarations carried serious penalties, including dismissal with loss of pension benefits. Those who were in debt were given six-month amnesty to make themselves debt free. Pecuniary embarrassment would compromise the performance of official duties. There were cases where senior officials who could not clear their debts were dismissed after due consideration. I knew of one senior officer in the ministry who was dismissed. It was sad. This is the background to the annual declaration of assets (including those owned by spouses) and declaration of indebtedness that civil servants have been required to make since.

EQUAL TREATMENT FOR WOMEN OFFICERS

An important early landmark reform was to abolish unequal treatment of women officers. In 1963, under the "Equal Treatment for Women Officers" policy, women officers were made equal to their male counterparts in all respects. Until then, female officers had lower salary scales, a lower retirement age (45) and faced few other discriminations. Singapore was then way ahead of many first world countries in implementing such a policy.

LAW AND ORDER

Criminal gangs with secret society connections were a serious problem (more details in chapter on nation building) in Singapore then. The Criminal Law (Temporary Provisions) Act that was enacted giving law enforcement authorities special powers to deal with them. The hard-core criminal network would frequently **kidnap** rich Chinese *towkays* (tycoons) for hefty ransoms. Those criminals did not target other races, not because they had a soft spot for them, but simply because they did not have the kind of money the criminals were after! Those who resisted kidnapping were ruthlessly gunned down. I remember reading in the newspaper that the President of the Watchmakers' Association was gunned down in his shop premises in North Bridge Road.

I witnessed one kidnapping operation while riding in a bus on my way home after school. As the bus reached the 11th mile on Bukit Panjang Road, we saw a car overtaking the bus rather recklessly and at very high speed with a police car in hot pursuit. All other vehicles froze and remained so for about an hour, I think, under police orders.

When we were finally allowed to move, we passed by a police car by the side of the road with its passenger side door open and we saw the victim *(towkay)* seated. His right leg was bleeding near the calf. According to the next day's newspaper reports, he was hit by a bullet in the shoot-out between the police and the kidnappers during the rescue operation. Often, the victims' families chose to quietly pay the ransom rather than risk the life of their loved ones.

In those days, no sane person would want to mess with the criminal underworld. Even the police had a little "respect" for some of them. There were few notorious ones and one such character was (if my memory serves me right) Oh Kim Kee dubbed as "two guns", He evoked such fear that some said even a crying child would freeze upon hearing his name. Many believed that he had no equal in the art of firing two guns simultaneously and with deadly accuracy. Finally, he was cornered in a house in Serangoon Garden Estate. In the ensuing shootout, he held the police at bay for a while, and true to his form, style and "infamy", he went down with both guns blazing. It was a massive police operation and meticulously planned, involving, as I understood, a few police divisions.

FINANCIAL DISCIPLINE AND ACCOUNTABILITY

Legislation (I think it was the Financial Procedure Act) was passed in 1959 which had provision to surcharge civil servants for the loss of public funds resulting from negligence in the performance of duty. In my Ministry (Culture), an experienced Executive Officer (EO), who took over the financial duties from me, was surcharged. The amount, if I remember correctly was about $560 and the loss occurred in less than a year into his job. The loss from the petty cash account was discovered during a surprise check by an audit officer from the Auditor General's Office. Actually, the EO did not personally operate the account but his subordinate, a clerical officer, did. Still, as the officer in charge, he was liable. **It was not**

uncommon then to see officers trying to avoid, if they can, jobs involving financial administration. More on this topic later.

ADMINISTRATION OF JUSTICE

Among other things, we inherited the **"Trial by Jury"** from the British. In a small place with a powerful criminal underworld, it was not easy to assemble a jury willing to serve, and that too serve impartially. Many would fear for their safety. In the environment then, it was not difficult for the criminal underworld to intimidate jurors and witnesses. The **Pulau Senang murder trials** were a good example. What happened in Pulau Senang ("island of ease" in Malay and a grim irony in the circumstance) was so horrific that it attracted worldwide interest and attention. Very briefly, Pulau Senang was a small island prison where the prisoners were free to move around within the island, unlike the prisons in Changi and in Outram in the mainland. It was said to be an experiment to rehabilitate rather than punish criminals. However, there were also other reasons circulating concerning this. Probably to gain prisoner confidence, the Superintendent, **Dutton,** a British man, decided for the guards and himself not to carry arms — a possibly enlightened approach that turned out to be a fatal mistake.

In 1963, all hell broke loose. The prisoners rioted and took control of the prison. They also seized the radio communication equipment, the only communication link with authorities on the mainland, which resulted in the outside world not knowing what was happening until much later. It was not clear at that time whether the prisoners had grievances of their own that drove them to riot. Dutton, along with a few of his senior staff, were gruesomely killed. It took a few days for the authorities to regain control. I think about 40 prisoners were charged; many for murder and others for rioting. A jury of about 7 (I cannot recall the actual number) had to be sworn-in before the trial could start and this caused a problem. I was then in the Broadcasting Division of the Ministry, as part of the team working on inaugurating television broadcasting service. My immediate boss, **M S Menon**, was called for jury service, and he reported at the Supreme Court wearing a full suit. When his name was called the prisoners took one look at him and immediately objected to him and that ended Menon's selection, much to his disappointment. A prisoner could object, without giving any reason, a certain number of times and with reasons some more. Many of the accused exploited this provision in the law. It took a few days to get the jury sworn in. Many of the accused were convicted and sentenced to death.

Trial by jury was abolished in 1969.

Appeal to the Privy Council, which had some judges from the British House of Lords and some Commonwealth judges, was another colonial hangover whereby, in certain cases, decisions of the highest court in Singapore could be appealed to the Privy Council, whose decision was final. Appeals to the Privy Council was abolished in 1994.

DRUG MENACE

Another serious problem that had to be dealt with was the increasing drug menace, especially among the youth. Tough legislation was enacted to punish drug pushers and peddlers and to rehabilitate addicts. The **Central Narcotics Board** was created to deal with the problem. Working together with the **Singapore Anti-Narcotics Association, National Council Against Drug Abuse (NCADA)** and with community support, a comprehensive policy and programmes were developed. The death sentence under **Misuse of Drugs Act** for those convicted of peddling certain drugs in certain quantities brought us international criticism. Nevertheless, we were not deflected from our core mission to rid our society of the drug scourge, and the results speak for our success. In many countries around the world, the political will to deal with the drug scourge was, and still is, not there. Instead, they have liberalised the use of drugs. It has become a trend in many Western countries, some even legalising the growing of drugs. Drug addiction has become widespread in many countries, including in the United States, creating serious problems for those communities. I have read reports that in some countries, lawmakers and police were in fact facilitating the illegal sale drugs in return for big fortunes! In one large country in Asia, one of its states has been so overwhelmed by the problem of drug addiction that head of that state government had to abandon a proposal to drug test public servants because of the sheer size and prevalence of the problem among them! In Singapore, the fight against drugs is a work in progress. I served in NCADA as a member for several years.

There were many other reforms designed to improve governance, by increasing efficiency and better coordination of government operations, teamwork and law enforcement, not only to improve the quality of life but also create favourable conditions for attracting foreign direct investments, which is a vital component of economic progress.

Chapter 7

BUILDING A NATION

From "God Save the King", God Save the Queen", "Negaraku" to Majulah Singapura" (and the "National Pledge")

Under the colonial regime there was no nation, only a collection of communities. We were required to sing "God save the King" and later "God save the Queen" but there was in general no enthusiasm for the British Crown, the symbol of dominance. There was no **emotional connection**, unlike for our **Majulah Singapura.** Even to this day, I get a rush of emotion, and sometimes get choked up with tears welling in my eyes, when I rise to sing **our** anthem. There are many reasons for this, and I will deal with some of them later.

The different communities coexisted, for the most part, with the minimal interactions necessary for a peaceful life. Growing up in kampongs, we children mixed among the different races and played rounders, spinning tops, flying kites and the like. We picked up languages and dialects at a minimum level necessary for the purpose but that was all in terms of racial interaction, not integration.

However, from time to time there were communal clashes. The Communists and the notorious secret societies readily exploited these, often inciting the mobs to confront the police by shouting *"pah mata"* (**"beat the police"** in *Hokkien).* Even schools were infiltrated by these elements. I can remember students belonging to secret society gangs **"throwing numbers"** — sign language using one's fingers — to let their opponents know which gang they belong to.

I have heard stories to that effect, in the early years following the founding of Singapore in 1819 by Sir Stamford Raffles, where the colonial governors would promptly gather all the policemen in his small police force (which largely consisted of non-Chinese immigrants) and lock them in the cells for their own safety while the members of the secret societies fought it out on the streets to settle their own scores. Such was the power of the secret societies.

EARLY "NATIONAL SERVICE"

In the early 1950s, the British introduced "national service", a sort of compulsory military training for youths. The population was, by and large, indifferent and had no emotional connection to Singapore, not to mention the British. Many Indian youths evaded the draft by leaving for India. The Indian Consul then reasoned that it was marriage season and they were going to India to seek brides, a practice not uncommon then, owing to the gender imbalance in the Indian community. The communists and their sympathisers in the Chinese community, influenced largely by events in China, saw no reason to support the draft and many youths left for the "motherland" to be part of the rising communist tide, rather than serve in a British colonial army.

However, it was not a total boycott, and some did enlist. It was a means of securing gainful employment for some and others liked the life in the army. My elder brother served part-time for about 2 years. On Fridays, he would go in the afternoon to the training ground in Beach Road to practice marching drills and be instructed on cleaning and maintaining out-dated rifles. Those who enlisted were not required to do much else during that "national service".

RIOTS

The PAP leaders were always acutely concerned about the fissures in the community along the racial, religious and linguistic divides. There had been many clashes causing strife, and the earliest I can remember was the **Maria Hertogh Riots in 1950.** The scene was at High Street just beside the High Court (later Supreme Court) which delivered the verdict giving the custody of Maria (Muslim name Nadira binte Maarof) to her Dutch Catholic biological parents. They had entrusted her to a Malay lady before they fled Singapore upon the approach of the Japanese military. Maria was brought up as Muslim and in Malay customs and culture.

The verdict, delivered by a British judge, drove many in the Malay/Muslim community almost berserk, resulting in vicious revenge killings. Not to miss an opportunity, the Communists exploited the tragedy to the hilt. To make matters worse, a lorry laden with *changkols* (hoes) and *parangs* (machetes) arrived at the scene, and rioters seized them and let loose the carnage that followed. I think around 15 to 20 people were killed, including several Caucasians who were the real target. Tragically also, many innocent civilians going about eking their meagre living were caught in the crossfire. A young newspaper boy, a son of our family friend, was killed on the spot by a bullet fired by Gurkha Rifles deployed by the British to quell the rioting which was out of control for about two days from 11 to 13 December. We were shaken. He was simply at the wrong place at the wrong time.

BUILDING COMMUNITY SPIRIT

In 1959, the Maria Hertogh case and its implications were still not distant memories and Rajaratnam, Minister for Culture, went to work immediately to bring communities together and increase tolerance and understanding. He launched many initiatives such as the inaugural cultural programme at the Botanical Gardens. The programme was known as the *"Aneka Ragam Rakyat"* ("Peoples' Concert"). As far as I know, the Peoples' Association (PA) that was created in 1960 had its origins in such beginnings. I saw a massive crowd participate with much enthusiasm. I watched the concert when it was later staged at the City Hall steps. I also had a duty to perform.

The **National Theatre** was built at the foot of the Fort Canning Park, near the junction of Clemenceau Avenue and River Valley, and directly opposite to a Hindu temple (Chettiar Temple). A trust — The National Theatre Trust — was established under the auspices of the Ministry of Culture. Public donations were sought, and the Government matched it **"dollar for dollar"**. As the Executive Officer in charge of finance, it was one of my duties then to issue official receipts (G56) for donations received. It was touching to see humble folks like manual workers, trishaw riders and taxi drivers donating a day's earnings.

The Theatre was completed in 1963 at a cost of about $1.5 million. It had covered seating accommodation for 7000 people and another 10,000 would be able to see the performances on stage from the garden in an open-air ambience. Apart from cultural programmes, important public meetings and events were also held there. The facilities were limited and it remained the venue for big gatherings until the state-of-the-art Kallang Theatre was built in the 1980s.

Community Centres (CC) were built rapidly in all the electoral constituencies, and became the focal point of community interaction. More often than not, they were wooden structures with corrugated iron roofs and had a fan and some chairs. When television was inaugurated in 1962, a black and white set was installed on wall mountings in the CCs. It would attract large crowds of all ages to watch programmes which showed government at work and entertainment segment like cartoon network. As in many other areas, these humble CCs gave way to state of the art buildings and equipment providing many more facilities. In fact, many observers have noted that they rival facilities found in posh clubs and resorts. Even the name was changed to Community Clubs to keep abreast of changing trends and lifestyles. The CCs had been the venue where Members of Parliament (MP) interacted with their constituents through many events.

Other grassroots organisations created were the "Citizens' Consultative Committee" (CCC) and the "Management Committee" (MC).

As a core grassroots organisation, the Peoples' Association (PA) helped to create harmony among the races and build a cohesive society in Singapore. I also believe that when race riots broke out in 1964 (widely believed to have be instigated from across the Causeway) in Singapore when we were part of Malaysia, organisations like the PA helped to contain the damage and prevent future riots. The PA had wide support from the populace, although there were few critics who thought that the PA was a tool of the PAP. However, in my view, the grassroots organisations were vital for the Government to get feedback from the people and to keep its ear glued to the ground to detect any electoral rumblings early. During my term as Chief of Protocol, I noted many visiting foreign leaders expressing interest in the PA. Some of them thought the PA was a "unique invention" and, in their experience, they had not seen anything similar elsewhere. It would not escape the attention of the readers that many countries were torn asunder for ignoring the importance of building communal harmony. As noted, the PA worked well for us, to maintain the communal harmony which was, and continues to be, vital for our national security and progress.

NATIONAL PLEDGE

Rajaratnam wrote the **National Pledge** that we Singaporeans recite on important occasions, especially on National Day. It is an innovative embodiment of what we are as a nation and emphasises the need for unity. During my service abroad, I found many leaders liked the idea of having a solemn pledge like ours.

Chapter 8

THE BATTLE FOR MERGER

I mentioned in the earlier chapter the serious challenge to the PAP mounted by the Communist United Front (CUF) and it was an increasing threat. As I saw it, the PAP faced an uphill task of confronting and containing them. If Singapore merged with Malaysia, the federal government would have to deal with them and the PAP could avoid the odium and the fallout from locking up all the key figures in the CUF, who were former comrades in arms in the PAP. Furthermore, it was also not in the security interests of Malaya, if the PAP lost to the communists. Therefore, there was convergence of interests of sorts. There were some loose bazaar talks later that the PAP "tricked the Malay leaders" into it. The economic benefit was also played up and prima facie it made sense. Singapore could tap into the resources of a larger federation.

Many of us, ordinary folks, not being political animals, thought (perhaps naively) that Malaysia was the pot of gold at the end of the rainbow and we were enthusiastic about merger.

THE CLASH

Thus, began the "battle for merger" between the government and the CUF, including the breakaway faction (from the PAP), the **Barisan Sosialis** led by **Lee Siew Choh**. Many believed that Lee Siew

Choh, though not a Communist himself, allowed the Communists to manipulate his party.

The "battle" was out in the open, face to face and the mudslinging was sometimes vitriolic. The "upper quadrangle" and the "lower quadrangle" in the then University of Malaya in Singapore (later University of Singapore and now the National University of Singapore) at Bukit Timah was the principal venue for the fiery speeches and debates between the opposing forces. My friends, N K Das (officer in the Income Tax department) and G Raman (then an interpreter in the courts), and I used to hurry after office hours to listen to the speeches and debates. It was our routine then that we would go to the university premises after work to pursue our part-time studies. Later, Das became an accountant and rose to the position of assistant commissioner and Dr. Raman became a senior lawyer respected among his peers. I worked at his firm when I started practicing law after I retired from the civil service.

We were especially concerned about how things would turn out when the dust settled. Nevertheless, for us it was exhilarating just to be there, and we tried not to miss any of the debates and leadership clashes in the epoch-making event. Leading the charge for merger were PM Lee and his colleagues like S Rajaratnam, Dr Goh Keng Swee and Dr Toh Chin Chye (chairman of the PAP). They took on **Lee Siew Choh** who was the very strident voice and public face of the forces opposing merger. He shared the stage with an array of comrades from CUF who also made their pitch. Ministers like **Ghazali Shafie** from Malaysia also threw in their lot. Prime Minister **Tunku Abdul Rahman**, Finance Minister **Tan Siew Sin** (MCA) and others were also seen in Singapore at that time. One notable chauvinist firebrand was **Syed Mohamad Jaafar Albar,** the balding UMNO Youth Leader, who, along with many others, was believed to have incited Malays on both sides of the Causeway against the PAP and, in particular, against Lee Kuan Yew.

Television broadcast was still at its infancy then but both television and radio (**"Radio Malaya in Singapore"**) were extensively used to promote a merger. I remember hearing a jingle in radio programmes like *"Malaysia as sure as the sun will rise"* and in the vernacular equivalents. Broadcasts also carried songs like "Malaysia forever, sing a happy song". More than that, there was proactive programmes to "sell" Malaysia, not only in Singapore, but also in Brunei, Sabah and Sarawak. As part of this programme, the Government sent a *"Rombongan Kebudayaan Singapura Ke Sarawak, Brunei Dan Sabah"* (**Singapore Cultural Mission to Sarawak, Brunei and Sabah**). I was the Secretary-cum-Treasurer of the Mission which consisted of big number of artists from Malay, Chinese and Indian Cultural organisations and was led by a Member of Parliament and Political Secretary, Buang bin Omar Junid, from the Ministry of Health and Law. I was still Executive Officer (Finance) in the Ministry of Culture. The Mission performed in the three territories from 24 April to 2 May 1962 — four months before the Referendum in September.

I enjoyed the experience immensely. It was the first time I was entrusted with duties and responsibilities that were entirely different from what I had done until then. Even more exciting and enjoyable was the flight. It was the first time I ever saw the inside of a plane never mind actually flying in one because doing it on personal expense was simply unaffordable for a *kampong* boy. It was a **Malayan Airways** flight and the aircraft was a "Comet", a new generation aircraft introduced into service not long before. I can still remember the mouth-watering meal served on board: delicious *satay and briyani* with aromatic local coffee brewed on board. Malayan Airways was then jointly owned and operated by Malaya and Singapore. With merger, it became the **Malaysia-Singapore Airlines** (MSA) and later it split into **Singapore International Airlines (SIA)** and **Malaysian Airlines System (MAS)** and they went their separate ways.

Meanwhile, the battle for merger was generating much heat and with it apprehension, concern and even a bit of confusion among the populace. The Government issued a White Paper on the "**Battle for Merger**" (a book in black and white print). My section in the Ministry was one of the principal distribution points. The White Paper detailed the communist threat and how the communists had been working against the State. In particular, there was an important revelation of a very important operative and a communist emissary identified only as "the **Plen**" However, to cut the long story short, Government decided that the people should be offered a **choice on the type of merger they wanted and not whether they were for or against merger.** As I saw it then, the government was most probably not confident that it would win, if the people were offered a straight "Yes" or "No" choice. The Communists and the pro-communists wielded enormous power and influence among the trade unions, vernacular Chinese schools, and in clan associations and, therefore, Government felt that it could not risk it.

In the Referendum conducted on 1st September, 1962, **three options** were offered for people to choose one. Very briefly:

➢ **Option A**
This gave autonomy in labour and education and other agreed matters with Singapore citizens automatically becoming citizens of Malaysia.
➢ **Option B**
Unconditional merger on equal basis with all other states in the Federation of Malaya.
➢ **Option C**
Enter Malaysia "on terms no less favourable than those given to the Borneo Territories"

As expected, the Barisan Sosialis and the CUF canvassed for a blank vote. They lost and 95.8% of the people voting chose Option A.

The voter turnout was about 90.6% of eligible voters. It was a resounding victory for the PAP. However, there was no victory parade. It was probably deliberate, in order to not provoke the communist tiger.

Putting politics aside, merger made sense for the common man. As a people, we were not much different: our economies were inter-linked, we both faced common security threats, had many cultural and linguistic similarities, including food and lifestyles, and had people with family ties on both sides. The British ruled Malaya and Singapore as part of one big administration although Singapore, Penang and Malacca had a different status as Straits Settlements. There were no passports and immigration controls. **My generation also sat for the common Cambridge International General Certificate of Education examinations.**

In later years, however, the Malaysian government pushed a policy that prioritized the Malay language at the expense of English. Since then their standards in English have dipped. Addressing the Lincoln's Inn Alumni in Kuala Lumpur in or about 2004, Sultan Azlan Shah, a respected former Malaysian Chief Justice and *Agong*, lamented the fact that judgments given in Malaysian courts were no longer cited in other Commonwealth courts, unlike before.

Our pioneer leaders also faced the language problem but took a very different and pragmatic route. My recollection is that when they took charge of self-governing Singapore in 1959, there were calls from certain sections of our Chinese community, which wanted the Chinese language (Mandarin) be made the official and working language of the administration to replace English. I believe the Communist United Front was also pushing the chauvinistic line. It must be seen in the context of the geopolitical events of the time. The leaders of the Peoples' Republic of China, founded in

1949, were not only exporting revolution but were also tugging at the heartstrings of overseas ethnic Chinese people, and extolling the glories and the virtues of the **"Motherland"**. One of their principal propaganda tools was **"The Voice of Malayan Revolution"**, a radio broadcast (believed to have been beamed from Peking, later name changed to Beijing) **calling for armed revolution to overthrow Governments,** and it targeted Singapore and Malaya in particular.

It was a difficult problem for our leaders who firmly believed that for Singapore to survive and prosper it must be plugged into the global grid, and that required competence in communicating in the global language — English. If I recall correctly, sometime in 1960, PM Lee addressed a large gathering of union leaders and probably also grassroots organisations and drove home the importance and the need to use English in the work place and gave many compelling examples for it. Driving home, the point that Singapore could not function, never mind prosper, without foreign investments, he asked the audience which foreign investor would want to set-up factories and assembly plants in Singapore, if his operation manuals had to be translated into Mandarin, Malay and Tamil just so that the workers could understand the process. In short, the message was that we must be competitive in the global marketplace. Also, in those days, the economic situation was dire and our policy then was that any investment would do, and was welcomed, in order to soak up the very high unemployment rate. Far from entertaining any thought whatsoever of downgrading English, the Government embarked on a policy of improving the standard of written and oral English — starting at schools, workplaces and all the way up. I also remember that PM Lee's opposition to the use of **"Singlish"** in oral conversations attracted some controversy (For the information of those not familiar with Singlish, it is language that uses English words with a few typical Singaporean slang words. For example, when a person says "no" they may typically say "no *lah*", often instinctively). Additionally, and more importantly, the Government also introduced a bilingual policy to make citizens more rooted in their culture which was necessary in modernizing Singapore. In schools, the medium of instruction was English, as before, but pupils were now required to also study another language, usually their mother tongue. They needed a certain level of competency in that second language to gain admission into university.

I end this part of my narrative with this thought. In my observations, the above example is one of the very many early stout-hearted policies, for the long-term interest of the nation, by our visionary and pragmatic leaders, especially the founding generation, that laid the strong foundation for our progress since. Around the same time, leaders in many other countries, big and small, near and far, simply found it easier to ride the populist train which took them to undesirable political and economic destinations. **In the latter cases, the political will was simply not there.**

Chapter 9

SOJOURN IN MALAYSIA: A FAILED VENTURE

A different work ethos and a clash of cultures.

The euphoria, excitement and expectation of better opportunities began to fade soon. One of the reasons for the merger was that, in a larger geographical entity, Singapore would be able to tap into natural resources for development. On the other side of the coin, Singapore's expertise in business, trade and banking, amongst others, would benefit other states in the new federation. In short, the selling point for going with Malaysia was **"Singapore the New York of Malaysia" and "Kuala Lumpur the Washington of Malaysia"**. It did not turn out quite that way. It appeared that Kuala Lumpur had planned a more subservient role for Singapore. A subservient role would have cut Singapore off from major political and economic decisions that would then have had repercussions on the internal and regional security, environment, trade and commerce and attraction of foreign investments. One could detect that there was an unspoken and unwritten expectation that the new kid in the block, Singapore, should always be deferential to the Big Brother. Inevitably, serious differences surfaced.

IMPOSING *BAHASA*

In the civil service we had to implement new policies, some of which were difficult to implement. Being in Malaysia, we were required to use Malay (Bahasa Malaysia) in all our official correspondences and that caused problems as the bulk of the civil servants and majority of the population was not literate in Bahasa. It did not pose problem for me as I had grown up in an environment where Malay was commonly spoken, and also, I had to study Malay and pass both written and oral examinations at a standard two level to secure confirmation of my appointment as Executive Officer. However, like me, there were many officers who were not too enthusiastic in implementing the new policy.

The permanent secretary was (and still is) the administrative head and internal correspondence from one ministry to another was usually by minutes.

In English it was addressed thus:

Permanent Secretary (Culture) to Permanent Secretary (Finance)

During merger with Malaysia the above was written thus:

Setiausaha Tetap (Kebudayan) kepada Setiausaha Tetap (Kewangan)

Explanatory notes:

- *Setiausha Tetap* = Permanent Secretary
- *kepada* = to
- *Kebudayaan* = Culture
- b/p (abbreviation for *'bagi pehak'*) = "for" or "on behalf of"

The initials of the typist, stenographer, or the personal assistant who typed the correspondence would appear at the bottom of the minute. In those days, typing was done on manual typewriters and was done by professional typists. Electric typewriters came later and computers decades later. Every department had a pool of typists. The officers then wrote the correspondence and sent it to the typists. The typed correspondence would be sent back to the officer concerned for their signature and then be despatched. If there were errors, it would be sent back to the typist to rectify them. The far bigger problem was when copies were required. The typist would insert additional sheets of paper and place carbon papers in between them. Only about 4 copies could be made this way and, if more were required, the process was even more laborious, time consuming, and sometimes messy. The typist would have to cut a stencil, meaning they would have to type it on a stencil which is a special coated fabric like paper with backing. When ready, they would have to load it on a drum with simple equipment, apply ink and then rotate the drum manually to produce the copies required. About 20 to 25 copies could be printed that way before the stencil tore and had to be discarded. We dreaded when the ink smudged the stencil and the copies became messy.

The above was just the beginning and the intention was that Bahasa should fully replace English eventually. The switch to Bahasa, to the extent we did, was short lived and was abandoned later upon our expulsion from Malaysia. Also, we no longer sang *"Negaraku"*, the Malaysian national anthem. Even on the very few occasions we had to sing it, not many understood the lyrics, much less had any enthusiasm for it.

DIFFERENT WORK ETHOS

Many ministers from the central government came down frequently for both official business and private visits. The performance of some of them paled in comparison to our own ministers. The Paya Lebar Airport was built by the Singapore government, but it was opened when we were in Malaysia. A senior police officer present at the opening ceremony observed that a senior federal minister (name redacted), who came to officially open the airport, went before the live microphone and pulled out a piece of paper from the breast pocket of his jacket. Looking at the paper and a little annoyed, he uttered loudly few obscene words (not suitable for print) followed by **"...*salah surat*"** (wrong paper). Many in the audience were embarrassed and others roared with laughter. We had the feeling that some of those ministers did not take their jobs seriously.

Some developments also affected our daily lives. For example, the Malaysian police on duty in our streets spoke only Malay and did not understand English or any other languages. Their behaviour was in stark contrast to our own. Many of them coming from *ulu* (remote) *kampongs* had no experience of life in a modern urban place like Singapore. They displayed crude behaviour like stopping cyclists and letting out the air in the bicycle tyres when they felt the cyclists did not *hormat* (respect) them by getting down or did not pay the small bribes, say 20 cents, that they expected. Clearly, they did not fit into our society. There was another side to this. At all levels in the administration in Singapore, there were many career officers who came from Malaya. In fact, ironically, our Police Force then was predominantly Malayan. Some of them rose to very high positions in the Force and were professional and efficient; the difference was in the culture of administration between Singapore and Malaya. I have alluded to this earlier.

There were also other problems that affected our daily lives and required adjustments.

Chapter 10

FOREVER INDEPENDENT & SOVEREIGN

"Singapore is 225 square miles only at low tide, and at high tide it is even smaller. It is only a matter of time that Singaporeans will come back crawling on their bended knees begging to be taken back and we will teach them a lesson they will never ever forget."

– **A Malaysian minister**

There is no need for me to go into the details as to why Singapore was expelled from Malaysia. They are well documented and there could not be a better account than the one given by the master himself, in "The Singapore Story" by Lee Kuan Yew. However, for those of us at the grassroots level who went through the emotions of euphoria and hope followed by despair, despondence and trauma, it was a difficult adjustment, especially because the exit was as sudden as it was unexpected. Historians might continue to examine and analyse the causes that led to our expulsion. However, one can analyse the ashes but seldom resurrect the flames.

IMPROBABLE BEGINNING

Thus, cast into the unknown and facing an uncertain future, we began our perilous journey as an independent and sovereign republic.

Here are excerpts from my article **"Starting from Scratch"** from page 247 to page 254 in the publication **"The Little Red DoT — Reflections by Singapore's Diplomats"**:

"That fateful day, 9 August 1965 started like any other at the then Land Office in City Hall where I was a Deputy Collector of Land Revenue. I was having a difficult time persuading a squatter to quit the State Land he was occupying, and I was not having much success. Suddenly, the whole office "exploded" with excitement. The news went around like wildfire that Singapore had separated or rather was expelled from Malaysia. Later in the afternoon, we gathered at the Padang to hear the Proclamation of Singapore's independence by Prime Minister (PM) Lee Kuan Yew from the City Hall steps. Thus, the Ministry of Foreign Affairs was born and Mr Sinnathamby Rajaratnam, who was then the Minister for Culture, became the Minister for Foreign Affairs operating from the same office on the 3rd floor in City Hall."

"I was among a small group of officers who volunteered for the "Foreign Service", not knowing much of what it entailed or how long it would last. **However, what we lacked in knowledge and experience was more than matched by the excitement and the iron determination to do our best for the country. There was no luxury of time".**

(Reproduced in the **Heart of Public Service on** page 25)

"At first it was like being thrown into the deep-end of a pool hoping that someone also tosses a float to keep you from drowning while you paddled to safety. We sought and received help from mainly Commonwealth missions — Indian, British and Australian among them — in Singapore. I remember attending a session conducted by the Australian High Commissioner. I think his name was Bill Pritchard. He covered a large amount of ground in great detail — about what to do from the day of arrival in the host country, to the day of departure on completion of the posting! In the following years, however, the Ministry sent a number of officers for attachments in New Delhi and Canberra, to gain first-hand experience in oiling the wheels of diplomacy."

(This publication, *The Little Red Dot*, was undertaken to commemorate 40th anniversary of Singapore's independence. It was a painstaking and commendable effort by the editors, **Tommy Koh & Chang Li Lin** and was published by World Scientific Publishing Co. Pte Ltd).

My understanding is that the Indians went out of their way to get diplomatic recognition for Singapore. One Indian diplomat, **Thomas Abraham,** who was Deputy High Commissioner then, was very helpful. According to one record, he was one of the few diplomats PM Lee spoke to almost immediately after our Separation from Malaysia. PM Lee had also sought India's help to train our fledgling Army. To my recollection, Thomas Abraham and Chia Cheong Fook became good friends and the latter would tap the former's expertise when necessary. Thomas Abraham came back to Singapore, this time, as High Commissioner and presented his credentials to President Sheares on 14 February 1973. During a conversation after the ceremony, he shared very interesting insights with the President. After Singapore, he remained active and, reportedly, rose to prominence in Indira Gandhi's administration.

What little initial excitement there was in being independent, it soon gave way to fear, concern and apprehension over how Singapore would make it on its own in what was then a troublesome and hostile environment. Suddenly, we felt everything had crashed and the shock was bone chilling. We grieved when we saw PM Lee shedding tears on television and many of us watching him could not fight back our own tears. I had never seen PM Lee shedding tears in public both before and since then. However, I must also state there were some who celebrated the event by letting off firecrackers. Many of them could have done so for no other reason than the dislike of being part of Malaysia; others probably had different reasons.

MANY REASONS TO BE WORRIED ABOUT THE FUTURE

- sudden loss of hinterland (needs no elaboration);
- security challenges;
    a) challenge from the Communists and communalists both within and without;
    b) the fallout from "K*onfrontasi"*(Confrontation).
       President Sukarno launched *Ganjang Malaysia* (Crush Malaysia) when Malaysia was formed. In the support of this policy, two Indonesian marines set off a bomb at the Hong Kong & Shanghai Banking Corporation in McDonald House in Orchard Road killing three people, two of them employees of the Bank. They were caught and tried and sentenced to death and were awaiting execution. This had caused severe strain in the bilateral relations with Indonesia although by then Sukarno had been eased out and was succeeded by Suharto.
- we had no army for self-defence;
- the uncertainty over continuance of British military presence; and
- we had no currency of our own

Not many in the world thought that we could survive and make it as a viable nation. Even not all Singaporeans were optimistic of our chances in this regard. These weighed heavily in our minds.

During an interview very soon after Separation, a reporter asked a senior Malaysian minister as to how Singapore with an area of 225 square miles would be viable without Malaysia. The minister remarked that **"Singapore is 225 square miles only at low tide and at high tide it is even smaller. It is only a matter of time that Singaporeans will come back crawling on their bended knees begging to be taken back and we will teach them a lesson they will never ever forget."** In fact, it was not just the Malaysians, who thought that Singapore could not make it. **Yap Neng Chew**, a senior civil servant, told me that a departing colonial engineer in the City Council rather cockily asked him how Singapore could survive without them. He had concluded that, without the likes of him in charge, Singapore government would not even manage municipal services, never mind govern an independent country. Such was the arrogance of some Westerners, who probably had the **"born to rule"** mentality.

One of the most important and immediate tasks was to have our own currency. I gathered the impression that in the immediate aftermath of Separation, some in the Malaysian leadership were trying to make things difficult for us in the continued use of the Ringgit as an interim measure. Therefore, having our own currency became extremely urgent. **Sim Kee Boon**, Permanent Secretary in the Ministry of Finance, was entrusted by the Cabinet with this task. I was serving in London when he came there and worked very hard, literally day and night over few weeks, with the **Crown Agents**, to make the necessary arrangements, and to have the currency printed and minted as quickly as possible. We at the High Commission assisted him in whatever way we could in the very important project.

At that time the staff was small — there were four home-based and six locally recruited staff who were with our Trade Commission, that has been in existence since before our independence, dealing with trade matters and disbursing pension to the British colonial civil servants who had served in Singapore. Among the local staff, there were a few Singaporeans who rendered valuable service. **Kelly Sim**, a brother of Sim Kee Boon, referred to above, was already serving in the Trade Commission and was helpful to us the newly-arrived home-based staff, a lady by the name of **Kay Parthasarathy** was an able front desk receptionist cum clerk, and **William Ho** who joined the High Commission (after I left London), initially assisted in student matters and later he headed the Information Section. They had the pioneer generation spirit and grit. In many cases, they all made their way to Britain to study and educate themselves and had very little money to do so. Many travelled on ships and a few worked on it to pay for the passage. There were rare cases of stowaways, as well. William Ho along with nine other fellow scouts **hitchhiked all the way from Singapore to London**, navigating through some of the wild and dangerous terrains and countries in the world. While travelling on a train which went through the **Khyber Pass**, a few local brigands were menacing William and his group. Our quick-thinking scouts pulled out their knives (the only self-protection tool they had) and moved the knives in a sharpening gesture. That saved the day. The brigands must have concluded that it was not worth their effort to take on such courageous hitchhikers, who usually never carried much money anyway. They started the journey with just 50 Pounds (S$491 at the then exchange rate) each and it took 14 weeks to reach London.

(William graduated with a Bachelor of Science in Sociology and obtained few other qualifications as well — all these while working and studying at the same time. Upon returning home, he did very well in many senior positions in the private sector, including as the Executive Director of the Singapura Finance Ltd. Whenever we meet, we reminisce those early years of our lives. Kelly went on to build a thriving marine engineering business in Singapore. Kay was one of those who helped me later in the running of the kindergarten that I started during my term as Chairman of Hindu Endowments Board. Sadly, she is no more.)

THE "PAPER FLOWER"

When we introduced our currency soon after independence, our one dollar was worth only about 90 Malaysian cents and the

Malaysians mocked us. At my brother's provision shop in the Malaysian Navy Quarters in Woodlands, I heard a Malaysian naval personnel deriding our dollar. He said loudly *"apa duit ini... keratas bunga sahaja"* which when translated is **"what kind of money is this... it is only a paper flower"**. He insisted that the change be in Malaysian currency. The paper flower was a reference to the picture of the orchid flower on our currency notes. Probably he, like many others, believed the Singapore Dollar would plummet and was not worth keeping. Some even started to hoard Malaysian Ringgits much to their distress later!

What has happened to the Malaysian Ringgit since then needs no mention. Its decline could not be stopped and in less than three decades it was trading, at one point, at 3.04 Ringgit to 1 Singapore Dollar! This was one reason that attracted (and still attracts) many Malaysians to work in Singapore — a bitter pill for the Malaysian establishment to swallow.

Another interesting experience of mine concerns the British Pound (Sterling) during my posting in London. The departing British had extracted an agreement with our Government that the pension for their officers who retired from Singapore would be paid at the rate of 2 shillings 4 pence to the Singapore dollar. At that time the exchange rate was S$8.57 to the Pound. Their concern probably was that our dollar could depreciate against the Pound in which case the quantum of pension (in Pound Sterling) would be reduced. They probably had good reason for this, based on their experiences elsewhere. But contrary to their belief and expectation, the pound devalued in 1967 to S$6.40 and pensioners were jubilant at the unexpected turn of events and the windfall they received. The pensioners called us to thank for the increase. Since then, the Pound has depreciated to below S$2. This was an unusual experience for Britain, since in almost all its other former colonies things went the other way — continuous depreciation of their currencies against the Sterling Pound. Singapore defied the odds against all predictions, in this and in many other respects, as well.

LEARNING TO COEXIST

The Malays in Malaysia, unlike our own Malay brothers and sisters, had an easy-going life. They gave the impression that time was on their side and there was no need to be overly concerned with anything. A big country with bountiful resources — oil, rubber, tin, timber, and with abundant land for cultivation — underpinned their confidence, perhaps not unreasonably considering the circumstances of the time. Singapore did not have those resources and had to have a different ethos and culture towards work. In order to overcome the lack of resources, which all our neighbours were so abundantly blessed with, we had to be more competitive, professional, efficient and walk a very tight rope. As our leaders often emphasised what we lacked in quantity must be more than made up for by quality. Given the constraints such as small land areas, and lack of resources, there was no other way for Singapore.

At a different time and on different occasions before the merger, PM Lee described the **Tunku** as a "wise man"– a characterisation widely held then. In my observation, the Tunku was also a kind man. He was generally forgiving of people. I remember that **Lim Yew Hock**, Malaysian High Commissioner in Australia, went missing for about two weeks. After a frantic and nationwide search, the Australian police finally found him in a seedy Sydney district where diplomats would not normally want to go or be seen (nothing to do with security).

The incident sparked widespread media attention both in Australia and abroad. Responding to the Opposition uproar in the Malaysian parliament, the Tunku asked the members not to be harsh on Lim Yew Hock saying "it could happen to anyone of us".

For the information of younger readers, Lim Yew Hock was a minister in the Labour Front Government of **David Marshall** (Chief Minister) elected under the Rendell Constitution in 1955. When Marshall resigned owing to serious disagreement with the colonial governor, he probably expected all in his cabinet to quit with him. Lim Yew Hock did not and took over as Chief Minister with quiet British support. He lost the 1959 election to the PAP, and later he moved to Malaya. The Tunku took Lim Yew Hock under his wing, bestowed on him the title "Tun", gave him a diplomatic post as High Commissioner to Australia, mentioned above. After his disappearance incident, and the consequent problems in his family, Lim Yew Hock converted to Islam, assumed the name of Omar Abdulla and moved to Saudi Arabia. With the Tunku's help, Lim Yew Hock joined the Organisation of Islamic Cooperation (OIC) in Jeddah and secured a job as special assistant to the President of the Islamic Development Bank, according to a source. Lim Yew Hock died in Jeddah and was buried there. The OIC was not considered influential in global affairs.

Chapter 11

RECOGNITION & INTERNATIONAL ROLE

"My working relationship with VK Rajan was superb, absolutely. VK Rajan, my number two (is) a first-class person. He became an Ambassador later. His last appointment was Ambassador to Cairo. First class fellow. Without him, I think I would have failed also. He was real help, big help. Plenty of initiatives."

— *Chia Cheong Fook, Permanent Secretary, Ministry of Foreign Affairs*

One of the urgent tasks for the infant Republic was securing international recognition. Singapore joined the Commonwealth in August 1965, was admitted to the United Nations on 21 September of the same year and became founding member of ASEAN in 1967. However, it was also important that the international community had a good understanding of our leaders, their pragmatic policies to attract foreign investments, the disciplined and hardworking work force and above all, the clean and honest government. In short, Singapore was a good place to visit, invest and live. Attracting international conferences and similar events were important building blocks in this strategy.

GLOBAL GRID

Our leaders realised from the beginning the importance of being plugged into the global economic grid. Rajaratnam conceptualised the idea of a **"Global City"** for Singapore long before globalisation took shape or was even heard of.

COMMONWEALTH SEMINAR

The first big event was the seminar in 1969 for senior officials from the Commonwealth countries, 34 in all. The title of the seminar was **"The Changing Patterns in the Conduct of Foreign Policy"**. It was held at the National Trade Union Congress Conference Hall, the only facility available then. Holding it was challenging on many accounts, most important being a very tight budget. We had to make do with limited facilities and assets and improvise where necessary.

I was appointed as the Administrative Secretary to organise the seminar. I was chosen for my experience in London where I gained familiarity with the workings of the Commonwealth Secretariat and experience in organising PM Lee and his delegation's participation in the Commonwealth Prime Ministers' Meeting (as it was known then) in 1966 and 1968. Mr Chia Cheong Fook, who was then Deputy Secretary in the Ministry of Labour was tasked by PM Lee to take on the job and he had asked for me to assist him. (We both were in the pioneer team posted to London.)

There was no proper conference table to accommodate the number of countries attending. In those days, furniture for government offices was made in government owned workshops and was standard issue. Meeting tables were long tables, and chairs were of two types; one without arm rests for junior officers and the other with curved half-back arm rests for senior officers. Limited number of swivel and tilting chairs were also made for superscale and higher office holders. All the furniture was made of wood and had rattan seat bottoms. The chairs for super scale officers had cloth cushions.

We had to deal with many problems. The swivel and tilting chairs were allotted to the heads of delegations. This chair had a central grooved iron rod fulcrum for height adjustment. Our chairs were designed for Asian weights and many of the delegates, especially from Africa, West Indies and Pacific Island nations, were bigger and heavier. On the eve of the seminar (a Sunday), PM Lee came to inspect the final arrangements and he tried out the chair (I had no notice of his coming). He told me that the chair did not appear to be sturdy and that it tilted a bit too much. He was concerned and exclaimed, **"You want Arnold Smith to fall down and cause an international incident?"** I told him that the degree of the tilt I could adjust but there were no other suitable chairs available to replace it. His response was to the effect of **"Let us hope there is no incident"**. Arnold Smith, a Canadian and the Secretary-General of the Commonwealth, was of big build.

After trying out the chair, PM Lee wanted to look at the floral decorations. Speaking in Malay and pointing to a few potted plants, which had leaves looking rather pale, he asked the Botanical Gardens worker whether they were the same plants that were there for the visit of Japanese Crown Prince that had taken place a few days before. The worker replied *"yah tuan"* (yes, sir) whereupon, he instructed me to replace them with fresh plants. I conveyed the instructions to the Director of Botanical Garden (**George Alphonso**) and he was furious with his worker. According to George, they were special plants and were placed there by the same worker the day before. I told him it was better that he replaced them, which he did. I asked the worker why he did not tell the PM they were new plants. He said *"saya takut tuan"* ("I was frightened sir").

In fact, I had heard of many senior officers, feeling nervous and fumbling in answering PM Lee's questions. Here are two anecdotes that were relayed to me by colleagues who had witnessed the scenes. A legal officer in another office would stand up whenever he received a telephone call from PM Lee. This officer assumed a senior position in the judiciary in later years. In another case, an Administrative Officer serving the PM also jumped to his feet whenever the telephone rang. He picked up the handset and placed the mouthpiece to his ear, uttered his name but pronounced it in reverse order, and as he jumped up his left foot went into the rattan waste paper basket! My colleague who witnessed this behaviour was a junior officer in the same office.

I was really concerned that night and did not sleep much, worrying over the chair. Before the start of the Seminar, I drew the attention of Arnold Smith to the chair's design and asked him whether he would like it to be replaced with the simpler and sturdier, but less comfortable, chair. He tried it, was happy with it, and insisted on having it. I kept my fingers crossed throughout the Seminar. There was nothing more that I could have done. I became more anxious when Arnold Smith really started to enjoy the chair, especially its tilt, and swivelled frequently, stretching it to the limit. He said he liked the chair very much. That was quite an experience. In a very small way, the chair also must have contributed to the success of the seminar. Upon his return to London, he sought out our High Commissioner, **A P Rajah**, to express his appreciation of our arrangements and the manner in which they were executed.

Our hospitality was modest. We provided hotel rooms in accordance with the agreed scheme. We transported the delegates from the hotel to the Conference Hall and back by a bus. Yet, the feedback from the delegates was positive — clean and green environment, orderly traffic, discipline in the workplace and in the streets, and the other aspects of life they saw, impressed them.

COMMONWEALTH HEADS OF GOVERNMENT MEETING (CHOGM) 1971

The experience gained and the lessons learned from the seminar served me well in organising the Commonwealth Heads of Government Meeting (CHOGM). In fact, the seminar was a dry run for this event. CHOGM was a very important international gathering of the heads of governments from all the six continents. There were very few, if any, other international events where so many heads of government assembled at the same time in one location.

One morning, sometime in January 1970, my boss, **Chia Cheong Fook**, was summoned by PM Lee and asked whether he could take charge and organise the event. He was told that he could name any officer(s) whom he wanted. According to my boss, he told PM that "I will take on the job and want VK Rajan". PM replied "You can have him." I told Chia Cheong Fook that it was an honour but I was also aware of the onerous responsibility. He nodded and said "I know and that is why I asked for you".

We had developed a good working relationship. When he was selected for his posting to London, he picked me (among the five Executive Officers selected for overseas posting) to be part of his team. He did not personally know me then but as the Secretary to the Public Service Commission, he had access to my service record and an assessment of my work experience, including in personnel and financial administration. He was very comfortable and confident to let me work with minimal supervision and interference and that imposed on me even heavier responsibility, in order not to let him and PM Lee down. For me, failing was not an option. In fact, quiet whispers reached me that it was a folly on my part to take on the job. Someone, without naming me, muttered, "fools rush in where angels fear to tread". There was no time to worry. I must state here that Chia Cheng Fook was, amongst all the senior officers I had worked with, one of the truly sincere, honest and humble officers and these qualities underpinned the foundation of our enduring working relationship through the years.

PLAN OF ACTION

My immediate task was to produce a "Plan of Action" with detailed descriptions of the minimum resources required, how all the components and the actions were to be coordinated within the required timelines, and to always keeping one eye on the limited finances available. It also required continuous contact and cooperation with the Commonwealth Secretariat in London.

STRUCTURE

To summarise, a Plenary Steering Committee (PSC) was formed consisting of:

- Chairman (**Stanley Stewart**, Permanent Secretary, MFA)
- Coordinating Secretary (**Chia Cheong Fook**, Deputy Secretary, MFA)
- Administration Secretary (**V K Rajan**. Higher Executive Officer, MFA)
- Several heads of departments from other relevant ministries and departments, each heading a Sub-Committee: Conference Facilities, Finance, Accommodation, Hospitality, Security, Transport, Publicity, Protocol and, Social Programme.
- A small Secretariat consisting of the Administration Secretary and 2 Clerical Officers.

The Administration Secretary, as a resource person, prepared the duties and responsibilities of the Sub-Committees and coordinated them on a daily basis. One of the other important tasks was to prepare the budget for the Meeting.

MODUS OPERANDI

Initially, the PSC met once a month and later more frequently to review progress and iron out problems. In the week before the CHOGM we met almost every day. The PM and the Cabinet were kept informed as and when necessary. In fact, PM Lee took a personal interest in the detailed planning, which drove home the importance of the CHOGM for Singapore and it also helped to ensure smooth cooperation among all those involved, both from the public and the private sectors.

INADEQUATE CONFERENCE FACILITIES

Many things had to be built from scratch. We designed an oval table enclosing a large empty space in the middle for floral decoration and seats around the table for all the delegates. Chairs were also designed for heads of delegation and other officials attending in a 1+3 format i.e. the heads of delegations at the table and 3 officials per delegation behind. Curtains were stitched and carpet was laid. All these were designed and made as investments to build up an inventory for future events, as it was our goal to make Singapore an international conference centre.

TRANSPORT

Unlike the seminar, we could not use buses to transport heads of governments for the CHOGM. The problem was that the government did not have the motor cars required; neither were there any private companies that had the resources to hire the vehicles. The only way out was to approach Cycle & Carriage (C&C) to loan the Mercedes cars they were assembling in Singapore for the duration of the CHOGM. There was a long waiting list for the cars and C&C had no problem in selling them. Yet, they obliged — a good gesture on their part. We allotted two cars per delegation — model 250 for heads of delegation and model 200 for the officials. I think, in total, about 80 cars were loaned to us by C&C.

Having secured the arrangement for the cars we had to find drivers and train them. Government did not have that many drivers to spare and in any case, to pull them out of their daily duties would disrupt government operations. MID (Ministry of Interior and Defence) helped out with regulars and national servicemen and we trained them to drive the vehicles, informed them of basic aspects of protocol, familiarised them with the routes, and other necessary skills and details, especially in serving VVIPs. In fact, the Transport Sub-Committee was headed by **Major Zee Chee Kiong** from the MID Transport Division.

SECURITY

Security was important even then but not to the nightmare levels it has become in the more recent times. Much of the terrorist organisations that threaten global security now, did not exist then. Still, as host, Singapore had to be prepared for any possible event.

Our police force took on the responsibility. An Assistant Commissioner, **Lionel Chee**, was the head of this Sub-Committee. His team consisted of Superintendent of Police, **Tan Kah Wan,** who was the head of PM Lee's security team and **R Shyamkumar**, Chief Inspector, among many others. Specially selected officers (male and female) were trained in personal security for the VIPs, securing the hotels, the routes, the Conference Hall, implementing identification tags, security passes, screening persons and belongings, executing ceremonials, and much more. I did not know Shyamkumar personally then, but we became very good friends later when we both were reading law. He narrated many difficult situations he had to deal with, especially getting the heads of government on time for the plenary sessions as precision timing was an important requirement. He had many interesting observations as well. Shyamkumar went on to practice law for more than three decades. We did not have equipment like scanners and x-ray machines and the work had to be done by trained and alert officers. The dedication and quiet efficiency of all in the team was appreciated by the delegates. The female police officers performing ceremonial and security duties in their smart uniforms, with professionalism and aplomb was among the many commendations in the unsolicited feedback we received. I would like to point out here that it was the first time the full CHOGM was held outside London.

PROTOCOL

We required Protocol Liaison Officers to be attached to the delegations to assist them on a variety of matters. Again, both the Ministry of Education and Ministry of the Interior and Defence provided a total of about 50 volunteers. They had to be trained in basic protocol and other requirements. They were also given a basic profile of the countries they were to be attached to and other related details. In those days, there was no internet and therefore no Google search. We had to get the required information from the Commonwealth Secretariat as information available in our libraries was not up to-date or sufficient.

CONFERENCE FURNITURE

A private firm was engaged under competitive tender to make the conference table, chairs and drapes required. Prototypes were made and tested before seeking PM Lee's approval. I remember demonstrating the chair for heads of delegation to the PM. As I manipulated the device to raise the seat nothing happened for several seconds and the **PM asked me whether I knew what I was doing. Without hesitation I answered confidently that I did** and just then the fulcrum started to rise. He tested the chair, including its swivel and tilt, himself. He had no complaints. For the information of readers, I always prepared myself well before I saw the PM and Ministers. That, I would say, has become a survival instinct for me. In this case, I tested the chair several times before taking it to PM. However, I do not want to give the impression to the readers that I did not ever get into trouble with PM Lee. I will refer to this later.

FINANCIAL CONSTRAINT

Owing to the financial constraint, we had to ensure that we kept well within the budget. I had to find some novel and innovative ways to do so, but also keep within the rules and regulations. The hotels were briefed on the type of expenditures by the delegates that was allowed under government's hospitality scheme: other expenditures not covered by the hospitality scheme had to be borne by those incurring the expenditure. Our officers from the Finance Sub-Committee started their work of going through the bills and sorting it out with the hotel accounting staff. They worked from midnight to 6 A.M. when all the bills would be in. This job had to be done sensitively and discreetly. We left it to the hotel management to speak to the delegates concerned, regarding expenditures not covered by the hospitality scheme. The hotel staff cooperated well and did a good job. Thus, we ensured that we were not left with any unpaid bills to settle after the delegations had departed.

GIFTS

One day on a late afternoon, Chia Cheong Fook stepped into my office and in a happy mood announced that there was someone who was prepared to donate money to make and or buy gifts for the heads of government and senior officials in the delegations. The purpose was to showcase that Singapore made high tech (relative to the time) products. I told him immediately that accepting any money from anyone for that or any other purpose was out of the question as it would contravene Government regulations. He said that there were no funds available in the budget for the event and, therefore, it would be difficult to get the gifts and souvenirs. I told him that whatever monies and the like received from well-wishers needed to be acknowledged by official receipt **(G56)** and essential details like the name of the donor and the purpose recorded therein. Most importantly, all the amounts thus received had to be paid without exception into the Consolidated Revenue Account maintained by the Accountant General. He told me that the donor wanted to remain anonymous. I advised him that would not pose a problem for issuing receipts; instead of the donor's name we could simply write "Anonymous" on the receipt in accordance with the financial procedure. It was accordingly done and duly accounted for, as required by the regulations. (More details about the rules and regulations concerning the receiving of gifts by public officers are dealt with in a later chapter.)

I also advised him that we could still solve the problem of the gifts by informing the Ministry of Finance of the donation received and seek the ministry's approval to pay for the cost of the gifts from the budget. If necessary, we could seek to increase the budget (allotted from the Contingencies Fund). The Ministry of Finance approved the request.

However busy we were in dealing with very many issues and problems in a tight timeline, it was always necessary not to overlook the need to scrupulously comply with the relevant regulations, especially those dealing with government finance. My early experience in financial administration served me well.

COMMONWEALTH DECLARATION

One of the highlights of the Meeting was the **"Commonwealth Declaration"**. In fact, the heads of government wanted to name it the "Singapore Declaration" but PM Lee graciously declined and suggested that it be named the "Commonwealth Declaration", instead. This earned even more respect for PM Lee and by extension for Singapore. Being the first time, there were a whole host of other issues we had to deal with, and we managed them, thanks to the enthusiastic cooperation of so many people and organisations involved.

Again in 1984 when Australia hosted CHOGM, PM Lee invited the Heads of Delegations to break their journey in Singapore for a few days either before or after the Meeting. It had an important objective. We wanted the leaders to see for themselves the changes and the progress Singapore had achieved, especially the economic transformation that had taken place since their first visit in 1971. Similarly, when Malaysia hosted the Meeting much later, many of the heads of government also visited Singapore at our invitation and thus, they were able to see the continuous developments in Singapore.

Once again, I was tasked to organise the visits and by now I was the Chief of Protocol. As before, I produced the **"Plan of Action"** for both these visits and the protocol team working with other concerned ministries and agencies implemented it. Our high-profile visitors were impressed with what had been achieved, judging from the unsolicited feedback we received.

The experience gained in organising was useful as these events formed a template for all high level conferences and large international gatherings that came afterwards.

FOREIGN LEADERS' IMPRESSIONS OF PM LEE

It was interesting to note the kind of impressions foreign leaders had of our PM Lee. The heads of governments who attended the meeting were very impressed by PM Lee's leadership and the way he managed the proceedings. On a different occasion in 1984, **Prince Charles**, the heir to the British throne, was on transit in Changi Airport en route to Brunei to represent the British Crown at a ceremony to mark Brunei's independence. While walking along the airport perimeter fence to stretch his legs, he told me that he heard that in PM Lee's presence the ministers and officials remained silent. My response was that the PM did not engage in small talk but he had no problems interacting with his ministers and officials. Indeed, he sought and expected to be advised and briefed when necessary. Further, from my personal experience, he would not stand on ceremony in that he would deal directly with officials when necessary, thereby by-passing the ministers and the permanent secretaries. However, it was also well known that he did not suffer fools gladly. One must be well prepared and always be alert when dealing with PM Lee. Prince Charles smiled and nodded his head.

PM Lee, on his part, made it a point to keep in touch with important and influential world leaders from a wide spectrum of fields, including political, economic, business, management, security and more. Many of them were invited to spend a few days in Singapore. He tapped them for their expertise and experience on a variety of issues. They stayed at the "Villa" and the "Lodge" in the Istana Domain. No programmes were arranged except at their request. Usually, there would be a poolside dinner with a pleasant ambience and very informal interaction and discussions. Often, PM Lee would also have few selected Singapore guests. It was his way of exposing our younger generation to world leaders and to learn from them, part of an overall programme to nurture the second-generation leaders. Many world leaders also came on their own to pick PM Lee's brains on issues of concern to them. Whenever PM Lee came to know some world leaders were making trips to other countries in the region or passing through Singapore, he would invite them to break journey for a brief rest in Singapore. Since they stayed in the Istana, it was customary for them to pay a courtesy call on the President.

A UNIQUE EXPERIENCE

As President's Private Secretary (1972–76), I had the privilege of being present at the calls. It gave me very good exposure and I learnt much from the unique opportunity. The conversations between the President and foreign ambassadors (when the latter presented their credentials to the President) were often interesting and informative. President Sheares radiated warmth and a keen interest in learning more about the countries the ambassadors represented. He made all those who called on him comfortable and at ease. As his Private Secretary, it was my job to prepare necessary briefs on the country concerned, as and when necessary. However, his general knowledge was more than adequate for the purpose and, with good insights, he would discuss particular issues with me.

These were also occasions that enabled me to gain valuable insights into the thinking of foreign leaders and, through them, their governments. Below I share two anecdotes.

The President asked the Italian ambassador why Italians had to carry large amounts of Liras in their daily life and why did they not just demonetise the currency in such a way to obviate the need to do so. (If I recall correctly, the exchange rate then was about 300 Liras to one US$). The ambassador's reply was quite interesting, if somewhat amusing. He said his governments had considered such a possibility but all of them gave up on it. He explained that psychologically the Italian people felt they were millionaires and, all things considered, they decided to leave the matter as it was. I read a report much later that there were 53 governments in 70 years in Italy and, therefore, there would have been plenty of other more pressing issues to deal with anyway! Since then, that country has been beset with a serious economic crisis and, more recently, the influx of refugees has caused social tensions and stress within the EU.

On another occasion, the visiting German Foreign Minister, **Hans Dietrich Genscher**, made a complimentary observation concerning our newspaper, The **Straits Times**. He said that when he read the paper during breakfast, he found that it had a good coverage of important events around the world. He went on to add that in his own country he had to read several newspapers to get a similar feel and that was very time consuming. Here, I would like to refer to a report I read in 2018 on press freedom in the world's largest democracy — India. It noted that there were more than 70,000 newspapers and more than 500 satellite television channels operating in that country. All chasing the not unlimited advertising revenue and each peddling a parochial agenda, pushing the interests of business patrons and their shareholders. Infrequently, they indulged in veiled opposition to each other, and in vitriolic attacks on anyone, including the government, whenever they deemed it appropriate to their interests. Since there was no self-control, it was open season in a country with about 30 major languages and countless number of lesser used languages and regional dialects. I leave it to the judgement of the readers whether the resulting "anything goes" situation will enlighten or confuse the average citizen.

It was my job to advise the President when asked and also whenever I judged that I should do so without being asked. As stated earlier, President Sheares always kept in touch with his friends (not limited to his medical fraternity) and many others whom he had known, including his students. The list he had, cut across social divide. Among the medical students he had tutored at the then

King Edward College of Medicine was Mahathir Mohamed. The President told me that he had been sending greetings to **Dr Mahathir** but stopped doing so after he assumed the office of the President. Apparently, my predecessor thought it would not be politically correct (in current language) to do so and gave the reason that Mahathir was controversial or something to that effect. I gave my opinion that he should continue to maintain contact with his circle of friends and others, whom he found necessary to keep in touch with. My reasons were that, as President, he was above politics, and that it was useful to keep in touch with them, in order to not isolate himself from the circle when he returned to private life upon completion of his term as President. He accepted my reasoning and expressed regret that he was wrongly advised! By then, it was too late to resume the practice after the lapse of a few years. Anyway, it would have been awkward to do so. Mahathir became prime minister of Malaysia.

President Sheares had a comfortable working relationship with me. He shared many of his inner thoughts with me. I was privy to much secret information and occasionally information graded with the highest security classifications. I adopted a policy of not discussing my job with others, not even with my family members, who understood and supported me. Cabinet papers on policy matters, including proposed changes to policies and many other related matters, would come to the President, usually for his information. However, as per constitutional requirement, laws passed by Parliament require the President's assent before it becomes law. Most of the time, these documents were conveyed in locked boxes (red in colour) by the Cabinet Secretary to the President through the Private Secretary. Another matter which comes to the President, and concerns life and death, literally, is the clemency petition from convicted criminals facing the gallows. As per the Constitution, the President acts on the advice of the Cabinet on whether to grant the clemency petition or reject it.

From time to time PM Lee and the President would speak on the telephone. Mr. Sankaran (PM Lee's Private Secretary) and I had devised a system to connect the calls without either of us having to speak to both or either of the principals in effecting the calls. PM Lee also would come to see President Sheares whenever he (PM) felt necessary to brief the President in person. I was also privy to very sensitive information, in cases involving national security and the need to protect the information remains, notwithstanding the passage of time since. It is the duty of every citizen to protect such information.

It is, however, no secret that in many large democracies (some in form only), very highly sensitive information and policies, both current and proposed, were discussed and debated so openly in the media, by political leaders, including those aspiring for high office. The general lax attitude to national security has helped the enemies of the nation (both within and out), thereby causing irreparable damage to their national security — all these in the name of "democracy", "freedom of speech", "human rights", "secularism", the "right to know" and more. Here it is not the fault of the media which, in a fiercely competitive environment, must make money to stay afloat. Therefore, they try to get what they want by any means possible and rush to be the first to "break the news". For the media, the more salacious the news the better it is for business. Largely, it is greed for money and, if I may say so, lust for power as well, that drive much of the businesses world-wide. The media actors employ a variety of tools, including snooping, covert and overt operations, blackmail, sex, corruption, and the cultivation of "useful idiots", the "loose cannons" and the plain "bumbling fools" in the establishment! And now, social media wreaks havoc in this regard. Governments in shaky coalitions are weak by nature, and the weaker they are the better for the media actors and foreign powers who seek to exploit them for their own national interest!

One day, about three years into the job, the President called me to his desk. After settling a few matters, he asked me whether I had a promotion since I took on the job. I was taken aback and paused for a while before responding. When I replied in the negative, he was surprised and his body language showed that he was upset as well. He said few other things but they were in confidence and therefore, must remain so. He did tell me that I had done well, especially compared to my predecessor and that he had made it known to the Chairman of the Public Service Commission (PSC). Next came one of biggest tests in my career. He asked me to get the Chairman of PSC (Dr Phay Seng What) to speak to him on the matter. It put me in a difficult position and without hesitation I pleaded with him not to do so. It was the only occasion I could not carry out the President's instruction. I explained to him that it might not be seen as proper if the President (Head of State), raised what was essentially a civil service matter with the PSC, the PSC might conclude that I had used the President for my personal benefit. (I had never done anything even remotely like that both before and since.) I also made the point that if he raised the issue with the PSC Chairman, he might promote me out of deference to the President but could stagnate me afterwards. The President felt the unfairness of the situation, but I assured him that I would be happy to serve him as long as he was satisfied with my performance. In the end of the conversation, I recall saying to the President "**... if the civil service cannot find one officer to serve the head of state, even in such circumstances, then it would be a sad indictment on the civil service itself**". The President's eyes kind of sparkled and he thanked and complimented me for my commitment.

As an aside, I state here that I did not project myself or lobby for promotions. It was not part of my character, belief and DNA. Many of my colleagues in the pioneer generation had a similar belief. In the dire circumstances of the time, it was a call of duty and pride to serve our beloved homeland and prove the purveyors of doom wrong — and that could only be achieved by single minded devotion and resolute action. I have narrated anecdotes on this in an earlier chapter. Frankly speaking, financial reward was not the motivation.

It had reached my ears that one senior officer had told a few of his colleagues that I was "a fool" in not "promoting and marketing" myself. He reminded me of the character in **Shakespeare's Othello,** named **Iago**, who said:

> *"...You shall mark*
> *Many a duteous and knee-crooking knave*
> *That doting on his own obsequious bondage,*
> *Wears out his time much like his master's ass,*
> *For nought but provender, and, when he is old, cashiered.*
> *Whip me such honest knaves. Others there are*
> *Who trimmed in form and visages of duty,*
> *Keep yet their hearts attending on themselves;*
> *And, throwing but shows of service on their lords,*
> *Do well thrive by them; and when they've lined their coats,*
> *Do themselves homage. These fellows have some soul.*
> *And such a one do I profess myself:"*

"The Heart of Public Service" published by the Prime Minister's Office in 2015 acknowledges the contributions of many pioneer generation civil servants and leaders. There is a passage on my contribution that highlighted a quote from my article published in **"The Little Red Dot"** referred to earlier. This is what I had said, amongst other things:

> **"...what we lacked in knowledge and experience was more than matched by the excitement and the iron determination to do our best for the country".**

In my article, I also stated that "There was no luxury of time". However, to say that we were not motivated by rewards, financial or otherwise, did not mean that we did not expect that in the long run our performance and the credentials would be fairly assessed and duly rewarded by the relevant authority, the PSC.

I have to state that I had several disappointments, especially when I was overlooked in promotions, even though my credentials and performance had no less merit than those who were promoted ahead of me. I cannot say that it did not pain me. Some senior officers who knew my work well told me that the fault was mine. In summary, what they told me was that "you did not market yourself". I began to realise that they were not entirely wrong. In a fiercely competitive world, good performance skills in the job alone were not enough; skilful marketing of oneself had its place. Such is the world! I knew of one officer, who was often described by his bosses as a "showman", gaining promotion ahead of me.

A curious thing in this was that the incumbent Chairman of the PSC, was often included in the line-up — consisting of our VVIPs, other high dignitaries and the heads of the diplomatic missions accredited to Singapore — to be presented by the Chief of Protocol to foreign heads of state and heads of government during ceremonies to welcome them during official visits. During my long term in the job, I discontinued the practice of my predecessors, of reading from the list of names of dignitaries in the line-up, sometimes stretching to 70 to 80 or more people. Instead, I made a point to memorise the names and the correct pronunciations well in advance, sometimes practising several times, well before the ceremony.

I had a protocol colleague to move in tandem behind me with the list of names in case I had difficulty and needed prompting. It was meant as a fail-safe arrangement. Happily, I did not require such assistance most of the time, and with every such visit, it became less stressful. This was not expected of me and indeed the practice of reading the names is standard in many countries around the world. However, I demonstrated our professionalism and it earned us respect form the visitors and the diplomatic corps. It was part of my firm belief that a small country needs to punch above its weight to earn respect and be relevant in global governance. The diplomatic corps was particularly pleased that I pronounced their names correctly without hesitation and without the aid of the list. This was one of the several practices that I introduced. The PSC Chairman present at one of those events was heard saying, while commenting on my performance after the event, that "his job is difficult".

As noted earlier, much of the work of the Chief of Protocol was out in the open, under public eye with television cameras rolling and for all to see. It was quite unlike the work of other officers who mostly worked within the confines of the Ministry building. In protocol operations, however, there was no similar cover for mistakes and lapses (actual or perceived), which many a time were magnified, with consequent pressure on the Chief of Protocol and his staff who work under stressful conditions. This is indeed a fact of life in protocol. This has been, in my view, one of the reasons for some officers shying away from a posting to protocol, especially for the position of Chief of Protocol. I have heard that many officers, including those in the Administrative Service, would rather choose to resign, if forced to take on the job. To them the risk of getting into trouble with ministers and VVIPs, amongst others, was not worth it.

Another problem I encountered during my term in the job was from some unenlightened senior officers, who berated the Protocol and Consular Directorate, of which I was the head, many a time by making snide remarks behind our back. We had a phrase for this: "sliming". I recall one such instance when there was a number of heads of government passing through the airport VIP Complex. In such cases, it was normal practice for senior officers to be rostered to assist ministers to receive the VVIP visitors, who often took the opportunity to discuss matters of mutual interest. It is the practice that the officer in attendance take notes, if necessary. A senior officer (name redacted and hereafter referred to as "X"), who was two grades above me then, tried to run me down by complaining to our minister in attendance that he was not advised properly on the arrival of the flight, which was false. He probably resented the fact that he had to do the duty during a weekend. I was not present in the room at that time as I was meeting the VVIP at the aircraft to bring him to VIP room where the minister was. Another senior officer of same rank as X, who was also present, later told me of what had happened during my absence.

That officer is Mr **Lee Chiong Giam, Deputy Secretary.** The next day, he sent me a letter in which he more than reproached X and stating, amongst other things, that I should confront X and take up the matter with him and if necessary, with higher ups. He also copied his letter to X. Chiong Giam is kind and an upright officer with a keen sense of justice. To my knowledge, he has helped many junior officers in serious situations to fight what he saw as injustice. Chiong Giam had a reputation of being the champion of the underdogs. He served with distinction as Chief Executive Officer of the very important grassroots organisation, the Peoples' Association (PA), for quite number of years. He took over the leadership at a time when the PA was without a leader at the administrative level. His predecessor left the job somewhat suddenly and it was not in pleasant circumstance for the PA. Chiong Giam was credited for many changes that lifted the PA's profile and also improved the grassroots administration. He acquired vast experience in people management.

It was a supreme irony that I defended X decades later. He was then our ambassador to an Asian county which had substantial relations with Singapore. I am not naming the country in order not to identify the officer and will refer to it as "country Y". **Mr and Mrs Lee Kuan Yew** made a visit to **Abu Dhabi** to attend a conference organised by the energy giant "Total". They arrived at about 1 A.M. in Dubai and I had arranged for police motorcycle outriders (in arrowhead formation) to escort our vehicles to the Intercontinental Hotel in Abu Dhabi about 100 km away. Seeing the outriders in action, Mrs Lee told me that when they were on official visit in country Y, the hosts did not provide any traffic clearance and X had told Mrs Lee that it was not the local protocol. She expressed surprise that I managed to get the outriders. I could have let the matter rest there, but I did not. I explained to her that in protocol Senior Minister X (as he then was) was not entitled to the motorcycle outriders. Usually the motorcycle escort, that I had secured, was given only to head of state/head of government on official visit. I explained to her why I had to impress on the Chiefs of Protocol in Dubai and Abu Dhabi on the importance of the outriders, so as to get them to relent. The stretch of road we were travelling was known for serious accidents involving many fatalities. (Not very long before the SIA staff was killed on that stretch, and at night it was even less safe.) I was able to convince them, and they made an exception. The Dubai escort handed over to a similar Abu Dhabi police escort at the halfway point. (For the information of the readers, United Arab Emirates (UAE) is a loose federation of six emirates who came together for the common purpose of defence, foreign affairs and common currency. Abu Dhabi is the capital. Except for Dubai, the other four smaller emirates depend on the immensely rich Abu Dhabi for cash injections. In other respects, they have autonomy and consider themselves "independent". I was then a non-resident Ambassador to UAE covering from Egypt.) My purpose was that I did not want Mrs Lee to form any adverse opinion of X in the circumstance. More on this visit is in a later chapter.

I now revert to the follow-up on the President's conversation with me. Months went by and one day Wong Chooi Sen (Wong) called me to his office. We would meet at his office frequently, informally, mainly to discuss and review matters as necessary. Without fail, he would offer a cup of tea or coffee to all who visited hm. Except in very rare situations, Wong was always calm and pleasant, and I had never seen him to lose his cool towards officers, whether in high or humble positions. Whenever he could be, he was always helpful to fellow officers and staff. To my knowledge, he, more than any other civil servant, was privy to all important matters of state and worked long hours under stressful circumstances. He served PM Lee and the Cabinet right from the beginning in 1959 until his retirement and beyond, continually, till his death sometime in the 2000s — a testimony to his loyalty, devotion and commitment. We had a comfortable working relationship and I think he also liked me as a person.

Once he shared with Chia Cheong Fook and I, a rare but very serious moment in his career. Sometime during what I would term as the "**survive or perish years**" from 1959–65, the PM, in a fit of anger, asked Wong to submit his resignation for what I figured was a slight delay in carrying out certain instruction. He went back to his office, typed out his resignation letter and sent it in. The PM summoned him immediately and asked him why he did that to which Wong responded; "PM you asked me for it". Then and there, the PM tore up the letter and threw it in the waste bin, saying that he should have known the pressure he was in, or something to that effect. According to Wong, the PM once called him on the telephone at 6 A.M. (I cannot recall whether or not it was a non-working day) and, probably sensing that he was not very alert, asked him whether he was still asleep to which Wong replied **"Yes PM, it is six in the morning"**. Probably, the PM did not realise the time of the day. These were among the rare insights Wong shared with a select circle of his colleagues. Sometimes conversations like these provided relief, if only temporarily, when the atmosphere was tense.

After I had finished drinking the tea (a good "Cabinet brew" I used to joke), Wong told me that the PM had asked him whether I wanted to continue in the job. He knew that by then I had been in the job as Private Secretary to the President for more than three years. I asked Wong what the PM was thinking. Judging from the tone in which Wong conveyed it, I had the impression that PM was not unhappy or dissatisfied with my performance in the job and, probably, he had my career development in the Administrative Service in mind. I told Wong it was not for me to say that I want a change, lest it be misconstrued that I was not happy in the job serving the President. However, I had always readily accepted postings to any ministry which Government deemed necessary for my career development and that I did not pick and choose where I wanted to go.

Few months passed before I had the news from Wong that the PM had decided that I should be posted elsewhere. Just about a week before, the PM saw the President in the latter's office. I did not know what transpired but I did not think much on it, the PM coming to see the President was nothing unusual. It was always as we used to say **"four eyes"** and as such I was rarely present. Later, I learnt that the President was consulted by PM Lee, and that he had agreed. Concerning the matter, the President told me that he reluctantly agreed to let me go in the interest of my career and complimented me on my performance. I was happy and satisfied that my service was much appreciated. Within a few days I had a call from Chia Cheong Fook, who had just been appointed as Permanent Secretary, and he said that he was arranging for my posting back to the Ministry of Foreign Affairs to help him out in the administration. Apparently, from what I gathered then, PM Lee was not happy with some problems in the administration of the Ministry and wanted Chia Cheong Fook to take charge of the Ministry and solve the problems.

I was not told more on this and I went back to the MFA. Among the officers we used to joke "ours is not to question why but to do and die"! Immediately upon my return to the MFA, I was put on "Special Duties". I was appointed **"Investigation Officer" to inquire into the loss of public funds in Singapore Embassy in The Philippines.** This could have been one of the several factors for why PM Lee wanted Chia Cheong Fook to take over the MFA and straighten out its administration, and why the latter asked PM Lee for my transfer to MFA.

There were many interesting factors concerning my posting back to MFA, which I came to know only decades later. About 10 years after Chia Cheong Fook's demise, I came upon his oral deposition in our National Archives quite by chance. Here are excerpts from his deposition and I quote:

> *"So, I went in, I saw the Minister for Foreign Affairs. PM asked me to sit down, without much further ado (he said) 'want you to take over Foreign Affairs'. I was stunned for a few moments. Then he went on to say that he wanted... The 'place was in a mess'."*
>
> *"Ah PM said 'Do you want any staff' I said I don't know yet. But straight away, I said if administration is (bad) I want VK Rajan I told him. Sir, I don't want to have any other staff transferred at the moment but I need somebody whom I can trust to help me in strengthening out matters, strengthening out the problems in administration".*
>
> *"So Wong Cui Sen comes in. I said that V K Rajan was the private secretary to the President; so daring of me asking for the President's private secretary but I do not want my head chopped of you see. One must get good man. So, I told..."*

"Wong Chui Sen came... 'Wong! He wants V K Rajan. Can you see to it and arrange for him?' 'Yes PM'. Then he went off"

"So, he (PM) told me, 'Ok Wong will see to it'"

"My working relationship with V K Rajan was superb, absolutely. V K Rajan, my number two (is) a first-class person. He became an Ambassador later. His last appointment was Ambassador to Cairo. First class fellow. Without him, I think I would have failed also. He was real help, big help. Plenty of initiatives."

Source: Oral History Deposition, National Archives Singapore. Reproduced with permission.

I did not know until then that Chia Cheong Fook had made his oral deposition and when I read the above, I was overwhelmed to know that he held me in such high esteem. I have not known of another tribute by a senior officer to his subordinate that is so sincere.

To understand the system and the policy of posting and transferring officers, one needs to understand the structure and organisation of the civil service back then. During colonial rule, the administration had two tiers: British Colonial Civil Service Officers and the local Civil Servants. Both were "common user" services, meaning that officers were rotated around to take on any positions within the service. The British officers were rotated to take on any position and responsibility in the British Empire. Therefore, they were "generalists" by nature. Most of them began their early education in elite grammar schools, then went on to Oxford and Cambridge where they studied arts and history, and then joined "His (or Her) Majesty's Service". It was said that handful of these officers were able to rule such a far-flung empire. They occupied all senior positions from Governor down to heads of departments. They introduced the "**Colonial Regulations**" and the "**General**

Orders" that governed government operations They were assisted by 'native' civil servants in subordinate positions.

In Singapore, as in other colonies, the civil service structure consisted of the Administrative Service, the General Executive Service, and the Clerical Service for general administration and the officers were rotated throughout the government. These were the "common users" and their services were pensionable. (As Executive Officer, I had served in several ministries, including on secondment to our High Commission in London. There were professional services like police, health, prison and others — mostly pensionable, but some non-pensionable with Central Provident Fund benefits. This was the system we inherited at self-government in 1959 and, with some changes, it continued up to mid-1970s when it was revamped substantially, but the general edifice continues. It should be noted that, at its inception, the system was designed to serve colonial interests, principally to maintain law and order. All services for the public, including services like refuse collection were performed by government employees. In the new environment, governance had become more complex and far reaching than the initial reforms that were undertaken. Statutory Boards and autonomous authorities were created to take on important functions e.g. Economic Development Board. Many other functions were privatised to increase efficiency and to reduce government expenditure to a desirable percentage of the GDP. In short, the objective was to enable Singapore to punch above its weight and, thereby, increase its global competitiveness. Under relentless reforms, ministries were made almost autonomous authorities in the sense that they operated on block budgets and could hire and fire staff without having to go through lengthy procedures. This did not mean that they were not accountable to the Parliament. There were no more **"common-users"** who moved across ministries, as the business of government became far more complex. However, the Administrative Service is regarded as a premier service and the administrative heads of ministries — permanent secretaries — are still the top rung officers from this service which comprises largely of technocrat scholars. Over time, the government has reduced the pensionable category of public servants, but as far as I can recollect, the Administrative Service and services like the Legal Service still retain their pensionable status along with other benefits, including the Central Provident Fund (CPF) contributions.

BACK TO THE FUTURE IN THE FOREIGN MINISTRY

I was then in the Administrative Service and Chia Cheong Fook wanted me to opt for transfer to the newly established Foreign Service, saying that I could contribute much to the Ministry of Foreign Affairs. He immediately proceeded to effect the transfer. A brief description of the structure of the civil service back then would be a useful background for the new generation civil servants. In the circumstances of our sudden independence, there was no time to create a Foreign Service as such. There was a compelling urgency to get started immediately in securing diplomatic recognition by as many countries as possible, and as quickly as possible, and to establish diplomatic missions in a few selected countries. And so we just answered the call to serve abroad and get our diplomatic missions operational, quickly, while learning the essentials along the way. Initially, we were just on "secondment" to the Ministry. There was no luxury of time.

With the experience gained and having studied the schemes of few other countries, including Malaysia, we launched our full-fledged **Foreign Service Scheme** sometime around 1974. A later development, however, troubled me. The remuneration package for Administrative Service officers was enhanced and they enjoyed better terms than their Foreign Service counterparts doing the same jobs, grade for grade and with equal responsibility. In my belief, it was a discrimination and the Foreign Ministry was, to the best of my knowledge, the only ministry where this anomalous situation existed. Other ministries had, as I understood at that time, managed to retain equal treatment in this regard for their departmental service officers doing similar jobs with same level of responsibility. There was unhappiness and some of us expressed our concern over this duality which objectively could not be justified. I remember Professor Tommy Koh (then Ambassador to the United States) raised this issue of injustice, if I may term it as such, during a heads of mission meeting. It appeared that the policy was by then deeply entrenched. **As it turned out my opting for the Foreign Service was a not a wise decision, to put it mildly.** In life, one must live with the consequences of one's mistakes that cannot be reversed. This was one of my few costly mistakes. In another context and in my private life, the most painful and difficult to forget experience was when my family's kindness and help was paid for by treachery. As **Baroness Margaret Thatcher** said, before going to see the Queen to tender her resignation, when her cabinet colleagues revolted against her: **"It is a funny old world"**.

Yet, I did not let all these affect me too much or dampen my spirit. It is important to look to the future and it cannot be found in the past. It must be noted that I was not unhappy during the rest of my career that followed. I must also state here that both my wife and I have been received with kindness and respect in all the countries we served, more so in the **Kingdom of Bahrain.**

Here is an experience which stumped me. One weekend, I was waiting for my turn to pay for the groceries I had picked up in an Al Jazeera supermarket in Bahrain. I was still in my cycling gear with my helmet on. At the cash desk, the staff on duty was checking out the groceries of a Bahraini lady who was middle aged. That lady signalled me to place all my groceries on the checkout desk. Taken aback, I did so, thinking that she was trying to speed up the situation. (Probably I must have been a little dense that morning.) Immediately, she instructed the counter staff (a Filipino lady) to include all my groceries in her bill. Shocked, I pleaded with her repeatedly not to do so, and insisted that that I would pay for my groceries. It was to no avail and the counter staff, probably not wanting to disobey the Bahraini lady, did as instructed. It happened very fast and all I could say by way of acknowledging her kindness was to say, "**may Allah bless you**". She thanked me and left promptly. I had never met her before or since. I must say that, as a people, the Bahrainis are tolerant, friendly and hospitable.

It is experiences like this that reinforce my belief that we should not to lose faith in humanity, no matter what problems and pain life throws at us.

A final note before I end this chapter. Both my predecessor and my successor in the job as Private Secretary to the President resigned and left the Service to pursue, as I understood, higher studies abroad. My transfer was slightly delayed because a few prospective candidates had declined the job. An Administrative Officer from the Finance Ministry, who was a grade higher than me, was offered the posting to take over from me. He came to see me in my office to find out more about the job. I answered all his questions and remember telling him that I enjoyed the unique experience. To my surprise, he too declined the job. I could only surmise that those who declined had probably concluded that for the risks involved the rewards were not commensurate. I had earlier mentioned the fact that many officers did not feel comfortable in PM Lee's presence. During my interaction with foreign VIPs, including Prince Charles, I noticed that they too had this impression that our officers were not at ease in the presence of PM Lee.

Chapter 12

SWIMMING AGAINST THE CURRENT

Many countries upon gaining independence from the colonial regimes adopted the policy of seeking reparations, wherever and whenever possible, from their former colonial masters and seeking aid by playing the United States against the then Soviet Union and vice versa while the Cold War lasted. Even after the end of the Cold War, many countries tried to continue this strategy in different formats under different circumstances.

Seek Trade Not Aid

The Peoples' Action Party (PAP) was a socialist party and for a while was a member of the **Socialist International.** In many newly emerging countries then, socialism was the flavour of the time. However, dogmatic attachment to socialist ideology had stymied economic development in many countries, including India. By and large the mantra of socialism had not worked as expected. So, the PAP chose a different route.

The Government drew up an economic development strategy that emphasised on attracting foreign direct investment, amongst other things. Pragmatic policies were introduced; institutions were created e.g. Economic Development Board; new laws enacted and existing impediments were removed.

Here is an anecdote:

Dr **Goh Keng Swee**, then First Deputy Prime Minister of Singapore, made an official visit to Australia from 23th-29th June, 1980. I was then Acting High Commissioner in Canberra and I accompanied him on a Royal Australian Air Force (RAAF) flight to Rockhampton. He told me that when he was the Finance Minister, leading Indian industrialist, **Tata**, saw him in his Fullerton Building office in 1960 and had asked what the conditions for investing in Singapore were. Dr Goh told Tata that the **only condition was his investment must make money — the more the better!** Dr Goh noted Tata was stunned and at a loss for words and wanted to know why. Tata narrated that he (Dr Goh) was the first finance minister ever to tell him that his investment must make money. Leaders in other countries whom he had talked to before had insisted on different conditions like 51% control and more, or having "informal" arrangements. Tata also related to Dr Goh of his own experience in his own country. Tata had written to his commerce minister, **Jagjivan Ram**, proposing similar investment. A year went by and there was no response. After several reminders, Jagjivan Ram invited Tata to his office in Delhi. When they met the minister asked him what his proposal was as they could not locate the file! After listening to Tata, the minister asked Tata since he (Tata) was very rich, why he wanted to invest in the project he (Tata) had proposed. The minister further said that Tata should give others (meaning smaller players) a chance to do so. Tata asked who else had shown interest. The minister's reply was "none". I thought then that India's loss was Singapore's gain!

Dr Goh said he insisted that Tata should make money for the reasons that:

a. Government wanted the swamp land in Jurong to take-off as a successful industrial complex and, if Tata's investment failed, it would be a bad publicity which could deter other investors; and

b. if he made profits then government would get its fair share of revenue and Tata get good returns; even more importantly, the workers would be paid fair wages and learn good skills.

It was music to Tata's ears. He was delighted and immediately committed his investment: **"Tata Precision Tools"**, which I understood was the first investment in Jurong Industrial Estate.

Not everyone in Singapore and abroad was very optimistic that Jurong would succeed. Even Dr Goh had concerns that it should not end up as **"Goh's folly".** Many years later when I was High Commissioner in New Zealand (1990-2)**, Robert Muldoon** (Prime Minister of New Zealand in the 1970s), shared his thoughts in this regard. During a visit to Singapore in 1961(or thereabout) Dr Goh took him and his few fellow MPs to visit Jurong. What he saw was a swampland and he quietly pulled his colleague aside and with a chuckle commented "Look at this. These fellows want to turn this swamp into an industrial estate". Few years later, he made a similar visit and he was astonished at the transformation. He said he could not believe his eyes. (Muldoon spoke to me frankly. He was known to be a pugnacious politician and dismissive of officials who to him did not measure up.)

The success of Jurong was among the factors that brought early recognition and respect for Singapore. Many countries looked at Jurong as possible model for their own development. Programmes for VIPs on official visits then included a trip to Jurong and the visits were commemorated by the VIPs' planting of *tembusu* tree saplings with a plaque bearing the name of the VIP concerned, the date and the occasion of the visit. One VIP, who came for a second visit many years later, told me how astonished he was to see the tree he planted had grown well and in good health! In many countries, after publicity photos were taken, things would have been forgotten!

Dr Goh was an able and respected economist. Many regarded him as the "father of Singapore's economic development". He was once an economic adviser to the Peoples' Republic of China.

Many countries, upon gaining independence from the colonial regimes adopted the policy of seeking reparations, wherever and whenever possible, from their former colonial masters and seeking aid by playing the United States against the then Soviet Union and vice versa while the Cold War lasted. Even after the end of the Cold War, many countries tried to continue this strategy in different formats under different circumstances.

SEEK TRADE AND NOT AID

However, our leaders chose a different strategy and went against the trend. At a meeting between the then Japanese Prime Minister and PM Lee in Tokyo sometime in the early 1960s, our officials present noted that the Japanese PM showed some unease and kept looking at his brief prepared by his officials. In a conversation after the meeting, our officials learned from their Japanese counterparts that in the brief they had prepared, they had advised their prime minister that, like many other leaders, PM Lee might raise the issue of war reparation. The officials had also suggested a response, including the amount that could be considered. However, PM Lee did not raise the issue despite pressure at home, especially (as I understood) from the Chinese clan associations and the Chinese Chamber of Commerce who wanted Japan to pay damages for wartime atrocities. Instead, he sought Japanese investment in Singapore. This surprised the Japanese PM and he did not know how to respond. Anyway to cut the long story short, Japan responded positively and, if I remember correctly, the Bridgestone Tyre factory was the first of their many investments that followed.

In response to the demand at home for war reparation, **PM Lee argued that it was better to get Japan to invest in Singapore, which would create jobs and enable workers to learn new skills and upgrade themselves, than to ask Japan to pay for war reparation, which in any case would not be much and would let Japan wash its hands off the whole incident**. This, in my view, was the starting point of our **"Look East"** policy which was adopted much later by other leaders in Asia and beyond.

As part of our learning process, upon return from his overseas trips, PM Lee would share with us the best practices, on a variety of matters, he had observed while abroad and instruct officials to find ways to implement them in Singapore. The practices we adopted over the years were the **"Koban Neighbourhood Policing", "Just in time delivery", Work Improvement Team (WIT)** and more, to increase productivity. I remember someone telling me that we adopted a yellow colour for taxis after PM Lee's visit to India.

Sometime in the early 1970s, PM Lee shared the observation he made in a Japanese factory. As the supervisor took him round to see the processes, he noticed the workers ignored him (PM Lee) although they were aware of his presence and knew who he was. They went about doing their work without any interruption in the operation. He contrasted that visit to a similar factory visit in Britain sometime previously. When PM Lee entered the factory there, the workers stopped their work temporarily and gathered around him, eager to know who he was and to engage him in conversation. He said that it showed why the productivity of the

Japanese workers was higher than their British counterparts. Whenever PM made these comparisons, the British were not amused. We politely pointed out to them that it was not our intention to disparage their work force but that our work force had to learn the best practices from around the world, including Britain, for our own survival.

Our **policy of seeking trade and not aid** instilled in our work force the right values, a sense of discipline and empowerment. The respect Singapore commands abroad is attributable in no small measure to the pragmatism of our work force.

Chapter 13

SETTING HIGH STANDARDS

> *Singapore was lucky that it had honest and incorruptible leaders with **"fire in their belly and iron in their soul"** taking charge right at the beginning, that is, upon self-government in 1959. They set the highest standards by personal example and insisted no less from those they led and from the bureaucracy. There was no magic formula, no secret recipe, no quick fix and no easy ride.*

During my postings abroad, I was often asked — in my interactions with host government officials, diplomats and in talks and lectures in universities and think tanks, and on other occasions — what was the **"secret"** of Singapore's success. I was also asked the same question during my lectures on **"Public Sector Reforms in Singapore"** at the Civil Service College for senior foreign government officials attending courses under the **Singapore Technical Cooperation Programme**. I have talked about this in a different chapter. Generally, the Singapore ambassador's job was a bit easier; Singapore's reputation as a successful country and PM Lee's international stature opened many doors, much to the envy of many other ambassadors, including those from bigger and wealthier countries. However, it also meant heavier responsibility, in that the Singapore ambassadors had to be professional and live up to expectations at all times.

Invariably, my response would be that Singapore was lucky in that it had honest and incorruptible leaders with **"fire in their belly and iron in their soul"** taking charge right at the beginning, that is, upon self-government in 1959. They set the highest standards by personal example and insisted on no less from those they led and from the bureaucracy. There was no magic formula, no secret recipe, no quick fix and no easy ride.

I was lucky that my duties in several positions gave me the opportunity to serve many pioneer leaders, including **Rajaratnam, Dr Goh Keng Swee, PM Lee, President Yusof Ishak and President Benjamin Henry Sheares, and President Wee Kim Wee** amongst others, to varying extents. It was a great learning experience for me quite early in my career, although not without some risks at times.

LEADERSHIP BY EXAMPLE

They led simple lives. Their offices were furnished threadbare and in those days the furniture was government issue from the Central Supplies Department in Kandang Kerbau, located beside the canal. There government-employed artisans made the furniture required for government offices. Broken furniture was also sent there to be repaired and returned. (I read in the newspaper that Dr Goh took with him soap powder when he went on visits abroad and he washed his own socks and under garments.)

Dr Goh had a reputation of being a tough task master. Statistics was his forte. A friend of mine serving in the Ministry of Finance told me that he had seen Dr Goh dismissing briefs prepared by senior officers with derisive comments, when he thought the officers were not thorough and up to the mark. Sometimes, his comments could be caustic.

Dr Goh was also a pragmatist. In an earlier chapter, I mentioned that **Kishore Mahbubani** gave lectures on communism. That was

Dr Goh's arrangement. In launching the programme (at the Civil Service Staff Training Institute in Pasir Panjang), Dr Goh made an interesting observation. He said that during his stay in a guest house in India, he saw a card on a desk which read "Truth will triumph". He commented something like this: only Indians have a mind for this, "if you tell this to a Chinese, he would ask you how much is that in dollars and cents"!

It was well known that Dr Goh was also a strict disciplinarian besides being a tough task master. I served in the Ministry of Defence from 1969 to 1971 as **Special Assistant to the Director of Manpower**, Chia Cheong Fook. Dr Goh was then the Minister of Defence. There was a group of graduate National Service men doing Reservists Training. One of the exercises was to jump from a high elevation. It essentially involved trainees climbing up a tall structure and then jumping down onto a large piece of tarpaulin held together and stretched very tightly by the other trainees on the ground. It was absolutely necessary that the tarpaulin remained fully stretched and very tight so as to cushion the fall of the jumper; otherwise the person jumping would hit the ground with force and risk serious injury.

The graduate trainees decided to prank their instructor — They refused to jump, protesting that it was dangerous to do so. The instructor, a sergeant, tried to convince them that it was safe to do so, provided they followed his instructions. Still, they refused and asked the instructor to demonstrate that it was safe. The instructor went up and as he jumped the trainees loosened the stretch. As a result the instructor was injured. Jubilantly, the trainees told him, "see we told you so".

When Dr Goh heard of the mischief, he hit the roof. He ordered severe punishment for the trainees involved and put them through extra rigorous drills to drive home the message that the Singapore

Armed Forces (SAF) would not tolerate such irresponsible acts. It was also meant to serve as a warning for all in the SAF, including and especially the future reservists. If I remember correctly, this incident also led to an amendment of laws regarding Reservist Training.

S Rajaratnam excelled both as Minister for Culture and as Foreign Minister. He had a deep, penetrative and analytical mind with a wit to match. His unrivalled grasp of issues in international relations endeared him to many foreign leaders, as well. For the information of readers, Raja did not eat lunch and slept late at night. He would spend all his lunch hour everyday browsing through the book collections in the nearby Ensign Book Store in High Street (later demolished to make way for the Parliament Complex) and return to office clutching a few books for nighttime reading. He would arrive in Office around ten in the morning and work until six or seven in the evening. This a habit developed during his prior career as a journalist. He used to brief us on important issues and we often looked forward to hearing from him. However, I must also state that the nitty-gritty of administration was not his cup of tea.

I can recall many interesting situations when Rajaratnam demonstrated his deep insights on issues in foreign relations and his skills in diplomacy.

Mochtar Kusumaatmadja, the Indonesian Foreign Minister in President Suharto's cabinet, would often say in public forums that "Raja is my mentor" and so would meet his mentor during his frequent visits to Singapore. Rajaratnam told us that we should try to seed our ideas into Mochtar and let them come out as Mochtar's own initiatives in managing relations with Indonesia and ASEAN.

Rajaratnam had kept up his contact with **Ngyuen Co Thac,** the diehard socialist Foreign Minister of Vietnam, even during the height of war in Cambodia when Vietnam and Singapore were at opposites ends of the spectrum. I recall in one of their meetings Co Thac admitted that there was poverty in Vietnam and asserted that it was being shared equally by all. Rajaratnam quipped **"why share poverty when you can share prosperity"**.

Referring to the then ongoing war in **Afghanistan** following the Soviet invasion, Rajaratnam told us that he had read a book by an English author (whom he named but I cannot recall now) in which the author had noted that Afghanistan throughout the centuries had known only two industries: "one is **shooting** and the other **looting**". Rajaratnam expressed the view that Russians would meet their "Vietnam" in Afghanistan. As it turned out, the Russians suffered a humiliating defeat and pulled out with nothing to show for their attempt, except heavy loss of about 15000 Russian lives, in almost a decade of fighting, and the enormous drain on their exchequer.

During the wars in Vietnam and in Cambodia large numbers of civilians caught up in the conflicts were fleeing in crammed, often leaky and unseaworthy boats to seek asylum in other Southeast Asian countries. Singapore, for obvious reasons, decided it could not take in the refugees who arrived at its shores. We were simply too small, had no space and would be overwhelmed. We had a policy that if any ship brought refugees, the government of the country to which the ship belonged must give a written agreement to take all the refugees away within 90 days to be settled elsewhere; otherwise they would not be let in. There were counties which reneged on their commitments and, if I remember correctly, Norway was one such country.

Many Western countries were very critical of our policy of not taking the refugees. The most strident was Australia, its media branded us as inhumane. Rajaratnam went to work immediately. He told the Australians that since Australia was huge and mostly an empty continent, the refugees would provide the much-needed manpower to develop the continent. Singapore could help Australia in this regard, by repairing their leaky boats, providing some supplies and a compass for the them to find their way to Australia! That quietened them down for a while.

We would be remiss if we do not contrast the above with Australia's own policy on refugees in later years. Refugees seeking asylum in Australia and arriving sometimes in unseaworthy crafts were intercepted by the Australian navy before they reached Australian shores, and transported to a desolate, and inhospitable island belonging to Papua New Guinea (PNG). A former Australian colony, PNG was reportedly pressured to agree to this, in return for cash amounting to about A$400 million. A documentary by a leading international news channel showed the inhuman conditions in which the refugees were being held in euphemistically termed detention centres. Another international channel aired a similar situation showing the detention of refugees in another island country used by Australia.

The inmates in the detention centres had no chance whatsoever of reaching Australia, and reportedly suicide was common. The PNG supreme court ruled that the detention centres in PNG were unconstitutional and a violation of human rights. Yet, the Aussies refused to take them out.

An Australian prime minister said on camera that Australia used **"imaginative ways"** to prevent refuges from reaching Australian shores and that he would **"keep them out at all cost"** and **"by hook or by crook"**. He also did not deny reports that his officials paid several thousand dollars to the owner of a boat crammed with refugees to turn back and head towards Indonesia. In this context, it is to be noted that a significant proportion of the original inhabitants of the vast and immensely resource rich continent felt marginalised by the wealthy mainstream population. In my view, it is a classic example of Western double standards when it comes to observing human rights and having compassion in dealing with refugees and displaced persons.

The hypocrisy of countries in the European Union (EU) in this regard was also laid bare when they erected barbed wire fences along their borders to keep out the refugees suffering in squalid and freezing conditions right at their borders. They were fleeing the conflicts in North Africa and Syria, for which the Western powers were largely responsible.

Every country has the right to determine its immigration policy; however, no country has the right to preach to others to do that which it itself is not prepared to do, to help the refugees.

MY FIRST POSTING

It was during my posting in London (1966–69) that I first had the opportunity of serving Prime Minister Lee Kuan Yew, and to learn from him and observe him in close proximity. It was a very good start to my career in diplomacy. That period was also a difficult one for Singapore. **Harold Wilson's** Labour Government had announced the pull out of British military forces from Singapore. It was part of a programme to reduce defence spending **"East of Suez"**. The impact of a total shut down of the British bases in Singapore at that time would have been very severe both in economic and security terms.

PM Lee made a few trips to London in those years to plead with the Wilson Government not to pull out precipitously and to delay it in order to give sufficient time for Singapore to adjust. Wilson was firm in his decision but was prepared to consider a slight delay. However, before all details could be settled Wilson lost the election and was succeeded by the Conservative Prime Minister, **Edward Heath**, who was equally firm on the pull out but was a bit more flexible in the implementation of the details.

As much as we did not want or like the British pull out, one could understand their reasons. There were already signs of economic decline in Britain and the cost of maintaining military bases east of Suez could not be sustained or justified to the taxpayer. One morning, I was following behind PM Lee and **Dennis Healey**, Labour Chancellor of Exchequer, who were discussing some points while strolling along Hyde Park. PM Lee noticed a British youth, looking unshaven and unkempt, strumming a guitar. He had a scrubby cap in front of him and some sympathetic people passing by tossed coins, often pennies into the cap. Visibly surprised, he asked **"Dennis, what's wrong with Britain? This fellow should be in school and not be like this."** Dennis responded **"Prime Minister, you are too puritanical"**. Disagreeing, PM Lee said **if the youth opted out, Britain will pay a heavy price later**.

Britain's economic decline was evident, and it was the Conservative party's policy, which the Labour Party could not stomach. Prime Minister Baroness Thatcher was dubbed as the **"Iron Lady"** and the joke that went around then was that she was the only man in the British Cabinet!

Thatcher and PM Lee had many similarities as strong leaders and had mutual respect. During Thatcher's official visit to Singapore in 1985, PM Lee commended her (in his speech at the dinner held in the Istana in her honour) for her courage in taking on the labour unions and her firm resolve not to give in to the unionists in the then ongoing industrial action which had paralysed London port for more than six months.

Infuriated by Lee Kuan Yew's comments, the leftist and pro-union (with Fabian influence) newspapers carried screaming headlines the next day: "Lee Kuan Yew should keep his stupid mouth shut" and slammed his **"arrogance to advise Britain"**.

The extremists in the British labour unions never forgave Thatcher for what they believed to be "anti-labour" policies, to the point that a few of them showed their back to Thatcher's cortege during its final journey through London streets before burial. Such was the depth of their bitterness towards her.

During the period I was in London, PM Lee also attended Commonwealth Prime Ministers' Meetings — the one in 1966 was his first. The Mission was quite busy with making all the arrangements. We were a pioneering team consisting of a small staff: High Commissioner, AP Rajah; Counsellor, Chia Cheong Fook; Administration Attaché (myself); and Joseph Chew, Personal Assistant to High Commissioner. Between us, we covered everything. When we made mistakes reprimand was swift, which was as expected. Nevertheless, it was a unique, valuable and enjoyable experience.

The **media in Britain** then took fiendish delight in putting their leaders on the dock, sometimes ridiculing and ensnaring them into making admissions which the interviewees would regret later. For the unwary and the incompetent, it was like entering a lion's den. However, they found Lee Kuan Yew did not play by their rule book; they had a sort of **"love hate" attitude** towards him but were always very eager to get him on camera. He was always well prepared and had vast array of relevant and up to date statistics at his command, quite unlike many leaders I knew then. I recall one occasion particularly well.

A journalist by the name of **Robin Day** was one of the ace reporters who stood above the pack. Watching him on the local television, I had the impression that he had built up a "fearsome" (for some) reputation as an anchor. He interviewed PM Lee Kuan Yew on the then ongoing **Vietnam war**. In response to one of his questions, Lee Kuan Yew said that many people in the West thought that the Viet Cong (Vietnamese communist fighters) were a "funny people as they came out in their pyjamas at night to fight". He then cited statistics about the alarming rise in US casualties and the many millions of US dollars being drained away daily. He cautioned Robin Day that in the circumstance "the Vietnamese are not a funny people". I thought Robin Day had more than met his match.

From my observation, Lee Kuan Yew had already begun to make a favourable impact on the British public at large. There were letters published in a leading newspaper wherein the writers, amongst other things, stated, **"let us swap Wilson for Lee"** (Harold Wilson was then the prime minister).

In another interview in London, Lee Kuan Yew punctured the ego of some Western journalists. I think it was a Dutch journalist who alleged that Lee Kuan Yew was dictatorial and did not allow dissent, an essential ingredient for democracy that had enabled the West to develop and prosper. Lee Kuan Yew cut him short and said that he would be prepared to implement Western style democracy in Singapore, provided the Western governments would guarantee admission for Singapore citizens into their countries and provide all of them the jobs, schools, hospitals, housing and security when Western style democracy failed to deliver in Singapore. If they could not get that iron-clad guarantee then he would do it in his own way. He warned them that **"time will tell who is right"**.

Time has indeed spoken, and it is not difficult to see in whose favour. Fast forward some 40 years, what do we see? Readers would note that Holland having lost the battle to control drug abuse has since legalised it — a growing trend in the West. Many countries in Europe are finding it difficult to balance their books; a few in Southern Europe are finding it difficult to even stay afloat without bailouts.

Greece, the cradle of western democracy, is unable to pay its dues and requires repeated cash bailouts from the European Union and/or International Monetary Fund (IMF). The economic health of other countries e.g. Italy and Spain has also come under severe financial strain at the time of writing. Even Portugal is not out of the woods. (It is not lost on the readers that these countries were former colonial powers.)

Democracy, freedom of speech and human rights are important, and they are a hallmarks of civilised societies. However, there is no one size that fits all. More on this in a later chapter.

Chapter 14

FORM VERSUS SUBSTANCE

"Mr Chairman,

With your permission, I will dispense with the pleasantries. Since we are all distinguished none is more distinguished than the other... And I have not come here to enjoy your hospitality, not that I am not grateful for it, but we have many important issues on the agenda to cover..."

PM Lee Kuan Yew's maiden speech at the Commonwealth Prime Ministers' Meeting in 1966 in London.

"if we are not serious nobody will take us seriously"

— *PM Lee Kuan Yew*

In Chapter 4, I briefly mentioned how our government decided against the use of honorifics. Our leaders did not use any titles in both oral and written communications. Dress codes were simplified both to suit local climate and to be in sync with the life style of the common man. Our leaders wore open neck shirts were the usual attire except when meeting a foreign dignitary, then they would wear a suit. This is in stark contrast to the culture in other countries, including many in our region. In this chapter, I deal with the behaviour of many leaders based on my personal experiences, observations, watching documentaries and reading of relevant reports.

There were countries emerging from colonialism that made the situation more complicated, never mind simplifying it. They probably wanted to satisfy their egos and had the misguided need to "impress" those over whom they wielded power. Still not content, they built expensive monuments (statues) to glorify themselves only to be toppled by succeeding regimes. Saddam Hussein's imposing statue was ignominiously toppled during the US led invasion of Iraq. Mubarak, the president of Egypt, insisted that the bridge across the Suez Canal built by the Japanese as part of their aid to Egypt be named "Mubarak Bridge", instead of "Japan-Egypt Friendship Bridge", as proposed by the Japanese. For all his much-vaunted power, he lost in the "Arab Spring" revolution and spent some time in prison on charges, including the use of force to quell the uprising and corruption.

The contrast to Singapore cannot be starker. I noted a very interesting thing at the Commonwealth Prime Ministers' Meeting in London in 1966. It was PM Lee's first attendance following Singapore' admission to the Commonwealth the year before. Many leaders, especially from Asia and Africa routinely indulged in long platitudes, often addressing each other as distinguished prime minister, praising the host for the hospitality and the like, and some of their speeches lacked depth and substance. I noticed from his body language that PM Lee was not impressed to say the least. When his turn came to speak, PM Lee began thus (as far as my memory goes):

> **"Mr Chairman** (Harold Wilson),
> **With your permission, I will dispense with the pleasantries. Since we are all distinguished, none is more distinguished than the other... And I have not come here to enjoy your hospitality, not that I am not grateful for it, but we have many important issues on the agenda to cover...".**

Momentarily, there was a stunned silence among those present. They had not expected this, especially from someone who had joined them at the table for the first time. His entire intervention was appropriately short with a critical analysis of the issues and he went straight to the core.

I thought then that the newest and the youngest prime minister in the Commonwealth (probably in the world then) had made his mark and earned respect, on his first appearance amongst his peers, who were far more senior to him.

(There were a few leaders who were not only long-winded but also not focussed when they spoke. I noted one leader (from a small country in South Asia), who deputised for his prime minister, was long on pleasantries but short in substance, and many began to dose off. One senior officer, I think he was a Financial Secretary from an important British colony in Asia), began to dose off with a lighted cigarette in his mouth. When the cigarette neared its end and began to burn his lips, he woke up, causing a stir which startled a few delegates seated beside him. Luckily, for him, he was seated two or three rows behind the plenary table.)

In subsequent Commonwealth Meetings, in which I was fortunate enough to be present, I noticed that PM Lee was often invited to lead the discussions, sometimes on difficult problems confronting the world, not just the Commonwealth.

Many of his colleagues in the Commonwealth looked forward to interacting with him and sought his views and counsel. **Ratu Kamisese Mara**, Prime Minister of Fiji, was among them. He observed that PM Lee had the unique ability to breakdown complex issues and articulate them with clarity and deep insights, "in a manner we could grasp and comprehend". Ratu Mara said, he and his colleagues in the Pacific island nations were very grateful to PM Lee.

Our founding fathers also shunned privileges and reduced them to the minimum that was absolutely necessary such as security considerations. No government housing, cars, drivers, domestic help, no free telephone, no free utilities and the like was provided to government officials. By way of contrast, in a large country in Asia, an audit report noted that hundreds of government bungalows were still being occupied by former minsters, MPs and other senior leaders who continued to enjoy all the perks associated with their former positions, long after they had left them. These former lawmakers had ignored all notices to vacate. Since all political parties were involved, no firm action had been or could be taken to evict them. A few of those over-stayers in government bungalows reportedly wanted the properties to be declared national monuments to perpetuate their rent-free occupation and associated perks! Many had also not bothered to pay their utility bills and it appeared that there were no serious attempts to enforce payments either.

Such a situation was not unique. I learnt that in a country in the Middle East, about 50% to 60% of the annual budget went to paying salaries of not very productive civil servants and political leaders, both serving and retired. The above-mentioned perks incurred substantial cost to the treasury. The head of state changed his cabinet frequently and it swelled the number of gainfully unemployed elite, who had to be catered for. The country had a highly educated, capable and talented manpower base but, due to lack of opportunities at home, many had to go abroad. As in many other countries around the world, this country also had problems in withdrawing the heavy subsidies. This country has become aid-reliant and without regular injection of cash from donors it cannot, in my view, remain afloat.

In 1972, I was posted to the Istana as Private Secretary to President Benjamin Henry Shears upon my promotion to the

Administrative Service. In briefing me, the Assistant Private Secretary (Patrick D'cruz) informed me, amongst other things, that I was entitled to exemption from payment of road tax for my car (which at that time was about $200 per year). I was surprised and asked him who else enjoyed the exemption. The list was: President, Private Secretary, Assistant Private Secretary, the two Aide de Camp (ADC) and the Butler (yes, even the butler). This was a carry-over from colonial days.

Years before, I had heard of accounts that gave some glimpses into the leisurely life under the colonial governors in the Istana (Government House then). There were chickens and goats reared by locals employed as domestic staff, orderlies, gardeners and the like. The chickens and the goats would do their daily rounds in the grounds searching and scratching for food. I gathered that the last governor, **William Goode**, was benevolent to those staff. About 30 pounds of flour would be baked daily into bread for the governor's household, European officers and their families, and also for the native subordinate staff living within the domain. In the evenings after dinner, the governor and family would watch movies in private screenings in one of the large function rooms and they would be surrounded on the floor by children of local staff.

Another interesting thing I had heard also was that the domestic staff who served guests during functions on the lawn, were sometimes tipsy and unsteady; obviously, they had helped themselves to the liquor even before the functions began. PM Lee put an end to this in 1959 and the staff were warned to behave on pain of disciplinary action. Thenceforth, all unconsumed liquor, especially wine, at the end of the function were to be poured into the sink. There was good reason for it. Apart from the need to maintain discipline and productivity, it was also necessary to prevent the staff from opening more bottles of liquor than necessary in the hope that they could help themselves to the unconsumed liquor, since they could not be returned to the cellar for future use.

Here is a bit of history concerning the **Istana.** The Istana was known as the Government House (GH) during the colonial era. In my recollection and understanding, the Governor resided in the main building where he also had his office. The top senior officials in his government such as the Attorney General, Financial Secretary and his Private Secretary also resided in separate bungalows spread within the GH domain. There were also very basic "servants' quarters" for the local support staff, such as butlers, maids, gardeners cleaners and other essential support and maintenance workers on call all the time.

As stated, things changed with self-government in 1959. The main building had the President's office and the Prime Minister's office was located in the Annex. Remainder of the rooms and suites, both in the main building and in the Annex, were suitably renovated and furbished to serve as accommodation for VIP **state guests** Also, as stated above, except for Presidents Yusof Ishak and Devan Nair, their successors in office chose to stay in their private residences. However, when I was posted to the Istana as the President's Private Secretary to President Sheares, I was allotted the Private Secretary's bungalow at No. **2 Edinburgh Road** which connected the main gate in Orchard Road to the main building. Having grown in a rural (kampong) environment, I enjoyed that very much. However, my wife, being an urbanite, did not much like it. The fact the bungalow was very quiet at night and "eerie" (to her) and the fact that we had to sleep under mosquito nets at night made her unhappy. Thus, I had to cut short our stay in the "palace grounds". We were the last residents in the bungalow which was demolished soon afterwards along with a few other buildings in the domain. As a reminder of those days, our elder daughter Revathi's birth certificate carries the address as "2 Edinburgh Road, The Istana". I must add that the accommodation was not rent-free. As per regulations for government quarters, I was charged rental, but it was not at market rate. Staying within the Istana domain had some advantages for me, especially for going on inspection rounds outside office hours and week-ends. I also had Revathi (then three years old) in tow sometimes when I worked overtime in my office during weekends.

Now reverting back to the road tax exemption, I felt immediately that it was wrong and could not be justified because no citizen should be above the law. I felt some unease and decided to bring it to the attention of PM Lee. The Cabinet Secretary, **Wong Chooi Sen,** who was also Secretary to the PM, was initially hesitant as it concerned the President as well. Wong was known to be a very helpful and approachable senior civil servant. At my insistence, he later agreed and sent my minute to the PM. I was told the **PM was very angry and asked "why Rajan did not bring this up earlier".** According to Wong, he told the PM that I did. The PM instructed that the exemption must cease forthwith. On my part, I was curious why no one else had raised it since 1959. In fact, I learned later from a friend of mine in the Income Tax Department (later IRAS) that my predecessor had even sought exemption from paying the Radio & TV Licence Fee ($24 per year) and it was turned down, quite rightly so.

During my term in Egypt from 1994 to 2001, I was also concurrently High Commissioner to Zimbabwe and Cyprus and Ambassador to the United Arab Emirates and Jordan.

I learned much from my experiences and observations in these countries. When I presented my credentials as High Commissioner in **Zimbabwe** (ambassador from one Commonwealth country to another Commonwealth country is known as a High Commissioner),

I noticed **President Robert Mugabe** arrive in a Rolls Royce escorted by lancers on horseback in front. The convoy was led by a military armoured personnel carrier with a machine gun turret. Mugabe was in a splendid and impeccably tailored suit with an array of shining medals pinned on his jacket covering much of his chest. (My fleeting thought then was who bestowed on him so many medals and for what?) Mugabe's chief of protocol had a rather unusual request. He told me that after presenting our credentials (my First Secretary was also with me), and after the very brief formal speeches, we should retreat by walking backwards several steps before taking our seats, with Mugabe and his officials in attendance. The practice of not turning one's back immediately after greeting a monarch was an old custom in the royal courts of Europe and it is not usually insisted upon these days, even in those countries.

Clearly, it was Mugabe's way of trying to impress or rather over-awe his people with his power. Mugabe, the freedom fighter, came to power in 1980 when **Ian Smith's** illegal regime, which had ruled Rhodesia (as it was known then) under **"Unilateral Declaration of Independence"** from Britain, was forced out by international sanctions and pressure. Rhodesia was once regarded the "bread basket" of southern Africa, with its good climate and abundant resources, but it was exploited by the white settlers.

It must be said that Mugabe, as a freedom fighter, fighting the white minority's oppressive and exploitative rule, probably had a few equals. He is an intelligent man and commanded enormous following among his masses for a while. However, he failed to make the transition from freedom fighter to administrator and, above all, make peace work for the country.

Within three decades of the Mugabe rule, Zimbabwe's economy plummeted; it went from being a bread basket of Southern Africa to become a basket case — unable to feed its people and provide their very basic needs. Its currency collapsed when he printed billion-dollar notes which nobody wanted. One commentator wryly said that the billion-dollar note was not even big enough to use as toilet paper! Commerce stopped and people survived by barter trade and using US$. When he took charge the Zimbabwe dollar was above par with the US$. The mismanagement was colossal, and the list of such mismanagement and corruption was very long. According to a report, the hyper-inflation was "230 million per cent". The few examples below can give the reader an understanding of the extent of corruption:

- Mugabe built an expensive mansion for himself known as "Grace Mansion", named after his wife, using public funds;
- ministers had flourishing businesses of their own using government facilities and connections; an ambassador-in-residence in Harare told me that government vehicles were not sent to the government workshops in the Public Works Department for servicing and repairs; instead, they were sent to the garage owned by a minister and billed to his ministry for payment from public funds;
- I was told by resident diplomats that the government budget would be exhausted by mid-year and the ministry of finance was forced to seek relief from other sources, including borrowing; and
- Mugabe and his senior party leaders used to go on expensive state-funded foreign trips, where they would spend lavishly. Mugabe's crackdown of the elected opposition led by **Morgan Tsvingarai**, led to sanctions being imposed on Mugabe and many of his close aides, by the EU and US, barring them from travelling to Europe and US. They switched to destinations in Asia and the Middle East. Mugabe's wife was also known to be a big spender with stacks of US$ drawn from government coffers.

There were abundant signs of the impending collapse and Mugabe either did not care or, if he did, had no clue how to deal with it. One of his biggest mistakes was to grab the white settler-owned lands and distribute them to supporters of his party, who were freedom fighters, not farmers, and were not up to learning farming skills. Agriculture mostly collapsed. They had no clue how to run the government, even at the routine level. They had no crash course to train the civil servants and others in managerial positions, including in financial matters. It was puzzling that there was no policy in place to learn the skills required from other countries.

I had accepted a request from the undersecretary (equivalent to our permanent secretary) to give a lecture to the staff in their Ministry of Foreign Affairs on public sector reforms. The lecture was slated for 2.30 P.M. and I, with my first secretary **(Desmond Wee)**, arrived at the ministry at about 1.50 P.M. There was nobody around. We waited and, about 10 minutes later, we asked a female staff passing by to inform the undersecretary of our arrival and the purpose. She was not aware of my lecture and not keen to find out either. Later, the telephone operator arrived, and we took it up with her. We repeated our request but she also did not know of any such arrangement. Her response was that "there was nobody around".

After more time lapsed, we asked her to try again. At about 2.40 P.M. the chief of protocol (a lady) arrived and met us, and to our surprise she also could not recall the appointment. Just then, the undersecretary came in and I reminded him of the lecture. He muttered something like "oh yes I remember now" and he instructed the chief of protocol to round up as many staff as possible to come to the conference room. Thus, I began my lecture about 40 minutes later than the scheduled time and, because no prior notice was given and no arrangements were made, a few senior officers who were supposed to attend were missing. A few months later, the chief of protocol sent me a letter with the request: **"Professor, we would like you to give another lecture during your next visit as we**

found it very useful". It did not enthuse me. It was clear to me that they were not serious in their work.

PM Lee once told us in London, when dressing down an officer for his lapse, **"if we are not serious nobody will take us seriously"**. On another occasion, he told another officer that he would not hesitate to "put officers on disciplinary charge". Those words and the serious tone in which he uttered them still resonate in my ears.

It was not surprising that Zimbabwe was not able to earn the respect of the international community and that it had a bad reputation. In a book on Mugabe by a British author, whose name I cannot recall now, there was a passage which detailed what happened at a dinner function in London for Mugabe, organised by senior British politicians. I think it was the initiative of **Christopher Soames**, the last Governor of Rhodesia. To get investment into Zimbabwe, they had assembled a few leading industrialists at the dinner. Mugabe, instead of listening to their views and seeing how he could get them interested in investing in Zimbabwe, gave a **lecture on Marxism**, much to the surprise and, probably, disgust of the guests. Thus, he squandered away whatever goodwill he had with the people who went out of their way to help Zimbabwe. It was probably Mugabe's biggest blunder and it set Zimbabwe on a course of self-destruction. People who have interacted with Mugabe had assessed him as very intelligent and with a sense of humour to match. Mugabe died in 2019. But observers began to note that increasingly senility was creeping in. Often, he was seen asleep in meetings and functions, including at the United Nations General Assembly, but still he would not step down. Finally, in 2018 and after more than 34 years in power, he was forced out of office by his senior "comrade-in-arms", with the help of the army. It was not a happy ending. He could have achieved much in developing Zimbabwe, a country with bountiful natural resources and an equable climate to match.

However, much blame for the general incompetence of African leaders' should also rest with their former colonial masters. In Congo, the Belgians were rapacious and extremely brutal to the natives. A television documentary on exhibits in a Belgium museum showed photos of young Congolese men almost half naked and without their right forearms. The absence of forearms was not the result of deformities or birth defects. Their Belgian masters had cut off their forearms for no other reason than the allegation that they did not meet the required daily quota of latex collection in the rubber plantations, while working for near starvation wages. Such widespread cruelty was inflicted on the natives to beat them into total submission and slavery. Many observers had noted that **Antwerp** could not have developed into the premier diamond centre that it is, without the vast wealth, particularly diamonds, plundered from the then **Belgian Congo** (name changed to **Zaire** and again to **Democratic Republic of Congo**) which had a land mass bigger than Europe and natural resources on a scale beyond imagination. An Egyptian ambassador, who had served in Congo, told me that if you kicked a stone anywhere in Congo the chances are that you would find diamonds underneath. At independence, it was reported that the only educated person was a postal clerk named **Patrice Lumumba** who became the prime minister of independent Congo and he was killed not long after. A former Belgian police officer (inspector rank) narrated in detail, on camera for an international television documentary aired sometime in the 1990s, how he killed Lumumba, chopped him to pieces and immersed the body parts in a vat of acid to destroy evidence. Reportedly, it took place in the breakaway province of Katanga ruled by a Belgian puppet named **Moise Tshombe**. One reason for the assassination was that the socialist Lumumba was not amenable to Belgian manipulation, Belgium had wanted to maintain indirect control and continue plundering Congo's immense resources. In the early 2000s, the Belgian government officially apologised for eliminating Lumumba.

Years later, a sergeant named **Joseph Mobutu Sese Soko** seized power through a coup and ruled for a number of years. Mobutu awarded himself many long and bizarre titles (their description, meaning and the language are not suitable to print here). Until then, I had not heard of a more corrupt dictator. Reports circulating then noted that Mobutu told his ministers that he would give them three years to make all the money they wanted. (According to stories circulating then, he expected favours from his ministers' wives and female relatives, if he took a fancy for them.) He, like many other dictators, also built huge, ornate and opulent palaces, sometimes in the middle of nowhere. Yet, somehow, he had support from the West. He was feted in the White House by **Ronald Reagan**. But the West was merely using him to advance their interests. When the political equation changed, Mobutu was unceremoniously dumped. He fled Congo after he himself was overthrown by Kabila, another dictator.

In contrast to the abovementioned African leaders, **Fidel Castro** of Cuba was a leader of great stature and was well respected by his own people and by many others abroad. He led a simple life. With his small revolutionary cadres, he fought to defeat the US-supported corrupt and decadent **Fulgencio Batista** regime, which was bleeding out the country. It was reported that Castro wanted to develop cooperative relations with the US but when he arrived in Washington, President Eisenhower refused to see him. It left him with no option but to turn to the Soviet Union. Despite crippling sanctions imposed by US over several decades, its failed Bay of Pigs invasion, the missile crisis and more than 500 CIA attempts to assassinate him, Castro achieved much **for all Cubans**, including quality education and affordable universal health care, an achievement that has eluded even the US, and is envied around the world. Castro outlasted eight US presidents and their sanctions. Another mark of this great leader was his contempt for personal glory. As per his wish he was cremated without fanfare, within a day of his death and his ashes interred at the remote spot (a swamp) where he first landed with his fellow revolutionaries to launch the revolution against the corrupt Batista regime in 1953. Also, to fulfil Castro's wish, the Cuban government enacted laws prohibiting any monuments, memorials and tributes like the naming of buildings, institutions and even streets in memory of Castro. Truly, he was an exceptional leader, even if some might not have found his policies very appealing.

Back home, my years with the President, in protocol and in overseas assignments gave me a very good opportunity to view matters from a vantage point, with a big picture perspective — especially those involving high level foreign dignitaries.

The strict standards and discipline set at home were also maintained when our leaders were abroad on visits, both official and private. Delegations were small and carefully picked. **PM Lee** would take with him a few people, usually new ministers and MPs, to expose them to foreign leaders, their thinking and politics. It was part of his desire to train the second-generation leaders. When appropriate, his delegation also included selected business leaders.

It was not difficult to arrange such visits, provided one had a mind for details and remained alert always. PM Lee's **"Likes and Dislikes"** were simple and detailed. For example, the room in the hotel was to be non-smoking and located away from lifts. The air conditioning was to be set at a certain temperature with no musty smell. Few other items, like a certain type of exercise equipment, was also required. In the years that I was in London, it was also my duty to collect **Singapore newspapers** from Heathrow airport, flown daily by British carrier BOAC, for PM Lee. (BOAC became British Airways Corporation and later British Airways.) Global television and global radio broadcasts came much later; and the internet was not yet invented then. It was a different world from today's instant news dissemination and "breaking news" that is made possible by the development of information communication technology tools like satellite communication. In those days, even to make an international telephone call you had to book the call with the local telephone exchange operator, who would contact the exchange operator in the country concerned, and then the call was only connected when the circuit was available. The cost was high and delays in getting connected was not uncommon.

Our leaders take commercial flights. Singapore does not have government-owned aircraft for travel. On a few occasions, I was asked by foreign leaders why our government did not have its own aircraft since we could afford it financially. My response was it was a deliberate policy in order to avoid wastage of public funds, since most of the time, the aircraft would stand idle in the hangar.

Conversely, leaders in Asia and Africa had their own private jets, for example, President **Kenyatta**, had special government-owned aircraft (I think it was known as "Kenya One') to fly around. In some countries, the aircrafts were purchased with aid money donated with the intention of fighting poverty. Allegedly, in Malawi, a fertile country with good climate, and yet, according to United Nations statistics, among the poorest countries in the world, a leader had his own private jet similarly financed! For some African leaders it would not be safe to take commercial flights as they were wanted by International Criminal Court (ICC) on charges like genocide and war crimes. It was reported that Sudan's President narrowly escaped being arrested in South Africa on Interpol warrant when he went there to attend the African Summit. He fled in his own private jet, probably with some help from the host, before the Interpol warrant could be executed. In general, they travelled with large delegations. Quite often they took with them generals and other key officials, not to train them, but to make sure that they (the leaders) would not be overthrown when out of their countries! President **Milton Obote** of **Uganda**, suffered this fate while attending the Commonwealth Heads of Government Meeting in Singapore in 1971. He was overthrown by sergeant **Idi Amin** who turned out to be a notorious and cruel tyrant. Obote spent more than a decade in exile in Tanzania before returning to Uganda upon the downfall of Amin.

Nearer home and on a state visit to Singapore in 1976, President **Marcos** and his wife **Imelda**, arrived separately but simultaneously in two Philippines Airlines jets which taxied one behind the other and came to a stop side by side with red carpet rolled out for both. Both disembarked at the same time. This arrangement was at the insistence of the Philippines protocol officials. I cannot recollect a similar arrangement for any other head of state who was accompanied by his spouse on official visit. Many had the impression that it was an ostentatious display of self-importance by a leader from a country with a struggling economy! (I was told that the two aircraft remained parked at the airport until departure at the conclusion of the visit. As a commercial carrier PAL was not very profitable. It was prone to delays and the joke then was PAL stood for "plane always late".)

Generally, there was no problem in managing the different strands of that visit. President Marcos and Imelda were easy going and cheerful and entertained themselves with singing at night. However, there was one problem which we were not used to before. It was our practice to budget as accurately as possible for the visit and to be efficient we needed to know, for example, the number of meals to be served each day in order to avoid wastage. Having obtained the relevant detail information from the guests, **Jenny Lim**, Controller of the Household, would do the marketing accordingly. In cases when the meals were catered from, say, hotels such details were also required. Our guests were surprised that Jenny even asked for this information and could not understand why. When Jenny approached Imelda she was very surprised and just pointed to her people around her. Jenny would do a quick arithmetic and prepare the number of number of meals to be served accordingly. Marcos had brought with him two cooks from his palace who prepared a large number of dishes daily. We learnt form the cooks that it was their usual routine to do so, just in case Marcos suddenly asked for any one of the dishes. The rest of the food were disposed of.

We understood from the cooks that in their palace, Malacanyang, there were quite a number of cooks preparing food and meals throughout the day not only for the VVIPs and their families but also for those who were around, including those who dropped in casually. We also noted many other examples which gave a glimpse of matters relating to arrangements in their personal lives. It also gave us an understanding of the cultural differences.

I had the impression that the visitors were also surprised the Istana was small, and that its furniture and furnishings were very modest. I have not been to Malacanyang and therefore, have no first-hand knowledge of how it looks on the inside. However, from pictures and video clips, the palace appears to be much bigger than the Istana with posh furnishings. I think the appropriate comparison of Malacanyang would be to the presidential palaces of many counties in South America. The Philippines and many of the South American states (excluding the biggest state Brazil) have a common heritage in that they were former colonies of Spain. In the case of Philippines, its very name was that of the Spanish king Phillip. From the pictures I have seen, some of the palaces in South America are very big, ornate and reflect opulent life styles. These palaces, which were the residences of the presidents and their families, were served by a large number of staff on state employment. In contrast, our presidents lived in their own private residences and employed their own domestic staff. Only exceptions were, as I stated in another chapter in this book, Yusof Ishak and Devan Nair who stayed in small bungalows situated within the Istana domain, and had very small number of domestic staff. These bungalows have been demolished since.

My observations during President Marcos's visit gave me a few clues on how a country, which is very richly endowed with natural resources and blessed with a vast and talented population, was not able to deliver the basic needs required by its people; The Filipinos are resilient people and always bounce back after the frequent natural disasters like violent and destructive typhoons and earthquakes.

In contrast, the Indonesian President **Joko Widodo**, travelled in economy class and waited in the queue for his turn for immigration and customs clearance during his trip to Singapore — a spectacle rarely seen anywhere in the world. This was very well received both in Indonesia and abroad. It certainly had its PR value; many observers thought that Jokowi (as he was popularly known) had not forgotten his humble beginnings. That he was able to connect with the masses in this manner must have been one of the factors that earned him his re-election as president in 2019.

Sometimes very powerful leaders become "prisoners" of their sycophants surrounding them. **Mohamed Reza Shah Pahlavi of Iran (Shah)** was perceived as both arrogant and very powerful. One British minister told President Sheares how Shah kept British ministers, who were visiting, waiting while he went skiing. On a stopover visit in 1977, enroute to Australia, Shah stayed at the Istana. We had offered him the suite with a veranda (which had a view) in the Annex, where VVIPs normally stayed, but his powerful secret service, SAVAK (much dreaded in Iran), made him sleep in a less appointed room in the centre wing, which had about 10 rooms separated by a small corridor in the middle and the wooden floor creaked a little sometimes. The Shah occupied a middle room and his secret service personnel surrounded him in the rest. Probably, they had thought it was better for Shah's personal safety and protection. At the courtesy call on President Shears next morning, I noticed the Shah's eyes were red and he admitted he had not slept well. His discomfort showed in the conversation. Had he stayed in the Annex he probably would have had a better night. (The practice of accommodating state guests at the Istana was discontinued some time later for a variety of reasons, including the fact that it was difficult to retain trained service staff and the inability to match the service and facilities available in hotels.) It was, therefore, not surprising that the Shah was out of touch with reality and life on the ground. He was forced to flee Iran hastily in 1979 due to very violent protests against his regime, supported by the spiritual leader **Ayatollah Khomeini**, who was then in exile in France. There were many early signs of the brewing problem, but he failed to realise that the ground was shifting under his feet. According to an international documentary made many years later, Shah believed that with his unrivalled power he could crush any challenge to his authority and the sycophants around him admitted that they were frightened to inform him of the shifts in the ground. When the mighty fall it is not often a pleasant sight. Even his good friends in America did not give him permanent asylum and not many countries wanted to take him in either, for fear of reprisals from the new rulers of Iran who had made it clear that any country harbouring the Shah would face serious consequences.

At the height of his power, he had an aura of invincibility, a fabulous jet-setting life, wielded enormous power and was courted assiduously by many Western leaders, who praised him lavishly with an eye on his enormous resources. He had all the riches. I had read reports that his crockery and even the toilet seats were made from gold (not gold-plated) — all this in a country where there was much poverty. In 1971, Shah hosted a gigantic party on a scale of opulence rarely seen before, for world leaders, to celebrate the 2500-year rule of the Persian kings and Shah's **Phalavi** dynasty. Included among the guests were more than 30 heads of states, royalties and others who were entertained in opulent splendour in more than 50 huge tents which were specially erected for the event. The things required to stage this extravaganza, including the food, spirits and gifts were sourced from the best overseas suppliers, principally from France. It appeared that no expense was spared for the spectacular show of self-glorification. His courtiers announced his arrival with his elaborate title, including **Shahanshah (king of kings)**. I watched the spectacle which was broadcasted on television in many countries around the world. Yet, for all his ostentation, power and predilection for grandeur, Shah died an extremely broken man at the early age of 59 in 1980, ravaged by cancer, in Egypt.

In contrast to Shah's self-inflicted discomfort at the Istana, **Earl Mountbatten of Burma** enjoyed his stay in one of the same rooms very much. He had asked to stay in the room when he came for a visit in 1974. On behalf of the British Crown, he had received the Japanese surrender in 1944 at the City Hall. On that occasion, he had stayed in the same room and he had fond memories of the Istana (then **Government House**). During a courtesy call on President Sheares, he narrated how a Japanese soldier had fallen through from the roof. He sent me a note to thank me for letting him stay at the same room. Mountbatten was also **the last Viceroy of India** and represented the British Crown at the ceremony marking Indian independence. Tragically, he was killed five years later in 1979 by the IRA (**Irish Republican Army**) when they blew up his pleasure boat in Ireland.

I referred to **Baroness Margaret Thatcher**, the **"Iron Lady"**, earlier. One could learn much from her. She, like Lee Kuan Yew, did not place over-reliance on officials. On our ride in the car from the airport to the hotel, she complimented our motorcycle out-riders and police personnel for the efficient traffic clearance and the sensitive manner in which they did it. She told me that, during an official visit to Italy, the Italians were kicking at the doors of cars to get them to give way. I informed her that the Singapore public would not accept such behaviour. At the airport VIP lounge before departure, she thanked me again for all the arrangements. It appeared as if she really appreciated them. I seized the opportunity to get her to meet the out-riders and she obliged readily. My team was very thrilled that she took the time to personally express her appreciation of their good work. In protocol, more than in many other activities, teamwork is very important for an operation to be seamless and successful.

Thatcher also shared with me her few other observations in her travels around the world. We took her by helicopter to Sembawang shipyard and on the way, she saw that the roofs of our buildings, including HDB flats, were clean and not used as storage space for unwanted items. On a similar visit to **British Forces on the Rhine** (BFOR) in Germany, she had noticed the roofs were cluttered with discarded items and used as storage spaces. I was shocked to hear that, knowing the German reputation for efficiency, cleanliness and thoroughness. Years later, during my posting in Cairo, I saw chicken, goats and sheep reared on rooftops which also sometimes doubled as dwellings.

It was obvious that Thatcher had a mind for details and took nothing for granted. Thatcher was impressed by our transport system which was a unique, pioneering and difficult undertaking that entailed much sacrifice from many people.

I recall the protests from the Diplomatic Corps that they should be exempted from the Restricted Zone scheme. Their argument was that it restricted their movements, that the fee charged was a "tax" and, therefore, the Corps should be exempted under the provisions of the **Vienna Convention on Diplomatic Relations, 1961 (VCDR)**. The Restricted Zone (precursor to Electronic Road Pricing-ERP) **scheme was built on the basis that no one would be exempted, not even the Head of State**. In fact, the Cabinet had reprimanded a Deputy Secretary in the concerned ministry for recommending exemptions for a selected list of high office holders. In the circumstance, the government did not accede to the Corps. As a compromise and in the spirit of VCDR, the Cabinet decided to pay for the cost of the decal for the flag-flying vehicle of head of the diplomatic mission. All other diplomats had to pay. Thus, the principle of no exemption was maintained which was very crucial for public acceptance and cooperation.

A few countries in the West, mainly in Europe, tried variants of our Restricted Zone scheme but did not succeed, owing to abuse of such schemes by leaders themselves and non-cooperation from the public. Some countries adopted a watered-down version of our policy. A few countries which failed to address traffic congestion and gridlock early had to resort to more drastic and desperate solutions later, to prevent total breakdown of their transport networks.

During my term as Chief of Protocol, I had to deal with a few diplomats who refused to pay, and thereby committed an offence. There was one French diplomat who was particularly arrogant and kept incurring summonses in this regard. He had about 70 summonses within a period of about several months. He thought that he could defy us, believing that VCDR would protect him and that we would be powerless to stop him. This was a blatant abuse of the diplomatic privileges provided in VCDR.

First, I tried the soft approach and reminded him that VCDR also required diplomats to respect the laws of the host country ("the receiving State"). He ignored me and continued to incur summonses. Then I called in his Ambassador and told him that the conduct of his subordinate was not acceptable and that he should appropriately counsel his subordinate to respect the laws of the host country. I did not know what action, if any, he took but the offences continued. I then decide to ask our Ambassador in Paris to take it up with **Quay d'Orsay** (ministry of foreign affairs) and he did. Soon after, the diplomat concerned got the message and he did not incur summonses afterwards. I must, however state here that overall, we had good relations with the French diplomats, who were generally always very professional. In fact, I personally knew a few of them who were well-disposed to Singapore. I still remember one French diplomat telling me that **"Singapore is condemned to succeed"**. He has watched Singapore climb up year after year in crucial international rankings.

As I said earlier, my stint at the Istana was extremely beneficial in gaining valuable insights into the behaviours of leaders and understanding the world. There are many more anecdotes that I can share but the above would suffice in giving a fleeting picture or rough sketch of some of the problems we had to deal with then.

Chapter 15

RELATIONS WITH NEIGHBOURS

"Some people say it (Malaysia) is near the Himalayas, some say it is in Africa because Malawi is there, others say we are in China, while some say we are near Singapore. The truth is that Singapore is near Malaysia"

—*Dr Mahathir Mohamed*

Our relations with Malaysia and Indonesia were, in my observation, coloured by the Malaysian and Indonesian perceptions that:

- we are a small country, merely a dot on the map compared to them;
- despite our lack of resources, which they are so abundantly blessed with, we have managed to punch above our weight and gain a better reputation in the world than them;
- we are a **"Third China"** in the Malay neighbourhood; and
- they have not been able to cow us into submission, especially our Chinese, as they had done to their Chinese communities.

MALAYSIA

The bitterness and rancour of separation left a deep scar and bedevilled our bilateral relations for years to come. The immediate years following our separation were particularly difficult. I have mentioned earlier that the Malaysian leaders believed that it was only a matter of time that Singapore would go on bended knees begging to be taken back.

Some policies pursued on both sides of the Causeway did have negative impact on the relations. We had a radio programme *"Suara Singapura"* (Voice of Singapore). In general, the Malaysians were annoyed with the commentaries and opinions that were aired on this programme. They perceived that our aim was to disparage Malaysia, not directly but by clever comparison of development statistics and trends in the region. In particular, there was a regular commentary under the title **"What Others Say"** which noted news, published by others, that was unfavourable to Malaysia. I remember they protested. As Singapore made progress (against their dire predictions), it made Malaysian leaders even more uncomfortable.

On their part, the Malaysians seized on every opportunity to hit back at us. In the 1960s, we had a policy against **males sporting long hair**. In fact, a campaign was launched (as we often did!) against it and posters in government premises warned that males with long hair would be served last. In a car park in Orchard Road, two overzealous policemen caught a man sporting very long locks and gave him unwanted hair cut on the spot. He turned out to be Malaysian and the next day the Malaysians went to town in denouncing us.

Despite having so many similarities in many areas, the gulf widened and spilled over into the political arena. Small pinpricks were sometimes deliberately magnified. Our faster economic development and increasing recognition and reputation abroad, only served to generate envy and therefore, antagonism. The continuous depreciation of the Malaysian Ringgit further deflated their ego. I could recall a comment by Tunku that, with the depreciation of the Ringgit against S$, Singapore's respect for Malaysia had plunged. Additionally, the fact that **by the 1970s, Singapore was more widely known abroad than Malaysia, riled Malaysian leaders even further**.

Once a Malaysian minister lamented that when he introduced himself to an Austrian official in Vienna, the latter was keen to know where Malaysia was. He told him first that it was in South East Asia; the Austrian looked puzzled; he then told him Malaysia was halfway between Austria and Australia and that still did not work. Frustrated, the minister asked the Austrian whether he knew where Singapore was and the response, without hesitation, was "yes, of course". The minister then told him that his country was just to the north of Singapore. The Austrian told him he should have said so from the start. **Mahathir** also had a similar experience concerning Malaysia's image abroad:

> *"Some people say it is near the Himalayas, some say it is in Africa because Malawi is there, others say we are in China, while some say we are near Singapore. The truth is that Singapore is near Malaysia":*
>
> Dr Mahathir Mohamed quoted in the
Straits Times (page A6), Friday 10 April, 2002

During my term as High Commissioner in New Zealand, a Malaysian diplomat there sent me a newspaper report in the Otago Times of July 25, 1992 captioned "Singapore link 'good' for tourism". It was based on one of the lectures I gave at the Otago University. In forwarding the report, he also sent me a handwritten note stating, *"It looks as if only what you say is important and comes out in the newspapers, what we say is not important".* As a Singaporean diplomat, it was part of my job to engage a wide spectrum of the host community on a variety of topics, in the countries I was accredited to. I undertook keynote lectures, dialogues and talks, participated in seminars, conferences and panel discussions and in other appropriate events, in order **for Singapore to be seen, heard and respected.** Some of these lectures were publicised in leading journals of the respective regions.

In my observation, Mahathir had uneasy relations with PM Lee and this coloured the overall relations with Singapore. I think he felt uncomfortable in dealing with PM Lee. It was also my observation that he became more bitter towards Singapore after his unsuccessful attempts to secure financial assistance from Singapore, when the financial crisis hit Malaysia severely in 1997. I remember his remark some time afterwards that we were prepared to pump more than $10 billion into Suzhou Park in China but not help Malaysia, a fellow ASEAN member.

VISIT OF CHAIM HERZOG

There was much stress and strain in our relations with Malaysia that needed to be managed. One very trying episode was the visit of the Israeli President, Chaim Herzog in 1986. It was one of the most difficult and sensitive visits I had to organise as chief of protocol. It was also a tense time in the Ministry. Our Muslim neighbours were against the visit. Brunei and Indonesia, while opposing the visit, did not press us that hard to cancel it. However, Malaysia whipped up Malay Muslim fervour. Mahathir, not wanting to miss an opportunity, let loose his tirades against Singapore and worked the **United Malay National Organisation (UMNO)** youths' emotions. Some said he was forced to act. Whatever drove him to that, the UMNO Youths were amassing in large numbers in Johor Bahru, the nearest land spot to Singapore, in a belligerent posture. Meanwhile, the Philippines caved in under the pressure and cancelled Hertzog's visit, due to take place immediately before the visit to Singapore. It was neither surprising nor unexpected.

Rajaratnam (who was Second Deputy Prime Minister then) handled it very cleverly. He went live on television and radio and gave reasons to demolish Malaysian objections. Our television and radio broadcasts reached sizeable parts of the southern states in peninsular Malaysia. Amongst other things, he asked **how it could be so wrong for secular Singapore to have diplomatic relations and contacts with Israel when it was alright for Egypt, a Muslim**

country, to have diplomatic relations with Israel and have embassies in their respective countries.

There were other problems concerning the visit we had to deal with. The Israeli ambassador, **Moshe Benyacov,** wanted us to arrange for his president to deliver a lecture in our prestigious Singapore Lecture series, and the government to bestow an award on his president. I told him that he must be out of his mind to even suggest that, knowing the situation we were in and the difficulties the visit had generated in the relations with our neighbours. He did not press the case. He had merely wanted to get the maximum benefit for his country and thus, increase his standing with his bosses back home. He could not be faulted for trying. One good outcome from that episode was that we (the ambassador and I) became good friends and have remained so. To this day, without fail, he sends greetings on my birthday. Sadly, he lost his wife a few years ago.

I also had another problem to deal with concerning the Israeli president's visit. On a Sunday morning, Minister **Dhanabalan** called me to ask my advice on a substantive issue. Our High Commissioner, **Maurice Baker**, in Kuala Lumpur was at Changi Airport to catch a flight back to KL. Apparently, he had second thoughts and had suggested to Dhanabalan that he should stay in Singapore until the visit was over, in view of the developing situation in Malaysia. Baker had cited a case involving Britain and Nigeria as a precedent (This was the *Omaru Dikko* case). Dhanabalan asked me "what is the protocol?". I informed him that in my view it was more than protocol and that Baker should return to his post. I explained to Dhanabalan why the *Omaru Dikko* case was not relevant to our situation. I gave a few examples to back up my view, including PM Lee's instruction to our Ambassador in Jakarta, **P S Raman**, to stay at the post when our embassy was attacked and ransacked following the hanging of the Indonesian marines in 1968. Dhanabalan agreed with me and asked me to convey his instruction to Baker, that he should return to his post. I did as I was instructed. Baker and his team in the High Commission did well in managing the boisterous protests outside our mission in Kuala Lumpur.

In the reverse direction, the Malaysian High Commissioner, **K T Ratnam**, a suave diplomat, called me about two days before the visit to seek my advice concerning his situation. He said he did not want to be in Singapore while the Israeli president was in town, but he was not sure whether he need to send a formal note (Third Person Note) on his temporary absence from Singapore. He told me that he would like to avoid sending a formal note. I advised him that he need not send a formal note but that he should inform the Ministry of his absence by a letter. Under the Vienna Convention on Diplomatic Relations 1961 (mentioned earlier) a head of mission was required to inform, in writing, the receiving state of his absence from his post and it was usually done by a note. However, there was no express requirement that it must be done by a note. He accepted my advice and sent me a letter accordingly. It was in our interest that the matter was handled quietly, calmly and unobtrusively in the context of the situation. The fallout from the visit caused strain in the bilateral relations for a few years to come. However, under the leadership of Rajaratnam and Dhanabalan, the Ministry managed the situation very well.

Rajaratnam was a supreme diplomat. He did not allow personal feelings and differences over policy, however serious, from maintaining cordiality and effective communication with other leaders. Here is an anecdote. On one occasion both Rajaratnam and **Mahathir** met at a suite in the Airport VIP complex while waiting to board different aircraft. During the conversation Rajaratnam told Mahathir that he was going to London to see his doctor there. Mahathir was curious and Rajaratnam told him with humour that he was going more "to find out how he (doctor) is doing"! (Rajaratnam was going for his medical check-up.) There was a small crowd to see him off and Mahathir asked who they were. Rajaratnam replied that they were his constituents from Kampong Glam and **"these fellows think that I might not come back"**! Mahathir quipped **"what a morbid thought"**. They parted wishing each other well.

There were many more valuable lessons I learnt from Minister Rajaratnam during his stewardship of the Ministry of Culture and the Ministry of Foreign Affairs. However, the above random examples suffice in giving a glimpse of his stature, his unrivalled grasp of issues and insights on a variety of subjects, his clarity of vision, and quick wit. In short, he laid a solid foundation for our foreign policy, which remains one of his enduring contributions.

The conduct of our relations with Malaysia, especially Johor, for obvious reasons always required special and deft handling. **Sultan Iskandar** was generally well disposed to Singapore, although sometimes he caused concerns. He used to speed quite fast on our highways in his "Bronco Billy" and once he arrived in his helicopter without prior notice and flight approval. Whenever he came by car, we handled it by giving him police outriders who would slow him down as necessary. It required coordination between the respective police authorities. The cooperation between the two police forces was very good. As for the flights, we insisted that his staff provided the required information in advance, including the purpose of the flight, and the clearance for the same and related details. Once, after his official visit, he invited me to his palace for a meal. I found the conversation warm and noted one interesting comment. He referred to the federal establishment as **"those northerners"** in a tone that implied that the Johor natives were superior to those living in the other States. I have also heard that he was quite informal and kind in many ways.

Sultan Iskandar loved fast cars and motorcycles. During his term as *Agong* (king) he was reviewing the march-past during *merdeka* (independence) celebrations in Kuala Lumpur. When a squad of motorcycles appeared, he promptly came down from the reviewing dais, commandeered a motorcycle, and went for a spin — thereby, temporarily stopping the proceedings. He came back a few minutes later and the march-past resumed.

He was also an avid golfer and used to play golf in Singapore. His golf partners often played diplomatic golf with him by letting him win. He was a bit unconventional in some respects. The Rolls Royce company could not meet a request from him concerning his Rolls Royce car and, out of pique, he decided to use his Rolls Royce car as a security escort car. I was told the British were not amused.

INDONESIA

Sukarno's **"Guided Democracy"**: Relations with Indonesia under Sukarno had never been easy, for several reasons. Although colonialism had ended sometime before, he did not change his anti-colonial agitator position. Sukarno had a reputation of being the greatest orator, after Adolf Hitler, and was charismatic, with mass appeal. Sukarno once bragged that he can tell Indonesians to eat grass and they would do it. He coined many acronyms and **neo-colim** (neo-colonialism) was his battle cry against the West. He was a master manipulator of various contending forces — leftists, communists, the military, unions, students, clerics and secularists — by pitting them against each other. He adroitly exploited the polemics and rivalry of the Cold War, then at its height. The occasional swipe at Singapore and Malaysia was a fair game for him. He was part of the **"Pyongyang-Hanoi-Jakarta" axis** (more in name than function). He also pursued the **"unfinished revolution"** which kept Indonesia in a state of flux. **We watched with growing concern**.

When relations with Britain were strained, the British embassy was attacked and the then ambassador, **Gilchrist**, was roughed up. Sukarno turned the heat against us as well. I have mentioned earlier the confrontation policy he launched following the formation of Malaysia. It was a tense situation and we felt it in our daily lives.

The sum total was, his guided democracy did not work: the economy faltered with massive corruption, hyper-inflation, unemployment, near valueless Rupiah and no foreign investments. His constant tirades against the US, his arch enemy, played well with the Communists, their sympathisers and left-wing elements, and diverted the attention of the masses from the grinding economic problems.

Suharto's *"Ordor Baru"* (New Order): In the putsch of September 30, 1965 started by *Partai Kommunist Indonesia (PKI),* the Communist Party of Indonesia, led by **DN Aidit** against ABRI (*Angatan Bersenta Republic Indonesia,* the Indonesian Armed Forces), the Army lost six of their top generals and PKI came close to seizing power. The generals were killed by PKI activists and dumped in a hole known as "Lubang Buaja" (crocodile pit). We watched the situation nervously. One man they missed out was the "smiling general" Major General Suharto (also spelt as Soeharto) then in charge of the Army's Strategic Reserve Command (KOSTRAD) based in Jakarta. Suharto swung into action, the putsch failed, and in the ensuing months the communists and those who supported them were hunted down and eliminated. That putsch was commonly known as *Gestapu* (*Gerakan September Tiga Puluh* or the September Thirty Movement). Suharto was the man of the hour and we breathed a sigh of relief. The atmosphere of tension, apprehension and uncertainty began to ease. Slowly, Sukarno was edged out of power and his role in the putsch remained unclear.

However, the toughest challenge to the newly independent Singapore came after Suharto came to power. It was a difficult legacy (of Sukarno) that he (Suharto) had to deal with. I mentioned the two Indonesian marines who were caught when the bomb they set off killed three persons at MacDonald House in Orchard Road, earlier. They were tried, found guilty and sentenced to death by hanging. The Privy Council turned down their appeal and upheld the sentence. Execution became imminent.

Indonesians rose up in uproar. The hanging of their "martyrs" by a "tiny Chinese island" was to them unthinkable, unacceptable and an affront to their "great nation", the *Indonesia Raya* (The Greater Indonesia). Indonesia launched a diplomatic offensive worldwide to get their martyrs back alive. Among their arguments were that the marines were prisoners of war and should be governed by the Geneva Convention which provided for return of prisoners. Or that, in the spirit of ASEAN (formed the year before), they should be pardoned. I recall the Indonesian ambassador in London making a presentation to our High Commissioner, A P Rajah, to spare the lives of the prisoners. Indonesians made similar presentations in other capitals where both countries were represented. Most importantly, Suharto made a personal appeal to our President.

It was one of the most difficult situations our infant Republic had to deal with. There were no legal grounds for the claim that they were prisoners of war. In the first place, the two Indonesian marines were in civilian clothes, not in military fatigue, when they carried out the attack. And when they were caught, they had no documents on them identifying them as Indonesian marines. Also, since Indonesia did not declare war and was not at war with Malaysia (including Singapore), the **Geneva Convention** did not apply in the circumstance, as Indonesia claimed. Importantly for us, giving in to mob pressure was unthinkable as it would have also set a dangerous precedent and threaten our sovereignty in the future. Our resolve was being tested to the full. Therefore, we had no alternative but to proceed with the execution. Meanwhile, anti-Singapore sentiments were rising fast, orchestrated by the Indonesian military and others inimical to us, with implied threats of violent action against Singapore, including invasion. It was a very tense time for all of us, but we went about our work as usual, despite the distractions and concerns.

The Malaysians seized the opportunity to make things difficult for us by appealing against the hanging. Probably, they did so at the behest of their big brother. It was, as I saw it, a wrong and unwise move on their part. It implied that they had accepted the **"prisoners of war"** claim by the Indonesians, thereby creating a bad precedent for themselves. It was like they were cutting the nose to spite the face!

In any event, the prisoners were executed on 22nd October 1968 and their remains were handed to the Indonesian Embassy which arranged for them to be flown on a special Garuda flight to a heroes' welcome in Jakarta and a burial at **Kalibata Heroes' Cemetery.**

All hell broke loose. Spewing venom and invective against Singapore, mobs attacked and looted our Embassy in Jakarta. We evacuated our staff to a hotel there. It was most important that our staff remained at the post to defend Singapore's sovereignty. Needless to say, our relations with Indonesia hit rock bottom.

At that point in time, Suharto was still consolidating his power and grip on Indonesia following the *Gestapu.* The military and those supporting it were orchestrating much of the violence and anti-Singapore sentiment. They portrayed the execution of their "martyrs" as an affront to their national dignity and pride and, therefore, said it should be avenged. Suharto probably found himself unable to rein in the mobs, even if he had wanted to do so. In any case, he could not be seen as a weak leader in the circumstances. On the contrary, it was probably an opportunity for him to show his seething masses that he was a strong leader who could stand up for them — and thereby, consolidate his power as he needed to then.

Nevertheless, and notwithstanding the above, I believe we were lucky that Suharto was at the helm and not the unpredictable Sukarno who had initiated the policies that eventually led to the hanging. Steeped in Javanese tradition and with his affable manners masking a steely interior and resolve, Suharto slowly moved towards normalisation of relations with Singapore, as he wisely chose the path of economic development rather than confrontation. In later years, Suharto was known as **"bapak pembangunan"** (father of development). As a gesture of reconciliation, PM Lee laid flowers at the graves of the marines during a visit to Jakarta in 1973.

In the succeeding years, both sides worked quietly to improve understanding and working relations. I witnessed many developments in this regard. PM Lee and Suharto developed a special working relationship demonstrating warmth and respect for each other. In fact, when the two leaders met, a **"empat mata"** ("four eyes") meeting was held, before their respective officials joined them.

This was also possible because PM Lee was fluent in Bahasa. It also made Suharto comfortable and confident to discuss sensitive issues. We officials from both sides would wait in the ante chamber to be let in when the leaders so decided and sometimes, they would conclude the meetings by themselves. We would be briefed by PM Lee later. In this regard, my assessment was the PM was much closer to Suharto than to the Malaysian leaders and I believed that the feelings were mutual. **For officials who were privileged enough to be involved in and to observe proceedings in those meetings, it was one of the best lessons in state craft and diplomacy *par excellence.*** PM Lee would always meet with relevant officials to seek their inputs in order to prepare our position on issues likely to be raised by either side, in such high-level meetings. I recall one such meeting to prepare for a visit by Suharto. I was then the assistant director in charge of Indonesia. PM Lee asked for suggestions on how he could be helpful to Suharto. When my turn came I suggested that in the context of economic development (which was the cornerstone of Suharto's **ordor baru** programme), corruption would have to be addressed by Suharto. PM's response was interesting and intuitive. He said his friendship (with Suharto) would not stand that, or something to that effect. Other officials present looked at me with much surprise. Later, I wondered whether what I did was wise. However, since PM Lee did not reprimand me, I thought it was his way of allowing honest views, even if they were impractical or difficult to implement in the circumstance.

I would also highlight the benefits of Suharto's elder statesman role in ASEAN. One such instance was the earlier mentioned visit of Israeli President Chaim Herzog to Singapore. Suharto was concerned about the deterioration in the relations between Singapore and Malaysia following this visit. In his typical Javanese style, he decided to send a message to both Singapore and Malaysia that it was time to move on. He made short trips to Malaysia and Singapore. What was unique was that Suharto came to Singapore via the Causeway at Woodlands after his visit to Kuala Lumpur. As far as I knew, this was the first time a head of state on official visit came to Singapore via the Causeway. The message was clear.

In my view, many negative commentaries on Suharto were biased and did not do justice to his legacy. Suharto's achievements under his new order policies, were substantial. He ended *Konfrontasi*, gave stability and security to Indonesia (an archipelago of more than 15,000 islands straddling a distance from East to West that longer than Europe) and to the region, which enabled the region to make economic progress. He also played a positive role in ASEAN. These achievements could not be dismissed as inconsequential.

Admittedly there was corruption, including allegations of his family's involvement. The quiet whisper making the rounds then was that Mrs Tien Suharto was referred to as **"Mrs ten percent"**. Suharto's fault was that, while it appeared that he himself was not personally involved in corruption, he allowed it. Corruption was one of the factors that probably contributed to his downfall eventually. Nevertheless, seen in the context of the circumstances of his coming to power and the downward spiralling economy he inherited, Indonesians had much to thank him for, like turning the Indonesian economy around. As noted above, the stability he helped to create in the region benefited Singapore and allowed countries in the region to concentrate on economic development.

Western hypocrisy and racism were quite evident on many occasions. Indonesia was hit severely in 1997 by the **Asian Financial Crisis** (AFC). I remember seeing a picture of Camdessus from the International Monetary Fund (IMF) talking down to Suharto in an arrogant tone, with his hands akimbo, insisting that Indonesia complied with all his terms in full and immediately. Contrast that behaviour to the way IMF and EU dealt with Greece, which unlike Indonesia had become an impoverished state despite repeated bailouts and had a debt mountain of about 320 billion Euros with little prospect of repaying it. The negotiations had been dragging for more than five years exploring every possible avenue to prevent Greece from defaulting. I have referred to this earlier. I also observed then that many in the West and even in the Arab world had a barely concealed glee that AFC had hit Asia. A few were not optimistic about recovery. At a panel discussion on the subject at the **American University in Cairo**, a lady professor asked me a question which had these undertones. My answer was that, as painful as it was for the countries that were affected, they would bounce back within a few years, after having implemented the necessary reforms. I gave the reason that the countries affected had enormous resources, both natural (Indonesia) and human talent and ingenuity (South Korea). Also these countries had experienced worse situation during the World War II Japanese occupation and had bounced back. I did not get the impression that the questioner was impressed with my reasoning, but she did not press the matter further.

I gained valuable insight, observation, experience and understanding of Indonesian politics and its leaders firsthand when (as mentioned earlier) I was assistant director in charge of Indonesia in the Ministry and later as the Private Secretary to the President and Director of Protocol. These enabled me to give advice on many issues and situations later in my career. During my stint at the Indonesia desk, I also gave lectures on Indonesia to SAF cadets at the Singapore Armed Forces Training Institute (SAFTI), as part of their overall programme of understanding our neighbours and the regional political landscape. In later years, few cadets from that group assumed very high political office and senior positions in the public service.

BRUNEI

We developed important relations with **Brunei**, and we did not have problems. Sultan Bolkia and senior members of the Brunei Royalty were frequent visitors to Singapore. We had minimised the protocol formalities to facilitate their visits and stay which were appreciated. Bolkia's father, Sir Omar Ali Saiffudin, had close relations with PM Lee and I understood that he used to seek the latter's counsel on many issues from time to time. The peg of Brunei and Singapore currencies becoming interchangeable at par also helped both parties. However, more valuable in my view, was the defence cooperation, especially the SAF training in Brunei.

Photo 01   My very first Letter of Appointment. Note the British Coat of Arms, salutation, the language, the terms and the ending. Missing at the bottom of the image is **"for Colonial Secretary"**. All official communications then were signed thus. (In those days the paper size was foolscap which was about 20% longer than the A4 size which came later with advent of computer.)

Photo 02   After he was sworn-in in December 1959 as *Yang di Pertuan Negara* (became president on August 9, 1965), Inche Yusof Ishak visited government ministries and departments to learn and familiarise himself with their operations. In this photo Ishak (centre) is speaking to Mary Bernard, a stenographer in my section. I am on his right (shirt & tie), behind the me is Lee Siow Mong, Permanent Secretary and on his right partially seen is S. Rajaratnam, Minister for Culture. Photos (02 above & 03 below) were taken when Ishak visited the Ministry in 1960. *Courtesy of Ministry of Culture.*

Photo 03 Ishak (second from right) at the Typing Unit speaking to me. Note the attire (*cheongsam and samfoo*) of the ladies and the typewriters in use then. Ishak's successor, Benjamin Henry Sheares, also made similar familiarisation visits. *Courtesy of Ministry of Culture.*

Photo 04 A sketch of a squatter hut by the Singapore River in the early 1960s. As could be expected, all waste, including human waste, went into the river. *Ong Teng Cheong Collection, Courtesy of the National Archives of Singapore*

Relations with Neighbours 187

[Prime Minister Lee]

Photo 05 PM Lee inspecting a squatter family dwelling in the early 1960s. It was a typical ***kampong*** scene in the 1960s. Dwellings in the rural areas were mostly wooden shacks with *attap* or corrugated iron roofs. Often, they had no running water, electricity and toilets. Some *kampong*s, the lucky ones, had standpipes for the public, installed by the Rural Board. Others depended on water from mostly communal wells. For many, toilets were bushes or holes in the ground. Owing to the mosquito menace, we slept under mosquito nets. Vector borne diseases, including Malaria, were endemic in the region then. Our family lived in a wooden house very much like this one, except the kitchen which was a separate structure and had a thatched roof made of *attap,* as corrugated iron sheets carried a higher cost. *Ministry of Information and the Arts Collection, courtesy of the National Archives of Singapore.*

[Location of hawker food stalls serving mainly officer workers then]

Photo 06 A view of and the Central Business District form the Singapore River in the early 1960s. The hawker food stalls we patronised were located by the riverbank very close to Fullerton Square (see arrow). The hawkers had no municipal water supply and they simply used the water from the river to wash their dishes, plates and the utensils. *Courtesy of the National Archives of Singapore.*

Photo 07 A view of the Central Business District circa 2010. *Courtesy of Shutterstock.*

Relations with Neighbours 189

ROMBONGAN KEBUDAYAAN
SINGAPURA
KE SERAWAK, BRUNEI DAN SABAH

SINGAPORE CULTURAL MISSION
TO SARAWAK, BRUNEI AND
NORTH BORNEO

24.4.1962 — 2.5.1962

Photo 08 Cover page of the souvenir programme. (Ministry of Culture publication)

SINGAPORE CULTURAL MISSION TO SARAWAK, BRUNEI AND NORTH BORNEO

Leader:	Inche Buang bin Omar Junid, Parliamentary Secretary, Ministry of Health and Law
Manager/Producer	Mr. Kuay Guan Kai
Secretary and Treasurer:	Mr. V. K. Rajan
Stage Director:	Mr. Yap Yan Hong
Publicity Officer:	Mr. A. Kajapathy
Comperes:	Mr. Foong Choon Hon
	Inche Mohd. Zain bin Haji Hamzah
Electrician:	Mr. Joseph Hoeden
Stagehand:	Mr. Somu Velayutham
Radio Singapore Orchestra:	Mr. Gus Steyn (Leader)
	Mr. Rufino Soliano
	Mr. Reynaldo Lachica
	Mr. Cesar Alano
	Inche Ahmad Jaafar
	Mr. Joachim Suares
	Mr. Olimpio Galaura
	Mr. Valentine Ortega
Artistes:	*Vocalists*
	Che Nona Asiah
	Che Siti Mariam
	Madam Khong Yoke Leng
	Miss Soh Eng Kheng
	Inche M. Bakri
	Dancers
	Lembaga Tetap Kongres
	Che Pon bte Bachik
	Che Hasnah bte Hassan
	Che Massamah bte Awi
	Inche S. Mohamad
	Inche Sulaiman Jeem
	Inche Ma'mon bin Mo'min

Photo 09   The full list has more names. The total number was about 50.

```
CONFIDENTIAL

P.S.(Culture) to Mr. V.T. Kanagarajan   -   2.1.63.


        With effect from 2nd January, 1963 you are assigned on
temporary transfer to assist Mr. M.S. Menon, Assistant Administrator
(T.V. & Radio), and your duties will include the recruitment of
staff for Radio and T.V. and personnel matters, such as renewal
of temporary appointments and acting appointments.


                                    (Kang Sek Eng)
/bw.                      f. Permanent Secretary (Culture).


c.c.  Administrator (T.V.)

                        Attention: Mr. M.S. Menon
```

Photo 10   The above minute is a sample of the internal correspondence, before we merged with Malaysia.

```
                                        A(TV)12/62

Setiausaha Tetap      kapada    Inche V.K. Rajan
  (Kebudayaan)                                      - 19.11.64.

            Owing to exigencies of service, your services
    are urgently required. I am, therefore, compelled to
    cancel your leave with effect from Monday, 23rd November,
    1964 and call you back for duty.

    2.      You are, therefore, requested to report for duty
    on Monday, 23rd November, 1964. The unexpended leave will
    be carried forward to 1965 if arrangements cannot be made
    to grant you the leave in December, 1964.


                                    ( M. S. MENON )
                                b/p Setiausaha Tetap (Kebudayaan)

c.c. P.44135

/iy.
```

Photo 11   The above minute shows the introduction of Bahasa during the short period Singapore was in Malaysia. With the separation from Malaysia, the administration reverted to status quo ante.

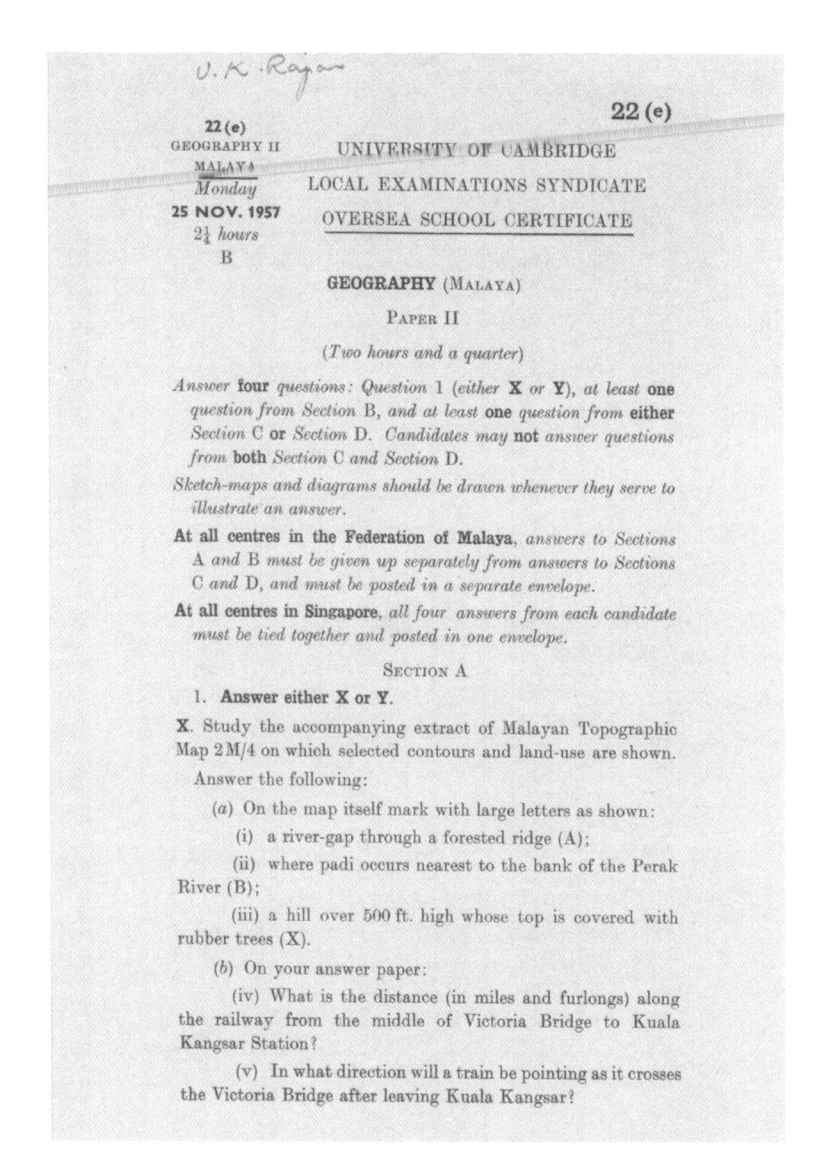

> U. K. Rajan
>
> 22 (e)
> GEOGRAPHY II
> MALAYA
> Monday
> 25 NOV. 1957
> 2¼ hours
> B
>
> 22 (e)
>
> UNIVERSITY OF CAMBRIDGE
> LOCAL EXAMINATIONS SYNDICATE
> OVERSEA SCHOOL CERTIFICATE
>
> GEOGRAPHY (MALAYA)
>
> PAPER II
>
> (Two hours and a quarter)
>
> Answer **four** questions: Question 1 (either **X** or **Y**), at least **one** question from Section B, and at least **one** question from either Section C or Section D. Candidates may **not** answer questions from **both** Section C and Section D.
>
> Sketch-maps and diagrams should be drawn whenever they serve to illustrate an answer.
>
> **At all centres in the Federation of Malaya**, answers to Sections A and B must be given up separately from answers to Sections C and D, and must be posted in a separate envelope.
>
> **At all centres in Singapore**, all four answers from each candidate must be tied together and posted in one envelope.
>
> SECTION A
>
> 1. **Answer either X or Y.**
>
> X. Study the accompanying extract of Malayan Topographic Map 2 M/4 on which selected contours and land-use are shown.
>
> Answer the following:
>
> (a) On the map itself mark with large letters as shown:
>
> (i) a river-gap through a forested ridge (A);
>
> (ii) where padi occurs nearest to the bank of the Perak River (B);
>
> (iii) a hill over 500 ft. high whose top is covered with rubber trees (X).
>
> (b) On your answer paper:
>
> (iv) What is the distance (in miles and furlongs) along the railway from the middle of Victoria Bridge to Kuala Kangsar Station?
>
> (v) In what direction will a train be pointing as it crosses the Victoria Bridge after leaving Kuala Kangsar?

Photo 12 Up to 1960 or thereabout students in Singapore and Malaya sat for the common Cambridge Overseas School Certificate. Papers were set by and marked in Cambridge University. The examinations were held in November and the results would arrive by early March. Under British rule, Singapore and Malaya had the same standard in educational qualification. However, with the switch to Bahasa in Malaysia during Dr. Mahathir Mohamad's first term, the standards dropped, especially in the English language.

Photo 13 My **Gilera** motor cycle, an Italian make. As a Deputy Collector of Land Revenue in the Land Office (Ministry of Law), I was in charge of State Lands in the North East, principally Yeo Chu Kang. I made field trips on my motorcycle to monitor unauthorised erections and encroachments. I could not afford a car then. I remembered an advertisement in the 1950s for a *Ford Anglia* car assembled at the Ford Company in Bukit Timah Road and its cost was about $3000, probably the cheapest then. My motorcycle was ahead of other makes in its class. It was my prized possession and I enjoyed it very much. My parents were not happy with it for safety reasons. One day my father came to my office just to check that I was safe. Apparently, someone had told him of an accident involving a red coloured motorcycle (the same colour as mine) in Bukit Timah Road.

> SINGAPORE 6.
>
> Date: 13th May, 1966.
>
> To: Mr. V. Kanagarajan
>
> Sir,
>
> I am directed to inform you that you have been selected for posting on secondment as **Executive Officer** to our Mission in **London** for a tour of duty of **two** years, with effect from 15th May 1966.
>
> 2. During your tour of service, you will be governed by the terms and conditions of service set out in the attached Memorandum entitled "General Conditions of Service for Officers posted for service in Overseas Missions". You will be entitled to the following monthly emoluments:-
>
> (i) Basic Salary : You will retain the salary and salary scale of your substantive appointment together with incremental date.
>
> (ii) Overseas Cost of Living Allowance (in lieu of Variable Allowance) : (Single:
> (Married:
> (Married with
> (children:
>
> (iii) Entertainment Allowance:
>
> 3. You will be eligible for an outfit allowance of $ which can be claimed by you before departure.
>
> 4. You will be required to go for a medical check-up for which the requisite medical form is attached. Your actual date of departure from Singapore will be notified to you as soon as possible.
>
> 5. In the meantime, you are advised to obtain all the necessary travelling documents and make such other travelling arrangements as are necessary.
>
> 6. This Ministry will be responsible for your passage arrangements.
>
> 7. I take this opportunity to wish you satisfaction and success in your assignment.
>
> I am, Sir,
> Your obedient servant,

Photo 14 My letter of posting to our Mission in London. The team comprising A P Rajah (High Commissioner), Chia Cheong Fook (Counsellor), me (Administrative Attaché) and Joseph Chew (Personal Assistant) established the High Commission in 1966. Until then, Singapore had a Trade Commission headed by an Englishman, Tony Hibberd, a retired officer from the colonial service in Singapore.

Photo 15 I travelled to London on 14 May, 1966 on this passport upon my posting as "Attaché Administration" to London.

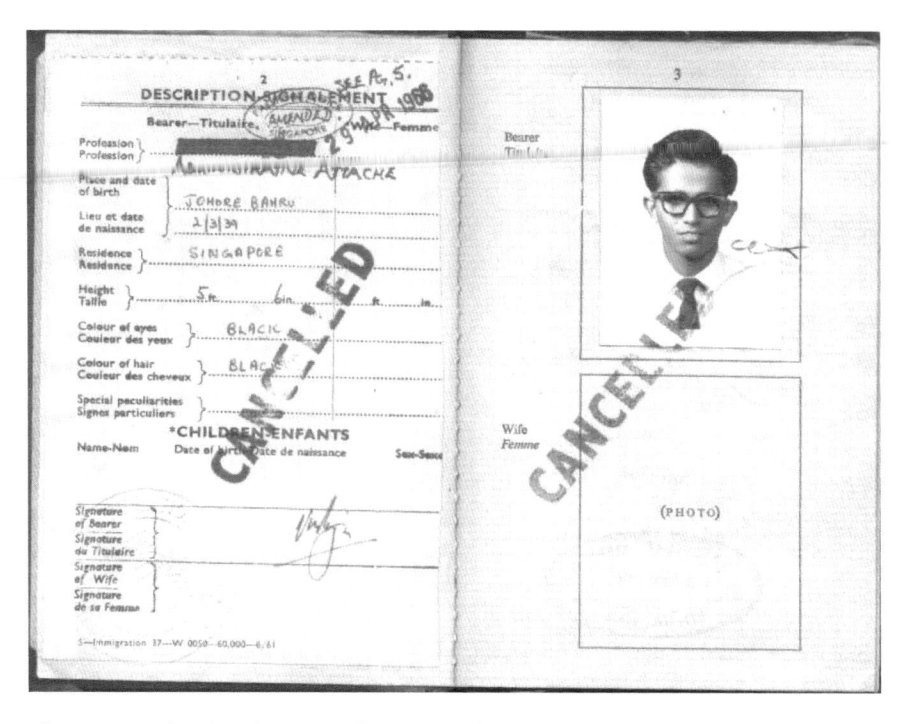

Photo 16 The details on inside pages. This passport was first issued to me in 1962 for the Singapore Cultural Mission visit to the Borneo Territories. Singapore passports were not ready in time for the trip to London. This was a transitional arrangement with the British and it worked well for Singapore. This passport was "CANCELLED" when I was issued with the new Singapore passport.

Relations with Neighbours 197

Photo 17 Me feeding the pigeons in Trafalgar Square during a lunch break in 1966. This was one of the popular sites for tourists. Not in the picture is the Nelson's Column which the Square is well known for. Our High Commission, then at 16 Northumberland Avenue, was only three minutes' walk away. This image appears on page 24 of the publication, **HEART OF PUBLIC SERVICE — OUR PEOPLE** published by the Prime Ministers' Office as a tribute to the pioneer generation public servants.

COMMONWEALTH HEADS OF GOVERNMENT MEETING
SINGAPORE 1971
(Mr. Lee Kuan Yew, Prime Minister of Singapore welcomes the Rt. Hon. P.E. Trudeau, Prime Minister of Canada on the opening day on 14th January, 1971)

Photo 18 PM Lee receiving Prime Minister P E Trudeau of Canada. Foreign Minister S Rajaratnam and Commonwealth Secretary General Arnold Smith are on the right. In the back row is Wong Chooi Sen and me. Almost fully hidden behind Rajaratnam is Chia Cheong Fook.

Photo 19   Commonwealth Heads of Government Meeting 1971 Prime Minister Lee Kuan Yew is seated 9th from the left. The traditional group photo was taken at the then Conference Hall foyer in Shenton Way, the venue of the meeting. Note the ships in the background. It was not part of the main harbour area as the waters were shallow. Only small coastal ships could be towed in to provide the backdrop. The idea was to portray Singapore as a global maritime hub. (**Note**: President Milton Obote, who was overthrown in a coup by Sergeant Idi Amin (later promoted himself to Field Marshal), is on the back row second from left). *Courtesy of the Ministry of Foreign Affairs.*

Photo 20 Attending a course on Development Administration under the Colombo Plan, organised by Department of Foreign Affairs Trade in Canberra, Australia, 1971, for senior officials from Asia and Africa. In the picture (left) is a small group from the total of about 20 participants. I am in the middle of back row. *Courtesy of the Department of Foreign Affairs and Trade, Australia.*

Photo 21 President Sheares in conversation with the High Commissioner of India, Thomas Abraham (in white dress) when he presented his credentials in 1975. I am on the right. Thomas Abraham was the Deputy High Commissioner in 1965 and in fact, he was one of the few diplomats PM Lee spoke to immediately after our separation from Malaysia. My understanding was that PM Lee had asked for India's help to get diplomatic recognition of Singapore as an independent state by as many countries as possible and as quickly as possible. I believe PM Lee also sought India's help to train our army. It is also my understanding that Thomas Abraham was helpful in our effort to get the diplomatic the recognition quickly. To my knowledge, he had also gave us informal advice on diplomatic practices during his earlier posting in Singapore. He was very friendly and approachable. Chia Cheong Fook had friendly relations with Thomas Abraham. *Courtesy of the Ministry of Communications and Information.*

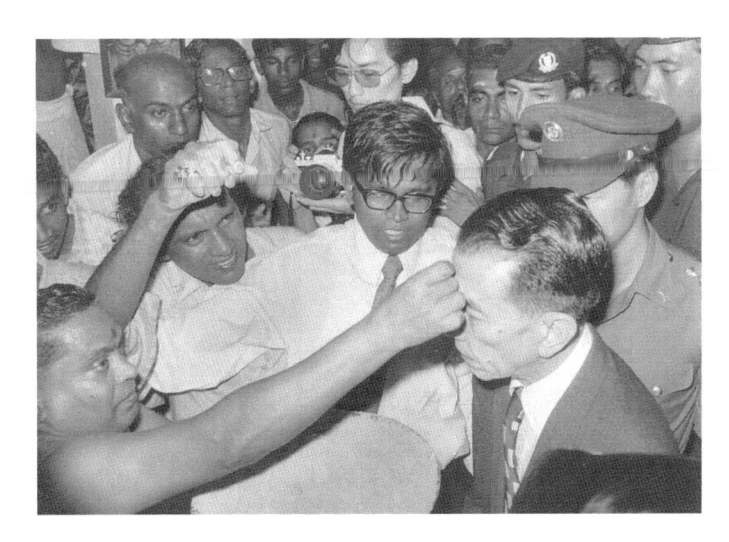

Photo 22 President Sheares receiving blessings at Thandapani Temple in Tank Road in 1973. The ADC and myself (in white shirt and tie) managed to get Sheares through the surge of enthusiastic devotees of the Temple. Sheares participated in all major events of different communities and was well received. He gave speeches when required and, as his private secretary, it was my duty to prepare them for his consideration.

Photo 23 President Sheares returning from London in 1975 after receiving the prestigious Fellowship of Royal Society of Medicine, the first head of state to receive the award. Sheares travelled on a scheduled flight without ADC and a security officer. I was the only official who travelled with him. This was in stark contrast to the way heads of state in other countries travelled. Also, a not very well known fact is that Sheares pioneered many surgical procedures in obstetrics and gynecology which were well-known internationally. A doctor from Yugoslavia came to Sheares for treatment for his wife, after having read of Sheares' pioneering procedure in a medical journal. (I think the procedure was named after Sheares to honour him.) When he saw Sheares' bill was just S$ 500 he was very surprised that it was such a small amount. The doctor was very much satisfied with the surgery and the results. He wrote a blank cheque and asked Sheares to fill in whatever the amount he wanted to charge. Sheares refused and told him that his charges were the same for all and insisted on the doctor paying only the amount he has billed. The doctor then told him that a similar treatment in Europe would have cost him at least ten times or more. Such was Sheares' commitment to ethics and honesty which was matched by his humility. Contrast this against the several cases of unethical practices and charges (including one case where the amount charged was considered grossly unconscionable), which the Singapore Medical Council had to deal with in later years. **I am proud to have served such a professional with very high integrity**. *Courtesy of the Ministry of Communications and Information.*

Photo 24 At the Istana lawn after a state function. In front from left to right: Mrs Lee, PM Lee, President Sheares and First Lady Mrs Sheares. In the background are OC Security, ADC and me. After the departure of guests who attended State function, PM Lee and President Sheares would exchange views and observations concerning the event and other matters.

Photo 25 President and Mrs Sheares with staff serving in the President's Office, the Prime Minister's Office and the Cabinet Office in 1974. Front row left to right: ADC (2), President, First Lady Mrs Sheares, Personal Assistant to Mrs Sheares, me (wearing tie) and Wong Chooi Sen.

Photo 26 Me (left) with the newly appointed Honorary ADCs. In many countries, the heads of state had several full-time ADCs in their staff to serve them at state functions. They had very big establishments, but we had no such luxury. We started with two, one from the Police Force and the other from the Singapore Armed Forces (SAF). Later, it was reduced to one. It was decided to have a pool of trained honorary ADCs, who could be called upon as when the need arose, for official and state functions when appropriate. Also, it was to enable officers to get experience in dealing with foreign dignitaries with confidence and aplomb. I initiated the training for the first batch of officers, mainly from the Services but it also included few from civilian ministries. They were senior officers and included among them was Dr Kwa Soon Bee (not in the picture above) who held a very senior position in the Singapore General Hospital. My training module consisted of protocol practices: how to address dignitaries, presenting guests to our principals, how and when honorifics and titles are used, the correct position to adopt when moving with dignitaries, assisting the guests in a correct way when the situation required, how to manage conversation with dignitaries, and much more. They were volunteers and served with much distinction. From what I understood, they found the experience useful in their professional lives, as well. *Courtesy of the Ministry of Communications and Information.*

ISTANA
SINGAPORE

12th August 1979

Dear Mr & Mrs Rajan,

I thank you and your dear children, Revathi and Bharathi for sending me a beautiful Birthday Greeting Card which arrived this morning. The sentiments it expressed touched my heart and I want all of you to know how much I really appreciated your kind gesture.

My wife and I take this opportunity to wish all of you the very best of Health, Happiness and Prosperity - always enhanced by the blessing of God Almighty.

Yours sincerely,

B H SHEARES
PRESIDENT

Photo 27 President Sheares was a humble and warm person. He always remembered his friends and kept in touch with them. Even after assuming the presidency, Sheares continued to teach medical students in O & G at the Kandang Kerbau Hospital. It was his continuing contribution to medical education. Among his friends were Dr Pinkerton, Queen Elizabeth's personal physician and Dr Michael Debakey, a very well-known surgeon in Mayo Clinic, USA. Sheares was also a caring person. He recommended a Malay medical orderly for a medal for keeping the pharmacy in KK Hospital open even while bombs were falling close to the Hospital during Japanese invasion. The orderly had shown exceptional courage and devotion to duty. The recommendation was rejected by the British and they gave the medal, instead, to a businessman who supplied alcohol to British officers.

Photo 28 My daughters, Revathi and Bharathi, during a stroll in Kampong Java Park in 1980.

This park has undergone many developments. It was a cemetery and probably burials took place there until early 1950s. Sometime in early 1970s, it was developed as a park, as seen in the picture. Later in 1997, the current Women and Children's Hospital was built and it reduced the park to about half its size. Here is an interesting story. There were two fast food joints — selling pizza, burger and chips — which set up shops in the park. I remember my younger daughter, Bharathi, who was then 6 years old, would recite an advertisement jingle very fast, without mistake, in 5 seconds, as required, and win a free packet of chips along with her meal order. However, there was a condition that school children in uniform would not be served. Bharathi circumvented that by making her grandmother go instead and do the same jingle, while she remained in the car when returning from school. She had trained her grandmother by insisting that she kept practising, until she could get it right. It was tough on the old lady but for the love of her grandchild she did it.

Both fast food joints did not do well and they ceased operation in a few years, despite the prime location and easy access. The pizza-joint with a curious name of "Shakey's Pizza" was in fact gutted by fire, if I remember correctly. The talk that was going around then was that the ghosts of the dead, who were buried there once, were still making their daily rounds and they were having the first bite of the foods served in the outlets!

Photo 29 Me receiving the **Public Administration Medal (Silver)** from the acting President Dr Yeoh Ghim Seng in 1971.

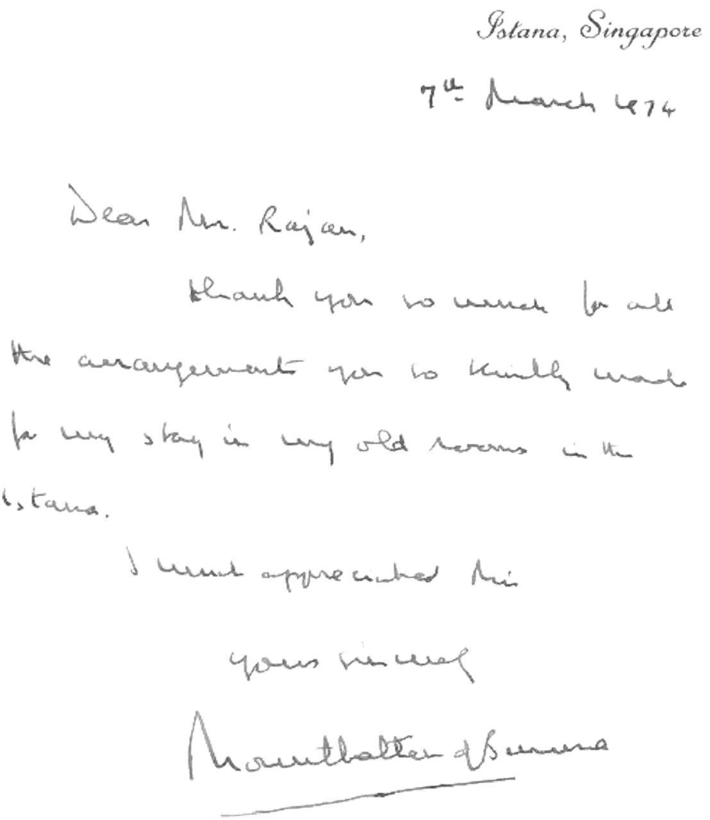

> Istana, Singapore
> 7th March 1974
>
> Dear Mr. Rajan,
>
> Thank you so much for all the arrangements you so kindly made for my stay in my old rooms in the Istana.
>
> I much appreciated this.
>
> Yours sincerely
>
> Mountbatten of Burma

Photo 30 Lord Mountbatten's letter to me. His stay at the Istana brought him fond memories. He told us a few stories of his previous stay, sometime in late 1940s, and some of them were quite amusing. Sadly, he met his tragic death when the Irish Republican Army blew up his pleasure yacht in 1976.

Photo 31 Me at the United Nation's Sixth Committee (legal) in 1977 making last minute changes to my speech while waiting for my turn to speak. In my first speech, I made the observation that meetings did not start on time and noted few other laxities. This was reported on in the Singapore newspapers. I and other members of the team sent by the Ministry of Foreign Affairs for United Nations General Assembly Sessions in 1977 worked under the guidance of our Permanent Representative to the United Nations, Professor Tommy Koh. He was well respected by his peers, especially for his contribution to United Nations Convention on the Law of the Sea (UNCLOS). He nurtured many of young diplomats (and not so young as well) in international relations, especially in multilateral diplomacy. *Courtesy the United Nations.*

Photo 32 Me during a weekend break with the Depperts, the host family, in Peoria, Illinois. It was US government arranged hospitality for delegates attending the United Nations General Assembly Sessions. The Depperts were very warm and hospitable. *Courtesy of the Depperts.*

HER MAJESTY THE QUEEN AND HIS ROYAL HIGHNESS THE DUKE OF EDINBURGH WITH COMMONWEALTH HIGH COMMISSIONERS AT THE GOVERNMENT HOUSE IN CANBERRA, AUSTRALIA ON 12 OCTOBER 1982.

Photo 33 I am on the extreme left in the back row. *Courtesy of the Department of Foreign Affairs and Trade, Australia.*

Relations with Neighbours 213

Photo 34 Left to right: Me, Dr Goh, Mrs Goh and the Australian chief of protocol, during Dr Goh's official visit to Australia in 1980. The hosts arranged a trip to Hayman Island near the Great Barrier Reef as part of the programme. The enthusiastic Australian anglers accompanying us demonstrated their prowess with these hefty catches! With encouragement from our hosts, Dr Goh and I tried to reel the fish in, but it was a futile attempt. We neither had the skill nor the strength to match these marauders of the oceans. *Courtesy of the Department of Foreign Affairs and Trade, Australia.*

Photo 35 Me getting instructions from PM Lee before PM Lee and Mrs Lee board the flight. *Courtesy of Mr Teo Chong Tee.*

Relations with Neighbours 215

Photo 36 Teo Chong Tee, an MP, greeting PM Lee. Teo Chong Tee was with the airport authority and was very helpful in achieving precision timing. PM Lee would have with him papers and books for reading, and to work on board the flight. I am in the middle. *Courtesy of Mr Teo Chong Tee.*

Photo 37 Mrs Lee travelled with PM Lee most of the time. She would help the officials with very useful advice and suggestions when necessary on certain matters during official visits of foreign heads of government and heads of state. *Courtesy of Mr Teo Chong Tee.*

23 Nov 88

Secretary to PM

Mr VK Rajan
We spoke on this.
[signature] 23/11/88

(15 Dec)

"I am supposed to give lunch to Mahathir and his wife, and Ministers on my side will be Mr & Mrs Goh Chok Tong, Ong Teng Cheong (no wife), Lee Hsien Loong (no wife), and Wong Kan Seng (no wife), may be also Jayakumar (no wife). Question is - Venue? Discuss this with Rajan. Decide which is a nice venue. He likes lobster.

Rajaratnam is giving him Supper the night before at the OUB Night Club or Penthouse, at the top of the building. Rajan is settling it.

So I will have to give him lunch somewhere else, may be Raffles City - Compass Room, but I have given him lunch there already, perhaps some other place. Check with Rajan and settle it so that Menu and his preferences and wife's preferences can be cleared. I do not know who he is bringing along for the Singapore Lecture and who has to be invited. I think it is not necessary because this is supposed to be very informal meeting to meet Singapore Ministers. Settle this with Rajan."

Photo 38 PM Lee's instructions to me were always precise, clear and usually not very difficult to implement. Infrequently, he would speak to me directly on the telephone. Time was always of the essence. One of my golden rules was to never let myself into a situation when PM Lee or his Secretary had to remind me on matters which I had to deal with.

Photo 39 Me (left) presenting the Singaporean guests to Baroness Thatcher, Prime Minister of the United Kingdom and Dennis Thatcher at the State Room in the Istana during their **official** visit in 1988. *Courtesy of the Ministry of Communication and Information.*

Photo 40   PM Lee greeting Baroness Thatcher during her informal visit at the Istana. Thatcher had admiration and respect for PM Lee and I believe the feeling was mutual. He had commended her for her stout-hearted and steadfast leadership in turning the British economy around and making United Kingdom regain its competitiveness. In doing so, he incurred the ire of the British Trade Unions. She often made it a point to meet PM Lee even when she was on route to other destinations, by breaking journey in Singapore. I learned from a source that Thatcher read all major speeches of PM Lee.

Relations with Neighbours 219

Photo 41 Me sending off Baroness Thatcher. *Courtesy of the Ministry of Information and the Arts.*

Photo 42   Me presenting Singaporean guests to President Suharto and Mrs Tien Suharto at the Istana State Room during their official visit. Behind them are President Wee Kim Wee and Mrs Wee. PM Lee Kuan Yew and Mrs Lee are at the head of the welcoming line-up near the entrance. Suharto and his wife came to Singapore via Woodlands Causeway after a brief visit there. It was the first time a head of state on official visit came through the Causeway. There was a message in that. Suharto made the visit at a time when there was a strain in our relations with Malaysia, resulting from the visit of Chaim Herzog, Israeli president. It was his very Javanese way of telling leaders of both Singapore and Malaysia to move on. *Courtesy of the Ministry of Communication and Information.*

Photo 43 Me (foreground) presenting ASEAN foreign ministers (from left to right) of Thailand, Malaysia, Indonesia and Brunei to PM Lee around 1985. Shaking hands with PM Lee is Dr Mochtar Kusuamaatmaja of Indonesia. Foreign Minister Dhanabalan is on the right (in white suit). ASEAN then comprised of the original five plus the newest member, Brunei, which was admitted in 1984. Not seen in the picture is the foreign minister of the Philippines.

Dr Mochtar often used say that his Singapore counterpart, Rajaratnam, was "his mentor" and would drop in frequently and informally to have meetings with the latter. *Courtesy of the Ministry of Communication and Information.*

222　　　　　　　　　*Serving Singapore: My Journey*

With HRH Prince Charles at Changi Airport
on Friday, 10 August 1984

Photo 44　His Royal Highness Prince Charles stretching his legs during his stopover at Changi Airport enroute to Bandar Seri Bagawan to represent the British crown at Brunei independence. Behind me is the President's ADC Major Richard Lim.

Photo 45 Me receiving President Corozon Aquino of the Philippines on her official visit in 1986. Behind Aquino is Francisco Benedicto, the Philippines ambassador. Benedicto was not a career diplomat. He was a very successful businessman from Cebu province and an ally of President Aquino. He appeared apprehensive that his lack of diplomatic experience could be a drawback in his mission. I assured him that he need not worry on that score, and that Singapore is an easy place to operate. I also offered him my help, if he needed it. He was very grateful and took me on it.

He would frequently call me seeking help on matters like trade promotion and enhancing political ties. At my suggestion, he worked on getting his President to visit Singapore in order for her to look at our relevant institutions and hold talks with our leaders.

By the time he completed his mission in Singapore, he had done very well by many accounts. He was a good example of a no-career diplomat doing well in the job. *Courtesy of Ambassador Francisco Benedicto.*

Photo 46 The Ceremonial Welcome for Her Majesty Queen Elizabeth the Second and His Royal Highness the Duke of Edinburgh at the Istana during their **State Visit** at the invitation of President Wee Kim Wee and Mrs Wee in 1989. *Courtesy of the Ministry of Communication and Information.*

Photo 47 The Queen during a visit to a school. Left to Right: Me, a female security officer, the Queen (with a bouquet), and Dr Tay Eng Soon, Minister for Education and Minister-in-Attendance. *Courtesy of the Ministry of Communication and Information.*

Relations with Neighbours 225

Photo 48 Pictured above is me presenting Singapore guests To Her Majesty as part of the ceremonial welcome. *Courtesy of the Ministry of Communication and Information.*

Photo 49 The Queen, the Duke of Edinburgh, President Wee, Mrs Wee and other guests at the **State Banque**t hosted by President Wee and Mrs Wee at the Istana. In front, on the left, is me. (Note the dress code for the occasion) *Courtesy of the Ministry of Communications and Information.*

Photo 50   Royal Banquet on board the Yacht Britannia hosted by HM the Queen and HRH Prince Phillip.

President Wee Kim Wee and First Lady Mrs wee (in photo above) and PM Lee and Mrs Lee (in photo 51) attended the banquet on board the Yacht. (Note the dress code and the medals worn.) The British have a long tradition in protocol and in ceremonies. Much of the protocol customs and practices in the international customary law have their origins in Europe.

Princely states found it necessary to minimise conflicts and safeguard Sovereignty by implementing certain minimum codes of behaviour in dealing with one another on equal footing. The royal houses developed elaborate rules for mutual compliance.

In this context, the British monarchy had contributed much. It is one of the few monarchies in existence continuously without interruption, except for brief interregnums, for example, when rebellious parliament, comprising mostly of wealthy landed gentry, chopped off the head of King Charles in 1649 for his refusal to cede some of his powers to parliament. The British conduct state ceremonies with much regal aura and aplomb. They also used these trappings to showcase their imperial power and to awe their subjects in their far-flung empire, while it lasted.

Photo 51 There was also a military ceremony when the yacht left port, on completion of its mission. It was known as "**Beating the Retreat**". HM the Queen used to make a very brief stopover at Changi Airport enroute to other destinations in the Asia Pacific and rested at the VVIP lounge while the aircraft was being serviced. We usually presented a box of orchids from our President both on the onward and return journeys. She told me that the New Zealand authorities did not allow the orchids to be taken out of the aircraft owing to their stringent agricultural policy. *Above photos courtesy of the Ministry of Communications and Information.*

H.M.YACHT BRITANNIA

At Sea

12th October, 1989.

Dear V.K,

When I jokingly said that I was disappointed how late we were (two minutes) at the end of our third afternoon in Singapore, I do hope you did not take me seriously. Knowing your perfectionism, it is just possible that you may have done. From the day I arrived in Singapore on my reconnaissance, I was absolutely confident that we were in the best possible hands with you in charge, and that confidence was completely borne out by events. The Queen's visit could not possibly have gone better, and your planning and programming were models of efficiency and comprehensive attention to detail.

It was a great pleasure to have travelled with you and worked with you and to have seen such an experienced hand in action. Thank you for your co-operation and for your example.

With every good wish.

Yours ever

Robert

(ROBERT FELLOWES)

Mr. V.K. Rajan.

Photo 52   Letter from the Queen's Private Secretary.

BRITISH HIGH COMMISSION

TANGLIN ROAD

SINGAPORE 1024

12 October 1989

Mr V K Rajan
Director
Protocol & Consular Directorate
Ministry of Foreign Affairs
250 North Bridge Road
#07-00 Raffles City Tower
SINGAPORE 0617

Dear VK,

I wanted to write and say how very grateful I am to you and to every member of your staff for the magnificent way you handled every aspect of the State Visit by Her Majesty, The Queen, and His Royal Highness, the Duke of Edinburgh.

I know how much of a burden the preparations have been, how much time and effort they have taken up, and how hard pressed you have all been not only in making arrangements for the State Visit but also for the visit to Singapore by so many Commonwealth Prime Ministers. But you have never flagged: every question was promptly answered; every problem handled without fuss; every possibility thought of and dealt with courteously and efficiently. As I told the Foreign Minister at the Reception on board HMY Britannia last night, Singapore could not have a better Head of Protocol (and he agreed).

With every good wish,
Very sincerely,

M E PIKE
HIGH COMMISSIONER

Photo 53 Letter from the British High Commissioner.

230　　　　　　　　*Serving Singapore: My Journey*

Photo 54　Me greeting His Holiness Pope John Paul II during his official visit to Singapore in 1986. As far as my knowledge goes, this was the first official visit of this or any other pontiff to Singapore. The visit came around the time when there was a controversy over alleged activities of a political nature by a priest from the Catholic Church in Singapore. *Courtesy of the Catholic Church, Singapore.*

Photo 55　Left to right: Premier Li Peng of China and PM Lee during the official visit of the Chinese leader in 1990. (Behind PM Lee is me.) I had a difficult situation to deal with during this visit. *Courtesy of the Ministry of Communication and Information.*

Photo 56 Prime Minister Noboru Takeshita of Japan greeting Mrs Lee at the Istana during his visit in 1989. I am behind PM Lee and behind me is the PM's Security officer, Kandasamy. I had observed that many Japanese leaders preferred to use interpreters even if they were proficient in English. (Takeshita's interpreter is on the left of PM Lee.) They used it as an advantage to give them more time to think and respond. *Courtesy of the Ministry of Communications and Information.*

THE ISTANA
Singapore

Dr & Mrs V. K. Rajan

*Season's Greetings
and
Good Wishes for Deepavali '90*

The President of the Republic of Singapore
and Mrs Wee Kim Wee

Photo 57 Greetings from the "people's President". Both President Wee and Mrs Wee were kind and gracious hosts and had an ability to make guests feel very much at ease. They took genuine interest in them.

Relations with Neighbours 233

Photo 57 **(Photo continued on facing page)** To my knowledge, only two presidents lived in the Istana compound. Yusof Ishak lived at "**Sri Melati**", which was later demolished and "**The Lodge**" was built on the same site. Devan Nair lived in "**The Lodge**". All other presidents lived in their own homes and commuted daily to the Istana.

The Istana grounds, about 42 acres with a pleasant greenery, was meticulously maintained by a curator and his support staff. It had a 9-hole golf course. Visiting VVIP guests, who were keen golfers, sometimes played a quick round of golf, and one of them was Dan Quayle, Vice President of the United States in 1986.

Photo 58 Me presenting Singapore guests to His Majesty Sultan of Brunei upon his arrival, after attending CHOGM in Kuala Lumpur in 1989. The Government had invited all heads of state attending CHOGM in KL to visit Singapore. *Courtesy of the Ministry of Communications and Information.*

Photo 59 President Wee Kim Wee (right) greeting His Majesty Sultan Bolkiah of Brunei. On the right is First Lady Mrs Wee. The ADC and me are in the background. At extreme right is the security officer. *Courtesy of President Wee Kim Wee.*

Photo 60　His Majesty Sultan Iskandar made a farewell call on President Wee Kim Wee at the Istana upon completion of his term as *Yang di Pertuan Agong* (King) of Malaysia in 1988. It was the first such visit by a Malaysian King. He and President Wee had a good relationship. He was a frequent visitor both officially and unofficially and was on friendly terms with many of our leaders. He has called on President Wee a few times.

For the information of readers, President Wee has served as our High Commissioner to Malaysia during his distinguished diplomatic career.

In the picture, the King is in conversation with me. He had a good memory. He asked me about a matter he had spoken to me about during an earlier visit. He was quite informal, warm and friendly to Singapore. *Courtesy of the Ministry of Communication and Information.*

Istana farewell marks end of Malaysian King's visit

WITH broad smiles and a warm handshake, the Yang di-Pertuan Agong of Malaysia bade farewell to his host, President Wee Kim Wee, at the Istana here last night.

Looking on is Singapore's Director of Protocol, Mr V.K. Rajan.

The King, Sultan Iskandar of Johor, ended a three-day state visit, the first by a Malaysian King.

Second Deputy Prime Minister Ong Teng Cheong, the minister in attendance, accompanied the King back to the Istana Bukit Serene in Johor Baru. — Picture by WONG KWAI CHOW.

• King takes in 3D movies: Page 24

Photo 61 A very warm handshake between the Malaysian King (right) and President Wee Kim Wee. The author is seen in the background.

Source: The Straits Times © Singapore Press Holdings Ltd. Reprinted with permission.

WEE KIM WEE
President of the Republic of Singapore

To

Her Majesty Elizabeth The Second,
by the Grace of God Queen of New Zealand,
and Her other Realms and Territories,
Head of the Commonwealth, Defender of the Faith

BEING desirous of making suitable provision for the representation in New Zealand of the interests of the Republic of Singapore and for the maintenance of the relations of amity and concord between the Republic and New Zealand, I have to that end made choice of Mr VELUTHEVAR KANAGARAJAN, a distinguished citizen of the Republic of Singapore, to be the High Commissioner of the Republic of Singapore in New Zealand.

I am confident that Mr VELUTHEVAR KANAGARAJAN is eminently worthy of the important Mission for which he has been selected and that he will discharge the duties of his High Office in a manner that will fully merit Your Majesty's approbation and esteem. It is with this conviction that I request Your Majesty to receive him with Your Majesty's usual graciousness and to attach faith and complete credence to all that he will say to Your Majesty on my behalf and especially when he will convey to Your Majesty the assurances of my high esteem and my constant friendship.

Given at the Istana, Singapore, the Third Day of July, One Thousand Nine Hundred and Ninety One.

WEE KIM WEE

Photo 62 My credentials as High Commissioner to New Zealand.

Photo 63 Me and my wife receiving my credentials as High Commissioner to New Zealand from President Wee Kim Wee. *Country of President Wee Kim Wee.*

Photo 64 With the Governor General, Catherine Tizard (centre) and Foreign Minister, Don McKinnon after I presented my credentials in 1991. McKinnon later became the Commonwealth Secretary General. I found New Zealand diplomats generally very well-informed, professional and respected in the international community — an important factor that enabled the country to punch above its weight globally. *Courtesy of the New Zealand Ministry of Foreign Affairs.*

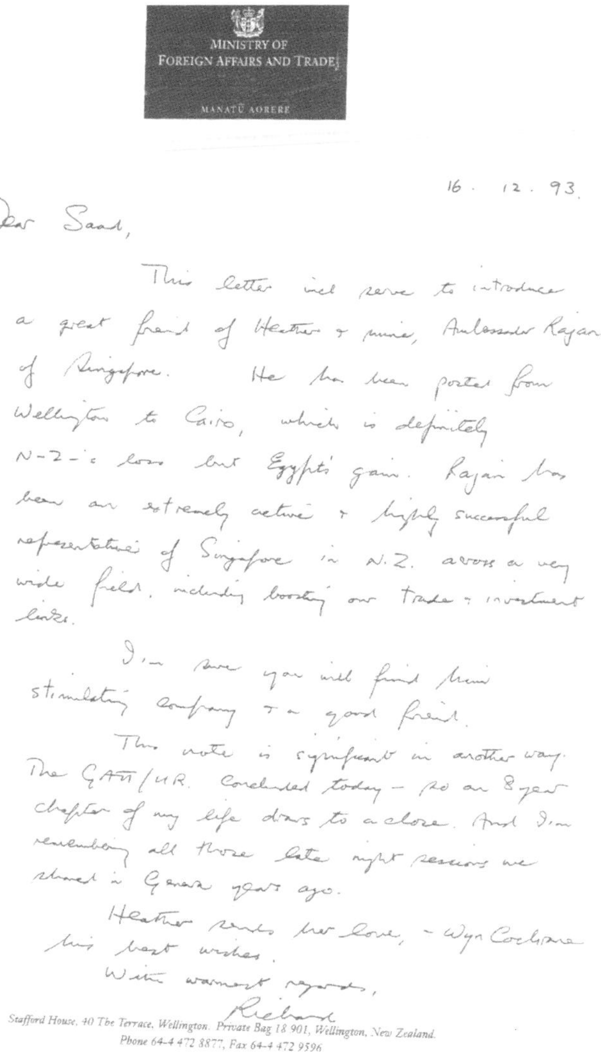

Photo 65 Letter from Mr Richard Nottage, a veteran diplomat and the Secretary of the New Zealand Ministry of Foreign Affairs. New Zealand was my first posting as head of mission. I learned a lot from both the establishment officials and the people of the country. My two daughters attended universities there and had enriching experiences. We are still fond of the country. We felt extreme sadness when a senseless extremist murdered so brutally, more than 50 innocent citizens of Muslim faith while they were in prayer in two mosques in Christchurch, a beautiful city, on 15 March 2019. That heinous attack was simply not the New Zealand we knew.

New Zealand Institute of International Affairs

c/- Victoria University of Wellington
P O Box 600
Wellington

Telephone 472 7430
Fax 473 1261

20 December 1993

The High Commissioner of the Republic of Singapore
and Mrs V K Rajan
Singapore High Commission
P O Box 13140
WELLINGTON

Dear High Commissioner,

Please forgive the typed letter but I am most anxious to get this away to you before your pending departure. There are a number of things that I would like to say, firstly how sad we are to see you leaving us so soon after the completely excellent, positive contribution you have made in this country to relationships between us. No doubt your new posting in Cairo will be one of considerable challenge and our loss is their gain.

Could I also thank you for your kindnesses and consideration during 1993 and say how much I have enjoyed my contact with you both, particularly you High Commissioner on so many occasions.

Thank you for including us in your invitation list at your recent farewell and again I would like to compliment you on the most positive comments that you made on such a moving occasion. A masterly and concise presentation, or should I say farewell, and I should add that we were all touched with the sincerity.

Thank you also for quite the most exquisite season's greetings card which has pride of place amongst those of our many friends and particularly our international ones.

There is little I can add to this without repeating myself apart from saying again that we are sorry to see you leave, we wish you well and we certainly trust that we will meet again in this rather small world.

In regard to your successor we look forward to meeting at that appropriate time but that is for the future. We more particularly wish to say goodbye to you both and thank you for being what you were.

Yours sincerely

[signature]
President

Photo 66 I gave several lectures at the New Zealand Institute of International Affairs. I was warmly received there.

PRIME MINISTER
CANBERRA

29 February 1984

Dear Mr Rajan

I should like to convey to you my appreciation for your part in the arrangements made for my recent visit to Singapore. My wife, my party and I were impessed by the courtesy and professionalism shown by all who contributed to ensure our visit went so smoothly.

I should be grateful if you would pass on my personal thanks to all of your colleagues and staff who assisted in making our regrettably brief visit both successful and enjoyable.

Yours sincerely

R.J.L. Hawke

Mr V.K. Rajan
Director
Protocol & Consular Division
Ministry of Foreign Affairs
City Hall
St Andrew's Road
SINGAPORE 0617

Photo 67   Prime Minister Hawke's official visit was the first major visit organised immediately upon taking charge of the Protocol and Consular Directorate. The visit went very well.

Relations with Neighbours 243

Photo 68 President Wee (5th from left in the front row) with our heads of mission and their spouses. This photo was taken during the Heads of Mission Meeting in 1992. Me and my wife are in the second row from the front, at 3rd and 4th positions from right, respectively. *Courtesy of the Ministry of Foreign Affairs.*

Photo 69 Me receiving my credentials as Ambassador to Egypt from President Ong Teng Chiong. *Courtesy of the Office of the President.*

Photo 70 Me presenting my credentials to President Hosni Mubarak in Cairo, Egypt in 1994. First in front and to the right of Mubarak is Foreign Minister Amr Moussa. During my term in Egypt, ambassadors would have to wait, sometimes for several months, to present their credentials. The US ambassador, however, would be fast tracked. This practice is not uncommon in many countries in the Arab world. *Courtesy of the Ministry of Foreign Affairs, Egypt.*

> **The Egyptian Gazette** MONDAY, APRIL 11, 1994
>
> ## Smug at home, Singaporeans build external wing of economy
>
> By: Tarek Fathi Rashed
>
> One cannot but envy this tiny island that looks like a glittering spot on the surface of the water. As the world seems to be on the brink of a trade war Singapore appears strong and adamant to such a looming ghost. Its tight and organised work policies sustain this position. It has become a model emulated by several developing nations. Over a period of less than thirty years, since gaining independence from Britain in 1965 Singaporeans have worked in full gear to create and build a nation, successful and prospering, out of the wreckage of occupation.
>
> "Our only resource was and still is the people. Adoption of a pragmatic policy, election of good and competent leaders, planning with long-term objectives, tolerating short-term sacrifices, have been the bases of a revolutionary march towards success. Tightening belts and encouraging saving were substantial development strategies", said Mr. V.K. Rajan, the ambassador of Singapore in Cairo, who has just taken office on March 24th. "Singapore's savings rate, which accounted for 46 per cent of the GDP in the last three years, is probably the highest in the world", noted Mr Rajan.
>
> Singapore learned the [...]
>
> *Every Friday, Muslims gather to pray at the mosque. The Sultan Mosque is one of the largest in Singapore as well as it is one of the 32 buildings declared as monuments.*
>
> The island, which stretches for only 42km from east to west, and 23 km from north to south is a thoroughfare for world communication. Its press is as free as national interests allow. The unique nature of its population composition has entailed that its press must be responsible. Its multi-ethnic motley of people have been living amiably under a meticulous constitutional and social system. "Every Singaporean is given an equal opportunity and the means to acquire [...] community of the 3 million (the majority of which are Chinese, followed by Malays and Indians) is given full freedom to practice its own beliefs and rites. Muslims are treated slightly better in the sense that every housing estate is endowed with a plot of land to build a mosque", said Mr Rajan. In a national unity more, the government decreed that all religious festivals be marked as public holidays for the whole cosmopolitan city.
>
> The unemployment rate is [...]
>
> 'Muslims are treated slightly better in the sense that every housing estate is endowed with a plot of land to build a mosque'
>
> agenda. Now, they are exploring opportunities for cultural engagements all over the world. The Singaporean minister of culture last year visited Egypt to sow the seeds of mutual cultural cooperation.
>
> The government charts out the broad vision of policies, provides services, and observes a commitment to high productivity and excellence. They provide free education for the primary and secondary stages. University education is subsidised 75%. However, nothing is for free in Singapore, where everything is imported.
>
> The economic system adopted since the birth of Singapore as an independent state has secured a constant growth and development. The government interfers only to

Photo 71 It is important for a proactive ambassador to be operational quickly after arrival in the host country, as soon as the necessary protocol formalities are completed, usually after presenting a "true copy" of the credentials to the foreign minister. I did it as fast I could and arranged to give the above interview.

It helped me to launch myself in the community. Among many other reasons were that I made it known to the wider community (not just the elite in the establishment) that the new Singapore ambassador is in town, and is keen to cooperate in upgrading the relations in all fields — political, economic (including trade and investments) and cultural, amongst others, for mutual benefit. Soon after the interview, I received an invitation for an interview on Nile TV. I also gave a few interviews to the well-known national newspaper the *Al Ahram*. The feedback was that they were well received in the community and among many members of the diplomatic corps. I worked proactively to engage all relevant and useful actors, state and non-state personnel alike. I was happy and satisfied over the returns on my investment to use the language of business.

Photo 72 Me presenting my credentials to President Robert Mugabe in Harare. Zimbabwe. Witnessing the ceremony are Mugabe's chief of protocol (in red tie), my wife, my personal assistant Ashok, and my daughters Revathi (partly visible) and Bharathi, respectively. *Courtesy of the Zimbabwe Ministry of Foreign Affairs.*

Photo 73 Me presenting my credentials to President Clerides [third from left] in Larnaca, Cyprus. *Courtesy of the Cyprus Ministry of Foreign Affairs.*

Photo 74 Some of the ambassadors in the Asia-Africa Group in 1997. I am at the sixth place from left in the front row and was then the Chairman of the Group. Egypt was host to one of the biggest diplomatic corps in the world. One senior diplomat who had served in London told me that the diplomatic corps in Cairo was as big as that in London. It was a reflection of Egypt's importance, not only in the Middle East, but also in the wider world.

Photo 75 Me being received on arrival at the Cairo University. On the right is Dr Mohamed Salim, Director, Centre for Asian Studies, where I gave several keynote lectures on a variety of topics, including Singapore's public sector reforms, economic and political developments in Asia and on global issues of interest, and participated in panel discussions on selected topics. *Courtesy Cairo University.*

Photo 76 Above is a section of the audience, comprising members of the Diplomatic Corps, government officials, academia and students. Inset, Professor of Economics in Cairo University, Ali Hilal Disoky, introducing me. I am in the middle and Professor Mohamed Salim is on my right. *"At Close Quarters"*, publication of the Ministry of Foreign Affairs.

Photo 77 Left to Right: Me, Prof Adel (AUC) and Carlos, Governor of the Central Bank of Chile. *Courtesy of the American University in Cairo.*

Photo 78 Delivering my address on the **"Asian Financial Crisis"** at the **American University in Cairo** (AUC) in 1998, before an invited audience comprising of ambassadors, academics, students and selected members of the local community. *Courtesy of the American University in Cairo.*

```
                                        CONSULATE
                                          OF THE
                                  REPUBLIC OF SINGAPORE
                                         CALIFORNIA
                                  2424 S.E. Bristol, Suite #320
                                  Santa Ana Heights, CA 92707
                                     Tel: (714) 476 2330
                                     Fax: (714) 476 8301
```

25 February 1994

Ambassador V.K. Rajan
Ambassador to the Arab Republic of Egypt
Ministry of Foreign Affairs
250 North Bridge Road #07-00
Raffles City Tower
Singapore 0617

Dear V.K.:

I just received a press statement from the Foreign Ministry in reference to your being appointed as Ambassador to the Arab Republic of Egypt.

I was hoping I could get to New Zealand to visit you while you were posted there. However, you were transferred so rapidly, I will have to go to Egypt to see you and Vijaya.

Shirley and I again want to congratulate you on your new assignment and I am sure that you will do an excellent job on behalf of the Singapore government. If you ever have reason to come to the United States, you are always welcome to stay at our home with us.

Yours very truly,

Daryl Arnold
Honorary Consul General

Photo 79 Ambassador Daryl Arnold and I shared a cordial working relationship. This helped in our negotiations on land isssues, especially relating to relocation of their chancery. Daryl also had many friends in the higher echelon of our establishment. Unfortunately, he and his wife Shirley met their untimely death in a road accident in their hometown. We miss them.

الجـامـعـة الأمـريكـية بالقـاهـرة
THE AMERICAN UNIVERSITY IN CAIRO
Office of Public Relations

November 19, 1998

19 NOV 1998

His Excellency Ambassador VK Rajan
Ambassador of Singapore to Egypt
Arab Republic of Egypt

Excellency:

On behalf of the American University in Cairo, I wish to express my gratitude to you for accepting to be an active part of the English Public Lecture Series for the academic year of 1998-99.

It was a great honor and pleasure to have you on campus last Monday. Your participation in the panel discussion entitled "Asian Crisis: Causes and Implications" was most inspiring and informative.

This series of monthly lectures was established in 1990, and has enjoyed an immense success among not only the AUC faculty and students, but also the English speaking Cairo community (foreign and Egyptian) including alumni, diplomats, intellectuals, businessmen and bankers among others.

The program is designed to serve the unique purpose of providing a platform for lectures and discussion of current affairs in a public setting as well as a forum for the exchange of ideas on important current issues in Egypt and the Arab World in an atmosphere of academic freedom.

The AUC Public Relations Office/ Cultural Programs and Special Events Unit, has been sponsoring the English Public Lecture Series for the last nine years inviting AUC faculty members and prominent thinkers and figures like yourself.

Your presentation and the following discussion shed light on the real issues concerning the Asia crisis and its national and international implications.

On behalf of AUC, I would like to thank you for your presence with us, and I look forward to continued cooperation in the future.

Sincerely yours,

Mona Zaki
Associate Director of Public Relations
for Cultural Programs and Special Events

Photo 80 I gave a keynote address on "Asian Financial Crisis" and participated in a panel discussion that followed. My contributions were very well received.

الجــامـعــة الأمـريـكيــة بـالقـاهــرة
THE AMERICAN UNIVERSITY IN CAIRO
John D. Gerhart
President

- 3 JUN

May 31, 1999

His Excellency Ambassador V.K. Rajan
Ambassador of Singapore to Egypt
Arab Republic of Egypt

Dear Excellency:

On behalf of the American University in Cairo, I wish to thank you for participation in our 1998-99 English Public Lecture Series. It was a great honor and pleasure to have you speak at our campus. Both your presentation and participation in the discussion following provided all who attended with a unique and insightful perspective.

The English Public Lecture Series, established in 1990, provides a platform for the exchange of ideas on current affairs in an atmosphere of academic freedom. In addition, the EPLS allows timely discussion on important issues concerning Egypt and the Arab world. The Cultural Programs and Special Events unit within the AUC Public Relations Office is pleased to be able to sponsor this special lecture series and hopes for its continued success in the coming years. Your participation this year has only added to its prestige.

Thank you again for taking the time to share your expertise as part of the English Public Lecture Series. All of us at AUC look forward to our continuing good relations, and we hope to see you at future events in the English Public Lecture Series.

Sincerely yours,

John D. Gerhart

113 KASR EL AINI STREET, P.O. BOX 2511, CAIRO 11511, EGYPT TEL: 357-5161/62/63 FAX: 354-1830
420 FIFTH AVENUE, 3RD FLOOR, NEW YORK, NY 10018 2729 TEL: (212) 730-8800 FAX: (212) 730-1600

Photo 81 A letter from the President of the American University in Cairo, a prestigious institution.

مركز دراسات وبحوث الدول النامية

CENTER FOR THE STUDY OF
DEVELOPING COUNTRIES

23 MAY 1999

Cairo May 22, 1999

His Excellency Ambassador V K Rajan
Ambassador of the Republic of Singapore,
Cairo
Fax no.: 3481682

Your Excellency

Your talk at the Conference on: " Political Conditions for Development: Transparency, Accountability and Good Governance" delivered as a keynote speech at the opening session of the conference last Tuesday morning was recognized by most participants as one of the major highlights of the conference. Your talk was quoted several times in nearly all sessions of the conference for what it contained as useful lessons on how corruption could be fought. One of those who spoke very favorably of your talk is Dr. Abdel-Aziz Hegazi, former Prime Minister of Egypt. Your country gives the world an eloquent demonstration that corruption is not an invincible enemy after all

As proceedings of the conference will be printed in a book form, I hope very much that we could get a copy of your very impressive lecture. I am very sorry that both shortage of time and traditions of the keynote speech did not allow much time for discussion.

Hoping to benefit from your wisdom in other activities of the Center.

Truly,

M. Al-Sayyid

Mustapha K AL-Sayyid,
Director, CSDC,
Cairo University.

Photo 82 Cairo University is one of the oldest institutions of higher learning in the world. It is renowned in the Arab world and beyond. The Centre for the Study of Developing Countries was very active in its field, especially in matters related to governance. I gave many lectures, keynote addresses and participated in panel discussions throughout my term in Egypt. I engaged with the academic establishment and student groups. Singapore was highly regarded and cited for its good governance.

Relations with Neighbours 255

> 19-APR-2000 09:42 FROM AIS EGYPT TO 3481682 P.01
>
> **the American International School in Egypt**
>
> 16 April 2000
>
> 1 8 APR 2000
>
> Ambassador V.K. Rajan
> Embassy of the Republic of Singapore
> 40 Babel Street
> Dokki, 11511
> Cairo, Egypt
>
> Tel 349 0468 / 5045
> Fax 348 1682
>
> Dear Ambassador Rajan:
>
> All of us at AIS-Egypt thank you for your keynote address at the Ninth Annual AISMUN. Please know that your comments were most well received by our audience. Incidentally, we counted 220 students from the conference and then brought in another 35 chairs for those that were invited. It was a pleasant surprise to find so many from the community in attendance. One student commented, "It was the best opening I have ever heard at an MUN conference." The visuals you used appealed to quite a number of others. The photo of the camel drinking Coca-Cola is an image that students will not forget soon - and, perhaps more important, they will remember the message of globalization. The speech was well thought out, polished and presented some good fodder for later debate in the conference formal session. Additionally, the insightful answers you provided to the questions were so valuable even if the students often basically asked you to somehow predict what the future holds.
>
> I was listening intently and appreciated very much how you wove the conference themes around the topic of *The Challenge of Change*. In fact, I am certain you recognize that we built the conference around your suggestion of the topic.
> I recognized some long research and preparation and we appreciate the time and effort you placed into the address. The time you spent with us truly made for a better learning experience and served to highlight a seasoned, professional diplomat in action. We thank you again.
>
> Kindest regards,
>
> Dr. Richard Green
> Social Studies Department Chair /
> AISMUN Director
>
> NB: when the report on the conference is aired on Nile Television I will see that the embassy gets a copy. Please look for the program to be aired sometime in mid-May.

Photo 83 Feedback from the American International School (AIS) on the keynote address I delivered to the **Model United Nations Conference** in Egypt in 2000. See first paragraph in Chapter 25 on "The Future". My address was also covered by Nile TV.

THE HASHEMITE KINGDOM OF JORDAN
Ministry of Foreign Affairs

المملكة الأردنية الهاشمية
وزارة الخارجية

Ref. No. _____
Date _____

His Excellency
Mr. V.K. RAJAN
Ambassador of the Republic of Singapore
Cairo-Egypt

Your Excellency,

On behalf of Ministry of foreign affairs and the diplomatic family in Jordan, I'd like to express my thanks and appreciation for your excellent presentation on 23 May 2000, at the Institute of Diplomacy in Amman.

The experience of Singapore in Public Administration and Foreign service, showed us a tremendous sense of responsibility and hard work of the leadership of Singapore and its people, also explained plainly the journey of success which Singapore achieved during these years.

We learned a lot from your experience, and assure you that we'll take it into consideration to modernize our institutions.

I congratulate you of being such an excellent promoter of Singapore.

With my best regards and highest consideration

Yours sincerely

Abdel-Elah Khatib

Photo 84 Letter dated 10 June, 2000 from the Jordanian Institute of Diplomacy. In the "List of VIPs in Attendance" attached to the letter, the attendees included **HRH Princes Wajdan Ali,** Patron of the Institute, and 14 others who were ministers and ambassadors.

Relations with Neighbours 257

Photo 85 United States Ambassador, Daniel Kurtzer, in conversation with my wife at our farewell reception in Cairo. Next to Kurtzer is Victoria Owen, the Australian Ambassador.

Photo 86 At a call on the Senior Minister Lee Kuan Yew (centre) by Jordanian Prime Minister, his ministers and officials in Amman around 1998. The Jordanian Prime Minister is on Senior Minister's right and I am Senior Minister's left. *Courtesy of the Ministry of Foreign Affairs, Jordan.*

Photo 87 Section titled "First Step" taken from "Heart of Public Service" (page 24) published by Public Service Division, Prime Minister's Office (2015).

Relations with Neighbours

In the years after Independence, Singapore's corps of Foreign Service officers worked tirelessly to safeguard our sovereignty by seeking international recognition and establishing ties with other countries.

Based on passages from *The Singapore Foreign Service: The First 40 Years* (Editions Didier Millet, 2005).

Singapore's Foreign Service was born at a moment of great uncertainty. Following Independence in August 1965, Mr S. Rajaratnam, the newly designated Minister for Foreign Affairs, got down to the urgent work at hand: to establish Singapore's status as a sovereign nation. This he undertook immediately by leading a delegation to the United Nations (UN). The mission proved successful and on 21 September 1965, Singapore was admitted to the UN as its 117th member.

It was a heady moment for the delegation, but much work remained. Having scored their first success, the officers now embarked on a whirlwind Afro-Asia Goodwill Mission. From New York, the delegation travelled to eight African and four Asian nations, as well as to Britain, Russia and Yugoslavia. By the end of 1965, Singapore had been formally recognised by more than 50 countries.

Back home, the new Ministry of Foreign Affairs (MFA) also began to take shape. Office space was secured at City Hall and a first slate of ambassadors, protocol officers and clerks was recruited, often directly from other ministries.

Despite a lack of resources, the new officers took to their tasks with vigour. Mr Francis D'Costa was among the few who could claim any diplomatic experience, having taken a Foreign Service training course in London in 1956. "I was 33 years old in 1965, working in the Ministry of Law," he recalls. "On 9 August in the afternoon, [Minister for Law] Eddie Barker called and said I was moving to MFA. I asked him where it was and he said I had better go and find out... Events were dictated by circumstances and we rallied together."

The new MFA officers were also grateful to get practical advice and support from other Commonwealth missions. "I remember attending a session conducted by the Australian High Commissioner," recalls Mr V. K. Rajan. "He covered a large amount of ground in great detail – from the day of arrival in the host country to the day of departure on completion of posting!"

Mr Rajan would go on to serve in various diplomatic missions as Ambassador to Jordan and the United Arab Emirates and High Commissioner to Cyprus and Zimbabwe. He recalls the pride of the young officers as they carried Singapore's flag around the world. "What we lacked in knowledge and experience was more than matched by the excitement and the iron determination to do our best for the country," he says.

Mr Chia Cheong Fook, who'd later serve as MFA's Permanent Secretary and Singapore's High Commissioner to New Zealand, travelled to London in 1966 to open a mission. Frugality was very much the order of the day. "I am afraid the property bill is tremendous," he wrote back. "I am fully aware that we have to cut our coats according to our cloth and that the Singapore government is not in the position to indulge in extravagances."

Overcoming these early challenges, MFA soon founded missions in Australia, Burma, Cambodia, Egypt, India, Japan, Malaysia, New Zealand, Thailand, the United Kingdom and the United States. By the end of 1969, 36 diplomatic missions and 14 consular missions had also been established here. Singapore had taken its first step onto the world stage.

> **What we lacked in knowledge and experience was more than matched by the excitement and the iron determination to do our best for the country.**
>
> Mr V. K. Rajan

CHAPTER 1 – INTEGRITY

Photo 88 Section titled "First Step" taken from "Heart of Public Service" (page 25) published by the Public Service Division, Prime Minister's Office (2015). *Courtesy of the Public Service Division, Prime Minister's office.*

Mr V. K. Rajan

13 November 2015

Dear Mr Rajan

In conjunction with the SG50 celebrations this year, the Public Service Division has just published *Heart of Public Service*, a two-volume book-set that honours the institutions and officers of the Singapore Public Service. Touching on key milestones in our history, *Heart of Public Service* brings to life Singapore's development through stories about our institutions and officers. It tells a story of our relentless effort to build the best Public Service for Singapore.

Thank you for sharing your experiences as a public officer with us for the *Heart of Public Service* book project. Your story is an inspiration. Thank you for serving.

We would like to present you with the enclosed package as a token of our appreciation. In addition to a complimentary copy of *Heart of Public Service*, we have also included a copy of *Pioneers Once More*, which tells the story of the Public Service from the time Singaporeans took over the reins of self-governance from the British in 1959; a commemorative SG50 umbrella; and a cupro-nickel coin that marks the nation's Jubilee celebration.

Thank you again and best wishes,

Chong Chee Yin
Assistant Director, Communications and Strategic Relations
Public Service Division
Prime Minister's Office

THE SINGAPORE
PUBLIC SERVICE
INTEGRITY
SERVICE
EXCELLENCE

Photo 89 Letter from the Public Service Division, Prime Minister's Office.

Relations with Neighbours 261

Photo 90 Me at the Mena House Golf Course in Egypt. It reminds me of the Egyptian saying, **"man fears time and time fears the Pyramid"**.

Photo 91 Me during a visit to Jerash in Jordan.

PRIME NEWS

'HE MUST BE AN INSPIRATION TO YOUNG LAWYERS WHO ARE HALF-HEARTED...'
— Mr Raman, with whom Mr Rajan (above) practises now

THE SUNDAY TIMES · May 25, 2003

From ambassador to practising lawyer at age 64

Life-long dream comes true for ex-diplomat who is among 168 called to the Bar

By ELENA CHONG

V.K. RAJAN had always wanted to be a lawyer, but his family could not afford to send him to university.

His father was a Public Works Department labourer, then a rubber tapper before he opened a provision shop in Marsiling Road. His mother was a housewife.

Their son, the would-be lawyer, joined the Civil Service

Former Chief of Protocol at the Foreign Ministry, once High Commissioner to New Zealand, Cyprus and Zimbabwe, and Ambassador to Egypt and concurrently to Jordan and the United Arab Emirates, he retired in December 2001.

Yesterday, he was the oldest of the 168 lawyers called to the Bar. The others are in their mid-20s.

His younger daughter, Bharathi, 28, a journalist, said of him: "He is dedicated to his work. He is a man of conviction. I am sure he will be a very dedicated lawyer."

Also present yesterday were Mr Rajan's wife, Madam Vijayalakshmi, 55, and their elder daughter, Revathi, 30.

In 1959, while doing the equivalent of the A levels now,

owner, Mr G. Raman, said: "He must be an inspiration to young lawyers who are half-hearted and who are becoming disillusioned."

Mr Rajan enters a profession that has been shrinking since 1999. Though new admissions bring the total to 3,366, that is still 306 fewer lawyers practising than last year.

The profession also faces multiple crises for the first time in history — the threat of a global economic downturn caused by the Iraq war and the Sars outbreak, as Chief Justice Yong Pung How reminded the newcomers.

Fees have been slashed and more competition looms.

When the World Trade Organisation fully liberalises the services sector, and the Singapore-United States Free

Photo 92 I was called to the Bar in Singapore on 24th May, 2003 and to the English Bar in 1977.

Source: The Sunday Times© Singapore Press Holdings Ltd. Reprinted with permission.

Photo 93   This was an honorary appointment. I led some of Singapore's business delegations abroad, including to South Korea, India, Sri Lanka and Malaysia. I resigned from this position about ten years later to take up my current position as **Adviser in the Ministry of Foreign Affairs, Kingdom of Bahrain in 2011.** *Courtesy of the Singapore Business Federation.*

A TRIBUTE TO OUR COMMUNITY LEADER

It was with mixed feelings that Hindus in Singapore received the news of the appointment of Mr. V. K. Rajan as the High Commissioner of New Zealand. Prior to his appointment Mr. V. K. Rajan had served as the Chairman of the HEB with rare distinction.

While the Hindus must have felt a sense of pride and satisfaction at the national recognition given to him, they also regretted having to lose a community leader who has ably guided them with complete dedication and exemplary leadership.

The Saraswathy Kindergarten, the first of its kind in Singapore and the catalyst for the emergence of many in future, was the brainchild of Mr. V. K. Rajan. The seal and enthusiasm he showed in the development of this project and the way he galvanised the support of the community to ensure its success has not only endeared him to all but also earned him lasting respect.

Sudar congratulates Mr. V. K. Rajan on his new appointment and wishes him every success in his role as the ambassador of our nation.

2/Sudar Vol 4. No. 2

Photo 94 I served first as Chairman of the Hindu Advisory Board (HAB) and later as the Chairman of the Hindu Endowments Board (HEB) for more than 10 years in the 1980s.

The appointments were made by the Minister for Law & Home Affairs. The HEB is a statutory board established under the Hindu Endowments Boards Act.

I resigned the chairmanship of HEB when I was appointed High Commissioner to New Zealand in 1991.

The tribute was published in a **"Sudar"**, a community run publication in August 1991. (August 1991)

Photo 95 Community Service: Me welcoming Prime Minister Goh Chock Tong at the Sri Sreenivasa Perumal Temple in Serangoon Road on the occasion of ***Thaipusam*** festival in 1991. I was then the Chairman of the Hindu Endowments Board.

Relations with Neighbours 267

Photo 96 At the Singapore Armed Forces Training Institute (SAFTI). I gave lectures on Singapore's political relations with our neighbours, especially Indonesia, to classes comprising of select officers in uniform. Many of them have since assumed very high public offices. I had also gave lectures on protocol upon request, to other audiences e.g. wives of ministers and members of parliament. As a Trainer at the Singapore Civil Service College, I conducted training courses on **"Public Sector Reforms in Singapore" to international audiences** comprising of senior government officials from Asia, Africa and South America, under the auspices of the Singapore Technical Cooperation Programme.

Photo 97 President Wee Kim Wee did much to promote closer friendship and understanding between our community and the Diplomatic Corps. Organising golf tournaments was one of the several activities he initiated events he initiated and was much appreciated by the Diplomatic Corps.

Long Service Award

Presented to

**Mr Veluthevar Kanaga Rajan
PPA(P), PBM, PBS**

In Appreciation of **5 years** of
Dedicated Voluntary Service
In the

National Council Against Drug Abuse

WONG KAN SENG
Deputy Prime Minister and
Minister for Home Affairs

17 NOVEMBER 2007

Photo 98   I served in NCADA from 2002 to 2011 before I left it to take up my current appointment as Adviser to the Bahrain Government.

Relations with Neighbours 269

Photo 99 His Royal Highness Prince Salman Bin Hamad Al Khalifa, Crown Prince, Deputy Supreme Commander and First Deputy Prime Minister receiving me at his *majlis* in Bahrain. *Courtesy of the Office of HRH Crown Prince, Bahrain.*

Photo 100 Me in conversation with His Royal Highness Prince Salman Bin Hamad Al Khalifa, Crown Prince, Deputy Supreme Commander and First Deputy Prime Minister. On his right (partly hidden) is the Foreign Minister Shaikh Khalid Bin Ahmed Al Khalifa 2014. *Courtesy of the Ministry of Foreign Affairs, Bahrain.*

Photo 101 Me addressing senior Bahraini diplomats during a training session. *Courtesy of the Ministry of Foreign Affairs, Bahrain.*

29 REVIEW Thursday 16, March 2006

The key role of Foreign Service wives

In the fourth of five excerpts from the new book The Singapore Foreign Service: The First 40 Years, the spotlight is trained on the women behind the men. Foreign Service wives played a big part in diplomacy too. The book, written by former journalist Gretchen Liu, is published by Editions Didier Millet and available at shops at $59.90.

FOREIGN Service spouses play many roles — the most obvious is that of hostess at official functions. It does not take much imagination to grasp that this kind of entertaining is extremely hard work.

Yet Singapore's diplomatic wives are frequently known for their culinary skills; in many capitals an invitation to dine chez Singapore is highly regarded.

Pioneering wives set the standards. In the '70s in Moscow, Mrs P S Raman grew bean sprouts under her bed and concocted innovative dishes with limited ingredients.

Food plays a central role in sustaining camaraderie abroad. Thus did Mrs V K Rajan win the hearts of staff and families during her husband's term as head of the Cairo mission. As one officer recorded: "Mrs Rajan's magnificent culinary skills have won her a loyal following at the mission. On the pretext of festivities, we would find excuses to visit their house. Although we are hundreds of miles away from Singapore, who has to feel homesick with food like this around?"

Photo 102 Throughout the ages food has been central to diplomacy. In this regard, the spouses of diplomats make a big contribution. Entertainment at the residence is generally preferred and appreciated by guests. Singapore cuisine combined with multi-ethnic food was always a hit, and guests expected it. Getting the spices and right ingredients required much effort. My wife used to bring them from home as part of her personal luggage at her own expense.

Source: The Straits Times © Singapore Press Holdings Ltd. Reprinted with permission.

GOVERNMENT HOUSE
New Zealand

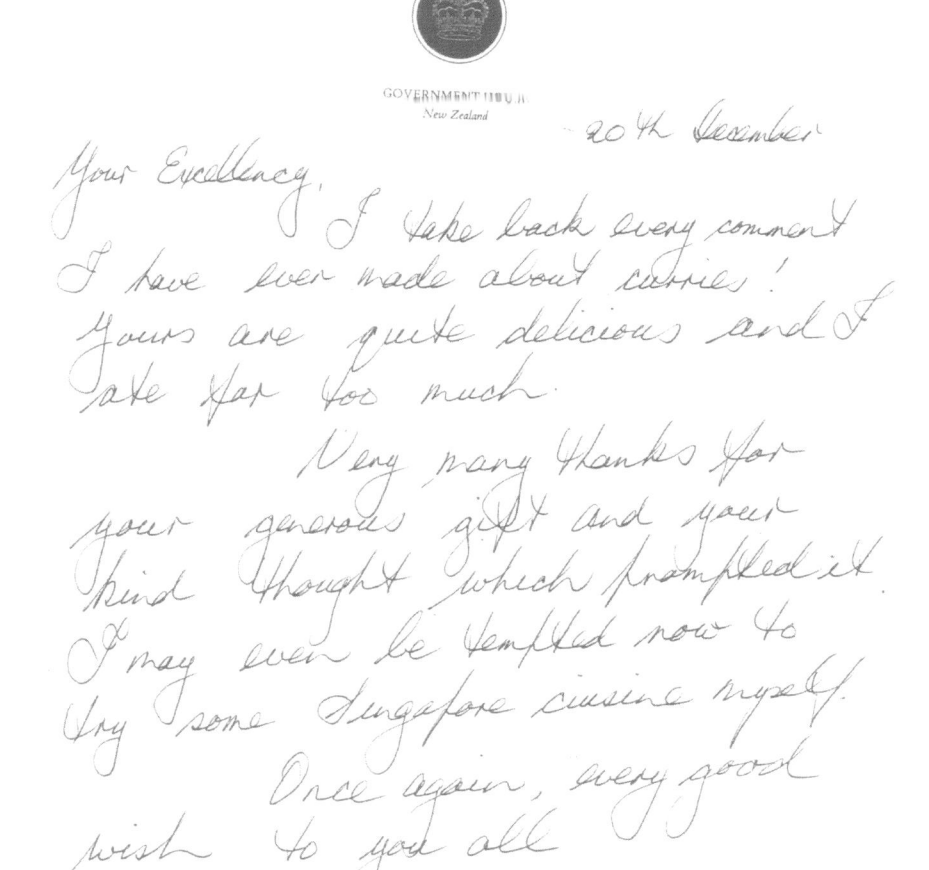

20th December

Your Excellency,

I take back every comment I have ever made about curries! Yours are quite delicious and I ate far too much.

Very many thanks for your generous gift and your kind thought which prompted it. I may even be tempted now to try some Singapore cuisine myself.

Once again, every good wish to you all

Yours sincerely
Catherine Tizard.

Photo 103   Letter to me from the Governor-General of New Zealand.

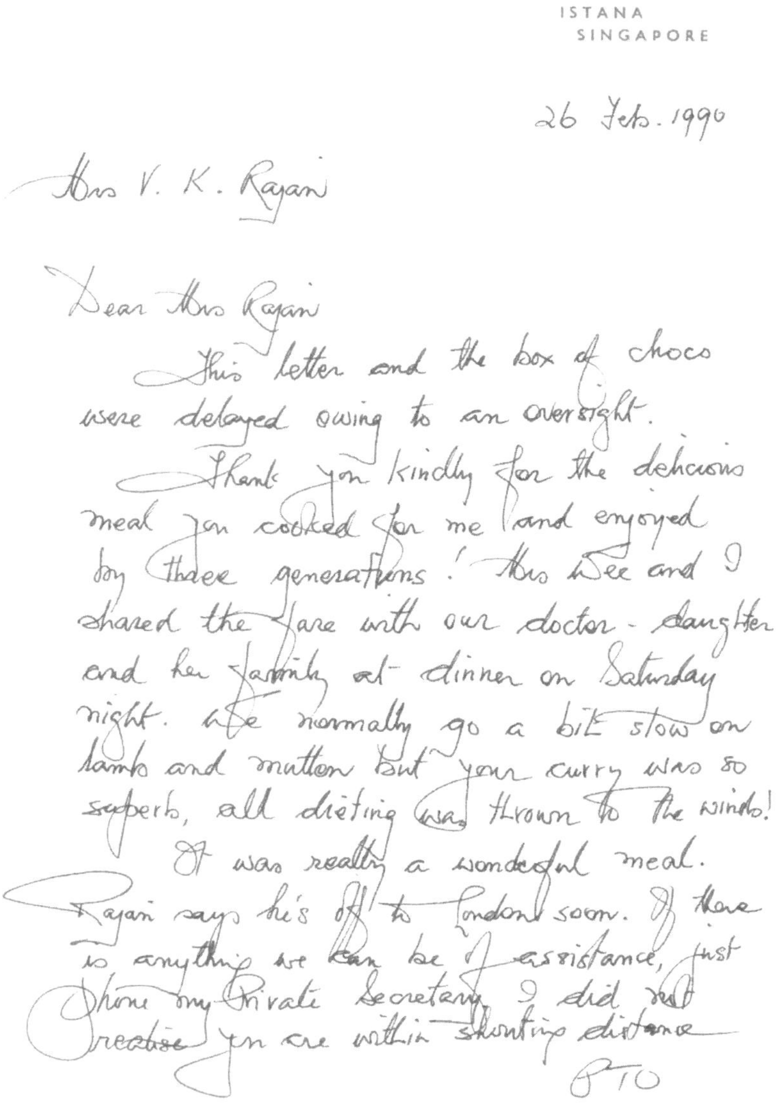

ISTANA
SINGAPORE

26 Feb. 1990

Mrs V. K. Rajan

Dear Mrs Rajan

This letter and the box of chocs were delayed owing to an oversight.

Thank you kindly for the delicious meal you cooked for me and enjoyed by three generations! Mrs Wee and I shared the fare with our doctor-daughter and her family at dinner on Saturday night. We normally go a bit slow on lamb and mutton but your curry was so superb, all dieting was thrown to the winds!

It was really a wonderful meal. Rajan says he's off to London soon. If there is anything we can be of assistance, just phone my Private Secretary. I did not realise you are within shouting distance

PTO

Photo 104 Letter from President Wee Kim Wee.

Wee Kim Wee

9 April '91

Mr & Mrs V. K. Rajan

Dear Vijaya & Rajan,

Thank you for the very delicious food you specially prepared for Mrs Wee and me. The whole family enjoyed it last evening.

Mrs Wee, as you know, loves cooking, especially spicy food, and if she says a dish is good the cook or chef is highly commended.

We hope to have a good chat with you before you go off for your next posting.

With warm regards,

Photo 105   Letter from President Wee Kim Wee.

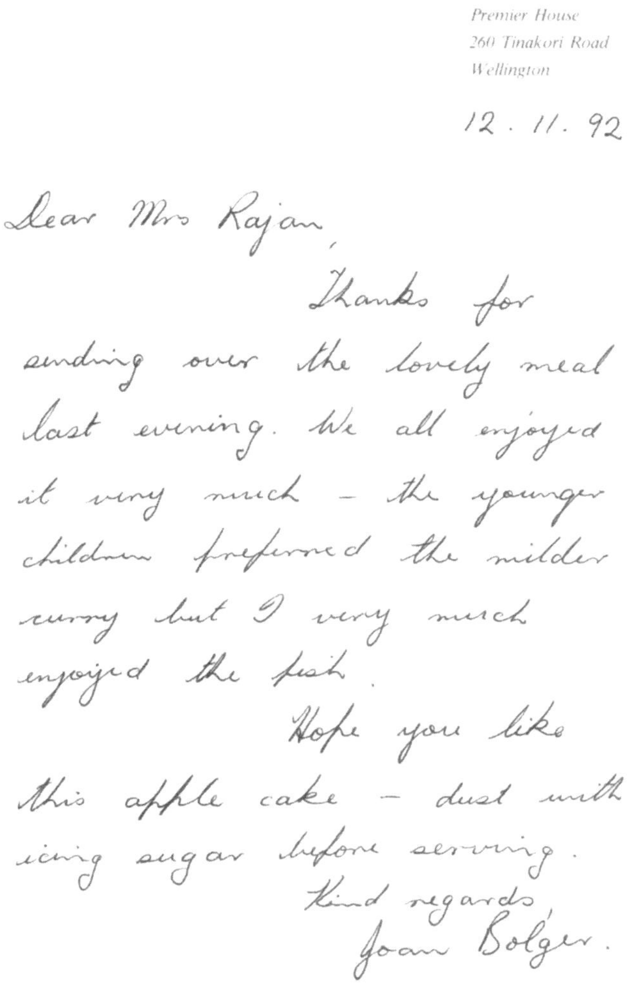

> Premier House
> 260 Tinakori Road
> Wellington
>
> 12.11.92
>
> Dear Mrs Rajan,
>
> Thanks for sending over the lovely meal last evening. We all enjoyed it very much — the younger children preferred the milder curry but I very much enjoyed the fish.
>
> Hope you like this apple cake — dust with icing sugar before serving.
>
> Kind regards,
> Joan Bolger.

Photo 106 Letter to my wife from Mrs Joan Bolger, wife of Prime Minister Jim Bolger of New Zealand.

"I have learned to look upon nature not in the hour of thoughtless youth but hearing often times the still sad music of humanity"

William Wordsworth

Photo 107   My ride through the beautiful **Bukit Batok Nature Reserve, Singapore** (circa 2004) on my favourite bicycle. (Note my skinny legs!) In the rustic background I was born into, learning to ride a bicycle very early in a child's life was necessary for both as a means of personal transport and to convey goods. I enjoy my rides and I took this bicycle (a rugged mountain bike which weighs not very much less than my own body weight) with me to Bahrain (*below*).

Relations with Neighbours

Photo 108 Me with the bike in Bahrain.

Photo 109   "*A thing of beauty is a joy forever, its loveliness increases and will never pass into nothingness*" English poet, John Keats.

These are pictures of the temple dedicated to Lord Shiva in Tanjore taken during first visit with my family in 1973. According to one account the Temple was built more than 1500 years ago. Above is a section of the Tanjore Temple complex with a close-up of the ***Rajagopuram*** ("king tower" in literal translation). I am most distressed to learn from widely reported sources that in recent years a large number of priceless deities including a large number of original ***Shiva lingas*** (as old as the Temple itself) have been removed (looted) and sold abroad for huge sums. In their place, fakes were installed. Several media reports have alleged that the crimes were committed by a group consisting of high officials, including lawmakers, trustees of the Temple, with the police probably involved. Many other ancient temples have also suffered a similar fate. **The nation is continuously losing its priceless and irreplaceable ancient cultural treasures. It is a crime against future generations.**

Photo 110   **(Photo continued on facing page)** high and placed with such symmetry and high degree of precision, and the whole structure still stands in sound condition, defying the vagaries of time throughout the many millennia. Every block is beautifully sculptured from top to bottom and carry ornate carvings of literature from the Vedas (believed to date back to 7000 years) in the language of the time. For all the "progress" man has made since, there is still much to know and to learn. **These magnificent works of art have stood the test time but will they survive the pollution that engulfs the world now?**

Photo 110 Me and my family made several pilgrimages to temples mostly **Tamil Nadu in India.** This temple and a few more, have been placed in the UNESCO heritage list. The pilgrimage also included another bigger and magnificent temple at **Srirangam,** and if I recall correctly, according to an international documentary it was built about 4000 years ago.

Just being in their presence is awe inspiring and exhilarating. They are much more than the ancient man's eternal homage to God. They are also a marvel of timelessness, combining absolute mastery of architecture, geology, engineering, astronomy, teachings of the Vedas, the Universe and more.

One account given by an official of the temple (shown in the pictures), a team of German archaeologists, architects and engineers who studied the temple structure were baffled. The team could not figure out as to how the thousands of granite blocks, each estimated to weigh about 80 tons, were lifted that

Chapter 16

SLUMS TO SHINING METROPOLIS

"Not all elected governments embark on housing programmes for the workers. In fact, the conspicuous absence of these programmes even after a decade of independence from colonial rule is a sad phenomenon in Asia. Some national governments after obtaining freedom from imperial rule followed the example of their imperial predecessors. They spent vast sums of public funds on prestige buildings and monuments, status symbols to satisfy their urge to immortality and to awe and overwhelm their voters into submission"

—*PM Lee Kuan Yew*

Many visiting high dignitaries were struck by the fact that they did not see slums in Singapore, noting that we were unique in this regard. **Tanin Kraivixien,** prime minister of Thailand, remarked to me during his official visit that he had not seen slums and asked me whether there was any. I informed him that we had them before but not any longer. He looked astonished and remarked that it was not typical of Asia. Probably, he must have wondered to himself how we managed to solve the problem when it had not been possible in many other countries, including his own.

A DIFFICULT PROBLEM

Our success did not come easy or without pain. Like slums elsewhere, there were also criminal elements embedded into ours and were a force to be reckoned with. However, unlike in many other countries, our slum dwellers were offered Housing Development Board flats and, as far as possible, jobs as near to their new locality as possible. Even then, there was resistance. **Politically it was a tough situation as the squatters were a significant vote bank for the Government. It was also not easy for the civil servants on frontline duty to clear slums.**

During **my term as Deputy Collector of Land Revenue in the Land Office from 1964 to 1966**, I was in charge of State Land in the North East (Yio Chu Kang & Pungol). Among my duties was dealing with encroachments and clearing illegal dwellings. It was not easy for the people affected either. They had been there for a very long time, two or three generations in some cases, earning their livelihood (many had thriving businesses), and being reliant on the locality for various needs, including schooling for children. In short, it was a very emotional issue, in addition to hardship arising from economic and social dislocation.

We had to be sensitive and patient. When a firm decision was taken by the Cabinet to clear illegal occupations, many government departments and agencies had to come together and work in coordination. Above all, **political will was the most important** factor. The Member of Parliament (MP) for the constituency concerned was a key factor in this regard. There were no quick fixes or easy rides. In a typical case, the people affected were informed well in advance of the plan to resettle them, told how it would be done, offered compensation if eligible, and given a Housing and Development Board (HDB) flat (not free but allocated on priority basis), as far as was possible, in a locality of their choice. Also, they were assisted in finding employment. By then of course the MP concerned would have met most if not all of them several times during his **"meet the people" sessions.**

Usually, some would accept the Government's offer and decide to move out, knowing that in their circumstance it would be better overall, especially considering their children's future. However, a significant number would stay put. Complicating the equation was the Communist dominated and Communist fronted political parties and unions exerting their influence on the squatters and others affected, to resist and to not move out. Therefore, it was a drawn-out process and had to be handled carefully and sensitively.

After several months, a formal **"Notice to Quit"** and a letter on the government's resettlement package were issued to those affected. At this point, I noticed growing antagonism towards us the civil servants involved, as, to them, we were the **"face of the Government"**. We continued to monitor the situation and usually there was no movement on the ground. Many would appeal both to the Land Office and to the MP and this process would go on for several more months. It was important they be given a polite and sympathetic hearing all the way, even if there was no way the decision to resettle could be reversed. When this stage was reached, we faced hostility and sometimes threats to our personal safety from those affected. There were also complaints against us, on one pretext or another, to the political leadership but we took them in our stride and remained unprovoked and undeflected from our duty. However, in cases where there was genuine difficulty in vacating the site by a given date, an extension of time was given, after very careful consideration by the higher authorities.

The above process took about year or more to play out before we decided to bite the bullet and fix the **Demolition Date** or aptly "D Day". Serving the **"Notice of Demolition"** was particularly difficult. As could be expected, no one wanted to accept it and we had to paste it on the structure itself, ignoring, in the process, the intimidation and the obstruction tactics of those affected. We (myself and the Land Baliffs) were accompanied by police escorts. Many a time the D-Day had to be postponed, due to pending decisions on the last ditch appeals to higher authorities. However, after a suitable lapse of time, we had to proceed with the demolition work. There was one instance when the last-minute decision to postpone the demolition came too late. At the very last minute, the Minister concerned decided to give the squatters affected a short reprieve, but that decision could not be communicated to me at the site in time. The demolition squad with protection from the **Police Reserve Unit** had already completed the task. I learned of the decision only when I returned to office later in the day. In those days there was no mobile telephones. Even landlines were a luxury for the average household and there was also a waiting period to get one installed.

Implementing the resettlement package went into high gear with utmost urgency. It was necessary to allow for a cooling off period after the demolition. We kept away from the site for a few weeks for tempers to cool before resuming our normal duties in that area. It was important that the vacant site was secured by appropriate means. Over a period of time, squatters generally became confident of the government resettlement policy and its fair deal, even if not everyone affected was totally satisfied.

My job then had another inconvenience, in that my field trips to state lands required transport. The motorcycle I bought, with a government loan of $980 to be repaid in three years, had limitations. The hot sun was not a problem but going on site visits in remote areas during wet weather was messy and risky. My salary was not high enough to qualify for a motor car loan. Later, pooling the proceeds of the sale of my motorcycle, my savings and a loan from the family, I bought a Volkswagen car.

On a personal note, my parents were not happy that I had bought the motorcycle. They thought it was too dangerous and always wanted me to get rid of it. They had known and heard of cases of fatal accidents involving motor cyclists. While I could understand their concern, I had no choice as I needed the transport for my work. One day my father came to my office to see for himself that I was alive and safe. Apparently, someone had told him that morning, after I had left for work, that there was a serious accident involving a motorcycle in Bukit Timah and that it was a red colour machine like mine. He then hurried to see me in my office then in City Hall. Like any youth, I liked speed (not reckless speeding) but I did take protective measures like wearing a crash helmet and a leather jacket, none of which were compulsory in law then.

HOMES FOR THE PEOPLE

The history of HDB and its very successful **"Homes for the People"** policy has been internationally acclaimed. A key factor in this was the clearing of the slums and resettling of the squatters in modern and affordable housing estates with comprehensive support facilities. As mentioned earlier, in the context of the economic, political and social conditions and tensions of the time, it was indeed a difficult task for the government, and it required much courage and political will. When a massive fire broke out in the slums of Bukit Ho Swee in 1963, troublemakers in the underworld spread rumours that the fire was lit deliberately by government agents to clear the squatter colony and not pay compensation. The truth was it was an accident waiting to happen. The colony was a maze of *attap*-roofed wooden shacks so closely packed that even the fire engines could not get access to the inner areas to douse the flames. It took much time to contain the flames. An exploding firecracker could easily have engulfed the slum colony within minutes.

LACK OF POLITICAL WILL IN MANY COUNTRIES

I would like to compare how other countries dealt or did not deal with the acute problems faced by its people in the margins of the community. During my term as Chief of Protocol in the 1980s, I had to deal with a problem faced by our High Commission in New Delhi. A squatter colony just behind the compound was causing hygiene and security problem for our mission and the staff. Every morning our staff had to contend with the stench of faeces and urine from the ablutions done during the night and early morning around the compound. The squatter colony consisted of rudimentary shacks with no water and no electricity, never mind toilets. Repeated requests to the Indian Ministry of External Affairs (MEA) fell on deaf ears. The dignity of our diplomatic mission was being violated and the failure of the Government of India, as the receiving State, to act was in this regard a contravention of Vienna Convention on Diplomatic Relations 1961 (VCDR).

I took it up with the Indian High Commissioner in Singapore, a political appointee, and again to no avail. However, he confided in me that the slum was a "vote bank" for the Congress Party (then in government). I noticed that, he being a leader in the Congress Party himself, had no incentive to resolve the problem. The bureaucrats in MEA probably felt embarrassed but were powerless to act, assuming they even wanted to. Far from acting as required, the Indian government dug a bore well to provide water for the squatters, thereby giving the colony semblance of permanence. It was done to secure votes in elections.

Many well-meaning commentators had pointed out that it was the perpetuation, and not the eradication, of poverty that served the interest of all political parties in the country. Come election time the ritual incantation and mantra of all political parties was the eradication of poverty, amongst other promises, if they were voted into power, only to be forgotten immediately after the election. This saga has been going on since independence and the masses had come to accept it. This is also the situation in many other countries in the region and beyond.

In some countries, the leaders did not want any reference to slums in their midst. During my term in Egypt, there was an advertisement for low-cost refrigerators with a rural setting as a background. Many thought it was quite humourous. However, it did not amuse President Mubarak and he ordered it to be taken off. Instead, he wanted the posh lifestyle of the very tiny upper class depicted in the advertisement!

There were also a few countries that adopted a knee-jerk and shock treatment to clear slums. They sent in demolition goons supported by the military, destroyed the dwellings and the means of livelihood with it, forcibly transported those affected and dumped them elsewhere without providing them with any housing, jobs and other means of survival. Before long, those thus evicted found their way back with more resentment and created even bigger problems.

In my observation, slum clearance does not succeed unless it is accompanied by a fair and honest resettlement package, including housing and job opportunities. Equally important, is political will on the part of the authorities to implement them fairly, firmly and with conviction.

In this context, it is worth recalling what PM Lee said:

> **"Not all elected governments embark on housing programmes for the workers. In fact, the conspicuous absence of these programmes even after a decade of independence from colonial**

rule is a sad phenomenon in Asia. Some national governments after obtaining freedom from imperial rule followed the example of their imperial predecessors. They spent vast sums of public funds on prestige buildings and monuments, status symbols to satisfy their urge to immortality and to awe and overwhelm their voters into submission."

(From the publication **"Towards Tomorrow"** a collection of Essays on Development and Social transformation in Singapore published by the Singapore National Trade Union Congress.)

POLITICAL CORRECTNESS

An important underpinning in our public housing policy not often realised abroad is the allocation of flats in a way that reflects broadly the racial composition of the population, in each block of flats. The objective was to avoid different communities forming their own enclaves based on racial, religious and linguistic factors. It was necessary to foster communal harmony through social interaction and integration. This policy was not without problems or even critics, mainly from the West, but it was necessary. Our leaders did not opt for the easier politically correct route. I have given several examples of this in other chapters.

Many European countries also had similar problems. According to a much-watched international television documentary channel, there were few unofficial **"no go areas"** for police in Paris. Sometime around 1996, Lee Kuan Yew (Senior Minister then) attended an energy conference organised by Total (French energy giant) in Abu Dhabi. Lee Kuan Yew was then an adviser to Total. I was then non-resident Ambassador to the United Arab Emirates. During the dinner hosted by Total, the French business leaders raised some problems, including security, caused by immigrants and the adverse impact on business climate in France.

Their minister gave an evasive response. I quietly asked the French guest seated on my left why they had allowed the problem to fester for so long, since the immigration started decades ago, and the problem could not have erupted overnight. His response: "Yes, you are right... please ask the minister". The corporate titans could not absolve themselves of blame either. They were happy as immigrants flooded in during the decades before, when the French economy was short of manpower, especially for the lower end jobs. But not only was there no efforts made to assimilate the immigrants, there were no serious attempts to address their problems, including unemployment and the lack of housing. Much of the immigrants were Muslims from the former French colonies in North Africa.

The frequent terrorist attacks in France in recent years, by **home grown religious extremists** with ISIS connections, claimed large numbers of civilian casualties and took a heavy toll on the people of **France**, who were facing frequent "lock downs" in affected areas and were often placed in a "state of emergency". **The question is "when" not "if" the next attack will come.**

Another serious problem hit France in November 2018 when protests throughout France erupted because President Macron introduced the fuel tax as part of his economic reform to improve France's competitiveness. Initially, the protests were peaceful but turned very violent later. They torched buildings and even national monuments were vandalised causing much damage to the economy. The protesters wearing yellow vests as their symbol increased their demands and continued their protests over several weekends accusing Macron government of being pro-rich and anti-poor. They caused massive disruptions in much of the country. Macron government was both stunned and shocked and one minister said it was "catastrophic". Macron government caved-in and was forced to withdraw the tax, grant wage rises and order benefits as well. In his statement, Macron blamed the past policies (read populist policies) which the population had become accustomed to over many decades.

Once the necessary discipline is lost, it is difficult for any leader to implement the reforms necessary. The **"yellow vest protesters"** appeared to be in no mood de-escalate and their actions are being adopted in few other countries in Europe, as well. At the time of writing, the yellow vest protests have spread to much of Europe and is still on going after 11 months. Unable to placate the protesters with concessions and subdue them by using the police force, Macron used the army to quell them without much success. The use of the soldiers has enraged not just the yellow vest protesters but many other sections of French society from across the political divide. As of now (September 2019), it appears that there is no light at the end of the tunnel. Even Macron's promise of big reforms to redress the imbalance between the wealthy elite and the struggling working class and an admission that his style of implementing of policies was wrong did not appeal to the demonstrators.

The Germans took in a large number of Turks during their boom years and, together with the German-born second generation, the number has increased to about two million. Many had risen to high positions, including law makers in the Bundestag (Parliament). However, with little assimilation, they remained separate, displaying their distinctive culture, religious practices and social network. It was reported that, by and large, their loyalties lay with Turkey, a factor **President Recep Tayyip Erdogan** of Turkey has skilfully manipulated in the conduct of Turkey's relations with Germany, much to the annoyance of the latter. Curiously, in 2015 or thereabout, the Germans opened their floodgates to welcome near million refugees from North Africa. For refugees wishing to settle in

Europe, Germany was and still is the number one choice! Needless to say, the frequent clashes in German cities since then between the locals and the refugees are the outcome of the German policy in this regard. All these in addition to the frequent terrorist attacks in German cities which claim many deaths and result in property destruction. I often wondered how the **German Chancellor, Angela Merkel**, who is probably the most effective and long serving political leader in post-war Germany, could have made a decision to welcome at one go so many refugees who brought with them very different religious faith, beliefs and cultural practices that were bound to create social problems, which in the event they did.

The irony is that it was the policy of the Western powers (principally US, UK and France) that created the refugee crisis in Europe. These powers intervened in Libya to change the regime of Colonel Muamar Gadhafi resulting in his killing rather gruesomely. The Western powers brought about the regime change which was not authorised by the relevant United Nations resolution. Whatever his shortcomings, Gadhafi was able to maintain peace and a level of prosperity for his people, and there were no refugees leaving through or from Libya during the long years he was in power. With Gadhafi gone and the country plunged into violent and destructive infighting between various opposing armed factions and groups (still ongoing and with no end in sight, at the time of writing), Libya has become, amongst other things, the exit point for refugees and economic migrants to Europe from Africa. Unscrupulous human traffickers were doing very profitable business using Libya as the base, sending the refugees in leaky and often not seaworthy boats. Large numbers perished and those who survived the perilous journeys faced uncertain future on EU shores. The relentless flow of refugees is causing strains in the relations among EU members. Just in May 2018 alone, more than 160 refugees were saved from drowning by an Italian coastguard vessel, but it was refused permission to land the refugees in Italian ports and was ordered to proceed to Malta, but Malta promptly banned the vessel. Finally, it was headed for Spain. The just elected prime minister of Italy warned that it was not acceptable that his country has become the **"refugee capital of Europe"**, and that European Union as whole must take responsibility for their resettlement. Pointedly, he noted that at the then rate of resettlement, of refugees who were already in, it **would take 100 years to get them out of Italy!**

It is pertinent in this regard to recall how we in Singapore avoided a serious refugee crisis at the height of Vietnam war, despite pressure and criticism from Western governments, liberals, and media. I have referred to the **Western hypocrisy** in this matter in an earlier chapter.

Chapter 17

"INNOVATE OR EVAPORATE"

"The Sun never set on the British Empire" and some locals parroted it as well. Years later, a Scotsman told me that the Sun indeed never set on the British Empire only because **"God did not trust the Englishmen in the dark!".**

HRH Prince Phillip, Duke of Edinburgh, *observed "...it looks like the whole of Singapore is under renovation". On a previous transit visit, he described Singapore as* **"a boom town".**

During his term as Finance Minister, Dr Richard Hu emphasised the stark choice for Singapore: **"either innovate or evaporate"**. According to the staff who worked under him, he prioritised financial prudence. His personal assistant used to double up as press secretary as well. He had minimal staff and to my understanding they were not unhappy in their jobs, very hard-pressed as they would have been.

The conventional thinking was that there could not be much room for innovation in the civil service owing to its traditions and the very nature of its operation. However, the age of globalisation and rapidly advancing technology which imposed so many challenges and demands, the civil service could not stand aside and allow itself to be overwhelmed. Innovation had many forms and shapes. Nevertheless, transparency and accountability are paramount and cannot be sacrificed at any cost. Notwithstanding the challenges, there was no alternative but to innovate as much as possible without undermining the core values of the civil service.

Here is an early example. For the traditional group photograph of the Heads of Government during CHOGM in 1971, PM Lee wanted the background to depict Singapore as a bustling maritime hub. The problem was all the big ships were in Keppel Harbour and could not be towed to the waters adjacent to the Conference Hall (in Shenton Way) because of inadequate depth in the water. The Port of Singapore Authority did the calculations quickly and towed in suitable size ships thus, providing the required backdrop.

Here are a few examples of innovation I made in the line of my duties.

AMBASSADORS PRESENTING CREDENTIALS

During my term as Chief of Protocol, I observed that some ambassadors, especially those who were ambassadors for the first time, were a bit uneasy and sometimes nervous during the ceremony of presenting credentials to the President at the Istana. We had a booklet on the ceremony, but it was not enough for some. Therefore, I decided to video tape the entire ceremony on VHS tape. There was no SD card then.

It was a big hit among the new ambassadors. When I played the video to a new Japanese Ambassador, he complimented me and said that he was going to recommend to the Imperial Staff in the Palace in Tokyo that they should adopt the same practice. I was surprised and I told him that it was Japanese technology. An interesting twist to this came about six years later when I was Ambassador in Egypt. I received a call from our then Chief of Protocol (name redacted) to find out how the video was made and by which government agency. I was told that the picture quality in the two videos I made had degraded to the point that it was unusable. I was surprised to note that no attempt had been made to make a new video. Anyway, I told him that I arranged it on my own and paid for it ($200) from my pocket, since I was told that "there was no financial provision for this purpose in the Ministry's budget". By the time this call came to me, SD card was easily available, widely in use and, therefore, cost was no issue at all.

Another change I made was in the announcement of the names of the ambassadors to the President when the ambassadors presented their credentials. Until then, it was the practice, as in many other countries, to read the name from a paper and sometimes only the last name in cases where the names were long and not easy to pronounce. This was to avoid fumbling as sometimes full names could be tongue twisters. I decided that the courtesy of announcing the name in full (and with aplomb) would be appreciated, and earn goodwill. There was a Soviet ambassador by the name of **Boris Vasilyavich Bezurukovnicov** whose name I announced in full. He appeared impressed and after the event he told me that in his previous posting the chief of protocol there only announced his last name and even then, not correctly. I also adopted this practice when introducing local and foreign VIP guests to the guest of honour and the host, respectively, during official and state visits. It was not difficult but required some effort.

VISIT OF QUEEN ELIZABETH

Another interesting case for me was the visit of Queen Elizabeth in 1989. It was a common practice in protocol then (and could be still in some countries) to erect welcome arches along roads, festoon lamp posts with buntings, banners and flags of both countries (host and guest), to announce the visit of a head of state from another country at the invitation of the head of state of the receiving country. During my term in London, I had observed that The Mall stretching from Buckingham Palace at one end to the Admiralty Arch at the other end had these ceremonial decorations during such visits, although I could not remember seeing special welcoming arches.

I do not think anybody can deny that the British with their long royal and imperial traditions are very good in protocol and in conducting ceremonies with much pomp, finesse and aplomb. It was, in my view, also an important instrument of policy to portray their sense of imperial power, glory and grandeur in ruling a vast and a far-flung empire. During my school years, the British teachers used to tell us very proudly that the **"The Sun never set on the British Empire"** and some locals parroted it as well. Years later, a Scotsman told me that the Sun indeed never set on the British Empire only because **"God did not trust the Englishmen in the dark!"**. The British teachers also made us sing **"Britannia rules the waves"**. In later years we used tell ourselves "Britannia waves the rules".

However, for the Queen's visit we had not erected arches or decorated the lamp posts. What we did was to have welcome cloth banners at the sites the Queen visited. Spontaneous small crowds of people gathered to greet the Queen.

Before the start of the visit the British were not very happy over what they perceived to be a lack of warmth on our part and they quietly made it known to my superiors. I was asked to explain by my superiors. I summed it up as follows:

- to my knowledge arches were erected during colonial times for British royal visits but not since self-government and independence;

- the Queen stayed at the Istana and arches along the very busy Orchard Road would impede traffic flow day and night;
- as a commercial hub we had to minimise traffic congestion; and
- that **what may be perceived as lacking in form we would more than make it up in substance.**

I could not be sure whether the British accepted the above explanation at that time, but I heard nothing further. (Another point to note here is the fact it was a tradition for the British monarch as head of the Commonwealth to open the Commonwealth Prime Ministers' Conference (later CHOGM) in London. The Meeting in Singapore was the first outside London and the Queen was not present to open it. Whether that factor played in the British mind I could not say. To my knowledge, all other subsequent Meetings whenever and wherever they were held, they were opened by the Queen.)

There was also another somewhat tricky issue to be settled. Apparently, the British High Commission had been making it known quietly that ladies should curtsey to the Queen when presented to her. Many, including wives of ministers amongst them, asked me what they should do. I advised them that they were not required to courtesy. My reason was that we are citizens of our independent and sovereign republic and not subjects of the British Crown, any longer. In the United Kingdom and in the countries where the Queen was still head of state, for example, Canada, Australia, New Zealand and Fiji, ladies generally did and probably were expected to do so. But even in those countries the practice was not universal, especially with the younger generation. I had seen television footage of Prime Minister Paul Keating escorting the Queen with his hand around her back during her visit to Australia and it raised many eyebrows. Be that as it may, the British officials were probably disappointed that our ladies did not curtsey to the Queen, but

I had the impression that they were not too concerned, at least outwardly.

The visit went well judging from the two letters I received from the British High Commissioner and the Queen's Private Secretary. Essentially, the Queen and her entourage were not unhappy over the way the programmes were executed and the achievements of the visit, in substantive terms. It also gave me and my team satisfaction that from then on what we did became a standard operating procedure (a template in IT jargon) for such visits. It was also not a difficult visit to organise, elaborate protocol notwithstanding. Both the Queen and Prince Phillip were punctual, kept to the arranged programme and related well to those around. I had a sense that they must have been impressed by the developments they saw. Here is an anecdote. We had arranged a lunch for the entourage at the Compass Rose restaurant on top of the Westin Stamford Hotel. While taking in the panoramic view and seeing large number of very tall cranes at construction sites all around, **His Royal Highness Prince Phillip,** observed "…**it looks like the whole of Singapore is under renovation**". On a previous transit visit, he described Singapore as "**a boom town**".

I was also happy that the British took particular note of how we presented guests to the Queen. We developed the practice of lining up guests in "U" formation beginning with Singapore guests followed by foreign guests all in order of seniority. I, as Chief of Protocol, introduced the Singaporean guests to the Queen and **Prince Phillip** as we proceeded along the line of guests. Our President, PM and their spouses were also with them. When we reached the end of Singapore guests, the British chief protocol stepped in and introduced their entourage to our VVIPs. (I had informed the British side in advance concerning this arrangement.) After that we arranged for selected Singapore guests to interact with the Queen and Prince Phillip and selected British guests to interact with our VVIPs, while other guests from both sides mingled among themselves. This arrangement enabled in depth conversation on matters of interest beyond mere pleasantries and enabled an efficient management of time.

The next day the British High Commissioner complimented me on the proceedings saying that it was a cross between the practices in **Buckingham Palace and Kensington Palace**. I told him that I was not aware of their practice in this regard. I explained that we developed our arrangement to save time, achieve a smooth operation and at the same time give enough time to the host and the guest of honour to interact with the selected guests from both sides. I gathered the impression from our High Commissioner in London that the British were considering the merits in adopting our practice. The **British High Commissioner** paid a big compliment to me. In his letter dated 12 October, 1989 to me, he said, amongst other things, *"As I told the Foreign Minister at the Reception on board the HMY Britannia last night, Singapore could not have a better Head of Protocol (and he agreed)"*. Coming from the British, it was a good compliment. As a team, we delivered.

VISIT OF US VICE PRESIDENT DAN QUAYLE

The visit of **Dan Quayle**, US Vice President during the senior **George Bush** presidency, was quite a contrast. The advance US Team consisting of their protocol and secret service personnel wanted our airspace closed for about an hour before the Air Force Two landed and wanted to freeze all movements in Changi Airport. The Americans also wanted the same arrangements for departure. I was aghast and told them straight away that Changi Airport was a vital component of our economy and its operations could not be disrupted. I emphasised that we had handled similar situations before, had no problems in that regard and that they should speak to their ambassador, Daryl Arnold, who had a good appreciation of the situation in Singapore. I also remarked that there were hundreds of airports in the US and closing even a few at any one time would not hurt them.

Daryl did come with the advance team but excused himself after introductions to attend to an "urgent matter". I knew it was diplomatic excuse and that he did not want to be with them when this difficult issue came up. In a private conversation after the visit, he confided in me that it would have been awkward for him to be there and not be seen pressing their case. He told me "anyway I was confident you would handle it satisfactorily". Seeing our resolve, their secret service did not press the case. Probably, they were used to having their way in other countries, in such circumstances and it had become a force of habit to insist on such arrangements wherever they went.

In my experience and observation, Daryl was one of the best US ambassadors who had served in Singapore. He had a thriving orange growing enterprise in California, was a Republican and a first-time political appointee. Yet, he did well to promote bilateral relations. He and his good wife, Shirley, had many friends and were well liked and regarded in Singapore. Frequently, we received boxes of good quality oranges as gifts from Daryl and Shirley.

I need to outline here the government rules with regards to public servants receiving gifts in the course of their duties. The rule is that public servants should not receive or expect to receive gifts from anyone. The reason is obvious, and it applies to all, **without exception**, from the head of state down to those in the public service. However, if in circumstances it would cause embarrassment to the giver, it can be accepted, and the gift sent afterwards to the

Accountant General (AG) for valuation. The "VALUATION OF GIFTS RECEIVED BY GOVERNMENT OFFICERS" form has five parts on a single sheet of paper. In **Part I** the officer states his relevant particulars, description of the gift(s), including the reason why the gift was offered and why it could not be refused and whether he/or she wants to retain the gift. This part is addressed to the relevant head of department, usually the permanent secretary, who then sends it to the Accountant General as provided in **Part II**. The AG acknowledges receipt and sends it to the permanent secretary as in **Part III**. After the valuation of the gifts, the AG sends the form back to the permanent secretary as in **Part IV,** who then sends it to the officer for his decision as to whether he wants to claim the gifts, paying for the cost as valued. In **Part V**, the permanent secretary sends the form back to the AG with the officer's decision, arranging for the collection of the gift concerned and "certify the $ — has been/will be collected from the officer's salary". Most of the time the gifts were left with the AG and in cases where they had special value to the officers concerned, they paid the amount valued and claimed it back. There also was no exceptions with regards to the type of gift received or its value and as I have said before the rule applies to everyone. Gifts not claimed are auctioned off by the AG and credited to Consolidated Revenue Account. Perishable gifts were distributed among staff or sometimes sent to charitable institutions, as appropriate. The oranges we received from Daryl were distributed among the Ministry staff and a record was made in the appropriate file.

In the Protocol and Consular Directorate which I headed, my protocol officers and I, as Chief of Protocol, received gifts quite often from dignitaries on official visits to Singapore. On occasions we received expensive watches like Rolex. They came with official certificates and in elegant boxes. I have heard from my staff that some those who received such gifts engraved their names on the gifts, for example on the back of the watches, before sending them for valuation. Their argument was since they want to retain the gift after paying the valuation, there was no problem. I did not agree and stopped the practice, in so far as my Directorate was concerned. I explained to them that if the gift did not come with the names already engraved when received from the VIPs concerned, it would not be right for the receiver to engrave the name before sending to AG. Also, once the name is engraved its market value would diminish. In such circumstances, we need to be absolutely correct. I purchased few watches that I received as gifts and none have my name on it. I did not also subsequently get them engraved, as there was no point in doing so. However, in one respect, I must admit that I was not far-sighted. I should have purchased the other watches I received as gifts during my long years as Chief of Protocol and they would have turned out to be a good investment!

I might also add here for the information of readers that an officer's duty is to declare **all** gifts received in the course of his or her duty, which includes all types of items, for example, cash, watches, paintings, cloth material, and more. (I learnt from foreign diplomats that in many countries there was no bar to accepting gifts by public officers; in other countries gifts up to certain value could be accepted. In Singapore the laws are strict and there is no discretion in this regard.) Public servants in Singapore are also not allowed to accept free air travel, free hotel accommodation and any form of similar benefits or gratification. I give below just three of the many examples which concerns me:

- For my journey home, **upon completion of my tour of duty** in New Zealand, I had booked air passages in premium economy class, at my expense, for my elder daughter and my mother-in-law, as they were not eligible for passage at government expense. The airline manager offered to upgrade them to a

higher class to be with me and my wife. The passage for my wife and I was paid for with government funds as per the rules then. The airline manager told me that it was nothing new in their operation. However, I did not feel comfortable. I declined it and wrote him a letter to thank him for his kind offer, and to explain that in compliance government rules, I had to decline. He seemed surprised;
- During one of my official visits to Cyprus (where I was a non-resident Ambassador), our Honorary Consul then, a very successful Greek Cypriot businessman, offered accommodation free-of-charge to me, my wife and the accompanying officer, in his own hotel. I politely declined his offer and in my letter to him thanked him for the kind offer and stated the same reasons as above as to why I had to decline. However, in this case, we did stay in his hotel but paid for our accommodation at the normal rate; and
- I was invited to deliver a paper at an international seminar on "Asia and the Gulf Cooperation" by the premiere think tank, **Emirates Centre for Strategic Studies and Research (ECSSR)** in Abu Dhabi. I was the non-resident Ambassador to the United Arab Emirates, as well. I was paid an honorarium of US$1000 and I duly sent it to our Ministry of Finance (through the Ministry of Foreign Affairs) for the money to be credited to Government revenue. The paper I delivered was published by ECSSR.

One of the most important and urgent tasks faced by our pioneer leaders, when they took charge of self-governing Singapore in 1959, was to enact laws and establish relevant institutions to fight corruption, in order to create an honest, clean and efficient Government. I have earlier mentioned the Prevention of Corruption Act and the strengthening of the powers the Corrupt Practices Investigation Bureau (CPIB). The rules and regulations concerning the receiving of gifts by public officials is just one component in the scheme of things.

However, at the core of this narrative is the integrity of Government institutions when it comes to dealing with citizens and taxpayers. Here is a good example of this. I read a report in our national newspaper that said **the Inland Revenue Authority of Singapore (IRAS) spent almost three months trying to locate a South Korean businessman to return to him a tax credit of about $100 which was due to him. Apparently, when that taxpayer left Singapore for good, he was not aware of the tax credit due to him and had not left his new contact details.** I also had similar experiences. On a few occasions I was informed by IRAS of tax credits due to me either owing to my incorrect calculation of the tax or overpayment of tax due. As a taxpayer, one can choose to receive the refund in cash or have it credited to their account to offset against future payment of tax. I must hasten to add that this practice is common in other Government institutions, as well. One foreign diplomat from a country in Europe, who had read the newspaper report, told me that he was amazed, and he praised our system. I think it bears repeating here that it is this integrity and the strict enforcement of the laws of the State that has enabled Singapore to punch above its weight in the global order.

RELOCATION OF US EMBASSY

The mark of a good and effective ambassador can be judged from the way he or she interacts with the host country — not just the government but with the wider community — and is able to find mutually acceptable solutions to difficult issues. During Ambassador Daryl Arnold's term, we had a thorny issue to resolve. The Chancery (office) of the US Embassy was then situated at Hill Street opposite the Chinese Chamber of Commerce. The Embassy had to be relocated because the site was required for road widening, to relieve severe traffic congestion. Under the Vienna Convention there was very little we could have done, if the US had refused to move. The US Government agreed to relocate but on certain conditions, and among them were, if I recall correctly, that they should get compensation for the Hill Street property at market rate, the Singapore government assist them in finding suitable alternative site, free of cost, be given sufficient time to build their new building. Our good relations with the US and the additional goodwill from Daryl played an important role. As could be expected, however, tough negotiations followed.

Daryl and I met often, both in the Ministry and at the sites. As could be expected in matters of this nature, it was a difficult and long drawn out negotiation. To maximise their bargaining position, Daryl would often claim that the State Department had no money in its budget to finance the project in Singapore and the Embassy had to find the funds required. My counter arguments went as follows:

- I could not believe that the world's number one economic superpower had no resources to build an embassy;
- the US Government already owned many bungalows in choice areas (in addition to the Hill Street property) which were occupied by the staff of the Embassy and if they sold just a few of them the proceeds would more than meet the cost of the land and erecting the new building; and
- I had noted that the US government built a new embassy building in the 1980s in Moscow at a cost of several million dollars only to tear much of it down and rebuild it again, upon discovering that the Soviets had bugged it extensively. I told Daryl that it was incredulous that the US Government had not anticipated that the Soviets would bug their embassy. Daryl sighed and said it was the mistake of the officers in his government who were dealing with the matter then.

In this regard, no country is totally immune. A staff in one of our embassies betrayed us to the receiving State (not very friendly to us then). The staff concerned was charged and duly punished with a long prison term. One of our diplomatic missions, in a country considered friendly to us, was bugged. Therefore, it is always of utmost importance that our staff concerned take every safeguard to protect the security of official documents, communication equipment, premises, personal security and other necessary precautions, wherever they operate, both at home and abroad. The point I want to make is that we cannot let our guard down. Vigilance without paranoia, should be the guiding principle.

Spying is probably the second oldest profession — the first is well known — in the world and is likely to continue, as long as mankind exists. There are no angels and no villains among nations in this regard. Only the methods vary; like in any other field of human endeavour, revolutions in technology and innovation have rendered many old methods and practices primitive. The array of the tools which are now easily available have enormous power and unimaginable sophistication. When an orbiting satellite deep in space can "read" the number plate of a car in the street anywhere in the world, then, there is no need to rely on those simple tools of an earlier era, except by those who cannot afford it or are not tech-savy. With the development of artificial intelligence there is much more to come in ways ordinary folks might not be able to comprehend.

But back to the US Embassy case, we identified a piece of state land in Napier Road suitable for the purpose, and then the question of valuation had to be dealt with. I must say that my previous experience as Deputy Collector of Land Revenue in the Land Office was helpful. When the negotiations reached a sticking point on the cost of the land, it could not be resolved at the level of officials. The cost of the land was finally agreed upon and the deal was struck by the political bosses, Minister Dhanabalan and the US Secretary of State George Schultz when the latter was in Singapore to attend an ASEAN meeting. As per our laws, the sale required Cabinet approval and we secured the approval. The Embassy sold several of its properties in Singapore to finance the building of their new Chancery. Both Dhanabalan and Schultz had good personal relations as well and were able to conclude the matter to mutual satisfaction.

When Daryl completed his assignment and returned home, Singapore appointed him Honorary Consul General of Singapore in the United States and to my understanding, he served us very well. Daryl and I had become very good friends by then. He and Shirley were to visit me and my wife in Cairo during our posting there and we were looking forward to their visit. By a twist of cruel fate, both of them met their untimely demise in a car crash in their hometown before they could make the trip to Cairo. Such is life.

RECIPROCITY

The core consideration in allocation of land for diplomatic missions is the principle of reciprocity, as stated in international law. There have been cases where Singapore did not receive full reciprocity. When the Soviet government bought a very big piece of land and built its very big embassy complex in Nassim Road, in the early years of our independence, we did not seek reciprocity. My understanding was that in Moscow, we were allotted a government owned apartment-like building. It happened very soon after our independence and we were still new to the game then.

In the 1980s, a newly independent and friendly country was allotted a very big piece of land in a choice area in Singapore to build the diplomatic mission complex, without securing proper enforceable reciprocity to build our diplomatic mission in that country, and we had to take our place in the queue there. Officer(s) dealing with the matter then had relied on verbal assurances given by the head of mission of the country concerned. In matters of this nature, such assurances are of little or no value. Government to government agreements by proper exchange of legal documents, simultaneous possession of land, and vesting of the legal titles to the lands in the respective governments, are necessary.

During my term as Chief of Protocol, an ambassador who had their country's embassy in a choice area, was sounding out a plan to develop part of their big land holding into a commercial complex, in collaboration with a big Singapore commercial developer. To do so, the embassy would need to move some of its operations to a new location and wanted our Government to help to find suitable land to acquire.

I did not have to think very much on this. Under the Vienna Convention the receiving State was obliged to assist the sending State in finding suitable premises to establish its diplomatic mission, including the residence for the head of mission. However, there was no such obligation to assist the sending State in a commercial enterprise, which was outside the duties and responsibilities of a diplomatic mission. I informed him straight away that we could not help in this regard. I believed he tried to bypass me and appeal to higher ups, but to no avail. I had briefed my superiors. At his farewell function, he made negative comments about Singapore, which is unusual behaviour for a diplomat. As it happened, I was posted about six months later to the same country (New Zealand) where he went after Singapore. I learnt from our staff, that he had bad mouthed Singapore there, as well. However, he appeared to change his tune after my arrival. He and his daughter congratulated me after one of the lectures I had given, which was also attended by members of the diplomatic corps.

DEVELOPING WIDER CONSTITUENCY FOR SINGAPORE

In my view, it is important for our diplomatic missions to engage with the wider community, for it to understand and appreciate

Singapore's policies and contributions to global peace and governance. During my posting in New Zealand, I gave several keynote addresses, lectures, talks and participated in panel discussions in universities, rotary clubs, farmers' group, at the invitation of their members of parliament, to speak to their constituents about Singapore. One of the keynote addresses I delivered in New Zealand was at University of Auckland, to commemorate the 25th anniversary of ASEAN, which was attended by people from many walks of life in the host community, diplomatic corps and the media. It was a very lively audience. I took questions both on Singapore and on ASEAN and my responses were well received. The message was not lost on the ambassador who had bad mouthed Singapore before my arrival.

Among those who engaged with me, was a senior journalist from the Auckland Herald newspaper. He asked me pointedly why Singapore was **"prickly and sensitive to criticism"**. I was expecting this and seized the opportunity to enlighten the audience about a political leader of a minor party in New Zealand, who had reacted to an article published in a Singapore tabloid — The New Paper. The Singaporean female journalist (who later became a Member of Parliament) wrote about 16 short pieces on New Zealand, after having toured the country. The articles were positive in appreciating the natural beauty and tranquillity of the country, and there was nothing in them really critical of New Zealand. There was, however, a passing mention of the increasing number of Kiwis on benefit (unemployment income). One article also noted that in the 1950s, the number of unemployed people in New Zealand could be counted in one hand. This irked the political leader concerned and it moved him to write a letter to the **Auckland Herald** stating that **New Zealand is a holiday resort compared to Singapore, which is a prison camp** or words to that effect. I told the audience that those who have read the letter in the newspaper would know who the leader was and in any case, the journalist must have known, or ought to have known. I asked the people in the audience: **"Now, you tell me who is sensitive to criticism?"**. The audience responded immediately with loud applause. After the Q&A, an elderly gentleman from the audience made his way to see me and complimented me on my performance saying that **"I always had high regards for Singapore and its people"**. In thanking him for the compliment, I asked him for his background, and he told me that he had served as his country's High Commissioner in Kuala Lumpur and was familiar with Singapore. I had no reason to be dissatisfied with my performance.

I received many invitations from universities, urban and rural communities, rotary clubs, members of parliament (for their constituency functions), business groups, and not to forget, the Singapore Club. I always asked the hosts for the topics they were interested in and usually they ranged from Singapore's development policy, bilateral relations, ASEAN and important developments in the regional and international landscape that could impact New Zealand and its relations with Asia. The next major keynote address I gave was at the Otego University in Dunedin (South Island) on the topic "ASEAN and New Zealand". Against the occasion was ASEAN's 25th Anniversary. There was a big gathering of academics and students of the University as well as, from other educational institutions, and members of the public. In a setting like that, I was prepared for searching, vigorous and not so polite questions, and they did come. One of the salient points I made in my address was that the "tyranny of distance" from teeming and "impoverished" Asia gave Australia and New Zealand in the past a sense of security. However, globalisation and booming economies in Asia had changed the dynamics. In fact, the first jolt for New Zealand and Australia came when their mother country, United Kingdom, joined the EEC (later EU) in 1973 and, in one stroke, both Australia and New Zealand lost their privileged access to export their agricultural produce to the UK, the mainstay of their economies then.

Therefore, the new reality was that both countries had to earn their living by exporting to the booming markets in Asia. I recall mentioning a New Zealand trade report which noted that the first harvest of Kiwi fruits went to South Korea and Singapore! To drive home my point more vigorously during my address, I quoted an article, from the University's noted and respected professor on international relations (Ramesh Thakur), that was published not long before, in the Auckland Herald, and probably in international media as well. In it, the professor had argued that while New Zealand in the past "sought security *from* Asia…. now it seeks security *in* Asia". (I remember reading this article during my car journey returning from Auckland to Wellington.) There was a momentary silence. The professor, who was moderating the Q&A session, said in his remarks that it was not often that a speaker would quote the chairperson, who was expected to stimulate discussion, in such a setting. Nevertheless, we had quite a lively session and after, I received another invitation to speak in Dunedin, to a different audience. The full text of my address was published in the **"New Zealand Institute of International Affairs Review"**.

Readers might be interested to know that my posting as High Commissioner to New Zealand was my first posting as Head of Mission. I learnt much and felt a sense of achievement from my mission. My family also enjoyed New Zealand. To round up, I would like to mention two anecdotes. One was my farewell reception, which a large number of invitees (selected government officials and from a cross-section of the wider community) attended, including the Foreign Minister Don McKinnon (who later became the Commonwealth Secretary General), who at that time had an extremely busy schedule. The other was a letter which the Secretary of that Ministry, Richard Nottage, a very experienced, able and respected diplomat, wrote to his friend, an assistant minister in the Egyptian Foreign Ministry. In introducing me, Nottage said, amongst other things, " …**New Zealand's loss is Egypt's gain**".

I received a similar gesture from another well-known and respected diplomat, our own Professor Tommy Koh. He wrote a letter to introduce me to his good friend, Dr Esmet Meguid, a veteran, respected Egyptian diplomat, and well-known former foreign minister. Introductions of this nature are useful in gaining access to the higher echelons of the government and the bureaucracy. They reduced my "running-in" period in the new environment. Learning from these courtesies so kindly extended to me, I also extended similar help to our diplomats whenever I could, and to foreign diplomats as well, in appropriate circumstances.

Reverting briefly to the need to engage with the wider community in the host country (receiving State), I noted that many diplomats, mostly from Asian and Middle Eastern countries, were not too keen to do so for fear of **"getting into trouble"**, especially with the media. In my view, this is wrong. In fact, it is the duty of the diplomats, especially the Ambassador, to seek an appreciation of his country's policies in the host country, not just among the government leaders, but in all influential sectors and groups in the wider community, in order to build enduring friendly relations for mutual benefit. At the same time, a vigorous defence of the policies of his home country, when appropriate and necessary, is very much part of the job. However, to be able to do so successfully, one needs to observe certain customs, norms, laws and conventions. My modus operandi for such situations was:

(a) to not react, either verbally or in writing, to **every** adverse report and article. I would, however, make mental and written note of it for later use, when circumstance warranted it;
(b) if it is a deliberate and orchestrated attack, or in circumstances when it was necessary to respond, I would act usually in consultation with Ministry headquarters. It had to be done quickly in order not to lose the impact of the response. If the attack was

not challenged when there was a clear necessity do so, it would amount to losing our good case by default. Each case must be considered on its potential damage to bilateral relations;
(c) to be effective in this job it was important to have a good command of up-to-date and credible information and statistics to demolish the allegations and insinuations;
(d) scrupulously comply with relevant provisions of Vienna Convention on Diplomatic Relations;
(e) there is a belief in some quarters that diplomats must **always** be nice and pleasant (soft) regardless of the seriousness of the situation. I do not subscribe to this view. On the contrary, I believe that it is the duty of the diplomat, as an official representative of his country, to vigorously prosecute his case using appropriate language in interventions (verbal or written), and in a body language that drives home the message intended, without causing offence, as far as possible. One must push the envelope to the very limit without breaching the relevant laws and customs; and
(f) as part of life, the diplomat should neither get carried away or be too pleased with accolades he may receive, nor should he be daunted by problems he may have to deal with. It should be noted that the credits he gets largely arise from his official position and not so much to him as a person. What matters, however, is the enduring respect he earns in the wider community and his success in achieving that is the real reward. It is also my belief that the good legacy he leaves behind will be helpful to his successors.

PROTOCOL IS BOTH A TOOL OF DIPLOMACY AND AN INSTRUMENT OF POLICY

The nature, purpose and importance of protocol in international relations had not been properly understood by many people, not just in Singapore, but in many other countries around the world, as well. When I called on the Egyptian Chief of Protocol immediately after my arrival in Cairo, one of the first things he said to me was that his "good work" was not being appreciated by the higher echelons in his Ministry. However, it must also be said that, like in most other professions, many chiefs of protocol contributed to such perceptions themselves. In the Egyptian case, I was not too impressed by his claim of the good work he had done.

When I first arrived, there was no one from their protocol team to receive me and assist through customs and immigration clearance, as is normal protocol. Our mission staff cleared me through the formalities and, when I was about to enter the car to leave for the hotel, an unimpressive and sullen looking man, probably in his thirties, turned up and identified himself as the protocol officer. He gave me the excuse that his car had broken down and later, ran out of petrol, as well.

As Chief of Protocol, I personally received the new heads of mission (HOM) on arrival at the airport. Also, I bid them farewell and sent them off at the airport upon completion of their tour of duty. It was taxing but the goodwill earned was worth it. While waiting in the VIP lounge for the immigration clearance and the arrival of the baggage, I would inform the newly arriving HOM of the programme, especially on matters relating to meetings and the details for their presentation of credentials. I made every effort for the HOM to call on our Minister and relevant senior officials, as quickly as possible, and then for them to present their credentials to the President, often within two weeks, or sooner. Usually, I received the HOM in my office the next working day to start the process.

The practice then was that only one HOM presented his/her credentials on a single day. This arrangement enabled the HOM to get operational very quickly, which often surprised them. For the information of readers, under VCDR the HOM cannot be fully operational until they are "accredited" by presenting the credentials to the head of state in the receiving State. However, pending accreditation, the HOM could present a copy of the credentials to the foreign minister and then carry on their duties, with certain limitations. Our efficiency was very much appreciated by the Diplomatic Corps. It is neither productive nor good manners to keep diplomats "in limbo".

It is important to make diplomats feel welcome and treat them well from the moment they set their feet on our soil. This is especially so for a small country. In my training sessions on protocol and diplomacy, both at home and abroad, I often emphasised the importance of very good understanding and cooperation between foreign heads of mission, their diplomats, and the host community. We should aim to "convert" as many of them as possible to be our **"ambassadors"** when they leave Singapore upon completion of their tour of duty. The goodwill we generate has many benefits. For example, some of them went out their way to be helpful to our diplomats when they were serving abroad. Also, their pleasant and enjoyable stay in Singapore has a positive effect when our diplomats interact with them in the many bilateral and multilateral forums around the world. I am a beneficiary of this during my postings abroad. For example, when I arrived in Cyprus to present my credentials as non-resident High Commissioner, the Indian High Commissioner and the Italian Ambassador went out of their way to brief me on the situation in Cyprus They also hosted dinners, for me and my wife to meet some of their diplomatic colleagues. Both these heads of mission had served in Singapore. They remembered their good experiences here as well as the assistance I had given them as Chief of Protocol. A very conspicuous and important example is the appointment of Daryl Arnold as Consul General of Singapore in the United States. I referred to this earlier.

While my team and I were always helpful, the diplomats knew very well that we would not tolerate deliberate violations of our laws. I have, in another chapter, given an account of how we effectively dealt with a French diplomat who incurred multiple summonses for violating our traffic laws concerning the **"Restricted Zone"**, which is the predecessor to **Electronic Road Pricing (ERP)**. The first duty of any diplomat is to respect the laws of the receiving State. We hold our own diplomats to a higher standard of compliance and behaviour. Our diplomatic missions were required to submit **regular returns** to the Ministry, giving details of any violations of local laws and breaches of privileges committed by our staff (diplomatic and non-diplomatic); they were also required to give explanations as to how and why the offences were committed and how they were dealt with. The returns also must include duty free purchases made by staff in the mission. Foreign diplomats with whom I had interacted, both at home and abroad, were surprised that we imposed such a requirement on our diplomats. I believe we were unique in doing this. During my days in London, I watched a regular splashing of statistics on violations and abuse of privileges committed by the diplomatic missions, on local television programmes. It was probably an attempt to shame them. There was one very large and oil-rich African country which continued to top the list of offenders, with more than 500 violations at one stage. Much of it concerned indiscriminate parking of motor vehicles and the rest was abuse of privileges in other matters. Diplomats misbehaving in this way bring disrepute to their country and results in host governments not taking them seriously.

Here is an anecdote which I believe could be illuminating, given the above context. In Egypt, diplomats were allowed to one duty free car every three years and, if I recall correctly, the wives of the entitled persons were also given this privilege then. In my observation, almost all diplomats availed of the privilege. The duty on cars was very high and it was highly profitable when sold at the end of the three years. As I understood, the nett profit was around US$20,000 or more, depending on the make and model of the car. Many of the diplomats kept their duty-free vehicles covered up in their garages, almost unused, to sell them in mint condition. They bought used vehicles for actual use. I was also aware that a few diplomats had sold the vehicles soon after purchase, in a clear violation of the rules. The diplomatic missions of two big countries (which will remain unnamed) in South East Asia landed in what the receiving State saw as a serious breach of the privileges accorded to them under VCDR 1961. In one case, the ambassador was alleged to have bought and sold eight cars that he bought duty free which was a clear violation of the rules. It became a scandal and the sending State was forced to withdraw the ambassador quietly. I understood, through the grape vine that he was kept in limbo in his ministry and passed away after a year. In the other case, the number of vehicles involved were even more. I think it was about ten. I do not know how exactly the problem was dealt with. However, soon after that ambassador was also withdrawn. A passing comment: the ambassadors from the countries concerned were also among the group who used to complain that they did not get much help in their work or respect from the host government. These instances underscore the point I made earlier: that in diplomacy, as in any other professional endeavour, respect must be earned.

I did not buy a car on duty free for personal use during my seven years in Egypt. I did not find it very necessary. My travels outside Cairo and within Egypt were not very frequent; I used to visit Alexandria, the business hub, several times to promote trade and investments and I made a few trips to Hurghada to attend functions organised by the host community. Furthermore, in our foreign service, ambassadors were allowed to use official vehicles for certain minimal personal use. In case the ambassador needed more use of the vehicle, for essential family transport in the country of his posting, there was a provision allowing him to do so, subject to reimbursement of the costs, based on a formula which took into account the mileage incurred (from the vehicle log book where every journey, official and personal, must be recorded by the driver and signed by both the driver and his supervisor), the overtime pay of the driver, the cost of fuel, insurance and other related factors. I found the reimbursement amount was fair.

Any visitor to Egypt, more so a diplomat serving there, cannot know or appreciate the country, if he or she does not visit the great archaeological treasures of the Pharonic past in the Valley of the Kings, Abu Simbel, Temples in Karnak, Hatshepsut, Kom Ombo and many more places which are in the south and quite far from Cairo. Except for the most adventurous, it was not possible to travel to those destinations by car, for several reasons, security being one of them. I have not known any diplomat who travelled to those destinations in their motor vehicles. Like others, my family and I flew down and picked local tours, which were quite well organised. It was fairly costly for us to cover many of them, but every dollar spent was well worth it.

I had no reason to buy duty-free alcoholic beverages and tobacco products because I am a teetotaller. (I drank the occasional glass of wine during functions hosted by diplomats in their residences, usually for purpose of toasting, and in circumstances, to show appreciation for the special occasion.) I have always been a non-smoker, as well. In Egypt, most guests did not consume alcohol at functions for religious and cultural reasons and, out of respect to the guests the hosts usually did not serve alcohol. Besides, upon my arrival, I found sizeable stock of wine and a few other items in the cellar and much of them were not fit for consumption, due to the lack of proper storage conditions. With official permission, the stock was disposed and written off.

In my observation and experience, drinking alcohol had no special advantage in my performing well at my job. The disadvantage was that, a lack of self-control could bring trouble. For example, during one of my dinner parties in New Zealand when I served there as High Commissioner, there a mixture of guests from the diplomatic corps and the local community and it was customary to serve alcohol, especially wine. The party went well or at least I thought it had. The next day, I received a polite letter from a local guest who attended the party, complaining about another guest, a diplomat, who, unknown to me, had misbehaved towards her. That diplomat was from a country which is among our closest neighbours and he even had more years of diplomatic experience than me. He embarrassed me and he was not a credit to his country. I apologised to the lady for his behaviour and I suggested to that diplomat that he should do so, as well. I immediately dropped him from my list of contacts and stopped dealing with him altogether. That diplomat was also among the small group of officers who were frequently complaining that they were not taken seriously by their host community.

I must repeat that, for Singapore, it is the impeccable character of our leaders and diplomats, both at home and abroad, that has earned us respect in the international community, and it remains one of the crucial factors for our progress and development.

President Wee Kim Wee made important contribution in forging close relations with the diplomatic corps. He organised several events for closer interaction between diplomats and our communities. For example, he organised golf tournaments (donated the "The President's Cup" trophy) for diplomats and selected golf playing members from across the spectrum of communities, and visits to rural Singapore, especially, to high-tech agro farms, including poultry production and fruit farms. Here is an interesting observation. During one such visit, most of the diplomats along with local hosts were relishing our king of fruits — durians. However, I noticed that the wife (an Asian lady) of a head of mission from a country in Western Europe, looked a little forlorn. When I spoke to her, she told me in a whisper that she liked to eat durian very much but her husband had forbidden her from eating it, whether at home or anywhere else. She said her husband was very serious and had threatened to divorce her, if she defied him. He just could not stand the smell and the mere sight of the fruit was revolting to him. I must say that he was not alone in the dislike of the fruit and I have known a few of our countrymen with similar distaste for the fruit, even with its "kingly" status among all the fruits! I felt very sorry for her and I stopped eating the fruit in her presence. The quality of the fruit served was very good indeed; any durian buff would not have left the scene until they had their fill and could eat no more!

In contrast, I knew of many countries that kept foreign ambassadors waiting for very long time, sometimes several months and, in few cases, more than a year, to present their credentials to the head of state. The first ever Chilean ambassador to Singapore told me that he was very impressed that he was able to present his credentials to our President so quickly. He said that in his previous posting to an African country (which he named) he was kept waiting several months. To satisfy my curiosity, I asked him why they did so. He said that that it was their way of "showing" that they were very important and to bolster their ego. The Chilean ambassador was a hardworking man. Being new to Singapore, he sought my advice on how Chile could increase trade with Singapore. I told him that I had heard that Chile had good wine and that the Chamber of

Commerce could help him to locate a suitable importer. Few months later, he saw me in my office and told me that he had succeeded in bringing Chilean wines to Singapore and thanked me for my help.

In another instance, a retired New Zealand diplomat told me that he was in a large West Asian country, which had just gone through a revolution and change of government, to present his credentials. He could not get a date to meet the head of state, and waited for some time. One day, without any prior notice, a protocol officer suddenly turned up at his residence at about 6 A.M., and insisted that the diplomat left with him immediately to present his credentials. The diplomat noted that the protocol officer was not appropriately dressed and a little unkempt. Thus, the diplomat's accreditation was rushed through. During my term in Egypt many heads of mission lamented the fact that in some countries they had to wait more than several months to present their credentials. A Bruneian ambassador in Cairo told me that he could not present his credentials in a Maghreb country, to which he was concurrently accredited, even after waiting for two years. Just before leaving Cairo on completion of his tour, he posted his credentials to the foreign ministry in that country! I can only say that cultural attitudes and values in these countries are not the same and differ greatly from ours.

As time went by, my first impression of the Egyptian chief of protocol was confirmed. He had a big ego. The inefficiency was to me was paradoxical. Egypt had well-educated and qualified staff in their bureaucracy. Their diplomats were skilful, competent, and many had excelled in this work. Boutoros Boutoros-Ghali, an Egyptian, was a UN Secretary General. Yet, Egypt then ranked below many developing countries in important development indicators. A renowned management guru, from a leading management institute in the United States, made an observation during a "Euro Money Conference" in Cairo. He noted that Egypt's bureaucracy was the oldest in the world, "yet it is the slowest now".

TAKING CHARGE OF THE PROTOCOL AND CONSULAR DIRECTORATE

It might be of some interest to readers to know how I landed in the protocol job. Sometime in 1984, I received a telephone call from Chia Cheong Fook, Permanent Secretary of the Ministry when I was serving as Counsellor (was number two then) in Canberra. It was a few months after my near fatal road accident in Canberra (I have referred to this earlier). He told me that he wanted me to return to Ministry Headquarters as soon as possible and take charge of the Protocol and Consular Directorate (PCD). It was an unusually lengthy conversation and he explained to me in much detail why it was necessary and also why he wanted me and not anyone else to take on the job. I had the sense that all was not well in the functioning of PCD. All I am at liberty to disclose is that the incumbent Director (Chief of Protocol) (whom I will refer to as "Q" to preserve anonymity), who had some experience serving both in the Ministry and in our overseas missions, had to leave due to circumstances where it was not possible for him to stay on, not just in the job, but also in the civil service as a whole. I also gathered that the deputy in the PCD could not cope and in fact, wanted out. In the circumstances, the PCD appeared rudderless. From Chia Cheong Fook's account of the situation, I realised the urgency of my having to go back home. In passing, I would like to say that "Q" was not the only casualty in the PCD, both before and since then.

Immediately upon my return, I had to organise the official visit of the Prime Minister of Australia, **Robert (Bob) Hawke** and his wife as well as a few more official visits of VVIPs from other countries down the line. I needed no more reason for why I had to be back. Bob Hawke's visit was a short one of few days' and we had to pack as much as possible into the time to achieve the best outcome for both parties. However, I did not find it difficult to plan, prepare and implement the programme with the precision required, in consultation with other concerned ministries. I had developed very good contacts in the Australian government and in the wider community there. I found their officials professional, competent, cooperative and, if I may say so, I earned their respect as well. Speaking of earning respect, here is an interesting anecdote. One Sunday, at about 8 A.M., my wife and I were driving from our residence, then in Torrens suburb, to a shopping centre in another suburb, Woden. About half-way, we noticed what appeared to be a stalled car and there was a lady and a gentleman standing beside it. I stopped our car and asked my wife to move it to a safe place. I went to their car and found out that the car's battery was flat. I asked the lady to sit in the driver's seat and keep the clutch pedal depressed while the gentleman and I pushed the car. I instructed her to slowly release the pedal as the car began to gather speed. It worked and the car burst into life. The couple thanked us and moved on. We did not think much about it afterwards. My wife and I resumed our drive to Woden to do our shopping. A few days later, I was in the foreign ministry as part of my regular visits to meet with host government officials. One officer whom I met said that he saw me pushing the car and helping the couple. Unknown to me at that time, he has seen me doing it while he slowed down to pass by. In time, the story had spread to other officials in that Ministry, and possibly beyond. Needless to say, those interactions were beneficial to me when I planned Bob Hawke's visit. I had personally known and had interacted with some of the officials who came with the Prime Minister.

Bob Hawke's visit went very well, and he wrote me a nice letter, dated 29 February 1984 complimenting me for the way we organised the visit, and all the arrangements that were made for his visit, short as it was.

The US government website describes the role of the Chief of Protocol thus:

"The Office of the Chief of Protocol seeks to advance the foreign policy goals of the United States by creating an environment for successful diplomacy".

Protocol is not set in stone. It evolves with time, albeit slowly, to take into account the changing patterns in diplomacy and the needs of the time, with regards to the conduct of relations between nation states. Skilful and intelligent application of the protocol tools, both in the customary and statute laws, are very important to achieve the nation's foreign policy goals, and thereby contributing to good governance at home and abroad.

There are many ways of achieving this. The President of Philippines, Corazon Aquino appointed **Francisco Benedicto**, a successful businessman of Chinese ethnicity from Cebu province, as ambassador to Singapore. He had never served as a diplomat before and was a bit apprehensive. As Chief of Protocol, I always tried to ease such concerns, wherever possible. I explained to him that it was not that difficult to operate in Singapore and that he could rely on me for guidance, if necessary. Also, I assured him that he need not worry that he had no experience as ambassador and told him that I knew many first-time political appointees, like himself, who had done very well in their jobs in Singapore. He wanted Aquino to succeed where Marcos had failed in the economic construction of his country, but he did not know how to go about in helping her.

I suggested to him that, in my view, it might be useful for Aquino to make a visit to Singapore and speak to relevant officials, to tap on

Singapore's experience, where relevant. If he agreed, he should then take it up with concerned officials in my Ministry. He did take up my suggestion and worked on it.

Aquino made an official visit to Singapore and held discussions with our economic agencies, in addition to political consultations with our leaders. I understood later that Aquino made an initial start to improve the administration, but the powerful feudal political clans deeply entrenched in the body politic and the pervasive corruption undermined her efforts.

By the time Francisco finished his term, he had done very well as his country's ambassador and earned the respect of his peers. His affable manners masked his steely resolve to succeed.

In my observation there are two important pre-requisites for innovation to flourish. The first is free exchange of ideas and information and the second, and even more important, is the acceptance of the fact that at all levels of the society, without failure there can be no success and certainly no innovation. If anyone in a position of authority says (as one actually did) that he would only remember the 20% failure of a person and not the 80% success he had achieved, then it cannot encourage initiatives, never mind innovation. As a society, we have to do more to nurture the spirit of innovation, encourage perseverance, and respect those who try and fail. I watched a video-clip in a Swedish museum devoted to failures — that is ventures, experiments, inventions and the like that did not succeed. The message is very obvious; most inventors did not achieve success on the first attempt. One extremely successful and wealthy technopreneur said any person would be very lucky to hit the ultimate jackpot, which he or she was looking for, even after 99 failed attempts.

Innovation requires an enabling mind-set and environment, whether in the public sector or in the private sector, on the part of all in the team, especially the leaders of the work teams. Here is an anecdote. On my first day of the job as Ambassador to Cairo, I sat with each of the staff to learn from them the work they were doing and how the office functioned. This is part of my work ethic, if I may so term it. I started with the Receptionist, an elderly Egyptian lady who was in the same job for about 10 years. It was part of my management tools to ask staff the following questions whenever and wherever I conducted such an operation:

- the purpose of the job;
- the description of the job and the details involved;
- how long he or she has been doing same job; and
- why he or she should continue to do the job.

I noticed some apprehension on the part of some of the staff. I quickly assured them that none of their jobs were in danger, and that I was merely trying to learn. Apparently, as I understood, no one else before me had taken this approach.

Going through the details, the Receptionist could not provide satisfactory answers on few things she was doing and why she was doing them. She told me that she did not know for how long it was going on before her and no one had talked to her about them. Probably, it had been going on since the mission was established in the late 1960s, after independence. I asked the other staff to also go through the details of their respective duties and come up with the answers to my questions, including whether they should continue to carry out the duties queried. I think I gave them 3 days. To cut the long story short, many things which they were doing for no other reason than what they said was "it was always done like that before" were discontinued and the opportunity was taken to reorganise and rationalise, as necessary.

Speaking generally, the perception of public service in many countries was (rightly or wrongly) risk-averse and many preferred to trod on the beaten path, "to be on the safe side". However, in the 21st, no country that wants to make progress can remain isolated, even if it feels that such isolation is splendid. An enterprising chief executive of a well-watched Indian international television channel summed it up very well when he said: **"going down the beaten path is for beaten men and women"**.

In the context of this narrative, one cannot ignore funding which is seldom unlimited. Reckless spending in the public service in the name of innovation will not bring about the needed innovation; on the contrary, it will result in national insolvency. I have alluded to this earlier. In the public service, prudent management of public funds and the financial discipline required to achieve that are vital, and that brings me to my next chapter.

Chapter 18

FISCAL DISCIPLINE

"Public funds should not only be spent correctly they must also be seen to be spent correctly. While you may have satisfied the first limb you have certainly not satisfied me on the second limb"

—*A Colonial Auditor*

In Global Competitiveness Rankings, Singapore was continually ranked among the top ten countries in the world. This could not have been possible without honest leadership, transparent procedures and **accountability,** amongst other factors. **Those found guilty of transgressions must be punished according to the law without exception.**

COLONIAL LEGACY

The countries that emerged from British colonial rule usually inherited a working administrative structure and machinery, underpinned by laws, an independent judiciary, law enforcement, and other institutions necessary for effective governance. The British installed the system essentially for them to hold together and manage their empire — in order to perpetuate British imperial power, dominance and interests. The benefits to the natives were more often consequential and incidental. Nevertheless, it had to be said that in this regard, the British were far better than other colonial powers; the Dutch who ruled the Indonesian Archipelago, for almost as long as the British did over Malaya and Singapore, did not develop an administrative system like the British did. However, in my observation, the Belgian colonisers deserve condemnation. In an earlier chapter, I have gave a short account of Belgium's systematic abuse and its rapacious conduct in Congo.

Overall, we inherited from the British a working administration with built-in transparency and accountability. In financial management, the procedures and requirements were adequate and clear. There were mechanisms to punish offending civil servants. They were generally effective in maintaining the administration in working order. The Corrupt Practices Investigation Bureau (CPIB) was set up by the colonial regime in 1952, and even if one might question its effectiveness in combating corruption then, it was undeniably useful. The system the British left behind helped us at the routine level to improve our financial discipline in the disbursement of public funds and the management of scarce resources. However, the priority for the colonial administration was maintaining stability, and serving its own imperial interests. Fighting corruption was incidental. Self- governing Singapore's development agenda, however, required a long-term vision and to achieve that, a total war on corruption, was necessary. In the dire situation we were in, failure was not an option. (If I may say so, at the risk of repetition, not eradicating corruption was the failure of the pioneer generation leaders of many other countries. It was the reason they were engulfed in the serious political, economic and social problems that followed, despite the enormous resources at their command.)

EXPENDITURE CONTROL

Every item of expenditure, big or small, had to be expressly provided for in the annual budget and each ministry or department would have funds allocated to it, under a Head of Expenditure in budget. Disbursements from the public purse (consolidated account) had built in checks and safeguards. Documentations required were elaborate, for example, every purchase, had to be made on an "indent" known as "Org Sec" which was in triplicate. (To my understanding, the term "Org Sec" was abbreviation for "Organising Secretary".) Relevant details were handwritten (or typed) on the original with (carbon sheets in between other pages). If my memory serves me right, the original went to the supplier, the first carbon copy was retained in the department's file, and the second was sent to Accountant General, together with the invoice from the supplier for payment. If I remember correctly there were several principal accounting forms (documents) and amongst them were:

- Org Sec 94 Letter of Appointment
- Org Sec 95 Purchase Order
- Org Sec 96 Requisition of Stores from government departments e.g. furniture
- Org Sec 97 Condemnation of Stores.

There were many other documents in use for financial control. These documents had to be kept securely under lock and produced for audit inspection

RIGOROUS AUDIT

The **Auditor General audited every item of expenditure** (regardless of the amount) by the government and, if he found any irregularity, however small, he would pursue the matter relentlessly until he was satisfied. If there was negligence or fraud, disciplinary action followed.

I recall an audit query concerning an overpayment of a very small amount (I think it was less than $5) and the matter could not be settled by correspondence stretching over a few months. My boss, **S T Ratnam**, and I (then in the Ministry of Culture) went to see the Director of Audit, a colonial civil servant by the name of Fell (if my memory serves me right) to explain the discrepancy. I had not forgotten what he said: "**Public funds should not only be spent correctly, they must also be seen to be spent correctly**. While you may have satisfied the first limb you have certainly not satisfied me on the second limb". In the end, he decided to let us off the hook with a strong warning. From that day on, I was always conscious of this requirement, throughout my career. Nobody liked audit queries and it was one reason why officers shied away from undertaking financial duties.

FINANCIAL CONSTRAINT

We operated on a shoe-string budget. Even the smallest item of expenditure had to be very carefully assessed.

When I joined the service, I did not have a telephone on my desk. The nearest telephone was some 30 feet away. In those days, offices had a PABX switchboard with few lines and officers were connected by extensions. The operator connected incoming calls to the officer concerned. To make a call, whether internal or external, one had to seek the assistance of the operator. The Ministry applied for a parallel extension for me. A Ministry of Finance official, **John Tan**, from the Organisations and Methods Branch came to assess whether the request was justified. He sat with me for a week or so to check the number of calls I had to make and receive for official purposes. He was satisfied and approved the request for a telephone extension to be shared with another officer, which meant only one of us could use it at any one time.

I mentioned earlier the **Singapore Cultural Mission to the Borneo Territories** and my position as its "Secretary-cum-Treasurer". I was given a cash advance of about $20,000 (if I recall correctly) for expenses for the Mission, including the allowance for artists, the construction of the stage, transport and miscellaneous expenses associated thereto. The Mission and its performances were well received. I disbursed the cash allowances to the artists as per the arrangement, paid for other expenses, and also doubled up as the photographer. I kept all records required for accounting. We returned home about a week later. I immediately prepared a **"Statement of Account"** to clear the cash advance.

The Accountant General (AG) decided that he should query me on why I changed Singapore currency into a Sterling Pound **Travellers Cheque** (credit cards and the like did not exist then). A few officers in my Ministry, who were envious that I was chosen for the overseas trip, were also quietly gleeful because they thought that I was headed for a surcharge. The amount of "loss" was very small but an endorsement of the surcharge in my Service Record would have been detrimental to my career.

I was undaunted as I knew the financial procedure well, having studied them in depth for my probationary examination. In those days, appointments in the civil service were on three-year probationary basis and appointees were required to pass written probationary examinations and maintain satisfactory conduct and performance to get confirmed. If not confirmed, they would have to leave the civil service.

I replied to AG that Financial Procedure Rules required that when public funds amounting to $2000 or more were carried by civil servants outside the office for disbursement in the course of their duties, then, they should be accompanied by suitable escorts, usually police personnel from the Guard & Escort Unit of the Police Force. I had no such escorts in the places we were in. Therefore, if

I had carried the whole amount in cash, I would have been in breach of the regulations and ran the risk of losing the money as well. The AG accepted my explanation and that was the end of the matter. I had a sense that my boss was quietly impressed.

When we established our High Commission in London, we submitted a very modest proposal to furnish the office. Among the items were the cost of carpets and curtains. The Finance Ministry queried us on the need for carpets and curtains contending they were "luxury items". We appealed explaining that they were a functional necessity and requirement in the London context. It was accepted. **At the time, with the very tight financial situation then, we did not consider the query as unreasonable, though it was inconvenient.**

Financial discipline and accountability have been among the factors that have contributed to the economic success of our nation. For many of us in the pioneer generation, financial discipline is in our blood. Switching off unused lights and turning off dripping taps came naturally to us. During my term as Private Secretary to the President, I received notes from PM Lee whenever he noticed that lights in the Istana had been left on when not required. He and Mrs Lee used to walk around the Istana domain after dinner. As it was well known, they lived in their private home in Oxley Road and not in Sri Temasek, the official residence, in the Istana Domain.

CHANGING ATTITUDE

With the succeeding generation of civil servants having experienced rising affluence, things began to change. The switching off of lights and the turning off of taps was not always observed; engaging in long conversations on the telephone was not uncommon. A US ambassador to Singapore told me that he had to personally approve all overseas calls by his staff, just to keep an eye on cost.

Well this was the situation at that time. It is to be noted, however, that the speed of change in communication technology had lowered communication costs. Other rapid changes, and especially with e-government, some controls used in the past are no longer practical.

Over the years, a changing attitude towards financial control and management was noticeable and those like me who expressed our views were brushed aside as "bureaucratic" or "out of date" or as "talking rot". In my view, it reflected the generational change. Also, as in many newly emerging countries, the pioneer generation in Singapore was challenged severely to make every penny count and doing that was in their blood. I have heard of one internationally known economist saying that **"saving is sin and spending is virtue". I do not subscribe to this view.** Maybe I am too old fashioned for some. Besides, there was nothing much to spend it on, even if we wanted to spend it away, when we started with almost depleted coffers. In my observation, it was our prudent financial management, defying such theories, that enabled us to prosper, much to the envy of others who did not make it! The younger generation officers in Singapore may see things differently. In recent years, I have read reports and watched programmes on international television channels on financial crises in many wealthy countries. Many health, education and other public service providers and experts have complained bitterly about the lack of funding to deliver quality standards to the consumers, and have warned of the possible collapse of some services to the public. Mind you, these are not Third World countries, they are countries in the European Union.

Government audits in many of these countries have revealed serious flaws in the administrations, especially in the disbursement and management of public funds. Furthermore, it should come as no surprise to anyone, the fact that audits in many multi-national corporations, have found serious financial irregularities, attributed to "**creative accounting**". These irregularities resulted in the collapse of leading financial power houses, that some considered 'too big to fail" and thus, triggering the global financial crises in recent decades. It is also to be noted that many of these wealthy countries had already gone for International Monetary Fund (IMF) bailouts and a few were depended on the IMF lifeline. The list was surprising and included many former colonial powers. **Singapore did not have the situation where it needed a IMF bailout and it is my fervent hope that we will never let it happen to us in the future.** However, we cannot take anything for granted and collectively we must work hard to prevent such a situation befalling us.

I give two examples here which are self-explanatory. However, at the outset let me make it clear that it is not my intention or purpose to blame any person or organisation concerned. It is rather to remind ourselves to always budget government operations in a cost effective manner, whatever the problems encountered are. It is also to remind us of the need to consider all factors and circumstances, so that we get the best deal and outcome. Also, learning from mistakes is an important factor in maintaining good governance and in this context, it is my humble view that if financial discipline loosened in prosperous years, then, it would be difficult to manage in leaner times when austerity is forced upon us.

Prime Minister Goh Chok Tong visited the United Arab Emirates (UAE) sometime around 1998 and I made the necessary arrangements with the UAE hosts. A day before the visit, a senior officer (name redacted) from our protocol office called me on the telephone asking me to change the hotel, the Crown Plaza, in Dubai that was allotted by the host government under their official hospitality. When I asked him for the reason he said both his officer who came to recce the place and the Consul in Dubai felt Crown Plaza was not suitable and insisted the delegation should stay at another hotel, the Al Bustan, a newer and a smaller hotel near the airport. I could not understand why and how he made that decision.

I stood firm. I gave my reasons which were that the Crown Plaza had all the necessary facilities, and many heads of government had stayed there. Besides, to reject the host's offer would not be in good taste. The Arabs are known to be generous hosts, and they could interpret our rejection of their offer of hospitality as a slight on them. Besides, if we chose to stay in another hotel, we would have to pay around $15,000. In his response, he made the point that he had changed hotels, under similar circumstances, during a visit to a country in Europe and that funds were no problem. I told him that I did not find it necessary to change the hotel and I was quite firm. He then said that I would have to be responsible for the consequences of my decision. I informed him that I had no problems with that.

On the last day as we were leaving for the airport, I asked Prime Minister Goh in the presence of the officer concerned, how he found the Hotel and he replied "very good". In protocol, it is customary for the host government to offer hospitality to leaders on official visit, and this has been the practice throughout the ages. If a UAE leader came to Singapore on an official visit, then our Government would extend similar hospitality. Anyway in this case, I had checked beforehand with a few resident ambassadors (I was a non-resident ambassador) and they all confirmed that their leaders had stayed there and found the hotel very comfortable. According to the British Ambassador, Baroness Margaret Thatcher had stayed there and had found it comfortable.

Another anecdote on being cost conscious: PM Goh made official visits to a few countries in southern Africa, including Zimbabwe where I was accredited as non-resident High Commissioner. I understood that someone had proposed to charter an SIA (Singapore Airlines) aircraft for the reasons that there were no convenient flights connecting the capitals, the airlines serving in the region were not known for their punctuality, and there were concerns about the safety of the aircrafts. I understood that Senior Minister Lee Kuan Yew, was against the proposal due to considerations of cost, and disruptions to SIA's schedules. It was a problem but thankfully, the Sultan of Brunei very generously made available his Boeing aircraft for PM Goh's visit.

CHANGES IN AUDITING

Hundred percent audit was abandoned, and the detailed nomenclature of the budget described above was discontinued, leaving control and management to the permanent secretaries who as Accounting Officers, managed to block vote provisions. It was done under the policy of devolution of powers to the ministries, to achieve greater efficiency in the management of public funds.

The Auditor General's scrutiny of disbursements of public funds in implementing the programmes, as approved by Parliament, is vital to maintain a clean, honest and efficient administration, which is the bedrock of our Republic. However, with the enormous increase in the volume of disbursements due to the implementation of many more government projects and programmes, since the early days of self-government, it was no longer possible to audit every item of expenditure, as before. The sheer manpower required and the cost of doing so would make it impractical and not cost effective. Therefore, in my understanding, the Auditor General had adopted selective random auditing of expenditure, amongst other measures, to scrutinise disbursements. In such a situation, it is **important that firm action is taken when irregularities, malpractices and frauds are detected.**

Here are two very different and contrasting cases:

In 1976, I was appointed as **"Investigating Officer"** to investigate the loss of public funds in our Embassy in Manila. I was then Director (Special Duties) in the Foreign Ministry. My investigation revealed a substantial loss of public funds (actual amount was ascertained) which occurred due to a lack of supervision of the incumbent Administration Attaché, and the failure to comply with rules and procedures in the Instruction Manuals and guidelines in circulars that were issued from time to time. The Administration Attaché was brought back home, charged in court with criminal breach of trust and was sentenced to a jail term. As per civil service rules, he was dismissed from the service upon conviction. In my observation, he was a unfit for the job. I was given to understand that he enjoyed a lavish lifestyle which his income could not support.

Many years later, a long-time friend of mine and a fellow civil servant, narrated a case whereby, in a transport claim, an officer claimed 18 km for a journey from his office in High Street to Suntec City and back. At most, the return trip should not have been more than 8 km. This was queried by the auditor and I was told that the only action taken was to merely tell the officer not to do that again in the future. It was not even a rap on the knuckle!

Upon my retirement, I was appointed as a consultant in the Ministry and in this capacity, I was tasked by the Ministry to audit our Consulates in Mumbai and Chennai in 2001, following an ongoing disciplinary action suit against a staff member in the Consulate in Chennai. I and my team of two MFA officers visited both Consulates and the High Commission in New Delhi, which supervised the operation of the Consulates. In my report, I made many recommendations based on the findings, and the most important one concerned a change in the criteria for selection and appointment of consuls. My recommendations were accepted and implemented. In the following year (by then I was in practicing law), I reviewed the operations of the Protocol Directorate at the request of the Ministry and in my report I made several recommendations which I believe were also implemented.

I would like to end this chapter with another anecdote to illustrate the point that "public funds must not only be spent correctly but also should **be seen to be spent correctly.**"

During my term in Egypt, our Government decided to build a new chancery (office) building for our Embassy, located in Babel Street, in Dokki. We located suitable land, not very far from where we were, and started the negotiations with the owner **in our office.** I had with me the First Secretary and the interpreter, a local staff member. I insisted that full record of the discussions was kept in the Mission. I had also kept the Ministry headquarters informed of this. The owner told me in one meeting at the office that he and I could discuss and conclude the deal quickly, without the need for others to be present, and hinted that he could come to my residence to settle it. I warned him straight away, and in no uncertain terms, that I would call off the meeting and stop dealing with him. (I had also informed our staff not to see or receive him anywhere but the office and that too, never alone. Any dealings with him was to be in the office with more than one officer present. I had also left a note to the effect in the relevant file.) The owner was surprised and claimed that it was how he did business with other diplomatic missions. He gave me the impression that it was nothing unusual and that we were odd. I told him that our laws were strict, and we could not proceed on the basis he was suggesting. It did not require much thinking to know what he was hinting at.

I left Egypt soon after, upon completion of my tour of duty. I enjoyed my posting very much and it was very satisfying, both in terms my performance and achievements, and the assistance and many courtesies extended to me by the host government and the wider community. **Egypt was as good a place as any to further my continuous learning in diplomacy and international relations**. Learning is the topic of my next chapter.

Chapter 19

LEARNING FROM THE MASTER

*In a very loud voice he (PM Lee) scolded me by saying **"are you daft"**. There was a stunned silence from all the VIP guests already assembled. I did not let it affect me as time was closing in fast and the rest of the proceedings had to be executed with clock-work precision.*

My generation started our service under difficult circumstances, but we also had the unique benefit of working with the founding fathers, especially Lee Kuan Yew (Prime Minister), Dr Goh Keng Swee (Finance Minister) and Sinnathamby Rajaratnam (Minister for Culture and Minister for Foreign Affairs). We learnt much from them. I was lucky that my duties, in various positions, brought me into contact with the pioneer leaders, especially with PM Lee. It all started in London. During his visits to London for the Commonwealth Prime Ministers' Conference, as it was known then (later CHOGM), and on other occasions, I assisted the delegation in several areas, gaining valuable insights into the way PM Lee dealt with people and issues. I have detailed some of my observations below.

TIME MANAGEMENT

PM Lee was very effective in managing his time. Everything had to be precisely planned and executed. Wherever he worked, whether in his office at the Istana, or in a hotel suite during travels, he had minimal furniture and very few papers, if at all, on his desk. He made clear, quick and firm decisions. When we had to refer matters to him, we would send a short note through his Secretary, and we did not have to wait long for his instructions. Often, we would get them within hours and many a time, immediately. I remember an occasion when I was Chief of Protocol, I sent a note to PM Lee around 5 P.M. through the electronic mailbox (internet came later) seeking instructions on a visit by a foreign head of government. I received the instructions I needed within 10 minutes! I used that example to tell my team in protocol that we had no excuses for delays.

In London, one of my many duties was to collect the Singapore newspapers, specially flown in for PM Lee on a BOAC (British Overseas Airways Corporation) flight which took more than 24 hours to reach Heathrow Airport. It was important that the papers reached the PM as quickly as possible, so that he could keep in touch with the news and developments at home. In those days, radio and newspapers were the only sources of news. Satellite communication and global television live news broadcasts aired by BBC, CNN and others did not exist.

To rush the papers quickly to PM Lee, I would go to the airport in the early hours of the morning and wait for the arrival of the aircraft, rather than wait at my residence for confirmation from airport authorities of the arrival of the aircraft. When I left London upon completion of my tour of duty, another officer took over this duty. For some reason, he decided that he would rather wait for confirmation of the arrival of the aircraft than to go so early in the morning and wait for the aircraft to arrive. Probably, he had concluded that it was a waste of time to wait at the airport. However, it so happened that on one occasion, the flight had arrived but the expected confirmation did not come and he assumed, that the newspapers had not arrived. He went to work as per normal still waiting for the confirmation that did not come. He had also not called to check on the flight status.

The PM's Personal Assistant, **A Sankaran**, an alert and efficient officer, asked for the papers. It was not clear what the officer told him. Not satisfied, he asked him to check and it was only then discovered that the flight had indeed arrived on time. By the time the papers reached PM Lee, it was very late in the day. Needless to say, the officer was severely reprimanded.

At this point, I would like to relate a situation which was, as some might describe, my run-in with the **British Trade Union**. We were in a hurry to get the High Commission premises (**2 Wilton Crescent** purchased from Lord Mountbatten) minimally furnished, and the telephones and the intercom system installed, in order to get the Office (Chancery) operational as quickly as possible. As Attaché Administration, it was my responsibility. Almost near the end, the "Post Office Engineers", as they called themselves, refused to lift a section of the carpet in order to pull the small cables to connect the telephone and intercom sets in the High Commissioner's office. They insisted that under their union rules they could not do it and that I must get the carpet people. They also told me that it could take a week or more to get it done, assuming we could get a carpet-layer that quickly. They left telling me to let them know when that job was completed. That was a Friday. It was quite ridiculous, and I was not going to be defeated by them.

I set to work the next day (a Saturday and a non-working day). I lifted the carpet, pulled the cables and made a small hole at the exact spot under the table and pulled the cables into the position required. I then pressed down the carpet neatly into the position it was before. I completed the job in less than an hour. It was not at all a difficult task for a handyman like me, even with the rudimentary tools I had then. The next working day, I called the post office engineers to tell them that the job had been completed and that they needed to come and connect the cable ends to the instruments, switch on the lines, and test the systems. Initially, they sounded sceptical, but I pleaded with them, telling them that it was very urgent that we got our communication system operational. They came a day later and were aghast that I had done it without bringing in the carpet-layers and protested that it was against union rules. I explained to them that the urgency was such that we had no alternative. Grudgingly they completed the last bit required from them. Frustrated at the inordinate amount of delay in getting things done, the High Commissioner asked the Trade Commissioner, Tony Hibberd, what was wrong with the country. Hibberd, an Englishman and a die-hard Tory with a wry sense of humour, said **"Sir, half the British labour force is permanently deployed in brewing tea".** Not to be outdone by Hibberd's wit, the High Commissioner quipped **"I suppose the other half is deployed in watching the tea being brewed".** Employers who wanted to keep industrial peace with the unions knew very well the importance of teatime in Britain then.

There was another concern as regards the property, 2 Wilton Crescent which as I mentioned earlier was owned by Lord Mountbatten. When we negotiated its purchase in 1966, the remainder of the lease was only about 40 years. I recall then High Commissioner A P Rajah mentioning this to PM Lee during the latter's visit that year. If did not bother the PM. If I remember correctly, he told us that if Singapore could survive that long it would not matter. As I have said elsewhere in the book, the odds were heavily stacked against our survival.

On a less serious note, there were instances when PM Lee tolerated us for our mistakes and we were lucky. Chia Cheong Fook told us about his experience in driving PM Lee for an appointment using his car, a Volvo (office car was not available at that time). He lost his way near Horse Guard Parade and asked the ceremoniol guard mounted on a horse and on static duty (remaining motionless), for directions. As part of his duty requirements he took no notice of Chia. When he returned to the car appearing dejected, PM Lee told Chia that he should have known that the guard on such duty would not speak.

I end my narrative of this experience with another observation. As part of bold economic reforms to the British economy, Prime Minister Baroness Margaret Thatcher (the "**Iron Lady**") hived-off the telecommunication component of the Post Office and established the autonomous enterprise "**British Telecom**" (BT). BT became very efficient, profitable, innovative and, as I understood later, it was able to compete for business abroad.

MY WORKING RELATIONS WITH PM LEE

In my observation, PM Lee's mind was always thinking of or working on something, except probably during his sleeping hours. Between the time he left office or home and arrived at the airport to board the aircraft, he would have thought of some issues or things that needed to be attended to during his absence, and would give me instructions as we went up the step ladder of the aerobridge. Most of the time the instructions were to be conveyed to his Secretary Wong Chooi Sen for action.

It must be said that implementing PM Lee's instructions was not difficult. His instructions, whether oral or in writing, were usually conveyed to me by **Wong Chooi Sen** (sometimes through **Sankaran**), except on occasions when PM Lee spoke to me directly on the telephone.

In organising the visits of foreign VVIPs, especially heads of state and heads of government, precision in implementing the programmes was important for many reasons. We had to pack in as much as possible, without tiring the visitors, to get the maximum impact and benefit for both sides. The programme also had to allow time for the visitors to see and feel what drives Singapore. Managing the various threads and pulling all of them together was important. At the core of the programmes was the session in the Cabinet Room in the Prime Minister's Office in the Istana Annex. Usually 45 to 60 minutes would be allotted depending on the issues to be dealt with. To control the time, I would knock on the door, enter and announce **"Sir, there is another appointment"** without specifying what the appointment was. PM Lee would say thank you or at other times he would ask me whether they could have little more time like "can I have 10 more minutes". I would simply say "yes sir' and come out and rearrange the next item on the programme, if necessary, for seamless operation of the rest of the programme. The whole thing was orchestrated carefully to make it easier for both sides to get through the business without delay and without causing any embarrassment. It helped visiting delegations as they could be waiting for the host to take the initiative to end the meeting. In fact, it served both sides well. Many VVIPs and ambassadors commented favourably on this arrangement. It should be noted here that this arrangement worked well for us because it had our leaders' support. It would be difficult to implement it in countries where royalties were involved. There the chief of protocol might not feel comfortable or confident enough to suggest it to his masters.

During my term as Private Secretary to President Sheares, I also implemented a somewhat similar arrangement. In those days, many state guests stayed in the Istana and it was customary for them to make a courtesy call on the President. Heads of state on state visits also did the same as customary in protocol. The President received those VIP guests at the State Room with two

ADCs and myself. The ADCs would just stand behind the President and not move. When all were seated the ADCs would leave. Usually about 20 minutes would be allotted and the same ADCs would re-enter and resume the same positions and remain silent. That was the signal for the visitors to take leave of the President. The visitors were briefed of this arrangement in advance. They found this to be an elegant way of conducting the proceedings. Years later, when I served abroad, one chief of protocol commended us for this practice.

I must state however, that it was easier for us to innovate in this regard. In the world of protocol, we were a new kid, having just become an independent republic. Starting from scratch also had its advantages; it allowed us to learn from the best, adapt, adopt and innovate to suit our circumstances with minimal departures from form and substance of international protocol. For countries with longer protocol tradition and in monarchies, it could be difficult to change. Among our many campaigns organised in the early years of our Republic, were **"Towards Excellence"** and **"Be the Best You Can Be"** and innovation was a key component of that strategy. A competitive economy requires continuous innovation and it will always remain as work in progress.

NOT ALWAYS SMOOTH SAILING

However, it was not always smooth sailing for me with PM Lee during all those years when I had the privilege of serving him. I recall two instances.

VISIT OF PREMIER LI PENG

One case was the visit of Premier Li Peng of China. At about 7.50 P.M. I received a call from Minister Ong Teng Cheong, Minister in Attendance to Premier Li, concerning an issue raised by the guests and he wanted to know our position before the Chinese guests arrived at the Istana for the official dinner. I asked our senior most minister present for instructions and he told me to ask PM Lee. Just then PM Lee arrived, and I conveyed the message from Ong Teng Cheong. In doing so, I volunteered a suggestion (in the spirit of finding a solution) which turned out to be both unwise and inappropriate — a big mistake on my part. PM Lee scolded me in a loud voice saying, **"are you daft?"** There was a stunned silence from guests who had already arrived, but I could not afford to get distracted. I had to act very quickly as time was closing in fast. With help from Wong Chooi Sen, we solved the issue and I sent a message to Ong Teng Cheong. The rest to of the programme was executed with precision.

On reflection, I felt it was a very serious mistake on my part and I deserved the rebuke. The next day I received calls from a few guests including members of parliament who were present at the function to console me. I did not hear further from PM Lee concerning the incident and neither did I sense any change afterwards in the way he used to deal with me. That was a close shave for me, and I learnt a good lesson from that incident.

VISIT OF PRESIDENT SUHARTO

The next incident concerned the visit of President Suharto that I have mentioned previously. To my knowledge, no other head of state on an official visit had come through the Causeway in Woodlands. The only exception was when the Sultan of Johor made an official visit to Singapore towards the end of his term as Yang di Pertuan Agong (king) in 1984. This was a special case and he was accustomed to coming to Singapore by road from Johor anyway. Receiving VVIP visitors at the Causeway had different problems, especially in getting the guest to arrive on time at our border. At the airport we were able to get PM Lee to arrive just as the aircraft taxied in. We had control over the whole process and could cut waiting time to absolute minimum, often to just a few minutes.

My suggestion was for PM to arrive at the small immigration building in Woodlands (CIQ complex was built later) 15 minutes before the scheduled time of arrival of Suharto. The Malaysian protocol would hand over halfway at the Causeway, on our side, and it would take only about one minute for Suharto to arrive, escorted by our motorcycle outriders, at the receiving point. Upon arrival at the checkpoint, PM Lee asked me in a somewhat angry tone why I had brought him to wait that long (15 minutes). I explained to him that I had very little control over the timing and that I was dependent on the cooperation of the Malaysian side to get Suharto arrive on time. That there was a possibility, however slight, that Suharto could arrive earlier, in which case he (PM Lee) had to be there to receive him. All he said was "huh". From his body language, I could not determine whether he was satisfied with my answer. He was quite accustomed to not having to wait that long to receive visitors. In this case, it would have been very risky to further trim the timings to such a fine degree. I had to make sure that PM Lee was there in case Suharto arrived earlier. I would have been in very deep trouble, if Suharto arrived earlier, and PM Lee was not there to receive him. The consequences would be too terrible to even contemplate.

As it turned out, the Malaysian protocol did a good job and Suharto arrived on time and the visit went very well in all aspects. The Police Officer, a DSP on duty, later thanked me for the way I handled the matter. He said he had noticed that I was interacting with all, from PM Lee to the outriders who were assigned to escort Suharto. In an operation of that nature, the enthusiastic cooperation of all in the team was absolutely essential for a successful outcome. It was always teamwork, teamwork and teamwork!

I must make the point that PM Lee, our ministers and in fact, all concerned personnel in any event were always punctual and adhered to the set timings. As Chief of Protocol, I introduced the **"Order of Proceedings"** which detailed the protocol order of arrivals of VIPs and others, as well as other details relevant to the event from beginning until the end. The timings were carefully worked out. It was carefully choreographed and meticulously executed to achieve clockwork precision. It was easier because of our leaders' respect for time and their insistence on efficiency. Such efficiency and cooperative working relationships was absent in many countries. In a few countries I have served, I noted that the leaders did not value punctuality and the officials serving them had no control over the timings. As usual of course, the protocol was blamed for the lapses though they were not responsible. That is part and parcel of life in protocol.

LEAN AND HUNGRY

I always thought to myself that I had a slight advantage compared to some other officers whom I knew, in so far as serving PM Lee was concerned. To my knowledge, PM Lee did not like very much officers with big bellies and pot bellies being the worst. I think he associated this condition and appearance with lack of discipline and, especially, in the light of his belief in being **"lean and hungry"**. As I mentioned earlier, I was skinny and had remained so throughout my life. In school and even later in adult life, many would make fun of me for this. I think it was my DNA (both my parents were very trim) and not so much the early hardship and scarcity of food. The next chapter is on food.

Chapter 20

FOOD IN DIPLOMACY

Food for thought.

My wife, to this day, has never understood why even after eating her good food, that I should still be "skin and bones" as she often used to say, causing her embarrassment. She was concerned that people would conclude that she was not feeding me and the children well at home! The irony was that she is a good cook and her cuisines were much appreciated by many, both at home and abroad. We found that serving a variety of Singaporean dishes were a great hit with our guests during the years we served abroad in different countries. In select cases, my wife even sent food to our friends' residences for their quiet family enjoyment. Generally, the useful contribution of foreign service wives to diplomacy has been under appreciated.

Throughout the ages, food has been an important and integral part of diplomacy. One instance from my experiences stands out. The US ambassador in Cairo did not go to residences of other ambassadors, especially those from small countries. I had developed good relations with three successive US ambassadors in Cairo. My wife took some effort to prepare several dishes and sent them to the US ambassador's residence for a family dinner. She had arranged to bring special items, including banana leaves, from Singapore. On one occasion, the US Ambassador, sent me a nice note to thank us for the **"feast fit for a king"**. (I have misplaced his letter.) My wife helped me very much in my duties in this way. Here is another interesting anecdote. The newly arrived Russian Ambassador called on me at the chancery (office). While signing the visitor's book he noticed that the two visitors before him, who had called on me, were the new US and Chinese ambassadors and he commented that **"only superpowers seem to call on you"**. Normally, the US ambassadors do not call on ambassadors of other countries except the "big boys", usually the P5 (Permanent Members of the United Nations Security Council). That is the reality and there is no point lamenting it. Cultivating contacts were necessary. My wife and I also had entertained most of our important contacts at our official residence.

I would like to state here for the information of the readers as to how, why and when such official entertainment is hosted or accepted, and above all accounted for, as public funds are involved. Necessary details and guidelines, including amounts allowed to be spent by the head of the mission and his diplomatic staff were set in the relevant circulars. Briefly, the objective for hosting official entertainment is to forge friendship with selected guests, as part of the on-going programme to develop and cultivate useful contacts in the host country, which are essential for the efficient performance of the mission to achieve its agenda. The entertainment takes a variety forms; it can be a breakfast, lunch, dinner, a cultural or a social event, or even participation in sports and the like depending on the purpose and objective. Equally, attending official functions also have broadly the same objective. A head of mission can host the function either at his residence or in a public place such as a restaurant. My wife and I preferred our residence for several reasons:

- that it creates a homely glow and a warm atmosphere;
- ensures privacy when it is needed:
- guests expect to be served authentic Singapore cuisine; and
- facilitates better interaction among guests.

When the function is hosted in a restaurant the accounting part is quite easy. Check through the bill and, if all the entries therein are correct, pay the bill, get the receipt and submit it with the detailed information required for reimbursement. However, home entertainment involves much more effort, especially for my wife. We found our reward in guests' appreciation of our efforts, the food served, and the enduring friendship we made which greatly helped me in my performance as ambassador and the mission as a whole.

Now comes the even harder part — preparing the accounts for the expenses incurred. Without wanting to sound boastful, I would like to say that our guests have always complimented my wife for her culinary skills and for her gracious manners. However, the nitty gritty of keeping records of purchases made, the amount spent on individual items, and other related administrative details, were not her cup of tea. I had to manage this. As necessary, an ambassador and other diplomatic staff who entertain on official duty, submit a detailed **Statement of Account** on the prescribed form, giving all relevant details such as the name and appointment of the officer, venue, number of guests that attended, purpose of entertaining, the items of food served, the amount claimed with receipts for each item e.g. fish, chicken, lamb, ingredients and other items. Where receipts were not given by the vendor, e.g. fish bought in a wet market, the officer claiming reimbursement has to state why a receipt was not available. Sometimes, we did not claim for some items which were taken from our personal stock, where it would be difficult to apportion the cost of the groceries used for official purpose. My wife also used to buy ingredients during trips back home and bring them to Egypt. On several occasions, she brought banana leaves to serve food for guests. It was a big hit, as I mentioned earlier. All officers were required to submit monthly representational activities undertaken by them and this included all activities, for example, calls made and received, meetings held and attended, talks and lectures given and attended, trade and investment promotions, and the entertainment functions hosted and attended. Nil returns were required where applicable in all these cases and the purpose of, say hosting a function, also needed to be given. After verification of the statement of account the officer would be reimbursed promptly.

On a lighter note, my wife was often asked, given that she is a strict vegetarian, how was it that she could cook non-vegetarian meals so well. She became a vegetarian some years after we were married, and I hasten to add that I had nothing to do with her decision to be a vegetarian. She has remained a strict vegetarian to this day. She acquired her culinary skills by learning from her mother and my mother, and both were good cooks in their own right. I watched my mother preparing tasty meals with the very little we had, using a wood-burning clay stove. I used to help her to find dry twigs and sometime chopped discarded logs to fire the stove. I am proud to say that the cooking skills I learnt from my mother have served me very well ever since, particularly during my posting in London when I was a bachelor. To this day, I do cook frequently at home. My wife excels in some dishes while in others it is me. By the way, I am not a vegetarian but I prefer vegetarian meals. I eat fish frequently, and meat like chicken and lamb occasionally, and even that at the urgings of my wife, strange as it might seem.

In my view, entertaining is one of the tools that oils the wheels of diplomacy. However, the ambassador must do much more than that, in order to excel in his mission, and to punch above his weight. The inescapable fact in this, is that the resources, both in terms of money and manpower are limited, and will always remain so for Singapore. Furthermore, our diplomatic missions usually covered larger geographical areas than many diplomatic missions of other countries. I have mentioned earlier of my concurrent accreditations from Egypt to Cyprus, Jordan, United Arab Emirates and Zimbabwe. To be effective in our representation and build good relations with those countries, I undertook on the average two visits per year to each country. I had to monitor the political, economic, social and security developments in those countries and report to Ministry as was appropriate and necessary. The constraints of distance had to be overcome by using the limited resources in innovative ways (I have mentioned some of these in another chapter). I read the relevant newspapers and journals, watched major international media channels, maintained close interactions with the concerned countries' ambassadors in Cairo, got briefed by the ambassadors of the P5 (permanent members of the United Nations Security Council) countries, which had very big diplomatic missions in the countries concerned and, usefully I also got frequent assessments from my friendly, knowledgeable, and obliging contacts in the Egyptian foreign ministry which also had sizeable diplomatic resident presence in all those countries. I found the Egyptian officials had a wealth of information and assessments about developments in the countries I was a non-resident ambassador.

I still remember what one of my teachers in my alma mater, Victoria School, told my class: **"There is no impression without expression".** In my observation and experience, this saying applies to diplomats as much as it does to practitioners of other professions. Before he can become effective and excel in his job, any diplomat, more so an ambassador, must be **seen, heard, recognised and respected,** not just in the official establishment, but in the wider community as well. One might ask, how to achieve this? Well, **there is more than one way to skin the cat**, if I may use the saying here. I have given many examples elsewhere in this book of how I used many of these tools, with much effect, to achieve my mission(s). However, one of the most effective tools, in my experience, is the proactive engagement of a very wide spectrum state and non-state actors in the host country: the government, the public and private sector institutions concerned with finance, economy, trade and investments; academia and institutions of learning, including schools, universities and IT institutes; political and social organisations; the media; NGOs; independent policy and research organisations, institutes of diplomacy, and the diplomatic corps.

My modus operandi was to undertake speaking engagements, for example giving talks, lectures, keynote addresses, participating in panel discussions, attending important seminars, participating in community events; giving interviews to media (both print and electronic), and any and all other avenues. After my first six months in Egypt, I believe I successfully managed to place myself in their radar and I received many invitations to address many of the abovementioned organisations and institutions, in Egypt and the other countries to which I was concurrently accredited to, throughout my years in there. Readers will find in the book a few selected letters (from a large number) expressing deep appreciation of my contributions to the organisations and institutions concerned.

I must, however, add a word of caution here. In order to perform well in the above task I had to keep abreast of the regional and global issues and problems, particularly those that have impact on the environment, have a lively interest in political, economic and security developments likely to impact regional architecture, have access to relevant and reputable international journals to read relevant reports, think pieces and analyses on topics of interest (I subscribed at my own cost to a few of these journals and still do), had at my command relevant, credible and up to date statistics on a variety of issues that were of concern to the different audiences. There is also no one-size-fits-all approach, style, delivery or way of interacting. The relevance of the subject matter to the audience, their expectations of me as the speaker, and the key takeaways were all important considerations. Even a well thought out and prepared speech or lecture may founder if not pitched at the right level and delivered with passion and commitment. An ambassador who is not well prepared and is out of his depth will soon be found out and side-lined. In my view, it would be unwise for any ambassador to accept such invitations, if he or she is not up to the task. It would be simply counterproductive.

Here, I would like to share a conversation I had with a very senior diplomat from a mid-sized country, on what he said about engaging with the various actors in the host country where we were both serving at that time. He lamented the negative perceptions of his country and the forceful and somewhat aggressive tone (read not so polite) and manners in questioning the diplomats, especially by the journalists and academics. He said that for him it was **like entering a lion's den** and that he preferred not to take the risk. I told him that, precisely for the reasons he mentioned, he should vigorously engage with them. I told him he should defend his country, put forward his country's case and seek a balanced appreciation of his country's policies. He did not respond to my suggestion, but judging from his body language, it seemed to have fallen on deaf years. All I can say is that, **in my experience and observation, an ambassador gets the respect that he earns.** Besides, I was always convinced that there was no law of nature that provided that small countries, like Singapore, that lack much political influence and natural and human resources, would necessarily figure or matter in the calculations of bigger countries and major global players. We simply have to make it happen, by mobilising the limited resources available to us and putting them to best use. In short, we must make ourselves relevant to them and the ambassador is an integral part in achieving that. It will always remain a work in progress.

I have given many examples of how I engaged the various sectors in the host countries to which I was accredited, including in countries where I was concurrently accredited to. It was my belief that building a strong and broad network of important and influential actors at all levels was, to use business language, a very important investment and I was more than satisfied with the returns. I give below a few more anecdotes to illustrate the point I am making.

That I managed to get Amr Moussa, Foreign Minister of Egypt, to visit Singapore, surprised many ambassadors, not just those from Asian countries, but also a few Western ambassadors, including the Polish and the Australian ambassadors. These countries had been trying for some time to get Moussa to reciprocate the visits of their own leaders to Egypt. The Egyptian leaders did not normally bother with small countries very much. Therefore, many ASEAN countries were not on their radar. US, Japan, China, Germany and UK, and France got better treatment because they were donors of aid. During my time, US aid to Egypt was about US$2.1 billion, which was second only to the aid given to Israel. There was no point in whinging that Egypt did not give much attention to smaller countries. Nevertheless, I served for seven years in Egypt and did it not find it a problem to build up our bilateral relations.

One day, during my usual and frequent rounds in the Egyptian Foreign Ministry, I called on the Assistant Minister (I cannot quite recall his name now, it could be Abu Gheit) who was also a senior aide to Moussa. While welcoming me, he said, "we were talking about you at the Gezira Club last night". Somewhat surprised, I jokingly asked him, "'why, have you decided to throw me out?". He laughed and said, "no, on the contrary, my colleagues were saying you are doing very well here". Noting my surprise, he told me that the talk I gave at the **American International School** (AIS) was very well received and people were talking about it. I asked him how he came to know about it. His answer was "my daughter studies at the school and she was present when you gave the talk". I quickly seized the opportunity. I thanked him for the compliment and told him that "my government would not be convinced of my good work until I am able to get Minister Moussa to return the visit of my Minister Jayakumar to Egypt". I also told him that I did not expect Moussa to make a separate visit to Singapore, but maybe he could stopover in Singapore during one of the many visits he made to Japan and China. (After US, Japan and to a lesser extent China were big aid donors to Egypt then.) As an incentive, I mentioned that both ministers could have a useful exchange of views on developments in their respective regions. As a further incentive, I mentioned that we could arrange for Moussa to give a lecture under the Singapore Lecture auspices. He said "leave it to me.... I will get back to you soon". He called me a few days later to say that Moussa had agreed to visit Singapore, and gave me a date. I quickly alerted my Ministry and it started the preparations immediately.

I had kept Moussa's visit a secret, for good reason. I informed my ASEAN colleagues only on the day of Moussa's departure for Singapore. Predictably, their reaction was disappointment and even, barely concealed anger, that Moussa was not visiting their countries, as well. The Malaysian, Indonesian and Brunei ambassadors appeared to be hurt that Moussa had not reciprocated the visits of their leaders, despite repeated renewal of their invitations to Moussa, over a long period. Had I informed my colleagues earlier of Moussa visiting Singapore, they would certainly have made strong representations to Moussa to visit their countries as well, and that may have scuttled his visit to Singapore. The Polish Ambassador told me that her government had been trying to get Moussa to go to Poland, without success, and was quite surprised that I succeeded.

Some of my ASEAN colleagues were surprised when some P5 ambassadors, including from US, were invited to the farewell dinner the Egyptian Foreign Ministry hosted for me and my wife. From the feedback that reached me, I sensed that there was some unhappiness over the fact that their ambassadors had not been accorded similar courtesy from the host government.

My success in this regard was a return on my investment. I generally knew that the Egyptian elite sent their children to prestigious educational institutions like AIS, American University in Cairo and Cairo University, amongst others, although I did not specifically know, until then, that the assistant minister's daughter was in AIS. During my posting in Egypt, I had also given several keynote addresses in their leading universities and other relevant private and government institutions, and this fact was known to the Egyptian elite. To my knowledge, none of my ASEAN colleagues bothered to cultivate constituencies outside the usual government and government-related agencies, despite the many advantages, such as large student populations enrolled in **Al Azar University**, a large number of staff in their embassies, and religious affinity and solidarity with the host community, that they enjoyed.

Another factor which helped me was that the Egyptian leadership knew that I was active in promoting trade and investment with Egypt. I give three examples below:

(a) Food security is important for us in Singapore and it is a good policy to diversify our sources as much as possible. I noticed that Picco, a high-tech farm in Egypt, produced good strawberries and the cost was reasonable. I contacted its general manager and told him to explore exporting them to Singapore. Upon his request for advice, I told him that to my knowledge the cargo space in Egypt Air flights to Singapore was mostly empty and that he could work out a good deal to transport the fruits. I advised him to visit supermarkets (I named them) in Singapore and negotiate the deal. I also told him that his strawberries, and other fruits like mangoes, could hit outlets at the right time in Singapore when other suppliers could not meet the demand, owing to different growing seasons in other producer countries. About a month later, he came to see me in my office and told me that he had already made shipments to Singapore and thanked me for my help. This is the background to the presence of Egyptians fruits in our sales outlets;

(b) The second was importing sand from the coastal desert in Egypt, for our land reclamation. For the readers' information, Egypt had abundant supply of good quality very fine sand which I understood was used in Hi Tec applications. I noticed very large ships (VLCC type) went empty from Egypt to Australia to bring back wheat to Egypt. I thought that the ships could easily unload the sand in Singapore on the way to Australia and the cost would be marginal. I discussed this with **Lee Ek Tieng** who was then in the Government Investment Corporation. He thought the idea was good but there could be technical problems. It would require ships with a special hull to drop the sand into the designated site in the reclamation area in Singapore. In short, the idea was not viable due to technical issues.

(c) The third was for investment into Egypt. I worked with the Egyptian authorities to get our Port of Singapore Authority (PSA) to participate in the Damietta port development. PSA was interested and **Goon Kek Loon** from PSA worked hard on it and, if my memory serves me correct, he submitted tender documents. Earlier, at my recommendation, the government invited the Egyptian prime minister to visit Singapore and an important component of the visit was a tour of PSA, our port operation, and its investments overseas in port management and development. The nearest PSA investment in the region then was Italy.

In his letter to thank me, he said he was impressed with what he saw in Singapore and gave me the impression that he wanted PSA's cooperation and investment in Egypt. However, I sensed that there was no political will to move. After very careful consideration, PSA decided to withdraw from the bidding process for the Damietta port development. I might also add here that I had arranged for the Governor of Alexandria to visit Singapore. In my discussions with the governor (a senior figure in the establishment and a Mubarak confidant), Singapore, with its developed technology in waste management, could offer solutions for the very serious waste disposal problems faced by Egypt. Also, I suggested a possible cooperation on developing the marina along the excellent seafronts in Alexandria that could draw a slice of the business from the across the Mediterranean, principally from Italy, Greece and Spain. Again, he came back seemingly with much enthusiasm, but nothing much came of it; and

(d) The Egyptian officials also knew that I had an excellent record and was scrupulous in my compliance of the relevant Egyptian laws, customs and the provisions in VCDR. (I have earlier mentioned the diplomatic missions that did not have a good record in this.)

It is important that we do not take this for granted and that we find ways to value-add to the bilateral relations for mutual benefit. Egyptians are warm and hospital people, and I was always treated with respect and courtesy by the whole community. It is this solid, deep, and mature relations which my team and I built-up across the spectrum in Egypt, that enabled us to ride out the problem that arose in our bilateral relations when Singapore imposed the visa for Egyptian nationals. Details on this are given in a later chapter.

I believe it is worth repeating here that the **"3Ps"** — **professional, proactive and productive** (in that order) — which I always emphasise in my training of protocol staff, diplomats and administrators.

A professional and proactive ambassador and his staff will achieve much higher productivity, than a laid-back mission. They will get recognised by and earn the respect of the receiving State, which are important requisites for developing a strong and rooted bilateral relationship. For this, there needs to be a great deal of teamwork between the ambassador and his staff.

Finally, I firmly believe that an ambassador should not become disheartened when every effort of his or hers does not succeed. I consider not trying as a bigger failure. Success and failure are two sides of the same coin. That is just the nature of things. This brings me to my next chapter: "Success and Failure".

Chapter 21

SUCCESS AND FAILURE

Success has many fathers; failure is an orphan.

It has been acknowledged around the world that Singapore has succeeded beyond anyone's expectations. It earned us respect and enabled us, as often said, to "punch above our weight". It was, in short, due to the cooperative partnership between the honest, incorruptible, and courageous political leadership, and the hard-working citizenry who were all willing to make the sacrifices that were necessary. Collectively, we **stood up for Singapore** and are proud of it.

However, in my view, success and failure are two sides of the same coin. In any "economic miracle" there are some sections of the population impacted adversely or feel disadvantaged.

BIRTH CONTROL

Controlling population increase through birth control was considered necessary back then, to address unemployment and housing problems, amongst others. The campaigns to control births were vigorous and relentless. The blitz through posters, radio, television and print media drove home the message of the two-child policy. The posters and other visuals carried pictures of two children with captions **"stop at two... the more you have the less they get..."**.

Punishment came in the form of "disincentives", of which there were many, such as increased hospital charges, including accouchement fees, for third and subsequent child, loss of priority for school admission and the like. If a couple ignored this policy, they were unofficially deemed anti-national. Many mothers were driven to voluntary sterilization just so that their children did not lose out.

Many families, including mine, and the nation as a whole has paid a price since.

The strategy of boosting economic growth through limiting the number of people entering the labour market made sense in initial years, but the policy planners left it too long on an **"autopilot"**. The population declined fast, thanks to the cooperative population, and when the planners woke up from their slumber, it was too late, and the damage had already been done — posing a serious risk to economic growth and ultimately, our survival as a prosperous nation. Attempts to reverse the decline, by pouring money into incentivising couples of reproductive ages to have more children, did not work as expected. Couples now face serious problems and hardships, which disincentivise them from getting married and raising families. Among them are:

- Work-related stress — I am personally aware of cases where people of marriageable age need to work 12 hours (sometimes 16 hours) at the workplace. Even during weekends and holidays, concern about work matters is never away from the mind. In such circumstances, they just "live to work" and it does not require a genius to realise the deleterious effect on health this has. It is like burning the candle at both ends;
- Cost of housing — The rising cost of housing and the high cost of bringing up children do not create an encouraging environment for young people to tie the knot;

- Longer life expectancy — with rising longevity of parents, there is an increasing cost, both in terms of time and finance to care for and support one's parents (while simultaneously balancing work and raising a family).

In Japan, which also suffers from a serious contraction in birth rate, all these problems have become even more serious. At the time of writing, there is an alarming rate of suicide reported among young Japanese people who were unable to manage work stress. There is a growing vocal demand for the government to legislate and reduce Japan's legendary long working hours, and punish the bosses who fail to comply. Many observers have expressed doubts as to whether legislation alone can solve the problem. As I have understood, the only government response, thus far, is to cap over-time work at 100 hours per month. Not everyone is convinced that this very modest measure will work. Many believe that it has become too late for Japan to reverse the decline.

We, in Singapore, must feel the urgency and bring together all our resources to arrest and reverse the problem, before it becomes too late for us as well. There are no easy solutions. However, we must try and find the solutions, for the sake of our survival as a nation.

Our success in lowering our birth rate has become, in my view, an albatross around our neck. Some have cited the trend in other affluent societies, and argued that the decline was inevitable, due to rising prosperity. However, it is my belief that our policies sped up that process.

I believe that the one person who perhaps could have reversed the policy in time was PM Lee. However, it is not clear if our policy planners had read the trend and alerted the political leadership in time about the consequences of continuing with the "stop at two" policy. It was implemented with great zeal and **collectively, we failed to anticipate the very serious implications of the "stop at two" policy on the long term well-being of our nation.**

IMMIGRATION

To make up for the shortfall, immigration rules were relaxed quickly to let in large numbers of foreigners in quick succession, and it was billed as attracting **"foreign talent"**. Soon foreigners comprised approximately 20% of the population, within about two decades. At that time, there were many senior officers who argued that immigration, in the way it was being implemented, was the right way to address the issue. Even a senior officer who I knew, wrote in the forum page of our national newspaper, arguing the same thing and he cited the United States (US) example in support. In a reply to that piece, **I argued that Singapore as an immigrant society would always need immigrants. However, immigration had to be calibrated by taking into account many factors.** The US example does not fit because US is a huge country spread over 17.1 million sq kms (compared to Singapore's mere 721.5 sq kms) and immigrants there were dispersed throughout that vast country. Even then, the US had not let in immigrants in the same proportion, relative to its population size, in such short a time, as Singapore has done. Despite these advantages, tensions between new immigrants and the established communities in the US have started to increase.

In recent years, there has been an increasing concern over widespread "hate crimes" being committed against racial and religious minorities in the US and Europe. An alarming trend of foreigners getting shot and killed, for no other reason than the fact that they were foreigners, have been reported in the US. US President Donald Trump's determination to build a wall along the border with Mexico to keep immigrants out and asking the Mexican

Government pay for the cost, reflects the seriousness of the problem. He insisted that he was prepared to keep the US Government partial shutdown going for as long as it took for the Congress to yield and approve more than US$5 billion to construct the wall. In the European Union (EU), the situation is not much better either. One of the major factors for Britain wanting to leave EU **(BREXIT)** was to stem the increasing flood of immigrants entering the United Kingdom, from mostly the rest of the European Union. It also has become a major sticking point in the ongoing BREXIT negotiations for the "divorce agreement". Furthermore, countries like US and Australia also appear to be adopting policies to further restrict immigration, toughen citizenship laws and reduce work visas, even for very highly skilled professionals from abroad.

Calibrated intake is essential to avoid social tensions and the stress on infrastructure that would inevitably arise in a small place like Singapore, if the flood gates are opened too quickly. There is a problem of overcrowding in buses and MRT trains. I remember missing two buses for a journey to Singapore General Hospital; the buses simply refused to stop because there were no more standing spaces in them. The buses were packed so tightly that the drivers found it difficult to close the doors. Recent improvements made to the transport system to relieve congestion has been welcomed.

EMIGRATION

Other factors that compounded our population crisis, apart from the declining birth rate, are the emigration of our young and talented to foreign countries (brain drain) and that many young people of marriageable age are choosing not to get married. There were many reasons given and among them were **"nothing to hold them here", "better life abroad", "being second class citizens in the land of birth", "rising high cost of living"** and **"problems in raising a family".** It was not certain whether enough efforts were made to address these concerns. It must be conceded that in a globalised world, people migrating to other countries has become a fact of life. The younger generation of Singaporeans are better educated, possess high skill levels, enjoy affluence, and are more competitive and mobile than the generations before them. Their skills are, to my knowledge, appreciated abroad and the respect and admiration Singapore has earned abroad opens many doors for them. In a way, we might be a victim of our own success. Therefore, strenuous efforts must be made to make Singapore citizens, especially the **Singapore born**, feel **rooted in Singapore** and **feel that Singapore is their home**. Replacing emigrating Singapore citizens with foreign talent is a relatively easier fix, but relying on such a policy on a permanent basis would bring in its train many long-term and serious consequences for the future of our beloved Republic.

Another problem was the bilingualism policy. Many would agree that it was necessary but applying the policy rigorously without flexibility has resulted in some damage. Many students with very high examination scores were denied admission into our universities because they did not have bilingual qualifications at a required level. My friend's daughter who had very high scores, well above the minimum requirements to study medicine, had her application rejected by the National University of Singapore because her Mandarin language score was not good enough. She migrated to the US for good, much to the disappointment of her parents. I have known other similar cases. I understand that there has been some flexibility in this regard, in later years, and it is now not as big a problem as it was then.

FOREIGN TALENTS

I had heard stories of "foreign talents" getting in based on fake qualifications that escaped the scrutiny of relevant authorities. In

Singapore, it would be very difficult indeed to forge documentation of Singapore institutions, and go undetected. This is not the case in many other countries, near and far. In some countries, fake degrees, diplomas and certificates are bought and sold without the person concerned ever having to step into the institutions concerned. Even some ministers were found to have faked their qualifications with impunity. Additionally, widespread cheating in examinations has been widely reported in some countries. It is an injustice to Singapore citizens when he or she loses out to an unqualified "foreign talent" in such circumstances.

A young citizen, a polytechnic graduate, had to work under a Malaysian supervisor who had a qualification from a *bumiputra* polytechnic, but had no idea of the skills required for the job to which he was recruited. To add insult to injury, the young Singaporean working under him was called all the time to fix the problems that his boss could not even figure out, never mind fix. In that particular case, the personnel manager who recruited the Malaysian "technician" was himself a Malaysian! This is an instance of foreigners bringing in their own kind, and getting them employed in Singapore, at the expense of Singaporeans. I do not think this was an isolated case. A secretary narrated to me that when she went for an interview in a foreign firm in Singapore, she was told to her face that there was no need for them to take in Singaporeans when they could bring in their own nationals and pay them far less. She was devastated and angry. I had the impression that some **employers went through the motion of interviewing citizens, only to claim that they could not get suitable Singaporeans for the job.** One swallow does not make a summer. Nevertheless, vigilance and tighter scrutiny on the part of relevant ministries is required, before approving the necessary permits to employ foreigners, to prevent such fraudulent practices. This is not a unique problem to Singapore.

In Singapore, the cost of living and commitments for Singaporeans is generally much higher than for foreigners and, therefore, it should be obvious that they cannot manage on wages that the foreigners can, especially in the middle and lower-end jobs. A citizen security guard at age 62 and having been in the job for more than 10 years, was replaced by a foreign national because the latter was "cheaper". However, this problem is not limited to lower and middle-end jobs. I have also heard that many able and talented Singapore born citizens, working under foreign talent bosses, (both in the public and in private sector enterprises), complain that their foreign bosses rode on the back of their hard work and achievements. These bosses, passed off the Singaporeans' hard work as their own and took credit for it. Thus, the Singaporeans felt that they did not get due credit or recognition from the management. Such a situation does not contribute to nurturing our own home-grown talent. Due to the nature of this problem, hard statistics are difficult to come by. However, **it would be unwise to assume that the problem does not exist**. Singaporeans in general are competitive and accept the need for it. However, they need to feel that the playing field is level and not tilted against them in their own homeland. Talent is crucial and Singapore should seek it abroad as a **supplement,** but it must be carefully calibrated, so that it does not undermine the confidence of our home-grown talent. It is a fine balance and is not an easy task by any means. Yet, it must be done in the long-term interest of our nation.

I have also heard of complaints from young Singaporeans about how they were discriminated against in the job market. Included amongst them were those seeking jobs after completing their national service, who felt they were unfairly rejected by employers, both local and foreign, who allegedly favoured foreigners for the cost advantage but also who had no national service obligations. It would be unwise to assume that all these were untrue accounts. Singapore citizens are our core and they should not be made to feel like "second-class citizens" in their own country by such unscrupulous practices and tactics of some employers. Our citizens are the ones who will **"stand up for Singapore"**, not the birds of passage. If indeed the above accounts are true, then, it would be difficult to find a similar situation in any other country.

MONETARY REWARDS

We had a campaign **"work for reward and reward for work"**. The idea that reward is pegged to productivity is undeniable, and it is necessary to maintain Singapore's competitiveness. The question is what the quantum of that reward should be. The quantum of rewards, especially for senior echelons had attracted controversies both at home and abroad.

During the years I served abroad as an ambassador, I observed, especially in Australia and New Zealand, their community spirit and pride in serving their nation. These countries had to battle frequently devastating bush fires, and more so in Australia where it is much drier. Bulk of the fire fighters in these countries were mostly volunteers and many of them had sacrificed their lives in battling the fires, literally in the line of fire. They were held in high esteem in the community and the bereaved families spoke with pride about how their loved ones sacrificed their lives, so that the others could live. Expectations of monetary reward never entered their minds and was not given either. I had also seen television news footage of volunteer fire fighters battling, along with regular fire service personnel, huge forest fires in US, Canada and in Europe. In the process, many made the ultimate sacrifice.

Even after factoring in the low cost of living, relative to Singapore, salaries in New Zealand were lower than in Singapore, where the disparity between top echelons and the rest was wide, quite unlike in New Zealand. Yet, New Zealand along with Sweden, Denmark,

Switzerland, and Singapore, had been among the top ten nations with the least corruption in global ranking. New Zealand had also consistently punched above its weight in international relations. Its former prime minister, Helen Clarke, was one of the contenders for Ban Kee Moon's job as the United Nations Secretary General, and a former New Zealand foreign minister, Don McKinnon became the Commonwealth Secretary General. I found the Kiwis were a proud and happy people. I have read reports that many young Kiwis who went to work abroad returned home for good, after successful careers abroad. It appeared that, for them, home was always New Zealand. It would be interesting to note what the statistics are for Singaporeans in this regard and what we could learn from the Kiwis.

Not everything in life should be allotted monetary value or seen in monetary terms. There is saying that **"not everything in life that counts can be counted"**. Sadly, many professions are no longer a calling but have become competitive and aggressive businesses. I recall one minister made a statement in the late 1970s or early 1980s to the effect that any civil servant who was worth his (or her) salt would have left for the private sector *to make more money* (emphasis mine). Taking his cue, a few senior civil servants did resign, and the statement was quickly retracted afterwards. Leaving all humility aside, a vast majority of my colleagues and I chose to remain in the service, not because we had no alternatives, but out of pride in contributing to the building of our nation. We never looked back and had no regrets, even if we had many disappointments in our career advancements. I entered law practice only after I retired and one very high public official asked me **"how is your business"** to which my polite response was: I was not in business but in law practice. I did not get the feeling that he was amused. Somehow, many in our society have come to measure success as the amount of money one makes from his or her work. **Money is important but so also are many other things in life.**

SUCCESS HAS MANY FATHERS, FAILURE IS AN ORPHAN

In the civil service, like elsewhere, there was a tendency to claim success and disown failure. The Israeli Ambassador, **Moshe Ben-Yaacov**, met me after the visit of his president, Chaim Herzog, commended me and my team for the successful visit and said the higher ups in the Ministry would be very pleased with my team's performance. I told him that in protocol success was taken for granted and shortcomings were often highlighted. With a smile he said "**success has many fathers and failure is an orphan**". In this regard, I would like to recall two anecdotes involving the community service I did.

The first was very early in my life. In the 1950 elections, I was a sort of unofficial election helper to the Liberal Socialist candidate, Goh Tong Liang, contesting in Bukit Panjang. I was in school then. The only other candidate who stood against Goh Tong Liang was from the Singapore UMNO. When Goh Tong Liang won, I wrote to him to install a standpipe to relieve the water problem in our area. He obliged and the standpipe was installed. Immediately, the defeated UMNO candidate went around telling our Malay brothers and sisters in our midst that it was he who arranged it and took the credit.

Three decades later in 1984, I was appointed Chairman of the Hindu Endowments Board (HEB) by the Minister for Home Affairs. HEB is a statutory organisation. HEB was responsible for the administration of four big Hindu temples and their property (collectively termed the "Endowments"). I was keen to involve the HEB in community work in order to serve the community as well. For example, I suggested operating a Tamil kindergarten, counselling drug addicts, and having family counselling in existing facilities. I faced opposition both within the Board and outside. In a telephone call, one high-ranking public officer told me that, as Chairman of the Board, my job was just to manage the Board's properties and not to do community work. Those who opposed me insisted that the legislation that created HEB had no provision for community service. I tried to get as many members as I could to support me and proceeded to implement them with the help of many other volunteers and well-wishers, who contributed much time and energy. I convinced them that doing community service was not against the spirit of the Hindu Endowments Board. I owe a deep debt of gratitude to all those in the Board and the community, who supported me in this undertaking, and all the volunteers who responded to my call to launch the projects.

The pioneering projects were well received, especially the kindergarten, which fulfilled a crying need of the community. There was a long waiting list to enrol and it became a model for a few other kindergartens that came later. Years later, when the government announced a policy encouraging different communities to do more to help the needy in their midst, those who had strongly opposed me, including the high official referred to above, were the first to claim credit for the projects that I started! Whenever one in their midst passed away, the others would attribute the credit to the deceased in the obituary. Indeed, there were many "fathers". Moshe Ben-Yaacov was dead right. However, at the grassroots level, I was recognised and respected, and that gave me and all my colleagues who had sacrificed much, immense satisfaction.

I involved the HEB in educational counselling because the Indian students were falling behind the other communities in primary and secondary schools. With the help of some dedicated teachers and friends, we held counselling sessions on Sunday mornings at the premises of the Kaliamman Temple in Toa Payoh, which was also the venue of the kindergarten. The temple premises were used because finances were tight. Many of my friends, including many busy professionals, gave much of their time to serve as mentors to selected students, who had difficult problems, both financially and socially. I owe a big debt of gratitude to all of them for their generous support. Limitations of space does not permit me to list the names of all of them. However, I would like to specially mention the valuable contributions of **Dr G Raman, R Jothi**, **KP Sivam, K Shanmugam, K Kannappan and A Palaniappan** amongst others.

There were frustrating times, as well. I remember a young lady who, with hard work, determination, and coaching from counsellors, managed straight "As" in all her subjects and, yet, could not get admission to study medicine in NUS. I appealed to a very senior member of parliament (who was also a minister) for assistance, but to no avail. The reply was that she "did not meet the usual criteria". We felt that we had let down that worthy candidate and it was especially painful for us. Many felt that in the context of the problems in the community then, the playing field was not level.

The **Singapore Indian Development Association** (SINDA) came later. I was in the initial pro-team group of persons, headed by **JYM Pillay,** that started the work to establish SINDA.

I end this chapter with this thought. There is a tendency to take Singapore's success for granted. Countless number of Singaporeans from all walks of life have made much sacrifice to create the conditions that are vital for our success. One such condition is our **national security**. We must not forget to thank the **Singapore Armed Forces (SAF),** in particular those who serve in the **National Service,** including the **Reservists.** It grieves me whenever I read reports of young lives cut short, due to mishaps during their training exercises. It is particularly hard for the concerned families to come to terms with such tragedies, nothing can compensate for the loss and grief that they must feel. We owe a debt of gratitude to all of them. It is their hard work and the sacrifice that enable us to sleep peacefully at night.

Chapter 22

POWER OF KNOWLEDGE

"It would not be impossible to prove, with sufficient repetition and a psychological understanding of the people concerned, that a square is in fact a circle. They are mere words, and words can be manipulated to clothe the ideas"

"If you tell a lie big enough and keep repeating it people will eventually believe it"

—*Joseph Goebbels, Adolf Hitler's propaganda chief*

In the conduct of diplomacy, depth of knowledge and good information is among the indispensable tools needed by diplomats. The foreign ministry never rests. There is always something happening somewhere in the world which could impact Singapore in some form or other. Therefore, our diplomats and other staff in the Foreign Ministry always had to be alert, to deal with developing events, both expected and unexpected, as they happen. In my experience, the foreign ministry is the best place to be for anyone who has a lively interest in current affairs, a flair for international relations, and a desire to excel in the rough and tumble of international diplomacy. I would not have exchanged my experience there for any other.

Knowledge also gives many advantages, like building bonds of friendship, gaining influence and power — all of which are good assets in diplomacy. However, the extent of satisfaction derived would depend on how resourceful and imaginative one is. Not being in the know has its perils.

Even seemingly ordinary and mundane news can be put to good use. I had mentioned earlier that during my term as ambassador in Egypt I also covered other countries — Cyprus, Jordan, United Arab Emirates and Zimbabwe, where I was officially accredited. It was also necessary for me to monitor developments in other nearby countries, which were important players in the region. I, at my own cost, travelled to some of these countries where I was not accredited.

It was my practice to read several regional newspapers (hard copies as they were not available online then) and watch selected television channels. One day, I read in the "Jerusalem Post" that Israel had decided to close its embassy in Kathmandu (Nepal). I knew the Nepalese Ambassador in Cairo, **Gopi**, was accredited to Israel as well and that he used to make regular visits to Tel Aviv. I called him to find out whether he had seen the report and why the Israelis had decided to take that action. To my surprise, he sounded shocked and concerned, and asked me to fax him the report immediately, which I obliged.

About a week later, he came to see me and thanked me for alerting him to the news. He said that when he contacted his ministry in Kathmandu, it was a shock to them as well, and he was instructed to go to Tel Aviv immediately and plead with the Israelis to reconsider and reverse their decision. It transpired that the Israeli decision to close its embassy was firm, but as a gesture of goodwill, they delayed the pull-out by several months. Gopi was grateful to me for the help. I was quite curious how such an important development in diplomatic relations could have gone unnoticed, why the Nepalese diplomats and their senior officials in their foreign ministry were completely in the dark and were taken by surprise. It is a normal practice in diplomacy for the sending State (Israel) to inform the receiving State (Nepal) well in advance of such decision, before making it public. Though Israel is a young country, their diplomats, to my knowledge and experience, were seasoned professionals. Probably, the Israelis gave the message in some form or other, and the Nepalese officials just had not picked it up, or that the note (or whatever the mode of communication sent) was lost in the Nepalese bureaucracy. It is my view, that in such circumstances, we should give whatever help we can, and it will help us to win friends in the wider international community.

When serving abroad, a diplomat has to make extra effort to keep abreast of developing issues. It is a fact that if a diplomat is not accredited to a State, he or she normally will not get access to the officials in that country. However, to overcome that, I developed good relations with all the diplomats of countries that were key players in the in the regional political, economic, and security landscape. I had to rely on other devices as well, including scanning major regional English newspapers (hard copies as in those days they were not available online). I also arranged for a local staff member in the embassy to monitor Arabic radio broadcasts, especially outside office hours, and alert me to important news and developments. I watched major international English news broadcast channels. I was put to the test when Israel's Prime Minister Yitzhak Rabin was assassinated in November 1995. My staff concerned called me around 11 P.M. to alert me to the news of Rabin's assassination. I assessed that the government would want to send an official to represent Singapore at the funeral which, in Jewish tradition, would take place within 24 hours. Therefore, time was very short. I called the duty officer in my Ministry (MFA) immediately. Thus, our government representative arrived on time and attended the funeral of Rabin. I was not accredited to Israel and made much of the arrangements required from Cairo.

Another situation in which I was again similarly tested, was in the case of the death of King Hussein of Jordan in February 1999. Unlike in the case of Rabin, Hussein was gravely ill, and his death was imminent. I was accredited to Jordan, but not residing in Amman. The problem was that I could not make arrangements for representation at the funeral until the official announcement was made. I advised MFA to hold provisional flight bookings, to enable our VIP to reach Amman in time after the announcement was made. Sensing that the announcement was imminent, judging from news bulletins on international channels, I hurried to Amman and made provisional booking for accommodation for our Minister in a hotel. The announcement was made the next day, around noon, and it was a Sunday. I called MFA immediately to put the plan into action. I was happy that I managed to pull it off. Minister Jayakumar attended the ceremony. Other world leaders who flew in their private jets were able to make it on time but many countries, including our neighbours, who had resident embassies in Amman, could not get their VIPs to arrive on time to attend the funeral. I also learnt that few VIPs were also not able to secure accommodation in hotels and had to billet with their ambassadors in Amman. I was satisfied with results of my efforts. I earned a commendation for my success in arranging the Minister's attendance:

> **"Minister has asked me to commend you for an excellent job in arranging his attendance at the funeral of Jordan's King. You have managed, under difficult conditions, to put everything in place in time for Minister to make a successful visit to Amman.**
>
> *(from Ministry's letter dated 5 March 1999).*

I will end this chapter with two anecdotes to illustrate the importance of keeping our leaders and diplomatic missions overseas, informed and updated of events at home as they develop.

Minister Dhanabalan, was in Sweden on an official visit when we announced the decision to expel the US diplomat, Eric Hendrickson, in 1986. I was leaving my office, then in Raffles City, at about 6.30 P.M., when I saw an ambassador, representing a country in North Asia, going to his car. Stopping very briefly, he mentioned "your government has taken a serious decision" or something to that effect. I had no clue as to what he was referring to. I replied "what needs to be done has to be done". Fortunately for me, he was in a hurry and left. I was then the Chief of Protocol.

When I reached home, I called the duty officer and it was then I learnt from him that a press release has been issued few hours before, declaring Hendrickson **persona non grata** and requiring him to leave Singapore. Out of curiosity, I called the hotel in Stockholm to check whether Dhanabalan was aware. To my surprise, the officers accompanying the minister told me that they were not aware of the expulsion or the press release. I gathered that Dhanabalan was getting ready to leave, to call on his Swedish counterpart and was due in about an hour from then. I asked the officer concerned to inform Dhanabalan immediately. By the time Dhanabalan met the Swedish foreign minister, the BBC had carried the news worldwide and, as could be expected, the Swedish minister raised the matter when he greeted Dhanabalan. As a cabinet minister, Dhanabalan would have known about the Hendrickson problem but not, as it happened, the actual announcement to expel him. The senior officer dealing with the matter in the Ministry had overlooked informing Dhanabalan. The next morning, I briefed the daily Directors' meeting on the action I took to inform Dhanabalan of the announcement. However, there was no reaction of any sort from those present.

It also happened to me when I was Ambassador in Cairo. Immediately after the 9/11 terrorist attacks on the Twin Towers in

New York and the Pentagon in Washington, Singapore, along with a number of other countries, imposed a visa for Egyptian nationals and nationals of few other countries. In the security context of the time, it was both necessary and urgent for us to implement the policy immediately. However, just before making the public announcement, the Ministry informed the Egyptian Ambassador in Singapore of the imminent announcement of the policy but I was not informed of the announcement. The announcement was made in late afternoon or evening (Singapore time). The next morning most of the newspapers and the radio and TV channels in Egypt reported the news, most of them criticising Singapore for imposing the visa. This was the first time we in the embassy came to know that our government had decided to impose the visa. There was one head of a sports group who was particularly emotional in his attack on us. He was joined by a few others who were asking their government to take up the matter with Singapore. At the embassy we were also taken by surprise and were flooded with calls, not all of them friendly to put it mildly.

I was summoned to their foreign ministry by a senior official who expressed displeasure at our policy and said that we should reconsider. I informed him that our Government had decided on the policy after careful consideration, to protect Singapore's security, following the 9/11 attacks that occurred in the preceding days, of which he was aware of. I had the impression that his Ministry was forced to act thus, to placate the boisterous crowd. The next day a few newspapers and radio and television channels reported the fact that I was summoned to their foreign ministry but in doing so they also stated incorrectly (perhaps deliberately) that the "Singapore Ambassador apologised" for the visa policy of his government. On the same day, I called the official concerned, referred him to the reports and reminded him that at no time in our brief meeting, I apologised for the Singapore Government's policy on the visa, as was being alleged. He knew that the reports were not true, but I had to make the point for the record. I kept my Ministry informed of all details. This was a temporary blip in our bilateral relations. With mature and professional handling of the matter, it did not become a problem. One of the reasons for the initial anger against our visa policy was the fact that to get a visa the applicant was required to get a Singaporean sponsor. The head of the sports group mentioned above told the media that a group from his sport were programmed to go to Singapore within a few days then and that he could not find a Singaporean sponsor to apply for the visa. Perhaps his anger was understandable in the circumstance.

There are few important lessons here for our diplomats:

- **Always** make sure that the ambassador and the mission is informed, as early as possible, and **before** the announcement of all policies concerning the receiving State (in this case Egypt), especially those that are likely to affect or have implications for bilateral relations. It is also a courtesy and a diplomatic practice to inform the counterpart ambassador (in this case the Egyptian ambassador) in Singapore at the appropriate time;
- The above lapse in communication can occur in any administration but for Singapore we must avoid it at all costs. In my training secessions on protocol and diplomacy for protocol officers and diplomats, both at home and abroad, I always emphasised the importance of **effective communication** between the ministry headquarters and its missions abroad. Failure to do so might embarrass the ambassador and the mission and affect their credibility and operational efficiency;
- An ambassador does not apologise to the host government for the policies of his own government. As the representative of his country, it is his duty is to implement the policy, as required, and defend it when necessary without reservation;

- It is of utmost importance also that the ambassador, working with his team, develops a broad-based constituency in the receiving State, which understands and appreciates his country's policies, administration and culture, amongst others. This must be done proactively by engaging, not just the political leaders and officials in the establishment, but a variety of organisations and actors both in the public and private sectors. They include business enterprises, institutions of learning, NGOs, media, think tanks, social organisations and others. Promoting trade and investment is very important in this regard. In another chapter I have given many examples of how my team and I achieved this task. It is, of course, always a work in progress. The point of this narrative is that with on-going solid and wide-ranging mutually beneficial relations, it would be easier to solve any problems that might arise in future; and
- It is in the nature of diplomacy and the conduct of relations between nations, that an ambassador **cannot expect an easy and comfortable ride all the time**. When problems occur, he and his team must be resilient enough to rise to the occasion and deal with them, to secure the best outcome for his nation, given the circumstances.

FAKE NEWS

Increasingly, diplomats, like their counterparts in other professions, have to be careful in deciphering **what is real and what is fake**. Fake news has become a tool for many, and social media is a minefield for the unwary. In fact, fake news is not actually a recent development. Disinformation has been around since ancient times and has been used as a weapon, both in war and during peace, throughout the ages. Here are some random examples:

- "It would not be impossible to prove, with sufficient repetition and a psychological understanding of the people concerned,

that a square is in fact a circle. They are mere words, and words can be manipulated to clothe the ideas".
"If you tell a lie big enough and keep repeating it, people will eventually come to believe it"
—**Joseph Goebbels, Adolf Hitler's propaganda chief**

- "Never believe anything in politics until it has been officially denied".
—**Otto von Bismarck, Germany's first Chancellor**
- "...political language is designed to make lies truthful and murder respectable, and to give appearance of solidity to pure wind"
—**George Orwell**
- "A lie can travel halfway round the world while truth is still putting on its shoes".
—**Unknown**

What is new and makes it dangerous is the power, speed and sophistication of social media, the internet and the digital world, enabled by the quantum leaps in technology revolution. We are in unchartered territory as to where the unimaginable power and sophistication of artificial intelligence (AI) will lead us. My question is who will control who?

Many governments around the world are concerned with the havoc that is being wreaked by deepfakes, perpetrated by a variety of actors, believed to involve state and non-state entities. The deepfakes feed an insatiable appetite for lurid and salacious stories in the global populace. This appears to be a new war in the information age. In my view, the genie is already out of the bottle and it would very difficult to put it back into the bottle and go for a good night's sleep! Dealing and coping with untruths (lies) on such a scale could well become an inevitable part of life for nations and individuals alike. As I see it, no country is immune to this danger, but small countries, like Singapore, with its global connectivity, multi-racial, multi-religious, multi-lingual and multi-cultural population, are particularly vulnerable. They need to be forever vigilant. Fighting a war in which the enemy is rarely visible will not be easy and requires the commitment of and cooperation from all who have an interest in keeping the state safe.

However, in my view, it would be unwise to conclude that social media as a tool is necessarily bad or evil. It is useful in exposing corruption, criminal behaviour and many other ills, plaguing society at large, and thus, bringing the leaders to account, in order to achieve good governance, both nationally and globally. That being said, social media is just like any other tool: it can be a shield or a weapon. If I may use the analogy of social media as a weapon, a well-known Indian leader, Krishna Menon, famously said in the United Nations in the 1950s that "**the gun that fires in only one direction is yet to be invented**". To put it in context, the acerbic Krishna Menon made that hard-hitting statement to demolish the claim by the then CIA Director, that the arms supplied by the United States to Pakistan was only for use against China. It is most unlikely that such a gun will ever be invented.

Nevertheless, and notwithstanding the hazards, diplomacy as a profession is as good as any other profession. A diplomat who is professional, well-informed and proactive will stand out in a crowd, gain respect and thereby will be more productive; others who prefer to enjoy the trappings of their office, positions and devote less energy to their work, could get marginalised and they will be not be taken seriously by their peers.

In my view, the moral, especially for diplomats, is to be wary of the pitfalls, and at the same time make every effort to master the game and use it skilfully to achieve the desired outcomes. In any case, social media is here to stay, and it is likely to get more sophisticated in its reach and operation. It can both reward and punish users. I believe that coming to grips with social media, and harnessing its energy for good while simultaneously curtailing its disruptive and destructive power, is likely to be the biggest challenge that democracies around the world will face, and this brings me to the next chapter: *"Western Democracy: Can It Deliver?"*

Chapter 23

WESTERN DEMOCRACY: CAN IT DELIVER?

"When the white missionaries came to Africa, they had the bible and we had the land. They told us to pray. We closed our eyes. When we opened them we had the bible and they had the land"

—**Desmond Tutu, the Archbishop of South Africa**

Why this chapter? I have two reasons.

FIRST REASON

Singapore's continued prosperity, well-being and global competitiveness depends on its ability to punch above its weight in the global marketplace. The foundation on which the whole edifice rests is **good governance**, which was painstakingly built beginning from 1959. In my view, if Singapore loses good governance, all will be lost.

The strong foundation for good governance in Singapore was laid by its pioneering, high-calibre leaders who were honest, incorruptible, and had an unwavering commitment to the progress of the nation. An important complement was the trust of the citizens, earned by the leadership over time, and also the willingness of the citizens to accept short-term pain for long-term national progress and well-being. It was a social contract. **This cannot be taken for**

granted and requires continuous vigilance, to maintain the integrity of the system.

As I saw it, we were staring at the abyss. We had to either survive or fade into oblivion, when we were cut adrift from Malaysia. We succeeded in reaching the level of development we enjoy now, against all the odds, defying the purveyors of impending doom, both within and outside. If not for that **iron will of our leaders right from the beginning, which has been maintained stoutly without compromise** ever since and surmounting at the same time enormous challenges along the way, I would not be here to write this book.

It is important to keep abreast of developments globally and **always learn the right lessons.** Therefore, it is important to adopt and/or adapt the best practices and policies and, at the same time, reject populist policies, soft options, and easy rides, however tempting they are politically. The latter course would send Singapore on a downward spiral. As the saying goes, mighty rivers begin with a trickle and end up in a flood as they flow downstream. We cannot allow our will to be sapped this way.

Departing colonial powers wrote and influenced the constitutions of their former colonies based on **their values and concept of democracy which is** underpinned by universal suffrage, freedom, human rights, independent judiciary and a need for vigorous opposition. Ironically, much of these were denied to their subjects during their long, oppressive rules. Notably, the framers of the constitutions had, to a large extent, not taken cognisance of the conditions required for the constitutions to work as envisaged. Some of the conditions are the natural geographic borders, homogenous population, minimum literacy, common language, religion, culture and race. With few exceptions, many leaders who assumed power had become tired out by long years of agitation against colonial rulers, and had also been deeply influenced by Marxist socialism, which was the flavour of the time, especially for revolutionary movements sweeping across Asia, Africa, South America and parts of Europe. I also noted an ironic twist of fate for the liberated masses in a few countries. When the native rulers assumed power, many of them also adopted the same trappings, practices and instruments of power which their former colonial masters used to awe the natives into submission. In a few cases, the excesses went further. One could say that it was not an ideal environment for Western democracy to bloom.

Basically, the leaders were eager to distribute the wealth to the masses even before it could be created. The privileges of democracy were emphasised while the discipline and responsibility required to sustain that privileges were underplayed or ignored. The United States **President Dwight Eisenhower** said that **"people who placed privileges above responsibility soon lose both"**. They chose idealism over pragmatism, erroneously believing that the newfound freedom, under a democratic umbrella, they had envisioned would by itself deliver the economic development that was so desperately needed. Thus, the stage was set for the political, economic and social morass that had since become so deeply embedded in many countries, and the much hoped for prosperity for all never arrived. As the saying goes, you reap what you sow. Exploitative as they were, the departing British rulers, in contrast to other colonial powers, did leave behind a relatively clean and efficient administrative structure and institutions necessary for minimum good governance. My narratives below outline some of the factors that led to the disappointing results in several countries, including those which Western economists believed were poised for a quick take-off.

My narratives are based on my observations, experiences, interactions with people and leaders across the spectrum, first-hand encounters, visits (both official and private), relevant reports by credible institutions, eye witness accounts, watching live feeds on many national and global television channels, videos footages, and reports and articles on the internet. Nowadays, it is not difficult to follow the developments of various countries from anywhere; all one needs is a bit of enthusiasm. My abiding interest in international relations, since secondary school years, was a factor that kindled my continuing interest in world affairs. I watched how political leaders, both near and far, often made generous, sometimes outlandish, promises to win elections, only to ignore them once in power. Over time, the political parties contending for power knew that the electorate also knew very well that much of the promises they made were not practical and could not be implemented for a variety of factors which had emerged since independence.

In my view, Singapore needed to draw the right lessons from the egregious follies of others. Because it is a global player, Singapore must continue to be relevant and useful to the world by making its contribution to global governance, especially in matters of peace, security and progress. The summit (noted abroad as the **"Summit of the Century"**) between US President Trump and Chairman Kim Jong Un of North Korea hosted by the people of Singapore on 12 June 2018 is a good example. At the margins of the 14th **Manama Dialogue** (Middle East counterpart of the **Shangri-La Dialogue**) in October, 2018, I had a very brief conversation with a United States veteran four-star general with much combat experience in the Middle East, and who still has influence in shaping United States policy for the region. He spoke very warmly of Singapore and made a special reference to Lee Kuan Yew. Referring to a leader of small Gulf state who spoke on the need for the Palestinians to look to the future and not dwell in the past in settling their problems with Israel, the General opined that that leader could become a visionary, a little like Lee Kuan Yew.

The key to maintaining Singapore's leadership role is good governance at home. Here I like to point out that my reason for giving the narratives below concerning the leadership failures abroad is not to denigrate any country. Nor are the situations reflected in the narratives, unique to any particular country. The purpose is to illustrate by actual examples (gathered from my experience and observations), how democracy has been subverted to serve the self-interests of those in power, thus, abandoning the masses who voted them into office in the first place! We in Singapore must never succumb to temptations of populist policies and soft options pursued by some leaders elsewhere. It is in this spirit of learning that I have decided, as far as possible, not to name any particular country and mask the names of the leaders, their titles and positions. While these particulars are relevant, what is more important, however, is to reflect on how, by acts of commission and omission, they have undermined governance, irreparably so, in some cases. As our leaders often warned that once Humpty Dumpty is broken it would be difficult to glue it back together.

We are justifiably proud, without being boastful, of our **unique achievements** that transformed Singapore from a Third World, sleepy, and poverty-ridden backwater state to a thriving First World state, **within one generation,** and that too in a hostile environment engulfed in a turbulent world. Often, there were voices both within and without, questioning why we must always be number one in whatever we did, saying that life would be much simpler and easier if we gave up this "obsession", and accept a lower peg on the totem pole. Well-meaning though some of them were, I strongly disagree. At the risk of forcefully repeating myself, I would say that if we had succumbed to this temptation and **threw the pearl away** (to borrow a phrase from **Shakespeare's "Othello"**) then we would have quickly descended into an abyss and become a mere footnote in history. Big countries with enormous natural and human resources at their command (which we Singaporeans cannot even dream of) could muddle through for some time and could still bounce back. Singapore simply did not, and still does not, have the necessary ballast.

RULE OF LAW

There are countries, both very large and small, where there is a continuous assault on the rule of law, by those who, in their oath of office, solemnly "pledged" to defend it. That set the stage for many other serious problems that followed, such as the criminalisation of politics, corruption and erosion of integrity in vital state institutions, including the judiciary, legislature and the public service. Both the criminal and anti-national actors claimed justification for what they did by invoking their **"democratic right"** and the **freedom guaranteed in the constitution**. Since all political parties were usually complicit, to varying extents, there was no incentive to stop the corrosion, forget reforming the system.

The Republic of India (hereafter referred to as India) is not only the world's largest democracy but as also a complex system. To me, it serves as good case study to assess how Western democracy has fared. India has followed the Westminster model of government since independence, except for a brief period of Emergency Rule imposed by late Prime Minister Indira Gandhi. Several credible reports noted that up to 40% of those elected to political office, had criminal backgrounds, including convictions for murder and rape, and even similar pending cases. Even in the later cases, they brazenly claimed they were innocent, since the charges have not been proven in court. The overburdened and short-staffed judiciary moved at a glacial speed and cases have remained not tried for more than 20 years. The accused could drag it longer, for several more years, through the many layers of appeal. There were cases that had remained without a final verdict for more than 30 years!

A senior judge admitted on camera that there was more than 3.3 million cases pending before the courts in 2018! It was not uncommon, for those with power — political, economic, underworld connections and celebrity status — to get privileged treatment in the system. Many had dragged out the cases against them by exploiting every loophole in the system, with compliant staff in the judiciary. The two topmost leaders of a major political party were on bail awaiting trial on serious charges involving criminal breach of trust. Yet the younger of the two (referred to as 'G') could become (as designated by the party) the head of government, should the party win general election. Many observers breathed a sign of relief when that party lost the May 2019 general election.

The serious character flaws and contempt for the law in their leaders did not seem relevant to the electorate. A sting operation conducted by an investigative media channel showed the horrific massacre of people belonging to the major religious group, to appease the people from the minority religious group for vote bank politics in 1990. The killings were reportedly ordered by the head of government in the large state and he had also ordered the police and other officials involved to falsify the facts on the casualties when preparing the official report on the killings. The documentary revealed that the official report claimed only 16 or thereabout were killed, whereas, in actual fact, more than a hundred had been killed and the bodies were buried in secret, thereby preventing the family members to perform the last religious rites. A retired senior police officer, who was at his job during that time, confirmed on camera, the falsification of the facts in the government's official report concerning the massacre. That head of government, who was out of office at the time of the airing, not only showed no remorse but also justified what he did!

Even in the rare cases of leaders geting convicted, they managed to avoid or reduce their prison sentence by, for example, faking serious illnesses and insisting admission in hospitals, where money could buy "five star" comfort, or falsely claiming family emergencies. A former minister from a major political party, who was being investigated for the alleged killing of his wife, promptly claimed heart problems and arranged for his admission and stay in a hospital. The media exposed the claim as false because the relevant hospital records showed that he suffered no such ailment and was in perfect health. In January 2019, I read in a Singapore vernacular newspaper that a female leader of a major regional political party, with ambitions to become head of government in that state, paid a bribe of 20 million in the local currency (about US$333,000) to the head of the prison administration and those above him to "serve" the 4-year prison sentence in a special 4-room accommodation (probably with air-conditioning) which included a kitchen as well, for her domestic staff to cater for all her needs! The same paper also carried another report on the same day. There was a picture of a senior police officer (in uniform), seated with his legs outstretched and an old lady (in her 70s as reported) on the floor, prostrating at his feet, and begging him to take action against those who were physically abusing her, while a large crowd stood and watched the pathetic scene. Still, the police officer did not take action as required. Such irresponsible derelictions of duty are not isolated incidents.

A scion of the powerful patriarchal family in power in a state, deliberately burnt down a newspaper office and its printing plant to settle a personal feud involving the siblings and extended family members. By chance, I was there on a short visit and watched on television the horror, in which three staff also perished. The police stood by idle and the fire engine was nowhere to be seen. I was told by a reliable source that they were intimidated. To my knowledge, the perpetrator of that crime was not prosecuted, not surprising as the family was ruling the state. Years later, the same person was elected as a law maker and went on to serve as a minister. Such contempt for the law is not an isolated incident.

In the rare event that they went to prison, many of them were able to enjoy special and separate accommodation with their own toilet and bathroom facilities as described above. In contrast, prison staff were abusing prisoners who could not afford to pay a bribe for even the most basic entitlements under prison regulations. As I have mentioned elsewhere in this book, the honest public servants were often punished for not carrying out the illegal and corrupt orders of their political masters. A female commissioner of prisons, who had an internationally noted record of honest and effective prison administration, became a political casualty and was transferred to another lesser job! Happily, for her, the new government (in opposition before) appointed her governor in one of the states. She again demonstrated her reputation as an honest and able administrator in her new job, though not to everyone's liking. Such comebacks have been rare indeed.

CONTEMPT OF COURT

There have been many cases from time to time where the judicial court verdicts, judgements, decisions and orders, including those of the Supreme Court, were not implemented by political parties, law makers, ministers, governments — both in the states and at the centre. All political parties were complicit, and the judiciary was powerless to enforce judgements. At the time of writing, the Supreme Court judgement ordering equal access for women to enter and worship in a famous temple was not only not implemented but was openly defied by all political parties and by both the state and central governments. There were also instigations by most actors involved to defy the court order. The reason was the general elections was upcoming, a few months from then. There are too many such cases and the above is the latest in the continuing process. Such has been the degradation of the rule of law.

CULTURE OF POLITICS

In my observation, the gradual debasement of politics by acts of commission and omission, began quite early after independence and over time entrenched itself in the political culture, which is unable to differentiate the **honest** from the **corrupt, legal** from **illegal, right** from **wrong, moral** from **immoral,** and **mere rule** from **good governance**. In general, political leaders at all levels focussed on short term fixes, thereby ignoring the serious long-term challenges, including matters of defence and national security. The naivety and indifference of some pioneer leaders was astonishing. In India, its first head of government summarily dismissed arguments to improve the poorly equipped and poorly funded armed forces, saying that the country **"does not need an army…it requires only a police force"**, and **"we have no enemies"**. Not long after, the country paid a heavy price for this with its devastating and humiliating defeat in a border war with its bigger neighbour — China. In matters of national defence, such policies are not a good option. In my view, the reason for this loss was the dereliction of responsibility, at the very least.

However, of more serious concern was the fact that, on average, the calibre of the candidates entering politics and seeking elected office was quite low, in terms integrity, commitment, level of education and ability to deliver in office, few exceptions notwithstanding. Increasingly, political parties were relying on those who could deliver the votes at the local level and many of those who could do so, often showed scant regard for election laws and rules. Using money (often unaccounted to revenue authorities) to buy votes, and intimidations by underworld elements, were tolerated as a necessary part of democracy. Even the organisation that conducts elections, once highly rated for its impartiality, integrity and efficiency, has been politicised, with the losing and disgruntled candidates challenging its decisions with street demonstrations and through the judicial process. Overt and covert intimidation of election staff has also been alleged.

In March, 2019, I watched on a major television channel beamed from that country, a video taken during a sting operation, showing a senior politician saying he needed a very big sum of money (he mentioned the amount) **"to buy votes"** in the elections that were due shortly and that he would accept cash from any source and by any means. The video clip was repeated. That paled in comparison to another, in which a head of government of a very populous state (the opposition to his party was the major party in the central government) sent his police squad to obstruct and prevent income tax officials (from the central government) from conducting their search of a premises where reportedly the cash that was unaccounted for, amounting to the equivalent of approximately US$20 million, was kept. The standoff between the tax officials and the police was played on all major television channels. Much of that money was shown to have been siphoned off from the state budget, including funds allocated to feeding poor and disadvantaged children. Allegedly, the head of government's close family member was involved. The cash was, as reported, to buy votes and to finance candidates in the elections, in a desperate effort to win back power at the centre. There were also several, very large hauls of cash that is unaccounted for throughout the country by election authorities close to the polling dates. I watched on television, at real time, a *mullah*, in his fiery speech, brazenly tell his flock not to vote for the party in government at the centre and give a warning that anyone who defied him would be treated as traitors. Not to be outdone by him, others with similar agendas also joined in. Law enforcement was strangely absent. Many feared that it was an ominous trend and did not bode well for the country.

I have, however, noted a common thread among politicians and lawmakers. Almost all issues, regardless of their nature and the subject matter, were made political, with all concerned relishing in seemingly endless debates that had little to no consensus. Even the loss of lives and destruction on a huge scale, resulting from unprecedented floods from rainfall, in a state in August 2018, was not spared of such politics! Serious warnings from environmental scientists (about four years before the tragedy struck) of impending disaster, predicting exactly what would and did happen, were not only ignored, but the experts were allegedly assailed and ridiculed. In my view, it should have been obvious to anyone that the uncontrolled deforestation, unregulated sand quarrying and illegal constructions over decades, would inevitably result in such tragedies and devastation.

In short, the able, talented, honest, and committed were largely shut out of the system. Many of them have excelled abroad in their chosen fields, rising to top positions in huge and powerful multinational corporations which have global reach and influence. (In this regard, Singapore's relentless search for high calibre talent to be inducted into politics, the civil service, public enterprises, institutions and undertakings will always remain a work-in-progress. Continuous nurturing of talent is very important for us, given the constraints we face.)

HUMAN RIGHTS

One of the fundamental requirements of democracy is the protection of human rights and dignity. It would be of little comfort or consolation to a starving person on the throes of death to be told that he should cherish the fact that democracy has given him all the freedoms, including free speech, and not complain about the hunger! Those in power need to provide basic human rights like preventing hunger, meaningful jobs for the workforce (not merely the right to work), access to quality education and health at an affordable cost, movement without hindrance, access (not merely the right) to equal justice under the law and, most importantly, a safe environment especially for women and children. With some exceptions, many countries have fallen short in meeting this standard. Again, based on my personal knowledge and observation of developments in countries, including India, over a long period, I list below a few random examples as illustrations:

- **Hunger:** Solemn undertaking given by the pioneer leaders to eradicate poverty and hunger within ten years from independence has largely remained unfulfilled after more than 60 years, even if the percentage of population below the poverty line has seen some reduction. The callous disregard of leaders, for the plight of those at the bottom of the heap, was cruelly evident when a minister said on national television, in response to a journalist's question, that a woman who died of starvation need not have died as she could have survived by begging for food in the city streets!
- **Crime:** Serious crimes including heinous attacks on women and very young children, resulting in rape and murder has reached alarming proportions, creating headlines around the world. A report from the UK, placed India at the top of the unsafe countries for women and young children list. Yet, the sex predators targeting the weak and the very vulnerable, in this case, young children and women, are largely roaming free. Several reasons were cited for this state of affairs and among them were that not all of these crimes were committed in the heat of the moment or by street people: in fact, in many instances, upper class children of the wealthy and powerful, who blatantly abuse their power and influence, have been implicated but not brought to justice.

I must make it clear that it is not just politicians, law makers, the rich and powerful, and the law enforcers who have committed such serious crimes. It is a very sad indictment that even the clergy (**all religions**) has been seriously implicated. Men donning religious robes and holding high positions in the respective hierarchies have not only abused the trust reposed on them by their respective flocks, but also committed despicable crimes on the followers and servants of God. The most recent case (August 2018) involved a bishop who was accused by a nun of repeatedly raping her (13 times) and unlawfully detaining her. The victim allegedly rejected large amounts of cash and a plot of land that was offered in order to buy her silence. When the offer was rejected, the bishop allegedly turned hostile to the victim and indulged in slandering her. Her name and identity were posted on social media, in clear violation of the law of the land. The police investigation established a prima facie case against the bishop but showed reluctance to proceed. In fact, it was reported that the police were pressuring the victim to withdraw her complaint! The bishop was seen on television claiming that it was "attack on the Church", thereby giving it a political spin! Law makers mostly from the same religious order joined with the clergy in slandering the victim, with posts on social media. Sizeable number of nuns were seen on global television protesting outside the church, claiming that their written complaints to the Church, the Vatican Ambassador and the Vatican (in Rome) demanding punishment, for not only the offender in this case but also the offenders (from the clergy) in many other similar cases of sexual abuse of nuns, which were all ignored by the authorities concerned. *(The same leading global television news channel which covered the Pope's historic visit to the United Arab Emirates in February, 2019 (the first ever such visit to the Gulf) reported that His Holiness the Pope acknowledged the fact that members of the clergy had sexually abused nuns.)*

Even if the prosecution proceeds, the case could be dragged out for decades, thereby increasing the chances for the accused to be declared innocent eventually. It is no secret that money, muscle, influence and connections in the right places can buy justice. Many people in high places, including law makers, have committed contempt of court by not attending court when required by court summons, to answer charges. Senior bureaucrats and political leaders not implementing court decisions when they consider it not in their interest to do so, is also not altogether uncommon.

Opportunistic political parties, activists and intellectuals went strangely silent in this case, unlike their vigorous protests in a previous and similar case involving a different religion. This was a cynical exploitation of "vote bank politics". The Church has a huge following and influence in the concerned state and its followers tended to vote as a block for the political party favoured by the Church. The Church also took on a political role, in that it openly on television and during its congregations, called on its flock not to vote for the biggest political party and the head of government of the country in the elections. The reason was its belief that the political party concerned was allegedly not sympathetic to the proselytizing and sometimes aggressive conversion carried out (allegedly with funding from abroad) by the Church in the country. The target of conversion has been the majority community. (Leaders in religious robes entering the political fray, and using religion to advance their own interests, are nothing new nor unique to any country. We in Singapore had this problem in the 1980s and it was dealt with effectively by our stout-hearted leaders. In my view, the timely enactment of the **"Maintenance of Religious Harmony Act"** in 1990, had served us well. In the countries I have served, I found admiration for the religious harmony that exists in our homeland.)

Conversely, where the prosecution deliberately brings a false case against a citizen, the prosecutors also play the same game. An eminent scientist was falsely accused of spying for a foreign power and reportedly, it took 24 years to establish his innocence in court, and to expose the conspiracy in the then state government. The court ordered the state to pay monetary compensation to the victim, a small comfort. Surprisingly, a few officials admitted framing the false charges, as exposed by the media. Allegedly, a foreign religious group was behind the conspiracy.

Premeditated attacks by those in high places, including those holding high political office e.g. lawmakers and ministers, have been exposed in the media. Adding insult to injury, they not only brazen it out, but also throw their weight to shield their family members and their election vote-getters. It was not difficult for them as they were law unto themselves. The law enforcement authorities, especially the police force, were ever willing to do the bidding of their political masters. A few rare and exceptionally honest officers, who respected their oath of office and their uniform suffered humiliation and adverse career consequences.

Many a time, police personnel were seen on television standing mute and seemingly helpless while witnessing the crime. The cruellest part in all this was that the police routinely refused to register complaints from the victims, when the perpetrators were politicians or those who were politically connected. A minister in charge of minorities was alleged to have killed an investigative journalist who was on the trail of massive corruption linked to the minister, and he allegedly did it with the help of a police inspector!

I have watched many more such exposés in the media. A lady inspector of police refused to register the complaint of a young lady (described as an "A Star" student) who was gang raped by men in high places. The video went viral and caused national outrage. If not for the relentless and courageous pursuit by a leading media channel in exposing the reluctance of the lawmakers to act, this case also would have met the similar fate of many other cases where victims were cruelly denied justice. A distressing cause for concern, is the fact that heinous crimes committed against women and very young children have been rising alarmingly in recent years. The international survey referred to in an earlier paragraph also highlighted the failure of the administration to provide adequate security and protection for women and young children.

In this context, I remind myself of the continuous vigilance of the Singapore Crime Prevention Council with its motto **"low crime does not mean no crime"**. It is such resolute and unyielding enforcement of the law, with the cooperation and the trust of the people, that earned Singapore its reputation as one of the few safest countries in the world. I served in the **"Home Team", in a** voluntary capacity. Here is an interesting anecdote. A female journalist, probably in her late 20s and either a US or Canadian national, told PM Lee Kuan Yew when she met him sometime in the late 1970s at the Istana, that she went out of her hotel (Raffles) for a long jog around the city at 3 A.M. in the morning. She told him that she enjoyed it very much and stressed the fact that she did not think she could have done it in any other city at that time of the night and in such safety.

CORRUPTION

There is no country on earth that can truly claim it is free of corruption. A senior United Nations official said, "corruption kills" and indeed it has killed, but not its perpetrators. It has become a very serious problem in the world and, in my view, corruption does not spare any country, big or small. The important factors are the attitude of the people towards corruption, their tolerance and indifference towards corrupt leaders. Television footages showed voters demanding bigger amount of cash from candidates in order to vote for them. At the very core is the betrayal by leaders while in power, and even afterwards. A head of government admitted, soon after leaving office, that he could not take action against his ministers, who were implicated in massive corruption scandals, involving mining and telecommunications, owing to the **"compulsions of coalition politics"**. The ministers who were from a regional party had threatened to pull out of the coalition and thereby, bring down that government. After many years, they were prosecuted by the succeeding government, but the initial conviction was overturned on appeal. They went free and enjoyed their ill-gotten wealth in opulent style. There was no outrage and it appeared that there was even a quiet admiration for their cunning and ability to defeat the law. It was as if it was a badge of honour for political office! They did what leaders there do best in such situations. Evade the charges, cry political vendetta, "take care" of evidence, witnesses, and staff in judiciary, and exploit every loophole in the law and the judicial process to drag out the case as long as possible. In one case, a former minister in oldest national political party was convicted after 34 years for his part in the in the killing of large number of people from a minority religious community, following the assassination of the head of government.

Both in scale and status, these cases were neither exceptional nor altogether infrequent. The long and inordinate delay in the cases coming to trial often resulted in the failure of justice. One flamboyant tycoon, who was a member of parliament and owner of an airline, a brewery and formula racing track, had allegedly defrauded the country and its banks of billions of dollars, in an elaborate scheme involving senior politicians, lawmakers and bank chief executives, who gave massive loans without the usual collateral. Much of the loans went into his personal bank accounts abroad. Not surprisingly, his enterprises collapsed with massive debts and a very large number of his employees were not paid for several months. Fraud on this scale must have been in the works for a long period. When the government finally decided to act, in response to public pressure, the tycoon fled to a Commonwealth country in Western Europe, and his flight was reportedly facilitated by cooperative officials at home. He was not alone; many others who also became fabulously wealthy through similar fraudulently corrupt schemes also fled the country, taking with them their vast ill-gotten fortunes, and leaving behind debts that ran into billions of dollars, to the exchequer. These fugitives led very conspicuous extravagant lives, and reportedly many in the establishment were recipients of their largesse. They comfortably settled abroad, enjoying their ill-gotten wealth, and cock a snoot at their government's inability, thus far, to bring them back to face justice at home. The extradition attempts since, have become protracted and difficult, involving many jurisdictions. Owing to the political patronage and connections they had in most political parties in the country, it would be an uphill task to bring them back to face charges, assuming of course that there would be enough political will to do so.

A litigant in a separate and much less serious case turned violent when the judge ruled against him and he tried to assault the judge. He was restrained by the court staff. It appears that the long growing cancer of corruption in body politics has undermined governance in all sectors and at all levels of the nation.

I have earlier stated that in many countries, corruption is pervasive and has become a deeply entrenched way of life. Here is an interesting and somewhat amusing anecdote. During a discussion among diplomats in Cairo, I mentioned the case of our former Minister of National Development, Teh Chiang Wan, who committed suicide rather than facing his day in court on a corruption charge. One Egyptian diplomat noted that in many countries, including his own, ministers could not be prosecuted thus because "there would not be any more left"!

However, an interesting development has taken place recently in India in the fight against corruption. The media reported that Palaniappan Chidambaram, a two-time finance minister and a one-time home minister in the previous government, was detained in August 2019 on charges alleging corruption and money laundering. The news garnered much interest and gave rise to controversies across the nation.

LEADERSHIP DEFICIT

Character: From the above examples, it should not be difficult to comprehend the flaws in the leadership. The head (G) and deputy head of a major political party in the opposition were, at the time of writing, on bail, pending trial on serious charges of criminal breach of trust. Also on bail with them there were several former ministers, senior officials and family members in the party for a variety of charges. There were some controversies over G's educational qualifications, as well. Most surprisingly, the aspiring head of government was seen on national television openly breaking the law by riding with two others on a single motorcycle and none of them were wearing protective crash helmets, as required by the law. G and his party supporters were on the way to participate in a demonstration by farmers which had turned violent. He did it against the advice of the police and forced his way through a road closed by the authorities in order to contain the protests which, as his party leader on site admitted, was done to "show solidarity" with the demonstrators. More often, the leaders did it for photo op, to serve their own interests, at the expense of national security. Readers might conclude that this event was preposterous but please read on.

Anarchists: I saw on television that, G along with many leaders from other opposition parties participated in a noisy protest, allegedly organised by extreme leftist students and anti-national elements within the university campus in the national capital. Reportedly, some academics in the university and like-minded outside anarchists, not one to miss an opportunity to ferment trouble, also joined in to support their anti-national agenda. That university was well-known as a hotbed of extreme politics, with many in it calling for a particular state to cede from the federation, showing an open defiance of laws, disrespecting the national anthem, displaying the national flag of a neighbouring country (hereafter referred to as B) that is not friendly to A because of B's export of terrorism to A. G and other leaders present unanimously criticised the government and accused it of "intolerance", "assault on democracy", "stifling free speech and academic freedom". The gravity of such offences was, in my view, serious enough to warrant charges of sedition and or treason and, probably, would have been acted upon accordingly by authorities in any other country, democracy or no democracy. By exploiting the corruption and the lax attitude to law enforcement, foreign powers and terrorist groups, have been able to implement their agenda of fermenting religious hatred, by targeting the religion of the majority in the population and sabotaging the national security and economy. Many terrorist attacks have claimed large numbers of lives. These foreign powers and terrorist groups have generously funded local proxies like NGOs and activists in return for the taking up the cause of the former. Emboldened by the inaction of the concerned authorities and the irresponsible support from some political leaders, the cancer of corruption is likely to spread. It had the hallmarks of **the Rip Van Winkle** syndrome.

Anti-National and Subversive Acts: Several sitting members of parliament (included among them former ministers) from G's party went over to Pakistan and in a television interview, sought help to bring down their own head of government back home. These very MPs were later seen on the television fraternising with hard core extremist members of state legislature who advocated rebellion, secession and open support for Pakistan. They refused to accept they were citizens of India, while enjoying the security and privileges given to them as legislators! G, and many leaders from other opposition parties who united in order to unseat the Government, questioned the integrity and the honour of the Armed Forces, when the Army successfully carried out an operation inside Pakistan in retaliation to country's earlier terror attack on an elite military base in India. Fearing that the Government might reap political dividend for the success, these leaders insisted that the Army must make all operational details public, including actual video footage and the results of the operation, in order to confirm that the operation was not "fake". Not wanting to show they were caught unawares, the rulers in Pakistan naturally denied the operation. When the Government did finally make public the actual video footage of that operation, several months later, the very same leaders changed their tune and condemned the Government for "politicising the Army" and "trying to seek political mileage". Another point to note here is that the same bunch of leaders had also criticised the Army's handling of the separatists' violence, even though it was clear from the real time coverage that the Army was very restrained and was forced to defend itself, sometimes retreating from raining missiles (mainly stones) from demonstrators, who were widely believed to be foreign inspired and funded. It appeared that most of the country's enemies were home-grown.

JUDICIARY

That the courts in country A moved at a glacial speed should be obvious from some of the narratives above. That they were also understaffed (not for lack of suitably qualified candidates or lack of funding) is a fact. The judicial authorities in **one** of the states admitted that more than 1000 cases of complaints involving corruption, abuse of power, contempt of court, and crimes committed by political leaders, including ministers and senior bureaucrats, were long pending. Many senior politicians in were reported to have ignored court notices.

As in other branches of the Administration, the judiciary has not been spared of corruption. One senior lawyer with 40 years' practice told me during my visit there that he gave up practice because of pervasive corruption; **lawyers were "arranging the verdict"**. Coincidentally, I also read a report in a leading newspaper at that time that sizeable number of practicing lawyers had no legal qualifications and were not registered with the bar council. It certainly appears that power — money, muscle, connections and influence — goes a very long way.

Politics also has not spared the judiciary. Four supreme court judges were seen on television criticising the chief justice. They vented their feelings to the journalists present and were seen receiving visits from opposition political party leaders, who were seen siding with the disgruntled judges. The real target was, as widely believed then, the political party and its leaders who were in government.

RESPECT FOR CITIZENS

The combined effect of the factors in the above narratives has been the lack of concern for the citizens in general and those at the bottom of the society, in particular. The elected representatives flaunted their power almost in all situations and insisted on and receiving privileged treatment, special facilities, and waivers from payments due. The variety of daily abuses were so extensive and continuous that it would be difficult for anyone to list them and it would not serve any useful purpose either. The narratives below highlight a sampling, taken at random.

- In general punctuality was not a priority. Routinely they expected the airline staff to wait for them before closing the gates, sometimes delaying the flight by 40 to 60 minutes. One legislator, in a video that went viral, was seen hitting an airline staff with his slippers 27 times for not waiting. They also demanded for themselves and their family members to be upgraded to a higher class. In one bizarre case, a legislator, who reportedly had 10 pending criminal cases against him, abused the airline staff, demanded to be upgraded to business class and held up the departure of the aircraft. He could not and did not accept the airline staff's plea that, due to the aircraft configuration, there was only economy class seats and no business class! They did not respect airline rules on smoking and a minister in charge of civil aviation even boasted that he had carried matches into the aircraft and lit his cigarette in clear violation of the law. Jobs in the national airline were not always filled by those with the best qualifications and experience, but rather by those with the right political and union connections. The fare-paying passengers' needs and requirements were of lesser priority. It was, therefore, not a surprise that attempts to privatise the heavily debt-laden national carrier did not elicit any response, despite extended deadlines and an unusually generous offer of 70% private ownership.

- VIPs demanded that their vehicles and that of their families be waived through without stopping at road toll booths and security check posts. One legislator's staff in the motor cade severely assaulted a toll gate official for daring to do his duty to collect the toll. Not content, his staff (more like thugs) destroyed the booth as well — all these in full view of bystanders and other road users. Yet, none intervened to protect the official. One senior legislator boarded a long-distance train without any booking or valid ticket and had a young couple holding valid tickets ejected from their seats, arrogantly ignoring their protests.
- Leaders abusing police personnel and deploying them on private and family matters has become very common. Traffic in busy city streets were stopped frequently for more than one hour to allow ministerial motorcades, consisting of several vehicles of security men toting assault weapons, to pass through, using blaring red beacon sirens and without stopping anywhere. In one case the traffic was stopped for more than two hours creating a traffic jam stretching back several kilometres. A patient requiring emergency treatment was unable to reach the hospital and died in the ambulance. Another speeding ministerial motorcade hit and killed a pedestrian and was noted to have sped away, without stopping to render assistance. In another case, when the public demanded police to prosecute a lawmaker who was accused of raping a woman while he was a sitting minister, the excuse given by the police was that the state

government would not "sanction prosecution concerned". The list is endless. The stock response of the VIPs had always been that they could not help it and the public had to endure it.

- In 1994, India's passenger aircraft was hijacked by terrorists, after it took off in Kathmandu on a three-hour flight to a city in India. The cabinet in India went into a huddle with all political parties to discuss how to respond. They talked and talked without arriving at any decision. The hijackers demanded that two of their comrades in India's jail be released and threatened to kill the passengers. To cut the long story short, the aircraft landed as scheduled and stood at the tarmac. The terrorists became violent towards the passengers, began to make good on their threat to kill and demanded that the aircraft be refuelled for take-off to Pakistan, known for its support for terrorists.

   Eventually, the aircraft took-off after a total of about 5 hours in India's airspace and on its soil. A few countries refused permission to land, the aircraft finally landed in a country not too far from India. Meanwhile, the terrorists had killed some passengers. Finally, the Government met all the demands of the terrorists, to secure the release of the aircraft, and its return, along with remains of the passengers who paid the ultimate price. I was then Ambassador to Egypt and remember the ambassador of India saying **"democracy has no answer"**, during a conversation concerning the incident among few of us at an informal gathering. Not to miss an opportunity to take a dig at his rival, ambassador of Pakistan said, in barely concealed glee, that India had all the time and the opportunities to take action when the aircraft was sitting on the ground "but they let it go".

   It is in an emergency like the above that the mettle of political leadership and the preparedness and efficacy of the security apparatus is tested to the limit. In a similar situation, a Singapore Airlines flight **SQ117** from Kuala Lumpur to Singapore was hijacked in March 1991 by four Pakistani terrorists, who demanded that the Captain (Stanley Lim) fly the aircraft to

Sydney. The Captain told them he did not have enough fuel and the aircraft would crash. He pleaded with them to land in Singapore. The hijackers reluctantly agreed to land in Singapore only to refuel and then take off for Sydney. They insisted that the aircraft should stay on the runway while being refuelled, threatened to blow up the aircraft, if any person approached it and if their demands were not met in full and swiftly. According to one account, the short flight from Kuala Lumpur landed at Changi Airport at 10.15 P.M. and the life and death drama began. In the ensuing negotiation, the hijackers made more demands, including arrangements for them to speak to Pakistani Ambassador in Singapore and Benazir Bhutto, their prime minister. Negotiations dragged on and the hijackers became agitated and restless; they pushed out two passengers and threatened to kill other passengers in quick succession. In order to drive home their seriousness, they made it known that they were priming explosives. Finally, our leaders gave the order to storm the aircraft and rescue the passengers, who were held hostages, with only about five minutes to spare. The Singapore Armed Forces commandoes stormed the aircraft at 6.05 A.M., the next morning, disguised as aircraft service personnel and shot dead all the four hijackers. Thus, they saved all the passengers and crew, 124 in all. How did they do it? As soon as the aircraft was hijacked, the commandos, quietly and in secret, went to work rehearsing the rescue operation simulating it in the interior of a similar empty aircraft parked away from the scene of action. It was to familiarise themselves with every important detail in the aircraft interior, including the seat configuration, and the likely location of the hijackers in the aircraft. It was a professional job and was noted as such abroad.

- A very big city, considered a financial centre in India, gets much monsoon rain in predictable regularity and strength during the season. With advanced weather forecasting technology, weathermen were able to give warnings weeks in advance and sometimes even pinpoint the actual date when the rains would occur. Within the first few days of the entire city and adjacent areas got flooded knee-deep and in some parts up to waist-deep. Over the years, I have watched appalling and worsening scenes in which people on foot and in vehicles struggled to get by in the flood waters that were mixed with overflowing sewers, putrid garbage and other items. The unmaintained and potholed roads, a common feature throughout the country, become death traps and claim large number of lives. Live television coverages showed potholes all over the city some measuring "30 inches" wide and as deep as "2 feet" submerged in water. A graphic video showed a mother with a young child on her motorcycle hit a submerged pothole and were thrown under a struggling bus. Both were killed instantly. The media reported more than 50 deaths within two weeks and an unknown number injured. The roads in the country were notorious for potholes.

- In typical fashion, the concerned officials and local government leaders launched into a blame game, so characteristics of the country's administrators, and did nothing to alleviate the sufferings and the paralysis of normal life for weeks. All modes of transportation had ceased creating food and water shortages. Reportedly, even the internet had stopped working briefly. Such recurring tragedies with increasing loss of life and destruction to property were due to callous and a cruel disregard for the citizens' wellbeing stretching back decades. One elected official in the local government blamed the British rulers, who left the country more than 60 years before, for not constructing drains that were wide and deep enough to drain the flood waters away!

The causes for the yearly visitation of misery and suffering were, amongst others, the lack of planning in all sectors, the unregulated orgy of building homes to meet the insatiable demand from the *nouveau riche:* non-compliance of building codes, destruction of water retaining marshes, unbridled deforestation, polluting industries in the city, lack of a maintenance culture and sheer arrogance on the part of those in power. In contrast to other countries, the concerned leaders did not wet their feet and were not seen at the scene of devastation and much suffering that brought the city to its knees. The apathy to disasters, natural and man-made, has prevailed in much of the country. During each such disaster, the concerned leaders promise much to implement the necessary measures but did very little. They have become quite comfortable in dodging any responsibility. The fact was the budget of the city administration was huge exceeding that of many state governments. One official proudly boasted of the huge size of the budget but refused to give details on how it was spent nor where the money went. It would not take much intelligence to know where it ended up. This state of affairs has been going on for a very long time and it is not likely to change.

GENDER

Gender inequality and the consequences arising therefrom, especially the loss to the economy, is a cause for concern. Regrettably, male chauvinism is widespread in the countries in this discourse. These countries maintain medieval practices and beliefs, for example, that the woman's role is in the kitchen and that her role is to produce children and to care for them. In rural settings, the burden is heavier indeed. In addition to these, the women also have to walk long hours to fetch water from ever dwindling water resources and gather firewood. The sad part is that women who are highly qualified in terms of education and technical expertise (especially IT), do not usually get treatment equally to their male counterparts in the work place, if they manage to land jobs in the first place. The result has been that the country has suffered enormous productivity loss. While this problem exists to varying degrees world-wide, it is, however, far more serious and acute in these countries.

In fact, as I see it, one of the biggest problems in India is the lack of respect for the dignity of women and children. I have given a brief narrative earlier of heinous crimes like the widely reported brutal gang rapes of women and young children in the country. The lack of law enforcement and connivance at high places to shield the perpetrators (not infrequently scions of well-connected families, including lawmakers) acts as encouragement to the depraved vultures! The paradox is that the country's religion revers women and both men and women worship goddesses *Laxmi, Saraswathi, Durga* (and few more) to seek blessings for wealth, education and health, respectively. I have made several pilgrimages to quite a number of temples, some of them dating back a few thousand years. (I could feel that the magnificent aura they projected is much more than spiritual; it is a marvel of human ingenuity and a triumph that combines religion, architecture, astronomy, geology, works of art, including the ornate carvings and *Vedic* inscriptions, deep insights into and knowledge of the universe and the celestial order. Several of the temples are UNESCO heritage list of monuments.) Each temple is dedicated to a particular deity (god or goddess) and it occupies the inner (the main) sanctum. When the dedicated deity is a goddess, the gods take a subsidiary position and I had observed that the ritual ceremonies involving the three elements — earth, fire and water — for the goddess were more elaborate in some temples.

The point I want to make here is that women were treated with much respect and enjoyed equal (if not more) protection in ancient times. It is, therefore, difficult to understand the kind of abuse and discrimination the women are being subjected to in present time. I am of the view that it could be insecurity of those unenlightened men, who are unable to accept the fact that women are not intellectually inferior, and can hold their own in the workplace, if given the opportunity in a level playing field. These fears and insecurity have no place in our globalised world. The nation will be the loser, if this unfortunate situation continues. Relatively speaking, Singapore does not have this problem but this state of affairs did not just happen to be. In an earlier chapter, I have given a short account of laws that were enacted, for example, the **"Women's Charter"** and the policies like "Equal Treatment for Women Officers" in the civil service that were implemented soon after our self-government in 1959.

OPULENCE AND GRINDING POVERTY

Few years ago, I watched a television programme which exposed extreme lavish life styles of the elected leaders and officials in the city administration referred to above, who were living in most expensive apartments with gold plated ornaments and fittings and the commentator likened their luxury life styles to that of "opulent Arab sheikhs". Even more shocking was the candid admission by one official that more than 80% of the concerned officials were corrupt. Unless the people hold them accountable, it is unlikely anything will change. It appears as if the people have resigned to the fact that what cannot be changed has to be endured. It is sad indictment on the city itself where the super-rich (some of them among the richest in the world) live surrounded by abject poverty, where the dispossessed live in ramshackle dwellings, in squalid slums without hygiene, sewers, piped water and other basic amenities necessary for survival. In contrast, a former law maker in a major political party reportedly spent US$70 million for his daughter's wedding. He flew guests by private aircrafts and helicopters and booked out all hotels, resorts and transport vehicles. Media footage showed many VIPs from across the spectrum in attendance. Many of the slum dwellers were victims of a shrinking rural economy and were driven to chase the elusive dream of making it big in the mega cities. The most painful part, for anyone with conscience, is the prevalence of child labour and child exploitation. I was moved to tears when I once saw a child, who could not have been more than 5 or 6 years old, struggling to carry a load of sand on his head at a construction site. It was not just boys; girls of similar age were also similarly exploited.

Two videos which were repeatedly telecast on their mainstream media, at different times, used to haunt me for a while. In one, a young man was seen running from hospital to hospital with his sick child slumped on his shoulder seeking urgent medical help. All hospitals he went to refused to treat the child for the simple reason that he could not pay the bribe that was demanded. The child died. In the other video, a man was seen walking with the corpse of his wife slung over his shoulder and with his young daughter in tow, from a hospital to the burial ground which was about 15 kms away. He could not afford to pay the cost of the transport. These were pathetic sights and many abroad were moved to tears. The head of government of Bahrain was so moved by the plight of the man walking the long journey by foot to the burial ground to do the last rites for his wife, that, in a commendable gesture of compassion, he ordered his embassy to render financial aid to that poor soul. It is a fact that generally the government hospitals were poorly funded, lacked proper facilities, including qualified staff and equipment, not to mention the lack of proper hygiene. Even many private hospitals did not meet the minimum standards required in this regard. In fact, "doctors" without proper medical qualifications were found to be treating patients in some hospitals. In some cases, hospital fires have claimed many patients' lives because emergency exits were securely padlocked. At other times, patients died because oxygen required to treat them was not available!

During a brain fever epidemic that broke out in one of the states in India in 2019, the media exposed the criminal negligence of the government in not treating the patients, especially children. The hospital building was crumbling had no qualified staff, no equipments, had abandoned wards, not enough beds for acute cases, no medicines and no running water. Few dedicated personnel tried their best to care but were greatly overwhelmed. As a result, about 200 children died. The government did not accept any responsibility.

LACK OF COMPASSION

During a visit to India in 2018, an acquaintance pointed to me a burnt-out shell of an old and narrow three-storey building in which more than 80 young school children perished in agonising deaths in a mid-sized city in 2004. I was shocked when I saw the totally gutted building that was the school. I remember watching from abroad that tragic fire in a live broadcast on their national television channel, which had international audience. Even though the building was totally unsuitable for use as a school and did not have the relevant permits from the authorities, the school owners and management had been in business for a very long time. According to reports, the fire was started from an open fire while the children's lunch was being prepared and it quickly spread to the whole building. The cruellest thing was that the only entrance and exit to the building were padlocked, and even more reprehensible was the fact that, the adults escaped through the very few small windows. As the height of the windows were beyond the reach of the young children, they died most agonising deaths. I learnt that many people in the neighbourhood had gathered and watched the unspeakable horror, hearing the cries for help of the innocent children. Either they were not able to help, or they had no proper equipment to fight the fire. The fire fighters had difficulty in getting access, and by the time they and the ambulance showed up on the scene, there was nothing much they could do.

Tragedies like this were not infrequent in the country. The underlying causes for their frequent occurrence cannot have escaped the notice of the authorities concerned. The parents were also culpable for their failure to hold their corrupt and incompetent leaders to account for the latter's criminal negligence. As it always happened, all who were concerned evaded responsibility and blamed each other. In my view, the people were equally complicit. During my above visit to the scene of the tragedy, I was given to understand that only junior officials were prosecuted and none of the senior responsible officials and politicians were held to account. Many have noted that appointing an inquiry committee has been the favourite trick of the rulers for the simple reason that it would take a very long time (sometimes years) to conclude and it often faced political pressure, thereby compromising its integrity.

Rarely, if ever, did political leaders or senior officials accept responsibility for such tragedies or faced any prosecution. In the unlikely event where public anger became intense, the well-known practice has been to "punish" a junior official by a transferring them to another slot in the vast and bloated bureaucracy. If and when the inquiry committee produced its report, public interest in it would have subsided due to apathy. In the event that the political revolving door threw up a new government, it would not pursue the matter. It would not serve the interests of political parties and their leaders nor that of the officials under their control. When faced with such situations all political parties and their leaders come together and cooperate to avoid responsibility.

In the context of this narrative, readers would be interested to note how other countries care for their citizens in distress and respond to calamities. The successful operation in June/July 2018 by the Thai authorities to rescue 12 boys and their football coach trapped deep inside a very narrow, dark and flooded cave three kilometres from entrance, gripped the world on television. There were many other factors, including lack of oxygen, making the rescue operation even more dangerous.

Yet, the Thais along with the foreign volunteer divers successfully rescued all those who were trapped. There is much other countries, including Singapore, can learn from the extraordinarily difficult and unique nature of the rescue mission:

- the enormous goodwill and support the Thai people received from the international community;
- international experts who spontaneously volunteered to help knowing fully the dangers to their lives;
- the professionalism of all actors, effective trauma management and the rehabilitation of all those rescued; and
- the courage and sacrifice of so many, including the army doctor who stayed with those trapped until all were rescued.

ACCOUNTABILITY

The essence of democracy is the accountability of the elected to the electors through free and fair elections. However, if the electorate does not exercise their responsibility to hold those, they elect accountable, democracy is undermined. Earlier in this chapter, I alluded to the inability on the part of the masses to differentiate mere ruling by governments from the duty to deliver good governance. The founding fathers of many countries did not instill these values by their own acts. Instead, in the culture of politics that developed over time, the electorate, by and large, were prepared to trade their votes for cash, and gifts e.g. mobile phones, household appliances and for promises to "serve" and "solve" their problems, which from experience they knew full well would not be kept. The result in many of these countries has been the criminalisation of politics and increasing corruption, thus, generally shutting out the able, honest and talented human resource from political office. Those who get elected thus, preserve their vote banks by polarising the country on narrow sectional, tribal, racial, religious and other societal divisions, totally disregarding the dangers to the national security and development that such division poses. Sooner or later, the masses pay the price.

In a rare case of total cooperation, all political parties in India united to oppose a private petition in the Supreme Court which sought to "decriminalise politics" by disqualifying criminals convicted of serious crimes, those who have been charged in court for similar crimes, and those without the minimum educational qualifications. Their outrage in this regard was palpable. According to a credible survey, all political parties in the land had in their midst significant number of convicted criminals and many more awaiting trial for serious crimes, including murder. The percentage of criminals in the parties ranged from 20% (lowest) to 63% (highest) and the party ruling the country (in 2018) in the middle with about 35%. One needs to be incurably optimistic to expect changes anytime soon. The Court ruled that it was a matter for the lawmakers to pass the necessary legislation. The decision was greeted with much jubilation by all political parties. The effect of the decision was like asking lawmakers to punish themselves! Difficult to see how the country can get out of this self-inflicted trap.

Another curious observation is that political leaders, including lawmakers and holders of high public office, routinely hurled abuses and accused each other as **"thief", "liar", "cheat", "corrupt", "incompetent" "psychopath"** and more, in a seriocomic display of drama. Shown on national television was a scene in parliament where the leader of the biggest party in the opposition crossed the floor and hugged the head of government, immediately after his vitriolic speech attacking him and his government's policies. He had on other occasions accused the same head of government of being a thief and corrupt in public meetings and in interviews with media. He even dared the media present to publish those accusations. The surprised and startled head of government reciprocated the hug somewhat awkwardly. Such war of words uttered mostly outside parliament and state legislatures were not protected by parliamentary privilege. Yet, none of the lawmakers and other high office-holders, to my knowledge, had resorted to legal action for defamation. The bottom line is that the people appeared not concerned. Probably, they welcomed and enjoyed the theatrics as good entertainment and a much-needed diversion from their problems.

The result has been that the electorate has lost both the inclination and the necessity to hold those whom they elect accountable. In some countries, including those above noted, the situation in this regard could be nearing a point of no return. **Here is the enigma. India the largest economy in the world about three centuries ago, according to some researchers. It has given the world, through its Vedas dating back to 7000 years, so much in terms of arts, literature science, culture, religion, philosophy, astronomy, mathematics, astrology, innovations, inventions, soft power, emphasising on a holistic approach to achieving a balanced life, by addressing the need for mental and physical well-being and, pursuing peace while forsaking violence for the sake of harmonious progress of mankind. These achievements were probably unprecedented in history.** Yet, India appears to have lost its moorings and stumbled in the contemporary world, despite it having enormous resources, natural and human, on a scale far more than ever before in its history. The disappointment is that the country has not been able to solve some of the basic problems (detailed earlier), including issues concerning national security. It is unable to punch at its own weight in international relations. The disconnect and the regress are difficult to comprehend.

In rare contrast, the leader of a relatively smaller country in our region, moved swiftly to fulfil his election promise to prosecute his immediate predecessor in office who was alleged to have stolen billions of dollars from state coffers by grossly abusing his powers in an elaborate scheme billed as the "kleptocracy of the century" and, at the time of writing, he had been charged in court. The leader also reportedly announced his intention to roll back the privileges and favoured treatment enjoyed by one ethnic community at the expense of the others. The paradox here is that he himself created the privileges and special treatment during his first term in office! Be that as it may, it is almost axiomatic that those enjoying such privileges and special treatment expect more and not less of the same. It would be quite difficult to get out of this trap as experience elsewhere has shown. It is easy to ride the "tiger" but difficult to control, much less to slay it. Nevertheless, his come back to power after more than 10 years in semi-retirement (and by then in advanced age) was itself seen as an extraordinary achievement.

There are countries, where men in uniform have ruled much of the time since independence by manipulating the elections, controlling the elected leaders and various other groups, including those aligned to terrorists in an entrenched "divide and rule" strategy. They also assumed direct rule from time to time by deposing the elected civilian government claiming it was "necessary in the national interest" and, ironically, to "safeguard democracy". One political analyst noted that usually "it is the country that has an army" but in country B "it is the army that has a country". It is also noteworthy that country B had earned the status of a "failed state" but still it had managed to convince the rest of the world that it is **"too dangerous to fail, while at the same time seeking international aid to keep its economy afloat"**.

EXTERNAL RELATIONS

There is a saying that a country's foreign policy is an extension of its domestic policy. If a country is unable to manage its internal problems and is bereft of long-term vision, it would not be able to safeguard its national interests in a tumultuous world in the long run. Often, the weakness and the confusion are taken advantage of by friends and foe alike. One tiny country, Mauritius, in the Indian ocean, which had long depended on India for its economic and security well-being, turned hostile to its benefactor in recent years, largely arising from India's inept handling of bilateral relations with Mauritius following serious internal political developments in the latter. This turn of event caused serious security concerns to India, as it is located in India's traditional and vital maritime security region. Reportedly India's not-so-friendly rivals were moving in to exploit an opportunity to advance their geo-strategic ambitions with designs to circumscribe India further in the process. Fortunately for India, relief came in the form of change of government in Mauritius. **In diplomacy, sleepwalking cannot be a good option**.

In this context, I would like to share a few thoughts with readers. In my training of diplomats overseas, I often engaged my audience to reflect on the following, amongst others:

- "We have no eternal allies, and we have no perpetual enemies. Our interests are eternal and perpetual and those interests it is our duty to follow" — **Viscount Palmerston**
- "Diplomacy without arms is like music without instruments" — **King Frederick of Prussia**
- The strong do what they have to do and the weak accept what they have to accept. **(Thucydides c.460B.C.- c.400B.C.)**; and
- Gratitude is lively expectation of favours to come.

FREEDOM

Freedom of speech, freedom of expression (especially but not limited to those in academia and the media) and freedom to participate in the political process are, amongst others, fundamental and necessary for the proper functioning of democracy. However, they do not operate in a vacuum; respect for and compliance with the constitution and the duly established laws of the state are necessary to maintain the balance that is vital for the nation to progress in peace and stability. Therefore, I subscribe to the view that **freedom is not absolute** and cannot survive in the long run without countervailing responsibility. In other words, they are two sides of the same coin. My observations reinforce my belief in this regard. Countries that went on the path of absolute freedom, and those regimes which enforced total or severe restrictions on such freedom, have both foundered. In my view, the balance has to be right for the country to progress.

I have given many examples earlier of freedom being grossly abused by a variety of actors, including politicians, religious groups, activists, NGOS, academics, students, extremists, and separatists — all these in the name of "democratic freedom", "secularism" "constitutional right", "it is my right" and more. Many of them have been exposed to have received foreign funding and consorting with enemies of the state, including hostile foreign powers, subversive religious extremists and terrorist networks, openly challenging the unity of the nation state and seeking to overthrow it, by unlawful means. They have exploited the impotence of the those in power and their lack of political will to enforce the law. I have also given examples of **universities** that have become centres for anti-national activities and hotbeds for terrorist propaganda and religious subversion. They have been infiltrated by generously funded foreign state and non-state actors in the garb of "Activists" and "NGOs". All political parties play along with them for short-term selfish gains, ignoring the grave peril to national security that they pose.

No country in the world can provide a perfect system where everybody is happy and contended. However, at the risk of repeating myself, the responsibility of the state to secure peace and security for all its citizens is paramount. In Singapore, our National Registration Identity Card (NRIC) (which was first introduced by the British in the post-Second World War years), was criticised by many foreign commentators as a serious violation of the citizens' privacy and human rights. Just look at what the Western democracies have put in place. They have gone for biometric identification and much overt and covert use of artificial intelligence to monitor almost every movement and aspect of their citizens' lives! Even with such measures in place, religious and racial strife have plunged many countries around the world into conflict. Our laws and policies have served us well in this regard. Countries that opted for the **politically-correct route**, found that it did not work. Few years ago, I was told of an alleged incident whereby a Member of Parliament in a west European country, who wanted to visit his constituency (as conscientious MPs often do), informed the police officer in the area of his intended visit, whereupon he was told by the policer officer that he (the MP) had to seek permission from the local *imam*. The MP was not amused, to put it mildly, and insisted on his rights as MP to visit his constituency anytime and unhindered. The police officer was equally insistent that the MP must get the *imam's* permission, as the area was under *Sharia* law and he (the police officer) had no jurisdiction in the matter!

In 2018, I read reports in our media about one of our academics who, along with an associate and a former citizen living in exile, approached a head of government in a neighbouring country to seek his help and intervention, "to bring democracy to South East Asia" (read Singapore). The irony in this was that head of government, during his long years in power, was noted more for promoting and perpetuating ethnic divisions than for his commitment to democracy! The motive of this group was suspect, to say the least. However, I hasten to state that many in the academia, media and from many other walks of life in Singapore have made important contributions in the service of our country and several of them have distinguished records in this regard. For example, our first and fourth presidents, **Yusof Ishak** and **Wee Kim Wee**, respectively, had distinguished and respected journalism careers.

Those who seek power to change society should seek that power through the ballot and accept the responsibility that comes with it. Seeking power by stealth and without the responsibility, undermines the state. **Stanley Baldwin** (1867–1947) who was a Conservative Party leader and Prime Minister of the United Kingdom noted, **"Power without responsibility — the prerogative of the harlot throughout the ages"**. (According to one reference source, the author of the quote was in fact Rudyard Kipling, the cousin of Baldwin, and the latter merely borrowed the quote.)

One might then ask how to strike the necessary balance? It is never an easy task and is fraught with danger. Several key factors come into play, such as the size of the country, its resources, the population make-up, racial, religious, linguistic and cultural divides, the geo-political environment, and the threats faced. In order to bring these centrifugal forces to work together, observing minimum and necessary restraints and limitations on the part of all those concerned, is necessary, to secure long-term peace and security without which the country cannot progress. It requires stout-hearted and courageous leaders, with unflagging stamina for the long haul, to convince the people why it is necessary in the national interest and, at the same time, be prepared to be thrown out of office in the next ballot, if the delivery does not match the promises made. This is why, I believe, many leaders in many countries opted for the easier and less perilous route, thus, ignoring the inevitable consequences.

SECOND REASON

At the beginning of this chapter, I said that there are two reasons for wanting to write this chapter. Having dealt with the first, now I come to the second reason. In Chapter 3, I gave an account of how I secured my first job in the Civil Service in 1959 through a highly competitive examination. I believed then, and still do, that it was the topic in the General Paper which I chose that qualified me for an interview by the Public Service Commission chaired by Inche Yusof bin Ishak (later President of the Republic). The topic was **"Is Western democracy suited to Asian countries? Discuss"**. To summarise, the thrust of my argument was that democracy, as understood and practised in the West, was unlikely to work in Asian countries, especially in countries that had just emerged from long colonial rule. Among the factors I cited then were many problems relating to geography, history, culture, race, religion and, most importantly, illiteracy. Overall, I believed that my arguments must have had some traction with the examiner, whoever he was, because during the interview, I was further probed on the topic by members of the interview panel, including the Chairman.

There was a bit of what one might consider a funny situation (not to me at that time) that arose just about two hours before my interview at the then Supreme Court Building. I finished school around 1 P.M. and was looking for a suitable place to rest since it was not possible to go home and get back in time to attend the interview. Just then, I discovered, to my horror, that my fountain pen (no ballpoint pens available then) had leaked, resulting in a sizeable black ink patch around my shirt pocket. There was no way I could attend the interview wearing that shirt. I could not go back home to change and come back in time for the interview. Much was at stake. Just at that time, my father and a close friend of his turned up to bless me for the interview. He had brought with him *prasadam* (holy white ash) from the temple where he had prayed earlier. (For the information of readers, some Hindus place the holy ash on their forehead when they pray.) I then quickly decided to buy a new shirt, pooling together our resources. The shirt cost about 3 dollars and was among the cheapest available, but good enough for the occasion. Curiously, the label read "Alsation Dog" along with an image of a dog. I did not think much of the label at that time and proceeded to attend the interview.

When I went home that evening my two dogs appeared more excited than usual in welcoming me home and kept jumping on me. That night while reflecting on the events of the day, I wondered if my dogs, in a way, had helped me in the decision to get that new shirt. Stretching sentiments too far perhaps, but the thought did cross my mind. I had reared many dogs from when they were young puppies and had developed very close bonds with them. Caring for them was part of my job in the family. They were fiercely loyal and would often await my return from work at night to greet me and escort me home, running around me excitedly. Later, when I bought my motorcycle, they would travel further along the dark and desolate road to await my return home and enjoyed the thrill of running along with my motorcycle, often crisscrossing my path, and sometimes even jumping on my motorcycle. They had an uncanny ability to know the sound of my motorcycle. Without doubt, dogs are among man's best friends. They give so much to us expecting very little in return.

THE VERDICT

Fast forward 60 years, one might ask how Western democracy has fared in the context of this discourse. More than half a century is surely sufficient time to settle the debate, especially on whether the rulers in the countries concerned have delivered good governance. However, there is, in my understanding, no single, universally-accepted yardstick to measure success and failure in this regard. Be that as it may, it is not difficult to see, feel, experience and to know and assess how lives of the masses have changed for the better, if at all, at least at the base level — in terms of lifting people out of crushing poverty, eradicating hunger, providing employment, shelter, freedom of movement, personal security, access to drinking (drinkable) water, basic and affordable health care, access to education, care for the severely disadvantaged, and other factors. It is the fundamental responsibility of any government to deliver on these, if democracy is to have any meaning at all. The question is, how responsible have the governments, in the countries concerned, been over the decades in this regard.

The picture that emerges from the many anecdotal narratives given above is not very encouraging. In my observations, I have noted that misunderstanding and misinterpretation (deliberate or otherwise) of democracy, and the emphasis on privilege over responsibility, the preference for short-term fixes for serious long term problems, disinterest in a long-term vision, and lack of integrity and necessary discipline are among the many factors that suggest that they have not delivered good governance. The above instead contributed, as the examples given above illustrate, to serious and pervasive corruption, leadership deficit, failure of justice, breakdown in the rule of law, brazen abuse of power, lack of accountability, appeasement, criminalisation of politics, increase in serious crimes, especially against women and children, disunity, anarchism and many more. In short, **those in power ruled but did very little to govern.**

Generally, this is the overall picture that has emerged in the countries concerned and it should not be a surprise. As noted earlier, the British wrote, guided or influenced the constitutions of most of their former colonies, but the British constitution itself remains largely unwritten. India's constitution was written by its own leaders soon after independence, but they borrowed many features from the constitutions of UK, USA, Australia, Canada, Ireland, USSR, and even Germany's Weimar Constitution. Perhaps, they were influenced by liberalism and the Fabian socialism of the time. However, the countries emerging from colonialism did not have the kind of underpinnings that established democracies in the West had, to support their constitutions. They had, as noted above, a high level of literacy, homogenous populations which are not riven by race, religion, language and culture, defined geographical entities and borders, amongst others.

To varying degrees and combinations, the necessary requirements were absent in most of the countries concerned. The reason for their absence was, for the most part, the deliberate action of the colonial regimes who drew and reordered political borders according to their spheres of influence, ignoring linguistic, religious, racial and cultural divides, existing natural geographic entities and enmities. In some countries, one of the major problems was land ownership and distribution. It was the result of the expropriation of land by the tiny minority of white settlers who came with the colonising and evangelical forces. **Desmond Tutu,** the Archbishop of South Africa described it thus: **"When the white missionaries came to Africa, they had the bible and we had the land. They told us to pray. We closed our eyes. When we opened them, we had the bible and they had the land".** Added to this, was the brutal suppression and exploitation of the native populations by the colonial regimes. In an earlier chapter, I referred to the rapacious and brutal exploitation of the enormous resources of Congo by Belgian colonisers and their settlers. The colonial powers built up their power and prosperity at home with the enormous resources they plundered from their colonies. It is, therefore, not a coincidence that with their empires gone, they face economic decline at home. Many of the former colonies had serious built-in obstacles to begin with, which were further compounded by the inability (or unwillingness) of the native rulers to lay strong and pragmatic foundations right at the beginning. I have earlier dealt with the leadership deficits in many of the countries that emerged from the colonial rule.

However, a few countries like Singapore, did exceptionally well in providing good governance, defying the great odds stacked against their very survival as a nation. The decisive factors for success were, and I repeat, honest and incorruptible leaders, who led frugal lives, were committed to the long-term vision of achieving national prosperity and resolutely confronted the challenges thrown at their way. They laid a solid foundation to nurture desired core values. They created a political and administrative system that promoted continuous economic and social progress, based on the ideals of meritocracy. All these required much stamina for the long haul. They chose the difficult path of **"levelling-up"** over the easier alternative of **"levelling down"**. Another important factor to be noted here is that they did it, not by abandoning democracy, but by adapting it, to make it work in the unique and very unpromising situation they inherited from the departing colonial administration. They practiced free and fair elections and firmly believed that delivery on good governance, and not empty rhetoric and promises at election time, would bring them acceptance, continued cooperation and respect from the masses. However, they were pragmatic and rejected the Western manual (that disregarded ground realities, compulsions and complications) on how democracy should be implemented. It was a demonstration of the fact that there can be no **"one size fits all"** democracy that the West very often prescribes for others.

Western democracy took centuries to evolve and develop the basic foundations necessary. Even then, those countries did not always have a smooth or easy ride, to say the least. The British wartime leader, **Winston Churchill**, noted: **"Democracy is the worst form of government, except for the alternative"**. Developments in recent decades, point to signs of stress and decline in some countries in many basic areas. A continuous thread in this saga is the duplicitous and hypocritical behaviour of some big powers, who by projecting themselves as "beacons of democracy", bully and punish smaller states, arrogantly alleging denial of "free speech", "freedom of movement", "equal justice" and "rule of law", which they themselves deny to varying degrees to their own populations, sometimes selectively to sections within their own populations. A senior official and an adviser to the US president threatened (on camera) the **International Criminal Court (ICC)** with sanctions, if it proceeded to investigate allegations of war crimes committed by US soldiers in Afghanistan. He further branded the Court as illegal. One of the cruellest frauds some countries have committed over the years, was to supply arms, sometimes expensive and precision-guided munitions, to many despotic and wealthy regimes to enable them to kill innocent and defenceless people and, inflict mass starvation and suffering on a scale comparable to war crimes, according to a report from a credible international organisation. Such is the record of their "commitments" to human rights and democracy! It is a very depressing sight to see needless suffering of the innocent, the weak, the defenceless and the deprived, inflicted by the abuse of power of powerful states which profess to be defenders of democracy and human rights. When I reflect on this during quiet moments, the words of an English poet, **William Wordsworth (1770–1850)** comes to mind: **"much it grieves my heart to think what man has made of man"**.

Before I bring this discourse on democracy to a close, it is worth taking a quick look at the political, economic, and social upheavals and unrests in the West, principally but not exclusively in the United States and in Europe in recent years and decades. Even a casual observer would not have failed to notice the continuing protests in the streets, many turning violent, resulting in much destruction of state assets. In so doing, they were challenging the legitimacy of the democratically elected governments and institutions, the very essence of democracy, for their failure to deliver political, economic, social and security well-being for the masses. The causes are too many to catalogue here. However, the most striking among them is the consequences of almost a half a century of unbridled and relentless globalisation which has fabulously enriched a very small minority and, at the same time, impoverished a vast majority of the people. The resultant despair and insecurity are cause for concern, especially for young job seekers pouring out of educational and training institutions. There is a body of literature arguing that the ground is shifting, and that the Western democratic century may be drawing to a close. If democracy is unable to deliver at home (the West) then is it be reasonable to expect that it can fare any better elsewhere?

Time to wrap-up this chapter but before doing so, here is one more anecdote. In my *alma mater*, **Victoria School**, we had many British expatriate teachers, and one of them was a Scottish lady, Mrs Campbell who taught us additional mathematics — a subject which I was not particularly fond of. Sometimes, she scolded me for not completing my homework. However, I remember that she insisted that after answering each theorem, we write the letters "Q E D" *(quod erat demonstrandum)* which in Latin roughly meant what needs to be proved has been proved. We also had a teacher by the name of C B Paul, who taught Latin and I attended his class for a few months before dropping out. My friend and classmate, **John Abraham,** also similarly dropped out, much to the disappointment of the teacher. However, the little knowledge I gained then was helpful in my law studies later. One of the subjects I did for my LLB was Roman Law.

In my mother tongue, Tamil, a saying goes thus: *"maatha, pitha, guru, theivam"* which in translation means "mother, father, teacher, God". I am grateful to all my teachers and, in particular, **Mr D S Samuel,** my Form Teacher who taught me in Standard Six in Victoria School in 1954.

Quod erat demonstrandum.

Chapter 24

SINGAPORE MODEL

"There is no law of nature that next year will be better. We have to work to make it happen"

—*PM Lee Kuan Yew*

"Your country gives the world an eloquent demonstration that corruption is not an invincible enemy after all".

—*Dr Mustapha Al-Sayyid, Director,*
Centre for the Study of Developing Countries,
Cairo University

"Without political will, nothing can be achieved. With political will, almost every problem has a solution"

—*Professor Tommy Koh*

The success of Singapore in overcoming enormous problems despite the dire predictions of impending doom when it was cast aside from Malaysia, earned Singapore great respect abroad, and Singapore was consistently rated highly in the narratives and commentaries of important global institutions. In an article on Singapore in October 1992, **"Management Today"** on page 112 concluded that **"Singapore is a successful human response to national disadvantage"**. At the 37th "Singapore Lecture", the Indian prime minister, **Narendra Modi,** said **"Singapore is a metaphor for dreams coming true".** There were many leaders who wanted their countries to be "the Singapore" in their region. **Yasser Arafat**, Chairman of the Palestine Liberation Organisation, told us, in a meeting at his office in the West Bank, that he wanted to develop **Palestine to be "the Singapore of the Middle East"**. There were many more accolades but the best of all is the **"China Reform Friendship Medal" bestowed posthumously on Lee Kuan Yew by President Xi Jinpeng in 2018 in recognition of Lee Kuan Yew's and, by extension, Singapore's contribution to China's economic modernisation and development.** In my view, the reason for China's meteoric rise was that, although it had a closed system, it had, at the same time, an **open mind,** which empowered the nation to learn from and adopt the best practices and policies of other countries, regardless of whether they were big or small. The Chinese leader Deng Xiaoping famously said: it does not matter whether the cat is black or white so long it catches mice! After his visit to Singapore (referred to in an earlier chapter), China sent a continuous stream of their officials, over many years, to Singapore to study our public administration and governance. President Xi Jinpeng also acknowledged this during his first term as President. Within a few decades, China has amply demonstrated to the world that it is a force to be reckoned with in the global economic and political landscape.

In contrast, many countries, including one which is not much smaller than China, which prided on its democracy and open system, had a **closed mind** in this regard. Whether for reasons of ego, or other factors, they concluded that there was nothing much to learn from other countries, especially small ones like Singapore. There is no need to dwell on this further and the results speak for themselves.

I delivered a keynote address at a conference on "Political Conditions for Development: Transparency, Accountability and Good Governance" organised by Cairo University during my term as Ambassador to Egypt. In the audience were many senior, former and current, officials and leaders, including **Dr Abdel Aziz Hegazy**, a former prime minister of Egypt. In a letter to thank me, the

Director of the Centre for the Study of Developing Countries said **"Your country gives the world an eloquent demonstration that corruption is not an invincible enemy after all"**.

CAN SINGAPORE BE A MODEL FOR OTHER COUNTRIES?

Often, I was asked this question during my interactions abroad and during my lectures on Singapore's public sector reforms given at our Civil Service College for senior public sector officials from developing countries in Asia, Africa and beyond. The training courses were organised under the auspices of the **Singapore Technical Cooperation Programme.**

NIMBLE AND AGILE

Many at home and abroad held the view that Singapore's small size enabled it to achieve success. A small country can be nimble and change course quickly when a situation requires. It is like the very small speed boat against the huge lumbering giant super tanker; the former can turn around within several seconds and the latter could take about 30 minutes to do so! In my view, however, it is only a small advantage. Many small countries have floundered, and it goes without saying that many big countries have, as well. Therefore, arguably, other factors are far more important and decisive. Furthermore, corruption and incompetence have no favourites and do not pick and choose based on size.

LEADERSHIP QUALITY

The quality of leadership was the decisive factor. We in Singapore were lucky that we had honest and incorruptible leaders taking charge right at the beginning, who set the highest standard in governance. By the standards of the time, they were also relatively young, compared to leaders of other newly independent countries, for example, Jawaharlal Nehru in India, and Jomo Kenyatta of Kenya. The relative youth and vitality of our leaders was complemented by their energy and conviction. Prime Minister Lee Kuan Yew was the youngest prime minister in the Commonwealth, if not in the world, when he assumed office, according to a commentary by **Vernon Bartlett** in the Straits Times, June 1959. On the other hand, the long and difficult struggle against British rule in many other countries had sapped the energy and vitality of their leaders, by the time they came to power. That they were idealists and not pragmatists also did not help, as previously noted. The situation was also not very different in some other Asian and African countries.

Right at the beginning, our leaders laid a solid foundation by setting a pragmatic course to mobilise the citizens in nation building. This was essential to prevent our multi-racial, multi-cultural, multi-lingual and multi-religious mix from igniting and combusting. They pressed on and did not lose courage in the face of hostility, initially from the communists and communalists from within, and then from so-called Western liberals, who did not think much of any development model, especially of developing countries, if it did not conform to their rule book. In contrast, many countries, both near and far, were plunged into serious strife by incompetent, corrupt and self-serving leaderships.

LONG TERM VISION

In Singapore, the PAP government worked out a **strategic and long-term plan** for the future, took tough decisions, and implemented them with single-minded determination to translate the vision into reality, while managing consequential problems in the process. It was able to do so only because of the trust it earned from the vast majority of people, over the years, which, in turn, enabled it to renew its electoral mandate in every election held since it first came to power in 1959. I cannot recall any other democracy, big or small, where the same government has remained in power for over half a century through fair and free elections, and continuously delivered good governance. This continuity in office was a major factor that enabled Singapore to plan and execute long term development programmes.

ELECTIONS

While there have been some critics who said the elections were not entirely fair, no international organisation has ever questioned the integrity of our election process, nor felt the need to send "election monitors" to monitor our elections, as they frequently do so in many other countries around the world.

There were also few critics at home who questioned the fact that our ballot papers carried serial numbers and suggested that government could trace who voted for whom. Having been involved in the conduct of polling in elections, I can say that, while in theory it is possible, in practice, it cannot be done, even if the government wants to do so. Votes are secret and the process of casting is observed by all stakeholders who are authorised to be present, to ensure that there are no irregularities. When polling closes, all ballot boxes are sealed in the presence of the same stakeholders, taken to the counting centres under police escort. After the votes are counted and the results announced, the ballots are put back in the boxes and sealed in the presence of the candidates and/or their agents, who put their seals. All the boxes are then taken to the supreme court vaults and kept there for the statutory period of six months, in case of an election petition contesting any issues concerning the polls. Nobody has access to the vaults once it is sealed. If there is any petition during the six months, it would be dealt with as per the law and, if none was received, the vault is opened, the ballot boxes taken out, and the ballots destroyed — all these in the presence of judges, stakeholders and even interested members of the public. A prior public announcement with the necessary details is made, informing all who are concerned. I cannot recall any election petition ever being lodged or if lodged, succeeding. The electoral system, including the numbered ballots, which we inherited from the British has, in my opinion, served us well. Also, it is to the credit of the citizens that in successive elections they elected good calibre candidates, although by quirk of politics a few able and proven candidates have also lost.

The serial number on the ballot paper is a safeguard against fraud (like stuffing ballot boxes) as each and every ballot cast can be accounted for. I am not sure how many countries have this additional safeguard and we should thank the British for giving us this system. In the elections of some countries around the world, stuffing ballot boxes to "achieve" over 90% support is not unheard of. During my service abroad, a retired ambassador in a large Arab country told me that when the polls closed, the officials in charge would get to work to fix the results to the percentage wanted by their president, usually anywhere between 95% to 99% per cent! Not surprisingly, that country with its enormous human and natural resources came to grief in 2011, when the president was overthrown in the Arab Spring uprising. In contrast, there has never been any violence during elections in Singapore, which have always been peaceful and orderly. To some, they were so peaceful and orderly, to the point of boring. Probably, these were the fellows who coined the term **"Singabore"**!

CORE VALUES

Usually long uninterrupted years in office has many hazards for a nation, such as complacency, lethargy and, more seriously, temptation to raid the public till. There have been many cases where big and prosperous countries went broke and, unable to pay the bills, had to seek repeated international bailouts. The PAP avoided this fate by steadfastly maintaining its core values of honesty, incorruptibility, and leadership renewal, and constantly reinventing Singapore. With its healthy financial reserves, painstakingly built up over the years, for any rainy days, it is unlikely Singapore would ever need a bailout, provided it is always prudently managed. Lee Kuan Yew and his colleagues planned and oversaw the smooth successions of the second and third generation leaders, **Goh Chok Tong** and **Lee Hsien Loong,** respectively, and their cabinets. They had to deal with different sets of challenges. For example, Prime Minister Lee Hsien Loong is faced with the tough challenges of the digital age, social media, changing regional security architecture, an aging population, and many newer complex problems. The way he has addressed some of them earned him ringing endorsement from the people in the 2015 election. Our leadership has been unique in many ways and I have given many other anecdotal narratives as illustrations, in my earlier chapters.

Even when the going was good our leaders would often warn the citizens not to take success for granted. I recall PM Lee Kuan Yew warning us that **"There is no law of nature that next year will be better. We have to work to make it happen"**. When the economy faced contractions in the 1980s, the government administered tough and unpopular medicine, including reductions in salaries across the board. The **National Trade Union Congress** (NTUC) chief explained to the workers that the measure was necessary in order to improve productivity, which was crucial for the economy to bounce back to growth. I recall an ambassador from a big a country in Latin America telling me when I was Chief of Protocol that he could not understand how a labour union chief could ask the workers to accept a pay cut voluntarily. He said that no labour union chief in his country would ever dare to ask the workers for a similar sacrifice. If he was brave enough to do so, the ambassador said with a throat slashing gesture, **"his throat will be cut immediately"**.

South America is an enormously resource-rich continent both in terms of natural and human resources. The continent is also immensely rich in minerals and has an abundant supply of water which enabled its prosperous agriculture sector, and more importantly gave the continent huge potential for hydro power. Added to these blessings was an equable climate. In my view, if the resources are efficiently and effectively managed, no other continent can match the level of prosperity South America can achieve for all its people. I always believed that **both prosperity and poverty are man-made.**

During my school years, I remember reading that up to the early 1940s, Argentina ranked about 4th among the developed nations. It was not surprising considering its bountiful natural resources and skilled manpower. It was one of the biggest economies then and it supported a high standard of living for its people. It was probably the envy of many countries in the continent then. It is no secret that despite all the resources it had, Argentina's economy began to falter. In my view, it started when **Juan Domingo Peron** was elected president with massive support from the labour unions, which he had courted during his term as labour minister in the previous administration. His development plans were based on **increasing workers' pay by legislation but not by increasing productivity.** He encouraged strikes against employers who resisted. One survey noted that in 1945 alone "50,000 working days" were lost! This was one of the pillars of what became to be known as **"Peronism"**. Argentina is still paying the price of this egregious folly. It is no secret that Argentina has been in and out of financial crises, requiring International Monetary Fund lifelines for support. The last such crisis was in 2018 and the IMF bailout was US$5.6 billion, according to one report.

A Brazilian ambassador used to boast to me that his foreign service had a very long tradition and only the best of the best in Brazil were taken in. I had the impression that he did not think much of our administration. He used to tell me how much he missed his home. Once he told a few ambassadors in my presence that he could not invite me to dinner because, I was a vegetarian and did not take alcohol, and he said that in a somewhat condescending manner. On a previous occasion I had told him that I did not take beef or pork and he found that strange. He had concluded that anyone who did not eat beef must be a vegetarian! The ambassador also told me that in his country, people ate beef for breakfast, lunch and dinner. (They must have been the wealthy ones in the country.) It was an unusual way for a diplomat to interact with the host community. Yet, when he left at the end of his tour, he was very close to tears and told me how much he liked Singapore and the life he enjoyed! It is worth mentioning here that Brazil, with 8.4 million sq. km of land (half the size of the continent of South America), with over 200 million people, and blessed with a scale of natural resources like no other country, had trouble in balancing its books! Corruption had engulfed the administration. Brazil's biggest corruption scandal involved PETROBRAS, Brazil's oil giant, which had an intricate web of corruption, allegedly leading all the way up to the head of state. President **Dilma Rousseff** was impeached for budget irregularities, although it was widely believed that she had not personally benefitted from the corruption. Many also believed that Rousseff was made a scapegoat by powerful families and lawmakers, who were themselves deeply entrenched in corruption, in an attempt to evade similar fate.

In the context of this narrative, it is worth recalling the frequent warnings of our pioneer leaders, especially PM Lee, that **once the humpty dumpty is broken it would be very difficult, if not impossible, to glue it back.**

It is worth noting here that recurrent industrial strife, involving governments, labour unions and businesses in antagonistic relationship, is a fact of life in many countries. Singapore **had** its fair share during colonial times and during the initial years of our self-government. I had watched that in some countries, the government response was to issue decrees and edicts mandating wage increase across the board, in some cases, just to buy a little peace and respite from the strident labour unions. It is my firm belief that meaningful wage increases to increase workforce prosperity cannot be achieved in this way. There is a proverb which goes something like this: *if wishes were horses than beggars might ride.* It does not require rocket science to realise that prosperity can be achieved only through continuous increase in productivity gains. **It is the rising tide that will lift us all.**

Singapore took a very different path to increase the prosperity of its citizens. Our pioneer leaders had firmly decided that meaningful wage increases could only be possible through sustained **productivity** increase of the work force in a fiercely competitive world. Very quickly the government went about creating an enabling environment, and established the necessary legislation, institutions, policies and productivity awareness campaigns and movements throughout the spectrum of the administration involving the public service, labour unions, business enterprises, and every other stakeholder. At the very core of the movement was the creation of the **National Wages Council (NWC) in 1972** which is a tripartite statutory organisation consisting of representatives from the Government, business community and the trade unions. Its mandate is to monitor the nation's productive performance continuously and recommend to the Government in July of each year the wage increase across the board based on productive gains in the preceding 12 months. Conversely, should the economy contract, it would recommend a wage freeze or even a reduction in wages to enable the economy to regain its competitiveness. In my recollection, there was one wage reduction across the board in the mid-1980s.

Crucial to the success was the acceptance of the policy by the population and its cooperation in its implementation. Several campaigns were launched to explain to the masses at the grassroots level the details of the policy and why it was vital for the survival and progress of the nation. Many other relevant organisations e.g. the **National Productivity Board (NPB)** were also created to take the message to the factory floor, government offices, business establishments, and others. NPB helped to implement relevant strategies and policies, and best practices across the board to increase productivity. It has always been a **"work in progress"** and will remain so. There was also a slew of schemes like productivity quizzes, competitions, staff suggestion schemes and the adoption of the Japanese practices of "just in time delivery" and the *Koban* system of neighbourhood policing by law enforcement officers. Those who excelled in these schemes were properly rewarded. Another important component of the productivity movement is learning from the best practices around the world and implementing them at home with the necessary adaptations. Singapore also has helped many countries around the world to set up productivity organisations and shared with them its expertise under its Technical Cooperation Programme which has more than 100 countries in its list of cooperation, not just in productivity but across a very wide field in public administration.

Productivity is important in every human activity, including for all professions and not any less in diplomacy. In my training of diplomats, amongst others, I have often emphasised on "3 Ps": the need to be **professional, proactive and productive,** as I have mentioned before. Based on my observations, if a diplomat is not professional <u>and</u> proactive, it is unlikely that he or she will be very productive.

SECURITY

A very important pillar in our development, as I mentioned before, has been the pragmatic and long-term vision of our pioneer generation leaders. Ever mindful of our vulnerabilities, we built security architecture involving interlocking security arrangements, with important strategic partners. We made it possible for the US to maintain a rotational naval presence in Singapore, despite our severe limitations of space. In contrast, few countries which closed their US bases in response to populist demands, reversed their position later, partly in response to the changing geostrategic equation in the vital South China Sea, especially China's increasing maritime presence in the area and the kind of response (or lack of it in some cases) from concerned regional states, including major Asian powers. US military and commercial presence had enabled many countries in the region to prosper. Its continued presence in this regard is necessary for regional security, which is essential to maintaining peace. However, a view that the US has not been a very reliable partner in the scheme of things also appears to be gaining some ground.

OPEN MIND AND INNOVATION

Keeping an open mind and an open system has been crucial to our success. In the continuous search for new ideas and solutions to problems, PM Lee tasked **Lee Ek Tieng,** Permanent Secretary in the Ministry of the Environment and Water Resources to turn the approximately 42 acres of Istana grounds into a catchment area, to collect as much rain water run-off as possible. Ek Tieng did a good job — a network of sunken drains and retaining ponds were created without disturbing or altering the garden scenery and the surroundings; pumps were immersed in water to pump out the water to the nearby Bukit Timah Pumping Station. This scheme was later abandoned because the cost of collecting and treating the water in this case proved to be uneconomical. I was then the Private Secretary to President Sheares and, after very heavy rains, I would go on rounds to see the functioning of the system. I was then living in government quarters, a bungalow (2 Edinburgh Road) within the Istana grounds. I had another experience in this regard. After I retired, together with **Tan Chee Wee**, my former colleague and a curator at the Istana, I met Lee Kuan Yew, who was the Senior Minister then, at the Cabinet Office and presented a proposal, on a possible solution to minimise the haze coming from Indonesia. Briefly, the proposal was to obviate the need to "slash and burn" by cutting the vegetation (instead of burning) and turning it into mulch which could have many uses, including use as organic fertiliser. The good timber could be recovered for better use. In short, the proposal would create environmentally sustainable farming and generate employment for the people concerned, with minimal environmental degradation. SM Lee thought the proposal was worth looking at and asked us to send it to the Ministry of the Environment and Water Resources, and we did.

SHARING EXPERIENCE

Over the years there were many study groups visiting Singapore to learn how we made it to where we were.

At the request of General **Olusegun Obasanjo** (then Chairman of the African Leadership Forum) to Senior Minister Lee Kuan Yew in 1992, the Singapore International Foundation hosted a conference on the theme **"Relevance of Singapore's Experience for Africa"**. **Obasanjo** headed a group of 17 very senior officials drawn from a wide cross section in 10 African states. At the concluding session, **Obasanjo** summed up the relevance of Singapore's development experience to Africa thus:

"One unique experience of Singapore that probably no African country shares is the smallness of the city state and the total absence of an agricultural sector. Also the geopolitical situation of Singapore during the height of the Cold War years of the 1960's may not be comparable to the situation in Africa".

"That being said, the recurring factor in the impressive performance of Singapore in the process of nation building and economic growth, is the issue of leadership, particularly political leadership, which is visionary, committed and honest. The leadership maintained stability, continuity and change without losing direction and bearing, if anything, with long-range planning. Analysis and planning are matched by execution and implementation. It has the courage of conviction and carries on in spite of irritating and unkind remarks from the foreign press. The leadership anchored the implementation of its policies on personal examples of integrity and self-discipline, human resource development, provision of infrastructures, political continuity, institution building, firm and serious sanctions against inefficiency and corruption, meritocracy, efficient and impartial civil service, accommodation of consensus, and interest of minorities, encouragement of private investment, and pragmatic approach to foreign relations.

These are lessons that cannot be regarded as irrelevant for African nations and African political leaders."

There were many examples of countries which adopted and implemented many policies that were pioneered in Singapore. Countries in our region adopted some of our policies, for example, in creating a **clean, green and a garden state** (we developed the **"instant tree"** widely used in other countries) and our EDB's **"one stop centre"**. The Emirate of Dubai made Singapore a model for its development. Dubai established an investment company (I think it was "Al Khaleej Investment") and stationed one of their senior officials, **Mohamed Alabbar**, in Singapore in the 1970s to study every aspect of Singapore's administration. They went about with zeal and determination to apply what they learnt from Singapore. During my term as ambassador to the United Arab Emirates, they would quite openly say then that they "learn from Singapore". At his request, I arranged for Alabbar to meet SM Lee Kuan Yew in Dubai (during the latter's visit there). He proudly displayed in his office many photographs of Lee Kuan Yew. Mohamed Alabbar is a leading entrepreneur and has been described as a "property tycoon". He played a significant role in Dubai's economic development.

When they started their airline — Emirates — they used the Singapore Airlines model and recruited some of SIA's staff as well. To cut the long story short, the Emirates Airline had become the largest airline in the world by around 2005 and Dubai has overtaken Singapore in many areas. Dubai has become a leading centre of innovation, excellence and a trail blazer in futuristic living in a desert environment due to relentless development and application of technology, including artificial intelligence. It has a small total population of about 2.9 million of which only 15% are indigenous Emirati citizens and the remaining 2.7 million or 85% are non-citizen foreigners. Yet, Dubai has managed to preserve its culture and its unique way of life intact and still maintain a high standard of living for all its citizens. Reportedly, Dubai Airport handles more flights than any other airport in the world. There are many lessons other countries, including Singapore, can learn from Dubai. Admittedly, Dubai, unlike Singapore, is well endowed with natural resources, including oil and a relatively big land mass. However, these alone could not have been the decisive factors for its continuing spectacular progress and push to be a world leader in many areas of human endeavour.

A few other countries, on the other hand, were not successful in applying Singapore policies. I understand that Fiji introduced our Central Provident Fund scheme but it collapsed within a few years when the government allowed contributors to make withdrawals from their accounts. **Jehan Sadat**, wife of President **Anwar Sadat** of Egypt, made a visit to Singapore in the 1980s (before the assassination of her husband). Impressed by our cleanliness and greenery, she introduced anti-litter measures, including providing litter bins, in Cairo. It did not take-off and within a few months the whole project was abandoned and forgotten. The will and the kind of discipline required in all strata of society was simply not there.

One of the important pillars of good governance in Singapore is the sensitive and effective management of our multi-racial, multi-religious, multi-lingual and multi-cultural population. It has attracted international interest and attention. At the 2016 Manama Dialogue (a premiere international security conference) in Bahrain, Defence Minister Ng Eng Hen's account of how this was achieved received favourable responses from the audience.

I have always taken the view that it was for others and not for Singaporeans to assess whether the Singapore model could be replicated elsewhere. However, in saying so, I have also emphasised my belief and experience that, while conditions in countries vary, there are, nevertheless, certain universal and time-tested norms, values and factors that are essential prerequisites for good governance. They are, amongst others, honesty, integrity, incorruptibility, and a visionary leadership that endeavours to earn the trust of the citizens in a cooperative dialogue. A very important factor has been the courage and determination of our founding leaders in fostering communal harmony in the volatile mix of racial, religious, linguistic and communal divides, through a policy of empowerment. They did not flinch from this even in the face of threats to their persons from communists and communalists. They adopted the difficult strategy of levelling up, rejecting the popular and easier option of levelling down, which would have created long-term danger. Many countries chose the easier option of levelling down by applying special privileges, reservations, quotas in every sphere of administration, including the judiciary. The countries which took this latter route were not only unable to roll back the reservations, quotas and the like, but were forced to give more and more for vote bank reasons. Not surprisingly, the pendulum has begun to swing the other way.

At the core of Singapore's success, which enabled it to punch far above its weight internationally, is, as stated before, its committed, pragmatic, visionary and high calibre leadership which took charge right at the beginning. Here is one of the many examples of this. The Cabinet was all set to expand the Paya Lebar Airport after an exhaustive study, including reports from foreign experts. Not convinced, PM Lee asked **Phua Bah Lee**, a grassroots member of the Party, whether the expansion would adversely affect the people in the area, especially the farmers. Bah Lee answered in the affirmative and gave reasons. PM Lee, then and there, decided that a new airport should be built at Changi which would enable aircrafts to land and take off, using the space above the sea as much as possible. It was a decisive and bold decision. (Bah Lee and I were Deputy Collectors of Land Revenue in the then Land Office located in City Hall. He later entered politics and became a Member of Parliament and a Senior Parliamentary Secretary. When that conversation took place, Bah Lee was the Organising Secretary of the PAP and PM Lee its Secretary General.)

GRACIOUS SOCIETY

Singapore, originally, comprised of a motley group of polyglot immigrants showing loyalty to respective "motherlands". They coexisted under the colonial rule and many returned "home" for good after having made small fortunes. Subsequent generations established roots, but they were still not a nation in the usual sense. Developments in their motherlands still held sway on them. By and large, this was the situation in Singapore when PAP came to power in 1959. Forging a nation was both urgent and indispensable.

As we progressed, our founding fathers were concerned that with increasing affluence, we could become, as **Minister Rajaratnam** said, a society of people who **know the price of everything and the value of nothing.** Policies were introduced to encourage a caring and a gracious society. There were many who made jokes about the policy, but the government persisted. The results are not disappointing. We have come a long way. I see many examples daily of Singaporeans coming to the assistance of the elderly in a variety of situations. For example, many young Singaporeans instinctively give up their seats in MRT trains and buses to the elderly and those with handicap. As senior citizens, my wife and I are accorded this kindness and we are grateful. They also come to the help of befuddled seniors in shopping malls, at escalators and the like. As a society, we are also welcoming of foreigners and appreciate their contribution, even if, as many have pointed out, "foreign talent" requires careful definition.

Here are interesting but at the same time contrasting anecdotes:

Sometime in February 2018, my wife and I were crossing Thomson Road from the side of Revenue House to Novena mall and MRT station. We noticed a Caucasian lady (in her mid-thirties) pushing a pram with an active toddler in it. After the crossing, we struck up a conversation with her and I asked her where she was from. She replied that she was from Hong Kong (HK). It made me curious to ask the next question — why she and her family moved to Singapore.

Her account was interesting in every detail. She was born in HK (her parents were in the British Army and long-term residents there) and lived there until recently. She was not accepted as part of the society and was never able to engage with the locals socially. Once she was in difficulty on the very long escalator that connected the International Finance Centre to the Mid-Levels, further up the steep slope, in the very densely populated part of HK Island. All the people in the scene passed by busily looking at their mobile phones and none stopped to render assistance. Somehow, she managed to prevent injury and moved on. On another occasion, when she was eight months pregnant with her toddler son, she was pushed around in the MTR and no one offered her a seat.

She then contrasted her HK experience to Singapore. She was very surprised how courteous and caring Singaporeans were. Even at the slightest sign of difficulty, Singaporeans went to help her. She mentioned several instances, such as guiding her to the right place in malls and in managing her pram in MRT stations and in buses. Seeing her with her toddler son, fellow passengers readily gave her their seats. I was not surprised by her HK experience. My wife and I visited HK several times when my daughter, Bharathi, worked in the leading bank there for over ten years. Bharathi once slipped and fell on the same above-mentioned escalator and no one came to help her; all hurried past her. Once she helped a very old homeless lady (who eked out a meagre living by selling vegetables on the roadside) to push her wooden cart up a very steep slope. The old lady had been struggling. Upon reaching the top, that poor soul hugged Bharathi and with tears she offered her what little money she had. My daughter was very touched and started to cry. Instead, she gave the lady some money and the lady again hugged Bharathi. The distressing part was that there were so many people watching, and none came to help the old lady. That day my daughter cried all the way to her residence and the experience has affected her deeply.

We also need to bear in mind that our generosity should not be abused by the unscrupulous and greedy, who seek to exploit the system. On 8 March 2018, my wife received an SMS in her mobile from **Tan Tock Seng Hospital,** asking her to settle an outstanding medical bill she had incurred in 2017. We were surprised and concerned. A contact telephone number was given in the SMS. My wife called the number and told the person at the other end that it must have been a mistake as she did not incur the bill. Not satisfied with the response, I went to the Hospital to sort out the matter on 9 March 2018.

Upon arrival at the reception desk, a courteous and helpful elderly gentleman took me to the Business Centre located two floors above. When my Q number flashed at about 11.30 A.M., I went to the counter as directed and explained to the lady (whom I later learned was not a Singapore citizen) that it was a mistake. My wife did not incur the bill as she was not even in Singapore on the date in question. I insisted that I needed to know the name of the patient who was treated. She checked the computer and gave a name which to me sounded foreign. I then asked her for the nationality, and she confirmed that he was a foreigner. I pursued the matter further and wanted to know why my wife was asked to pay and what action had been taken since to recover the debt owed to the Hospital from the patient. She appeared not very happy and said she would check the records and come back. She did not come back, but after a short while another lady (a pleasant Singaporean) attended to me and she apologised for the mistake. With regards the action to recover the debt, she said both the patient and his employer(s) had not responded to the telephone calls. I told her it was quite simple. Get the required particulars from the relevant authority and cancel the residence permit and Work Permit/Employment Pass issued to him to work in Singapore, and deport the person concerned. Such unscrupulous foreigners who exploit the system in this way cannot make any meaningful contribution to Singapore. Furthermore, his employer should also be dealt with as per the law. It is not fair or even justified that citizens should carry such burden.

COMPLACENCY

However, one of the biggest problems for many countries, Singapore included, in maintaining high standards is **complacency.** By way of an anecdote, in 2003, I drew the attention of the Ministry of the Environment and Water Resources (MEWR) a few times to roadside drains being clogged with leaves and mud, which impeded drainage of rain water. I received polite replies thanking me for the observation and stating that relevant contractors would be instructed to clear the blockage. However, the problems continued, and it appeared that the contractors required more effective supervision. I also noted that the cleaning workers engaged by the contractors were foreign nationals from countries where litter, leaves and other thrash were routinely swept into the drains, or not at all, and to them that came naturally. In my humble opinion, the chocked drains also contributed to the severity of the floods that occurred in many areas in the city in subsequent years. It does not require one hundred percent check of drains and other installations, which is impossible anyway. However, **effective and random surprise checks carried out efficiently with punishment of offenders strictly as per the law could solve much of the problem**.

Revolutions in information technology has made it possible to view situations, places and events from a remote location. In a more recent case, a senior MEWR official's reported response to citizens' concern over food poisoning cases cannot be considered satisfactory. His alleged response was that there were 39,000 restaurants in Singapore and he could not supervise all of them. MEWR licenses the food outlets and has the responsibility to ensure food safety in this regard. Besides being very important to ensure the health of our citizens and visitors, it is also necessary to safeguard Singapore's reputation abroad.

Many citizens have expressed their concerns over what they see as slackening in the implementation of policies and observance of relevant established protocols, especially in the SAF training of servicemen, health screening of foreign nationals seeking employment in Singapore, power outages and many more matters involving many ministries. The lesson is that **vigilance needs to be continuously improved,** to deal effectively with whatever problems are thrown at us.

In 1956, when I was in Standard 8 (Form 3), I was asked to give a talk to my class. I spoke on the sinking of the **"unsinkable" Titanic**, the most luxurious passenger liner of the time, while on its maiden voyage from Southampton to New York in 1912. The mighty Titanic plunged to its icy grave in the bottom of the North Atlantic Ocean, carrying with it more than 1500 passengers, who were mostly from the wealthy British upper class. That tragedy shocked the world. My information then was based on an article in a well-read monthly magazine which I borrowed from our family friend. I gave an account of why it sank. I also remember telling the class that, according to the article, an elderly female passenger asked an official from the owners of the liner, "is it true that this ship is unsinkable?". The official's reply was **"Madam even God cannot sink this ship".**

One might ask what is the relevance of the Titanic tragedy to the narratives in this chapter? Since giving that talk in my beloved Victoria School, I had read quite widely on this tragedy. One of the major factors that contributed to the tragedy was almost an irresponsible **complacency** at various levels of the establishment which owned and organised the voyage of "a lifetime". They mesmerised themselves with the unshakeable belief that the technologically advanced construction of the ship made it unsinkable under any circumstance. This complacency probably led to the series of most elementary lapses and failures. Since it was "unsinkable", they probably had not devoted as much attention as was necessary to practice evacuation drills to deal with disaster at sea. According to reports, there were also problems with lifeboats. The two staff who were on watch duty to look out for dangers, especially ice bergs, which were common at that time of the year, could not see very far with their naked eyes, owing to poor visibility. Someone whose duty it was to provide them with binoculars, as per operating procedure, apparently forgot to bring them on board when the ship left Southampton. Iceberg warnings from other ships in the area were not attended to with the urgency the situation required. (At that time radar was not invented.) Finally, in spite of all these signs and warnings, everyone including the Captain in command of the ship were utterly shocked and numbed when the ship slammed into the massive iceberg (much of its mass was below the water level). The rest, as they say, is history. I have always emphasised that, in any operation, **the devil is in the detail**. Those who ignore this rule, do so at their own peril.

Often, I have heard bureaucrats priding themselves on the system they have put in place to deal with problems. Clear, effective and user-friendly systems are very important for efficient administration. However, equally important is a regular review of the working of the systems, and their continued relevance and effectiveness, in the face of changing dynamics. I read in a British newspaper some time in 1966, or thereabout, that their Ministry of Defence (MOD) had put in place an arrangement whereby there were two soldiers on sentry duty (at any one time) on a strategic vantage point at Dover Cliffs to look out across the English Channel for **enemy German ships and aircrafts approaching the British coast during the Second World War.** According to that report the soldiers were still on duty in 1966 looking for the Germans, some ten years after the War had ended! This fact came to light only when the Auditor General (or his/her equivalent) queried the expenditure for the sentry duty and the continuing need for it. Obviously, someone in the MOD who was responsible for approving the funds for the sentry duty has not done his job to review the policy.

Now I revert back to the question whether the Singapore model and success can be replicated in other countries. I believe that, in a suitable setting and environment, much of our policies can be adopted and adapted to create the growth necessary. However, it should be obvious to the readers by now that the important factors that I repeatedly visited in this book are political will, accountability, discipline, commitment, etc. of the leaders and the other people concerned. These are the important determinants of success in the context of this narrative. It is the absence of these factors to varying degrees that have stymied progress in many countries, not the lack of resources, both natural and human, which most of them are so abundantly endowed with. Here is an interesting and telling anecdote: On 13 February, 2019, I heard on the BBC Radio news bulletin that the 300 new luxury cars bought for the VIP delegates attending the Asia Pacific Economic Cooperation (APEC) Summit held in Papua New Guinea (PNG) in November, 2018, had gone missing, barely two months after the event! (These cars were probably bought with aid money from donors, probably from China. China has been increasing its footprint in PNG, as part of its strategic penetration of the Asia Pacific, and thereby causing concern in the West, especially in the United States and Australia.) If so many new and expensive cars can go missing without a trace, so soon after their purchase, then that says it all.

Professor Tommy Koh, Ambassador-at-Large in the Ministry of Foreign Affairs, summed this up eloquently, thus: **"Without political will, nothing can be achieved. With political will almost every problem has a solution"** (from "A MARITIME FORCE FOR A MARITIME NATION" published by Straits Times, SPH holdings).

The anecdote below is one of the many clear examples of a stout **exercise of political will by our visionary leadership.**

I have earlier mentioned how polluted the Singapore River was in the 1960s. In those the days everything that was unwanted was simply tossed out into the drains and on to the streets, which was then carried by rainwater and dumped into the waterways. Food and human waste were also found in the river. Such a situation was not unique to Singapore. We started the anti-littering campaign followed by laws to punish offenders. Many in the West thought it was draconian, but it helped us to clean up the environment.

It was, therefore, both urgent and crucial that our waterways were cleaned up, as part of an integrated master plan to recover as much of the water as possible, to increase the water stock and have a clean and healthy environment. In 1977, Prime Minister Lee opened the Pierce Reservoir and in his opening ceremony speech he said:

> "The day we achieve that (clean river), whoever has been in charge for the last ten years or for the next ten years, if I am still around, I will give each one of them — both the Minister, the Permanent Secretary and the head of department — a real solid gold medal, one troy ounce. I don't care what the price of it will

be... But if it isn't done... if I am still around and in charge in 1986, I will find out where it went wrong and whoever and whichever group of people made it go wrong and failed... Well, I have got special pieces of lead — not for striking medals — I think I'll add it to their water supply".

> *taken from "Heart of Public Service" (page 69) published by Public Service Division, Prime Minister' office 2015.*

I was present at that event and attended to the foreign diplomats who were there by invitation. I recall that many ambassadors were amazed at PM Lee's speech, especially the reference to lead. They told me that it would be unthinkable that their heads of governments would be able to say that under any circumstance!

Those who were put in charge of the project accomplished it well ahead of the time limit set by PM Lee and they received their gold medals! I also remember PM Lee saying at that time that he wanted to see fish swimming in the clean waters. Indeed, I saw fish breeding and swimming while walking along a section of the river near Kampong Java Road.

Even while grappling with the daunting immediate problems, our pioneer generation leaders were always conscious of the fact that **Singapore needed to continually reinvent itself to make it in the future.** The final chapter (a very short one) that follows is on "The Future".

Chapter 25

THE FUTURE

"The Future is unknowable"

—Alan Greenspan

I was invited by the American International School (AIS) in Cairo to deliver a keynote address to the **Model United Nations Conference** organised by AIS with support from local authorities. AIS left it to me to decide the title of my keynote address and I decided that I should speak on **"The Challenge of Change"**. The very lively audience repeatedly engaged me to predict the future. My response was:

- "Uncertainty is the only certainty..." —John Allen Paulos; and
- "change is the only constant" —Heraclitus.

I quoted **Allan Greenspan**, the Chairman of the United States Federal Reserve, who said that the **"future is unknowable"**.

The audience was in excess of 250 persons, comprising mostly of students (16–19 years old) from universities and schools in Egypt, Italy, India, Syria, Turkey and Tunisia. Additionally, there were also invited leaders from the wider community and the Diplomatic Corps. My address was very well received and the feedback was very good and satisfying. (See AIS letter dated 16 April, 2000 reproduced in the book.)

In my view, nothing much has changed in substance since then. Even Greenspan could not foresee, let alone predict, the 2008 financial meltdown which occurred just two years after he left office. (Interestingly, there was also a view that some of his policies were partly or fully responsible for the meltdown.) Considering the recurrent bouts of economic and financial crises, continuing political upheavals, increasing security threats and the rising power of social media in the global landscape over the last several decades, some analysts fear that the world might be heading towards a **dysfunctional future**.

Since the future is unknowable, there are no guideposts to point the way ahead. What is knowable, however, is that the future generation of Singaporeans will face many challenges which would be different but no less exacting than those that confronted the pioneer generation. They face a different and more complex world, which is enmeshed in ruthless competition for profit, power and wealth, driven by increasing automation, robotic technology and artificial intelligence, that is displacing humans even in highly specialised and skilled jobs. As I mentioned in a preceding chapter, artificial intelligence is an uncharted territory and, as of now, there is no telling where it is likely to lead mankind to: reasonable living standards for all, or immense wealth for a few and despair for the vast majority?

In a short 10-second clip on the **"Future of Work"** telecast by BBC global channel in March 2018, a man asks a lady what her strengths were. Her response was that she excelled in high volume tasks and had an excellent memory. His next question: "where would you be in the next five years?". The lady replied: "I will be more intelligent than you and I will be doing your job." Startled, the man asked: "Where will I be?" to which the lady smugly said "Well, that is up to you". I think readers would have realised by now that the man was real, but the lady was not. She is the product of artificial intelligence, which of course is the creation of humanoids. If I may add, the man certainly looked Caucasian, but the lady looked more Asian, possibly Chinese. Is there a subtle message in that as well? Maybe, but I am not sure.

In addition to geopolitical challenges, the present and future generations will also have to deal with the dangers arising from climate change, from global warming, and the degradation of the environment, owing to a variety of factors. Island nations, like Singapore which are surrounded by sea, are at much greater risk in this regard than bigger countries.

Worldwide, the youth are angry and very concerned over the future. A young passionate Swedish teenage climate activist Greta Thunberg, told the crowd in a hard-hitting speech during a climate strike demonstration in New York on 20 September, 2019 (not far from United Nations where a special session on climate change was being held):

> **"Why should we study for a future that is being taken away from us? That is being sold for profit."**

The problems posed by our declining birth-rate and the policies that contributed to that outcome have been noted earlier. Whether Singapore citizens — by birth or naturalised — will rise to answer the call to increase the birth rate, only time will tell.

Notwithstanding the challenges and the odds, there is no reason to believe that Singapore cannot continue to punch above its weight globally, provided both the lessons of the past are not lost and the nation continues to reinvent itself.

President **Devan Nair** noted:

> "The essential ingredients which went into the making of modern Singapore will remain essential for the future of Singapore. The cooks in charge of the Singapore broth must, of course, change with effluxion of time. But if they temper with the essential ingredients of success in our compact urban society — secularism, multi-racialism, pragmatism, incorruptibility and high standards of public life and social discipline — we will gravely imperil the future for everyone in our Republic". (Excerpt from "Towards Tomorrow — Essays on Development and Social Transformation in Singapore" published by The National Trade Union Congress.)

Challenges also bring opportunities. With the global economic tide shifting to Asia, Singapore can ride the tide in order to seize the opportunities and reap the benefits, if we prepare ourselves towards that end. **This century is most likely to be the Asian Century and could be an exciting one in many ways.**

However, and unlike in the past, the future generations will be challenged by far more complex and unforeseeable problems and achieving success in every endeavour will not be easy or guaranteed.

Therefore, I think it is relevant for them to reflect on the following:

> **"Success is not final, failure is not fatal. It is the courage to continue that counts."**
>
> *—Winston Churchill*

A saying attributed to the famous (or infamous depending on one's perspective) **Genghis Khan** goes something like this:

> **"An army is defeated if it loses its morale; a nation is finished if it loses its confidence."**

I recall reading that one of the defendants in the **Nuremberg Trials** was heard saying, as he was being led to the gallows, **"a nation that believes in itself will not perish"**.

Stand-up for Singapore!

And my journey continues… a citizen's duty to serve the nation never ends.

Majulah Singapura!